	Nov 24/25	First night r... Fire Service ... time, and th...
London bombed for 76 consecutive nights. Part of 9 months of night-raids on our cities	November 25	IBs Hick's G... 20 HE in Ke...
	Dec 2/3	15 HE Keynsham – Queen Charlton area
	1941	
Greece occupied	Jan 3/4	4 HE, several IB Bungalow damaged. First issue serge battle dress to H.G. Sensational.
Hitler attacked Russia	Jan 29	Hurricane(?) crashed Stockwood Flats
	Feb	English trainer plane crashed Cameroons, Park Road, crew of 2 died
	Feb	Issue of military commisions and ranks to H.G. 20 leaders accepted commissions (Later – Dr N.D. Gerrish became Captain as M.O. of No. 2 Company.)
	March	Many incidents
	April 11	3 HE
	April 13	17 HE, numerous IB in Keynsham-Whitchurch area
	May 5	1 HE Hick's Gate
Pearl Harbour bombed	August	
	1942	
Crimea falls to Germans Fall of Singapore	Feb 15	
	Feb 16	H.G. became part of Armed Forces & subject to Military Law. Free use of cinema for H.G. training films.
N Africa Rommel's drive for Cairo	Feb 22	Inspection of H.G. at Drill Hall by General Churchill.
	April 3	1 HE on Frys. 2 boys hurt
	April 25	House and bungalow Stockwood Vale damaged. 1/2nd attacks on Bath. Great damage. Keynsham N.F.S. and Heavy Rescue ordered into Bath.
	April 27	Another heavy attack Bath
1,000 bombers raid on Cologne	May 1	Warship week. H.G. inspected by Admiral Dicken & Mavis Tate, M.P.

CU00659891

To Carol Meurnane,

with best wishes,

Michael E. Fisher.

January 16. 1996.

THE WAR OVER KEYNSHAM

**The companion volume to
'Keynsham in Grandfather's Day'**

Michael C. Fitter

Foreword by Mr. LESLIE CROWTHER

**THE AMMONITE PRESS
KEYNSHAM**

ADDENDA

To Volume I, 'Keynsham in Grandfather's Day'

Page 27   The 'new P.O.' was between Milward House and the former
            dairy (later Jean's Wool Shop, now closed.)
Pages 68–71 The 'unsigned document' was the work of Elizabeth White.

ERRATA

Page 128   For 'Edward Charles' read 'Charles Henry'.
            The photo was taken at his father's golden wedding.
            For 'eldest daughter' read 'youngest daughter'.
Page 135   For 'brother Christopher' read 'brother Percival'.
Page 143   For 'Haig' read 'Kitchener'.
Page 187   For 1987 read 1887.
Page 279   The photo is almost certainly J.S. Fry's (1767–1835) great-
            grandson Francis Rhodalph Fry (1862–1923).
Page 280   For 'Jack Tetley' read 'Jack Titley'.
Index   For 'Tetley' read 'Titley'.

All rights reserved. No part of this publication may be reproduced, stored in a retrieval system, or transmitted in any form or by any means electronic, mechanical, photocopying, recording or otherwise, without the prior permission of the publishers.

Limited edition 1995. ISBN 0 9523202 1 5

The copyright of this book is with the author.

Published by, THE AMMONITE PRESS, KEYNSHAM,
    'Greensleeves', 6 Avon Road, Keynsham, Bristol, BS18 1LJ.

Typesetting by 'Anneset', 25 Back Street, Weston-super-Mare, Avon.

Printed by J.W. Arrowsmith, Winterstoke Road, Bristol, BS3 2NT.

DEDICATION

This book is dedicated to the forty-three servicemen, many only in their twenties, who, in World War Two, courageously laid down their lives for their families, friends and freedom, and for the very different Keynsham of those days that was their home.

FOREWORD

When Michael Fitter asked me to write a foreword to 'The War over Keynsham', the companion book of his 'Keynsham in Grandfather's Day', I leapt at the chance. I am constantly reminded of my daily debt to Keynsham. I have, after all, married one of her daughters.

Had the W.W. II. German fighter plane been a little more accurate in its attempt to mow down a group of young Keynsham boys and girls in the Manor Road playground (Incidentally, the playground is still there and I can distinctly remember my wife Jean describing the excitement as the pilot stitched up the grass by the side of her as she ran for cover), and had the German bombers not missed St. John's church (Oh God, thy hand was here, much the same as St. Paul's Cathedral rising from the rubble and dust of the City of London as a phoenix from the ashes), I would have never have married my wife Jean at all. That would have been a pity!!

Today Keynsham bears little or no sign of the aerial fury that was hurled at Bristol, a much larger city but a few miles away, which proudly displays its scars. Gone are the ration books and the evacuees in the days when Hurn Lane really was a lane, and Rockhill was an Army centre. Only the lives of the locals are permanently affected, and ever will be, by the bereavement that war brings. To them this foreword, and indeed the entire book, is dedicated.

I can heartily recommend 'The War over Keynsham' as a good read, coming as it does from Michael Fitter, the author of that other grand book, 'Keynsham in Grandfather's Day'.

Leslie Crowther, C.B.E.

November 1994, Corston.

INTRODUCTION

This book is the companion volume to 'Keynsham in Grandfather's Day', and therefore it is also written from the standpoint of local history. Consequently, a number of chapters which conclude with World War Two are often preceded by a longer account of the earlier life of the person concerned. The title, 'The War over Keynsham' is an attempt to bring a little order to a miscellany of unrelated biographies and events. Again, where possible, I have encouraged people to write their own accounts. Those who did so were Gladys Dyson, Edward Joll, Harry Wakeling, Monty Veale, Bert Robe and William Sherer.

This book makes no pretence to being the definitive record of the experiences of those who during World War Two were in the Royal Navy, the Army or the Air Force, or engaged in the 'War on the Home Front'.

Far from being an authoritative work on the war, it is a collection of personal accounts, with particular emphasis on the second war. I regret that the record of the 'blood, toil, tears and sweat' of so many local servicemen has not been told. In Keynsham probably each service has a sufficiently large number of members to fill a book with their memories alone. So the stories of a few representative servicemen have been chosen from the three forces.

The ill-fated Derek Renshaw, Monty Veale and the decorated Herbert Phelps, speak for the Navy. Michael Sparey, Les Harvey and Geoff Sherwell represent the Royal Air Force. Fortunately all of them survived. John Wood deceased, Harry Wakeling, William Williams and Roy Williams (no relation) represent the Army, while Leonard Hall and Chris Wiggins suffered as prisoners of war of the Japanese. Later Desmond Crease was killed fighting the Japanese. Ron Headington fought the Germans in Egypt and in Italy, with personal distinction. Howard Jefferies and Bill Cotter went over on D-Day. Bert Robe was at Dunkirk. Les Harding, another old soldier, is sadly no longer with us.

Jean Williams has written her own moving account of being a wife and mother left behind with her conflicting emotions when her man went away to fight the Germans and endure the D-Day landing. Diana Carbery (nee Woods) and Sybil Benoy (nee Wiggins) were in the ATS; Dinah Ruttledge was in the WAAF; together they symbolise the young single girls who went away on active service. Many a local woman remained behind and served as backup staff to the Home Guard, the ARP, or the National Fire Service, as telephonists, like Mrs Delia Pillinger (nee Wiggins). Others, such as Isabel Andrews (nee Ollis), were auxiliary constables, while some were the vital Land Girls. When the sirens went, nurses reported to the First Aid centre at Temple Street School.

From the blitzed City of London, evacuee children were hurriedly brought West for their own safety, some to Keynsham. Many left behind weeping mothers. How did the evacuees travel, and who supervised them?

How did this influx of street-wise children, 'they Londoners', integrate into a rural community? Were the children happy here, and how did the housewives manage? After the war, did the evacuees all rush back to the Capital? An attempt is made to answer these questions. Just what it was like to 'take in' evacuees is described by Sydney Holborn and the late Mrs Eunice Ollis, while Iris Lerpiniere and Samuel Olive record their experiences of being 'taken in'.

Following the invasion by Londoners, came the occupation by the United States Army. They were warmly received and many homes entertained them. Their music, money and charm made them doubly attractive to the local girls, and the streets of Keynsham bulged with these lively young men. A few elderly ladies felt a little threatened by the tall, coloured Americans with funny accents.

On the Home Front, after a full day's work, many of the local men like Jim Ollis, Edward Cannock, Fred Bees, Les Whittock, Sydney Fairclough and many others, would turn out to fulfil their Civil Defence duties. Some were ARP wardens and fire watchers, while others plotted planes in the Observer Corps. A number were auxiliary firemen. Many faced rigorous training in the Home Guard, or were special constables. As leader of the Heavy Rescue team, the late Reg Willey was decorated for his bravery.

Despite the fact that no local people were killed in the town, there was still considerable disruption of life here. This was due to the efforts of the Luftwaffe, intentional or otherwise, and the many tiresome and sometimes frightening air raids, night after night. Keynsham was not unscarred. Mrs Leslie Crowther records her own memories of those days.

There is a brief note on the servicemen who made the supreme sacrifice, as far as I was able to trace their relatives for information. Often this was not possible due to the limitations of time, people moving away, others marrying and thus changing their family name, and some dying. The book concludes with the Roll of Honour of all those who from Keynsham and Saltford fell in WWI and WW2.

I am grateful to all who have contributed their own accounts, and could say 'I was there', and to others who have trusted me with their confidences and memories of the war, not to mention their photographs. In a book of this size, mistakes are inevitable, so let me apologise for that in advance. I am not responsible for any inaccuracies or contradictions in articles supplied by contributors, or for their views.

I am indebted to the following publishers for permission to quote from their books:

'Somerset at War', by Mr Mac Hawkins, Dovecott Press, 1988.
'Attack Warning Red' by Mr Derek Wood, 1976.
'Forewarned is Forearmed', by TE Winslow, 1948, Wm Hodge and Co.
'North Wansdyke Past and Present', No. 3, 1990, by Keynsham and Saltford Local History Society.

I am also grateful to Barbara Lowe for permission to quote from her books:

'Keynsham in old picture postcards', European Library, 1983; and,
'Around Keynsham and Saltford', by Barbara Lowe and Tony Brown, Alan Sutton, 1988.

The Somerset Record Office, Taunton, most kindly helped with information concerning evacuees and Civil Defence.

My thanks go to Cadbury's and Brian Davies for permission to use an article from Somerdale Magazine, and for the loan of some fine war-time photographs. I am indebted to the Bristol Press for the memorial photograph, to Ian James for his outline of Luftwaffe attacks on Keynsham, and to John Penney, the aviation war specialist on Bristol, for background information.

Again I would express my very sincere appreciation to Chris Wiggins for initially reading the script; and even more so to Bert Robe and Donald Hiscox for again undertaking the onerous task of proof reading. Their painstaking work and attention to fine details, together with their shrewd and helpful suggestions, leave me greatly indebted to them.

Doug Dyson, with his love of aeroplanes, graciously enlightened me as to what was involved in being a member of the Observer Corps. Ron Headington, with his admirable ability to tell a story, made the Egyptian Campaign with the 'Desert Rats' (of the 8th Army under General Montgomery) really come to life. Edward Cannock kindly provided material and photographs. My grateful thanks are also extended to all those who so kindly helped with information and stories.

In addition to those already mentioned, I must record my sincere appreciation to the following people for information and help: Brian Woodham Fred Balcombe, Frank Passco, Phyllis Clayfield, Ann Randall, Alfred Paget, Les Whittock, William Down, Doreen Wiltshire, William Sherer, Rosemary King-Smith, Sheila McGrath, Elizabeth Linssen, Brian Keeling, Minnie Bates, George Morley, Janet Snart, Rick Brand, Jeff Whittock, Doreen Gyles, Ernest Wiltshire, Ken Bye, Leonard Dunn, Mary George, Charles Gerrish, Hubert Hall, Eileen Phelps, Brian Renshaw, Percy Kilburn, John Clarke, Gerwyn Thomas, David Wilson, Rosemary Thurlow, Joyce Knight, Kathleen B. Watts, and many others. I am also grateful for the help of Dorothy Warren, Professor McGrath, and Jack Smith, all of them, sadly, being no longer with us.

Again I am deeply indebted to Mary Fairclough for eye-witness accounts, considerable information, and for guidance and encouragement over the long years spent in research. She co-founded the Keynsham and Saltford Local History Society. Its chairman, Elizabeth White, meticulously ploughed through the lengthy chapter on the Home Guard. From the depths of the archives of the Local History Society, Margaret Whitehead dug out early material by Sydney Fairclough. I am grateful to these ladies.

Much of the material of this book was collected and written several years ago. Since then, sadly, some of the people involved have died. I have tried to edit the text accordingly and this accounts for the difficulty of the text in places.

In addition to all the above, I gladly acknowledge the sound advice, the helpful suggestions and the whole-hearted support of my wife, Margaret, in encouraging me and enabling this venture to come to fruition.

On May 8th we shall be remembering the event 50 years ago, when as a nation we rejoiced at last at Victory in Europe, VE Day, and soon after that at VJ Day, Victory over Japan. This book is offered as a tribute to all that the local people suffered and endured, both on the home front and at the battle front; and in the hope that their descendants might understand a little about 'The War over Keynsham'.

Michael C Fitter
RKC (London), Cert Ed (Bristol)
Keynsham, Bristol.

November 1994

CONTENTS

'THE WAR OVER KEYNSHAM'

CHAPTERS
PART ONE – ON THE HOME FRONT

PART TWO – ON THE BATTLE FRONT

PART ONE

ON THE HOME FRONT

Chapter 1

Early memories of Mrs Gladys Dyson and Mr. E. A. R. Joll

The childhood and career of a Keynsham nurse

My first impression of life in Keynsham was of a very happy childhood living in Durley Cottage, Durley Hill, with my mother and father, Gladys and Gilbert Veale, and my sisters Doreen and Marjorie, and my brothers Jack and Monty. Doreen (Mrs E Wiltshire) was born in Keynsham before my parents emigrated to Toronto, Canada, where Jack, Marjorie and I were born. Monty was born in Durley Cottage after we returned.

The cottage had no gas and no electricity in those days and lighting was supplied by paraffin lamps, and we used candles to go to bed. Coal and logs provided the heating. Cooking was done on a primus stove and a fireside oven. The surrounding fields, the humpty dumps, streams, paddling, picking conkers from Durley Park, provided many exciting activities. I picked black-berries and crab apples which mother made into delicious jams and jellies. The ferry across the Avon which was run by Mr and Mrs Payne, who punted us across in a small boat, took us to a favourite place for picnics. The highlight was the ride to The Chequer's side and back for one penny, which was our pocket money for a week.

Milk was delivered daily by Mr Exon by horse and cart, in which we had a ride as far as his shop opposite St John's church, if we were lucky. Otherwise it would be three of us on the one bike, Jack in the saddle, one on the crossbar and one on the step by the back wheel. Delicious hot crusty bread was deliv-ered by Mr Ollis, also in a horse and cart. The bread was covered by a large tarpaulin.

My father was a bespoke tailor and worked for a firm in St Pauls. He also had a shop at 10, High Street, where he took orders for made-to-measure men's and women's clothes, which he measured, cut out and tacked, and then took to Bristol for finishing. The work was seasonal and times were very hard in the early years but improved later.

The shop had a frosted front window and was fitted with a tailor's long table for cutting out, a sewing machine, and gas light and a gas ring which was used for heating a tailor's large iron. The workshop had no front window display. There was a lino floor, with stove heating.

Dad's specialist knowledge of tailoring was of great advantage to my sister Doreen, who at the age of seventeen used this shop for dress making and found his advice invaluable.

Behind the shop lived Mr and Mrs Mansbridge and their son and daughter, Joan and Jack. There Mr Mansbridge ran a barber's shop.

Mr Gilbert James Veale and his wife Gladys, in 1912, with their eldest daughter Doreen in the centre, and only just visible, their son William, always known as Jack. Gladys Dyson's (nee Veale) photograph.

We left the cottage when I was seven and moved to 50, Temple Street, which was owned by my uncle Horace and Aunt Edie, who owned the grocer's shop next door. They worked very hard late into the night, packing up sugar and tea. Butter was weighed and patted up. They ground their own coffee while you waited. My uncle was also a well-known piano tuner.

There were many children to play with. Many hours were spent in the recreation ground, where there were swings, a sand pit and a much used maypole. We also had tops and wooden hoops. The boys played football at the top of the field. The Hawthorn's sheltered housing estate and Hawthorn House are now on the site.

My uncle Harry had a butcher's shop at 70, Temple Street and cattle were driven up Carpenter's Lane into the slaughter house.

Characters that I remember from Temple Street were Mr and Mrs Waters, who went to Bristol fish market every morning with their pony and trap. There was Mr Stephens, who was renowned for his faggots and peas, and fish and chips, and Mr and Mrs Frank Ogborn and his sister Kathleen, who also had a fish and chip shop. Mr Beck was the blacksmith who practised his craft in Godfrey's yard, Temple Street (now a car business), and Mrs Williams sold home-made pickle. Mr Williams and Courtney Sherer were butchers, while Mr Sweet and Mr Hine were chimney sweeps. Mrs Ruddick sold sweets, where on Thursday evenings there was always a big dish of home-cooked chitterlings on the counter for sale.

I attended the Baptist Church Sunday School. Among the many activities run by the churches were the Brownie Pack led by Miss Belsten, the Girl Guides by Miss Richards, and the Cubs and Scouts by Mr Reg and Mr Vivian Turner. I attended Temple Street Infants' School, starting at four years of age. The head teacher was Miss Brown. Later I went to Bath Hill Cof E School where the head master was Mr C Mycock. I loved it at both schools. I studied shorthand, typing and business studies at the Civil Service Institute at Westpark, Clifton, but later decided to be trained as a nurse.

I commenced my general nursing training at the RUH Bath. Except for the first six months, all my training was done during the Second World War. At the outbreak of hostilities, there was much reorganisation as half the hospital was taken over for the military and was run by Queen Alexandra's nurses and VADs. The remaining wards were rather congested by extra beds. Blackout conditions were very strictly adhered to, and we were only allowed pencil torches covered with blue litmus paper to perform all treatments.

There were many anxious times when, during an air raid alert, we could hear the hum of the German planes, our ack ack guns, bombs dropping and see the resulting admission of casualties.

Back in Keynsham, the iron railings were taken from around St John's church, from in front of the banks and outside some of the old shops. Old utensil were collected so that all the metal could be melted down to produce planes, tanks and shells. Ornate garden gates were removed, with hardly a word to their owners. The story is told of how Mr David Sherwell, who was a member of the LDV, was in his pickle factory in Bristol Road early in the summer of 1940 when his neighbour Mr Tom Davies of Milward Lodge came running in to say 'Hitler has arrived'. David reached for his rifle, only to be

A close look at a small part of old Keynsham in 1930, outside Mr G J Veale's bespoke tailor's shop at 10, High Street, opposite St John's church. The ladies are, from the left, Doreen Veale, Mrs Joe Wiltshire, Marjorie Veale and Connie Hitchings. His shop was first on the right down the corridor. Further down lived Mr and Mrs Mansbridge with their family. He was a hairdresser, hence the pole outside the shop. The photo belongs to Mrs G Dyson, nee Veale.

told, 'The Council have come to take my railings away'.

People were encouraged to grow their own vegetables, and so 'Dig for Victory'. Potato peelings and household scraps were regularly collected in round old-type aluminium containers, placed outside people's houses, for feeding pigs to provide more meat. If you worked in a factory, or received news of a serviceman being posted overseas, you were reminded by posters that 'Careless talk costs lives'. (Don't provide the Hun, or his spies over here, with information that could be useful to them.)

I commenced my midwifery training at Southmead Hospital in 1942. The majority of patients were wives of servicemen, who if it was possible had compassionate leave when their babies were born. Inevitably, sadly, there were some for whom home leave was impossible, being injured or dead, or who had been taken prisoners of war, which was extremely traumatic. There was also the elation when there was good news.

I finished my midwifery training at Bristol Maternity Hospital at Southwell Street, which was a very old building, with many stairs. At night, all the babies were taken down to the nursery in the basement for safety. Three months of our training was on the district. I was based at St John's Lane, Bedminster. Bicycles were our only means of transport except when there was an alert, when we were driven by the WRVS. Sometimes we had to relieve as far up as Knowle West or down to Hotwell's tenements, and to Cathay.

After completion of my training and qualifying, I returned to Southmead Hospital for some time. Also I worked at Cedar Hall, Frenchay, which was owned by a member of the Cadbury family. During my stay there we met some of the American nurses who were stationed at Frenchay Hospital, which was built for and used by American servicemen.

I was back at Southmead Hospital when the Armistice was declared, and well remember the feelings of relief, the joy and the celebrations. We were invited to many parties. Everyone decorated the outside of their homes with red, white and blue and all the flags were brought out. Although rationing was very strict, the cooks always managed to make a variety of mouth-watering refreshments.

Old Keynsham as seen from 55, High Street

In response to my request, Mr E A R Joll has kindly written the following account of his family's connection with Keynsham.

Edward W Joll came to live in Keynsham in 1927 at Rockhill Villa, Wellsway, and commuted by train to his father's menswear shop at 108, Victoria Street, Bristol.

In 1933 he bought the business of J Newport Brothers at 55, High Street, Keynsham, and moved with his wife Florence and their only child, two year old Edward, to live over and behind the shop, in that year. It had been a menswear shop since at least 1896 but is a much older building dating from 1700 and was described in the original deeds as 'a merchant's house, on the Great West Road'. The property had mains water and gas lighting only, with a WC in the small back garden.

The house is double the depth of the others in the terrace with a single storey rear extension for a kitchen, where there was a well, which was promptly covered over to keep young Edward out. There was a solid fuel boiler in one corner to heat laundry water and water for the tin bath which was brought in from the shed when needed, usually on Monday and Friday evenings. The suit room of the present shop was originally the dining room.

The menswear shop catered for the local and surrounding farming community, E W J having a country round. He visited virtually every farm and hamlet in the area each month, driving a 1934 Morris Minor two-door saloon, with a sun roof.

When the war came in 1939 with petrol restrictions and later rationing, a special allowance was made for this purpose of half a gallon a week. This was saved up to enable a grand tour of the district to be made with the family, incorporating a picnic lunch and mixing business with pleasure.

E W J was called up to serve in the Auxillary Fire Service, and due to his business, was stationed at Keynsham. The fire station was where the Black Horse Estate Agents now is, where it housed one Albion engine, 1937 model. The station office and living quarters were behind the Lamb and Lark Hotel, now Rontos, in the old Masonic Hall. There was soon a large number of per-

Keynsham between the wars, circa 1930, showing on the right, next to Lennards, G Veale's tailor's shop. A woman Salvationist stands by his window. On the left, part of the Railway Tavern can just be seen. Until recently it was the SWEB's shop. Further along on the same side is a covered horse-drawn cart, without the horse. The road appears to be still untarmacked.

sonnel present as it was a full-time station, working three shifts. Though prepared to fight great fires at large buildings, that was not to be for E W J in Keynsham, where any fires there were described by his son as purely 'mundane'.

The AFS even organised their own pantomimes, which were much enjoyed by their families and friends, and numerous understudies were necessary in case of a call out. Additional appliances joined the original engine, including a Bedford which carried a 400 gallon watertank.

During this period the cellars of the High Street were used by some as air raid shelters, including numbers 55 and 57 (now Oxfam), where a hole was knocked in the three foot thick dividing wall to provide an escape route, by their neighbour Mr Heal, who was a builder. He thought it would take him about three hours, working in the evenings; it took him three weeks! It is still there today with a heavy metal door. In the early days of air raids, they took shelter under the dining room table, but, with the escape route provided, during raids they used the cellar, which was provided with electric light, bunk beds, chairs and even a radio.

One night in August 1940, the nine year old Edward was rudely awakened by the loud thud of a German oil bomb dropping on the house of their neighbour two doors down, at number 59, which caught fire and was severely damaged. This was the home of the two spinsters, the Miss Wallaces. One of them

This photo shows Mr E W Joll with his new 1948 four door Morris Ten car at Greendown, Litton, early in October 1948. He recorded that 'It was equal to a midsummer day, and I picked six pounds of blackberries'. The photo belongs to Mr E A Joll.

played the organ at the local Methodist church. The other sister, of ample proportions, was only rescued with difficulty from her upstairs bedroom by the firemen, down the narrow twisting stairs

When the 'all clear' sounded, although it was three o'clock in the morning, young Edward, wide awake, was allowed outside for a while to watch. There was still a lot of smoke, but the flames were well under control. The street was lit up, and there was a glow from a burning Bristol not far away. A fire engine was outside, but not the water carrier as the busy firemen were using mains water. Across the road, residents watched the fire being fought, many in their pyjamas and dressing gowns. Fascinated, they had never seen anything like it before in old Keynsham.

The only other bomb which fell nearby was in the park, now the Memorial Park, which was a much bigger explosion and made quite a large crater just a hundred yards from number 55. Apart from the odd plane crash and a few stray incendiaries, Keynsham saw little of the war, except the red glow in the sky from the blitz at Bath and Bristol. Children were frequently disappointed to find their schools still standing in the morning.

Confectionery was very scarce, especially before rationing, but no one went hungry in this country town where there were many productive gardens and the district was surrounded by farmers. The garden of 55, beyond the Back Lane, contained several brick buildings belonging to the Throsper Factory (now the Halifax), so E W J grew vegetables in part of the large garden of his neighbour, Mr Heal.

Bartering was an accepted way of getting rid of something one could spare for something one needed, and this included children swopping almost anything for something. 'Swop you this incendiary case for that tracer bullet.'

By this time, Edward had left Bath Hill School and attended Redland Hill House School, Clifton, as a day boy. In those days children had respect for their elders and fear of the headmasters, and the crime of scrumping apples was the worst any youngster got up to. The park had apple and damson trees, a long way from the owner's (Mr Clothier) house in Abbey Park, so there was plenty of time to get away. Kids played in the fields and coppices around the town, and the Rivers Chew and Avon were great favourites for tiddler fishing and generally getting wet muddy shoes.

Even with WWII going on, the most popular game was cowboys and Indians, and of course, kicking or hitting a ball about. In the summer months many went swimming in the canal locks and the River Avon near the White Hart, now the Lock Keeper.

After the war there was no sudden or noticeable change in Keynsham. Food, clothes and petrol were rationed and cars were at a premium. The new Austin 8 that E W J ordered in 1939 arrived in 1946 at the garage of Bailey and Matticks, (St Keyna Motor Works) now Halfords. Cars could drive from the High Street over the pavement into the garage and down a ramp, across Back Lane and into a very large corrugated iron building. The new Austin 8 side valve, two door, was really the same as the 1939 model. It cost £345 and E W J sold his immaculate 1934 Morris Minor for £185, which had cost £85 in 1936. Cars were in such short supply that offers of £100 more than the new car had cost were numerous.

It was not until the 1950s that things in Keynsham began to change, but that is another story.

* * *

Oil bombs
One morning in the early days of the war, Mr W J T Tookey was walking over the fields that are now the Chandag Estate, when he came across a clutch of unexploded high explosive bombs, which as an air raid warden, he referred to as 'UXBs'. Of greater interest was an unexploded oil bomb, stuck in the soil. He described its basic shape as that of the familiar red pillar box. It was about six feet tall and a foot and a half across, being of thin steel plate and containing old sump oil. A small nose cone contained an explosive, which both ignited the oil as well as spraying everything with the burning fuel. No wonder Number 59 was so seriously burnt.

Chapter 2

Major John Wood, 1913–1983

The Red Cross in World War Two

During the 1939–45 war, Dr Fox's wife from Brislington was the Commandant of the Keynsham branch of the Red Cross. They had a First Aid Post in part of Temple Street School in case of casualties from the bombing. According to Mrs John Wood, 'It was manned by the VAD but chiefly by its members Miss E M Wood, Miss Claire Jeffrys and Mrs Edith Mills. It was probably not open all day, but it was operational from 9 pm Saturday night until Sunday morning. There was probably a duty rota of members, with camp beds for when required.

'The Medical Officer was Dr Peach Taylor, and the two single ladies would argue in a friendly manner as to who was to make the coffee for the MO.' Dr Taylor, Dr Gerrish and Dr Claude Harrison (the son, not the father) were the three MDs in Keynsham during the war, and they all worked very well together.

Dr Taylor's surgery was at 2, Station Road. Mrs J Wood said that during the war, neither Dr Gerrish nor Dr Harrison took fees from mothers whose husbands were away in the war; 'but the doctors' lives were very hard.'

The Fear Institute on a War-Time Footing

Mrs D Carbery said, 'Strictly speaking it was not a YMCA centre, but rather a canteen for the troops. It was started by Miss Dolly Jacques of the Avenue, with a body of helpers. These included Miss Alice Stacey, a blind lady who lived at the 'Cameroons' in Park Road for many years and who was in the Red Cross. I helped there before I enlisted.' Many other Keynsham ladies and even young girls helped out there in the kitchens, and Mrs I Andrews mentioned that after being on duty as a police woman, she would then help out at the Institute for a few hours.

Actually John Nelson Fear was born on August 2, 1839, and owned both numbers 30 and 32, The High Street. A devout Christian and a member of the Victoria Methodist Church, he donated the site and provided the money, in his will, for the Institute. The late Mr Swain, in 1980, as part of his biography of Mr Fear, wrote of the building in, 'North Wansdyke, Past and Present, No. 3'.

'This was requisitioned in September 1939 for use as a First Aid Post but at the end of that year, mainly through the efforts of the YMCA, the building was released for use by the members of His Majesty's Forces and at the same time membership was still open to residents of Keynsham. During the six years that followed the Institute was the principal place in the district where the soldiers and ATS girls stationed in the area spent their leisure hours, and during most of those years the capacity of the building was strained to the uttermost. The canteen, which was run by a band of voluntary helpers, acquired a great reputation among those stationed here and those who were passing through.'

Major John Skidmore Wood, 1913–1982

Bereft very young of his father's love, (Gunner Charles Henry Wood, 1881–1917, was killed at Ypres), John, who was born at number 1, Priory Road, was a rather delicate 'blue baby'. Later, as his wife, Corena (nee Church), wrote, 'He attended a number of small schools in Keynsham and then went to Monkton Combe Junior School, where life was tough under the Rev and Mrs Eastman. Each term he would go by bus to Bath and there caught a tram to Combe Down, where he was a boarder for the term. There he passed the examination for the senior section of this prestigious public school.

'Not an academic, John, like his sister Diana, was very athletic,and was in the school's First XV for Rugger, was a team leader, and won the coveted Victor Ludorum cup and medal which his son now has. Boys were not mollycoddled at Monkton! Also he was in the school's 'Officer Training Corps'.

'When he left school he joined Lloyd's Bank in Milsom Street, Bath, and not only played rugger for Bath, but for Somerset too and was capped. He and his sister enjoyed tennis at the St Keyna Club with its excellent courts and bowling green. In 1938 he left the bank and volunteered for the Territorial Army with several friends from the Rugger Club and joined the TA Royal Engineers.

Miss Corena Church had two elder sisters, Mary and Dorothy, and a younger brother Edward. Edward trained as a doctor in London and became Captain W E Church, RAMC. Corena wrote, 'My brother was in the 6th Airborne Parachute Regiment and on D Day they were one of the first to be dropped but unfortunately in the wrong place. The doctor with him was killed and many others. Edward was taken to a POW camp in Germany where the conditions were ghastly. Red Cross parcels were retained and given out in rations, and medical instruments sent by the Red Cross were not given to him. When they were freed, all these things were found. He was down to six stone!'

Corena was educated at Lowther College in North Wales. She wrote that at the beginning of the war, 'I was living in Headcorn, Kent, with my parents on a smallholding with lovely small Dexter cows, chickens, turkeys and ducks, etc. During the war Dorothy and I both worked for the National Provincial Bank at Maidstone where I was secretary to the manager.

'I really was terribly lucky to meet John. If we had worked late and there was a raid on, instead of the 12 mile journey home, we would stay at the lovely huge Turkey Mill House, with its extensive gardens and a large lake in the middle. There our friends, Mr Brooke-Wright, the manager, and his wife, had invited the Officers of the 260th RE Company to a party, where we met. We were both attracted to each other and a friendship developed. We were

13

married at Headcorn Church on July 25, 1942.

'John's company was then moved to Canterbury. While there he was detailed to meet the Red Dean of Canterbury to go up to the Cathedral's roof to see what was needed to camouflage it. John hated heights, but it was fortunate that this was done, as quite soon afterwards Canterbury was bombed.

Lieutenant, later Major, John Skidmore Wood, of the Royal Engineers, 1913–1982.

'John was then posted somewhere in Kent until D Day. He had a narrow escape coming to Headcorn when he was stationed at Cranbrook. Convoys travelled at night with little or no lights on, and John on his army motor cycle went into the back of one, and arrived with a nasty cut leg which mother noticed, to which our doctor came.

'John had leave to come to Queen Charlotte's Hospital, where there was a special Officer's Ward, to see his first child Anne. The Registrar arrived before John, and I had to decide on names. There were too many Annes about, I thought, so she would have to be Angela Corena, but John did not like Angela, so Anne it has always been to us – and Angela when she trained at St Thomas's Hospital.

'John was transferred to the 183 Field Company and went over to France on D Day. He phoned me from Southampton, but could say little. From Normandy he closely followed the infantry, building bridges for the 43 Division, under General Montgomery, as he fought his way through France into Belgium and finally into Germany.'

He was finally demobilized in mid 1946, and was awarded five medals. These included the Defence Medal, the 1939–45 Star, the France and Germany Star, and lastly, in 1950, as the citation said 'the Efficiency Decoration conferred upon you by His Majesty . . . in recognition of your service in the Territorial Army.' Earlier in 1946/47 he had participated in the march past in Queen's Square, when the Royal Engineers were honoured by being granted the Freedom of the City of Bath.

'The question now was where to live? Eventually the maiden aunts at Ladbroke (now an Abbeyfield's Home) in Westbourne Avenue, said we could have Granny's former room if we stayed for two years, but of course, we never left. We had happy and sad times – three generations living together, but John had a wonderful sense of humour.

'Our daughter Celia was born in 1947 at Mrs Gill's Nursing Home in West View Road, which is now Dr Nutt's surgery. Snow lay inches deep that year but we managed to walk there. The home could only take a few mothers at a time, and Mrs Gill ruled with a rod of iron. Mother came from Kent, but it was a struggle to keep warm, and at Ladbroke the oil stove in Celia's room was never off and she scarcely went out for a month. A year later Henry was born.'

Bombardier Diana Wood

Like the father she never knew, when the war commenced, she too rallied to the colours. She joined the ATS, in the 13th Somerset Local Company, which was started in Keynsham by Captain Mrs Diana Thomas. Miss Margaret Hickling from Chandag Road and Miss Joyce Clarke (Mrs Scott) of West View Road, were also members.

Diana was posted to Larkhill, on Salisbury Plain in September 1940. After a week's training in clerical work at Aldermaston, she applied successfully to rejoin the 13th Somersets at Larkhill. There she met and later married Master Gunner Denis Carbery, after which she was sent to the 13th City of London Company at Bulford, near Larkhill.

'I found the work quite interesting as I was in the Instructor's Office, and so typed out the week's training course. I worked from 8.30 am to 5.30 pm and rose to become a bombardier with two stripes, working for the Chief Instructor, who was a Major. Our daughter Susan was born in 1943, so after two years' service, it was back to Ladbroke.'

Life after the war

Later, in 1945, Diana and Denis moved to the bungalow at 240, Bath Road, which backed on to fields and she recalled that, 'Before Wellsway School was built, we could look across and see there a fine field of corn waving in the wind. We lived there for 39 years. When the wind was in the right direction, we could hear batsmen hitting cricket balls during matches at the F Taylor Memorial Ground!'

Corena wrote, 'Sunday was a family tea-party day at Ladbroke. Granny, the aunts and friends made us very welcome . . . John and Diana loved tennis and Mrs Braithwaite of Hamleaze, Bristol Road, who had a large house and a garden, had a hard court which she allowed us to use. There were Men's Four with Ken Gibbons, Harold Dowdney (of Cooper and Tanner), Hugh Statham and John. They played one or more evenings in the week and every Saturday. Diana and I became friends and were allowed to play once a week.

'Later Hugh Statham made a gorgeous tennis court at Rivermead and was then sadly killed piloting Brittania.

'John went daily to the Lloyd's Bank in Lower Weston Road on his 'buzz bomb', a cycle with an engine fitted to it and had some scary minor accidents. Sadly he did not enjoy banking but soldiered on and was delighted to retire. He joined the Bank's Rugger club and appeared in the Tatler.

'John was the Vicar's Warden for ten years with Padre Trevor Wright. The Vicarage garden was huge and the Padre asked John to have a plot there to grow vegetables. This was invaluable as we could get away to their garden, and aunts and all had vegetables, as there was still rationing. Miss Cooksley produced plays in the vicarage garden, which was a perfect setting.

'Sadly John died in hospital on May 22 1982 from heart trouble. By then all three of our children were married and John was a grandfather.'

Of the large Wood family, with many maiden sisters, it seems that Gunner Charles Henry alone had a son, that is, Major John Wood. As we have seen, John had a son bearing the ancient family name of Henry, who alone carries on the family name of Wood. He is not a farmer nor does he live in Keynsham, but today Henry is an architect working and living in California, with his wife Nina and their 11 year old athletic daughter. Their very musical 18 year old son Daniel came over in 1990 with the Californian Youth Orchestra who played in Bath, Winchester, the Barbican and Canterbury. 'Henry Wood' would be proud of them.

Chapter 3

Evacuees in Keynsham

From the River Chew, a steep pull up the hill brings one to the charming old Bath Hill School. Built in 1857, it is one of the few unspoilt Victorian buildings in the town, its three original class rooms retaining most of their distinctive early architectural charm. However, Miss Mary Fairclough pointed out that in 1939 'the washing facilities in that school were sub-Roman'. Linked to the school is the home of earlier successive headmasters, even though it has never boasted a bathroom. To the rear it has a fine view over the park, and its rooms are now used for school administration.

Mary Fairclough remembers

The day war broke out, about 20 billeting officers and their devils, of whom I was one, were sitting on the steps of Bath Hill School waiting for the evacuees who were supposed to arrive about dinner time, but who did not arrive until about 5 or 6 o'clock. It was probably the WVS who supplied them all with some tea. Though it was light when they arrived, by the time we had given them a meal, and divided them into groups for different areas of the village, it was beginning to get dark. It was the first night of complete blackout, and we were trying to billet unaccompanied children, some 40 or 50, who had come by train accompanied by a small number of mothers with their babies.

By the time that my group got to St Ladoc Road, it was darker still. We took the children round and knocked at a door and said, 'Mrs Smith, you said you would have three. Can you take these three?' Most would say 'Yes, come on in', and we would gratefully leave them and go on with the remainder to the next house.

The children came from Wapping and Soho mainly and were nice kids mostly. We managed to find the people who said they would billet them and left the poor little kids with them. They were dead tired, poor little brats, and scared out of their lives, a lot of them. They seemed to be all ages from seven years onwards and a few younger still, I would have thought, and some up to teenagers.

Next morning most people who had taken them in had the same experience as I had, for early next day they phoned up to ask what they could do, as they could not keep the children with their own as the Londoners all had lice. It hadn't occurred to any of us that we might be up against that. So one of our billeting officers, Jean Sharman, tackled George Ashton, the town clerk, in his lair, and he said, 'It can't be lice' so she opened her hand and deposited a said creature on his blotting pad, where he drew a circle around it. By 5 pm he had arranged a de-lousing centre down at the old gas works building at the bottom of Dapps Hill, which had really been put by to be a mortuary if we needed it. So that gradually, with a lot of hard talking on our part, we got over that particular difficulty. It was the lice, more than the fleas, which had really upset the mothers.

Mother, Father and I were living at a biggish house at No 43, Charlton Road, and were expecting to take evacuees. We did not have any the first night, for which I was profoundly grateful, but the second night we had a mother, a boy of 14, a girl of 8, and a baby of 9 months not house trained. She was a dear soul was Mrs Beale. They had never been in the country before, and the thing that fascinated them most of all was when, a few days later when things weren't quite so hectic, we took them for a walk down to Chewton Keynsham where they saw cows being milked in the byre of the Manor Farm. This so fascinated them that whenever anyone had time to take them for a walk, this was always where they wanted to go. The farmer had one of the earlier milking machines. Dolly, the little girl, had not realised that milk came from cows.

They stayed with us for four weeks, while we tried to get them a house of their own, which was easier for them than having to fit in with us. Eventually we got them a flat, but soon afterwards we heard that they had gone back to London, which quite a number of families did in the early 'phoney war' period. A little later Dad received a letter from the boy, who must have lied like blazes about his age and had got into the Royal Navy. He knew Dad was connected with Wills and asked if there was still such a thing as a Woodbine, so we sent him some. We lost track of them after that.

In charge of distributing the children was Mrs Jack Hickling and Mrs Jean Sharman second. The only billeting difficulties were in the early days, when the operation was set up. Before the war started, we had to do a complete survey, house to house, of the whole of Keynsham, though in those days there was no Chandag Road Estate, no Meadow Park and no Federated Homes Estates. We had to see who had accommodation as billeting could be compulsory, though most people were very good. My own impression was that you had more trouble with the bigger houses than you did in areas like St George's Road who had very little accommodation, but who said 'Yes, of course we will take some'. My chief was Miss Richards and I think most of the responsibility came on George Ashton.

I don't think we had soldiers billeted on people here. For that purpose the military took over the Drill Hall and Rockhill House. When the real war started, they found that Keynsham was not a good place to send evacuees, as we were the fighting ground for Bristol.

I got to know two or three of the London teachers later, who said, 'If the authorities had only let us open the London schools a week or two earlier, we would have got the children organised, deloused, etc, because we always had to do this at the beginning of the autumn term in our district. But we were just not allowed to open any earlier than usual, and on the second day of term we were just sent off.

We had about the whole of one school from Soho, and possibly part of another school from Wapping, so there might have been some 150 or more evacuees. I think the small group of mothers went back, apart from an Italian family who were sent to Queen Charlton, and a red-headed Irish family. I still see one of the daughters about, who is quite unmistakable. The bulk of the children remained behind. One of them, Marie, was adopted, I believe, by Dr Charles Sharman and his wife Jean, as something happened to her parents. I painted a picture of her. She was a darling.

I would say that, by and large, the evacuees didn't shape up too badly in the schools and mixed happily with the local children. The few Londoners that I met seemed to be a pretty bright lot.

As time went on, I got to know two or three of the teachers from London, and particularly a delightful little woman, a Jewess, Esther Freedland, who was hungry for books to read. As there was no library in the village in those days, she used to come up to our home for books.

The only primary schools in Keynsham then were Temple Street and Bath Hill, and the established secondary school, Broadlands. The two junior schools could not possibly have absorbed all the extra children, even though a few evacuees probably went to Broadlands. All the chapels had classes in them, that is, the Baptist's, Victoria, Bethesda, Zion chapel and probably the Old Church School in Station Road. At that time, all the Sunday schools, and the additional rooms, were all small. Actually they were using anywhere they could get. The Fear Institute had been taken over for the 'duration' by the Army. The evacuees must have almost doubled the school population, and Bath Hill had no extra class rooms in those days. The children would have been in the schools as far as possible, and the London teachers spread as thinly as possible in the outlying buildings.

I would think that the London teachers kept to their own classes as much as possible to give the children continuity and reassurance. The three teachers I knew were all women, and I think there were another two teachers, also women, from London.

* * *

If each of these five teachers brought a class of 35 children with them, this would have amounted to 175 children. But it appears that there was more than just the one group of evacuees. A lady from Woodbine Terrace spoke of the arrival at Bath Hill School of two bus loads of Londoners. Another lady, herself an evacuee, recalled how she was just thankful to get away from the bombs on the city, and she did not travel here by train. That was probably in 1940.

At the end of the war, most of the evacuees went back to London, though a few remained behind, including the Italian and the Irish family. Mary thought a girl named Iris Kilburn also remained and married soon afterwards, around 1945. She could not recall any London teenagers working in the local shops, only local youngsters and those recently returned from the war.

Mrs Rosemary King-Smith, a dear soul, lived at The Towers at Kelston during the war, and billeted a number of children. She recalled, 'It was a mistake for them to have been sent to the isolation of small country villages, as all they wanted was the pub and the fish shop. I think that some went back quite soon, though others stayed and a few remained after the war and worked locally.'

19

Professor McGrath's wife, Sheila, who was at Redmaids' School, Bristol, during the war, has a delightful memory of that time. As early as 1938 and more so in 1939, business firms and government departments, including the BBC, were evacuated to Bristol, where their children attended many local schools, including Redmaids. The landladies who cared for the adults were paid three shillings a day board money, making twenty one shillings a week, so the Bristolians wittily dubbed them 'The guinea pigs'.

Mrs Isabelle Andrews (nee Ollis) recalls that the Police Force in Keynsham during the war consisted of an Inspector, a Sergeant, a plain-clothes detective, with a regular male staff of two men on motor duty and four on the beat. The Keynsham police area was a large one, with several villages, including Woollard and Pensford, with Headquarters at Long Ashton. To release men for military service, women officers were recruited. So it was that Miss Ollis was visited at her home at the top of Bath Hill, where she was asked if she would consider joining the force. This is how she became 'Auxiliary Police Woman 45,' one of the village's two APWs, stationed at the fine stone built Victorian Police Station on Bath Hill, constructed in the same charming style as Bath Hill school, and also sited close to the road.

She remembers the arrival of the evacuees, and thought that they fitted in well with the local children. She suspected that possibly it was not only the London children that suffered from lice! [Before you rise up in anger at her dreadful suggestion, can I just say that on to my desk at school on December 1, 1989, came a pile of four-page yellow leaflets from the Avon Education Dept. for distribution in the class, entitled, 'You don't have to go to school – To Catch Headlice'.]

APW 45's uncle was Mr Henry Willcox, who lived with his wife Sarah at the family home of his father, the well-known builder, Mr Willcox senior, at 86, Bath Hill, Keynsham. 'Henry accepted an evacuee girl of about ten, who in effect became a member of the family, and remained happily with them right up to the end of the war. The family almost adopted her, and kept in close touch with her and later attended her marriage in London,' recalled Mrs Andrews.

She thought that among the evacuees there were only about six mothers with babies, and that they were billeted in the large houses in Priory Road. However, they seemed to have missed their London friends greatly, and after a short time returned to the capital, as Mary had thought. It seems, perhaps surprisingly, that no Londoners were in trouble with the law.

A wider look at the evacuation procedures

My colleague, Elizabeth Linssen, B.Ed(Hons), in her excellent degree dissertation on 'Evacuation Procedures and Experiences in the Bristol Area', states that only 69% of London's mothers with children under five registered for evacuation in 1939. She wrote: 'When war finally came in 1939, the government had made provision for four million people to leave the cities, but in fact only one and a half million took advantage of the scheme. A further two million people made private arrangements to move out of dangerous areas. (p 10.)

'Evacuation from Bristol had been recommended on Dec 20, 1940 for children between five and fourteen years, by the Bristol Education Committee. . . . On the 7 February 1941, it was reported that the parents of 7,111 Bristol children had assented to evacuation (34.9% of those eligible).

'It was agreed that evacuation should take place over four days, starting on Tuesday 18 February. Forms for parental consent were circulated to secondary schools for possible consideration later on, but in the first instance evacuation was only offered to children between five and fourteen. Each party being evacuated was to be accompanied by a first aid kit, and a list of recommended clothes was to be sent to parents. In cases of hardship, approaches were to be made to the Lord Mayor's Relief Fund and the WVS. Where it was necessary, children might take gymnastic shoes supplied by the Education department. Parents were to supply their children with enough food for two meals, and the Committee was to supply and pay for a bottle of milk for each child to drink on the journey.

'Schools were to be used as assembly points, and were therefore to be closed for normal schooling . . . The Chief Education Officer had asked for 500 volunteers to help with the evacuation, and 1,000 people had come forward. . . . The WVS and The Lord Mayor's Distress Fund supplemented the supply of boots and shoes for distribution to the children . . .

'A second evacuation of children to Cornwall was organised for Easter week in 1941. . . . 2,248 elementary children went to Cornwall . . . and arrangements were also made for 95 secondary school children to go to St Austell so they might continue their education.

'The Committee spent some of their time considering expenses claimed by teachers for their removals . . . The maximum weekly allowance was to be 14/-, with 5/- extra for teachers who found their own accommodation. It appears that married teachers were expected to leave their families in Bristol.

'In July 41 the Committee received letters deprecating the removal of children by their parents before they had settled down, and stressing the undesirability of children having large amounts of pocket money. It was agreed that parents should be asked to give only small sums to their children . . . As early as 1941 it became apparent that 35% of evacuees had returned home to Bristol . . . Following an attack on Exeter in May 1941, a party of children was re-evacuated to Bideford.' (p 100.)

Elizabeth relates how sad it was for the evacuees who waited in vain for letters from their parents, and how some of the younger children who had been away from home for years felt that, on the rare occasions that their mothers visited them, they were really strangers. Also there were the occasions when in the initial rush to find homes for the "vackies", a term commonly used, usually in a disparaging way, the social background of the child was not matched to that of the host, to the distress of both parties.

Householders, with 'habitable rooms', contribute to the war effort

Keynsham obviously received the same request as that recorded in the Clutton RUDC Minute Book on 13 Jan 1939, stating, 'A circular has been

21

received from the Ministry of Health asking that a 'detailed survey be made of the district to ascertain accommodation available for housing persons evacuated from congested areas in times of national emergency.'

'It was suggested that officers be appointed to direct the survey, and that expenditure properly incurred would not be a charge on the rates and that no extra staff would be needed to carry out this survey. The survey was to be completed by 28 February and the Clerk to the Council was appointed to direct it. He arranged that all houses in the district should be visited and that particulars should be obtained as to surplus accommodation, on the basis of one person per 'habitable' room. Householders should be asked whether they would be willing to receive unaccompanied children or teachers. On the basis of this survey (14 April 1939) the Ministry of Health proposed that 5,800 persons could be accommodated in the district.'

Elizabeth continued that at Taunton the Evacuation Committee on 9 June 1939, 'agreed to the use of schools for the reception and distribution of evacuees. It appears that the initial evacuation went very smoothly, although a tribunal had to be set up to consider appeals against billeting (11 Aug 1939) . . . Throughout the war it became more difficult to place evacuees and there are instances both in the Clutton RDC Minutes and in the Somerset Guardian, where reluctant householders have been prosecuted. A 71-year-old man 'claimed that his beds were damp and that he was too old to look after children. He was fined 10/-'.

'A Frome woman was fined £2, after claiming that an evacuee upset her nerves and she had to see a doctor. The boy had no laces in his shoes and his shirt was outside his trousers,' (page 13, quoting the Somerset Guardian of 26 July 1940).

'Clutton's Minutes Book, dated 14 February, 1941, records that although the District had received 3,000 evacuees, 1,700 of these had returned home or transferred to other areas. In addition to child evacuees, there was evidence that many aged and homeless people were being sent to the area. The clerk reported that it was difficult to get hosts to accept more evacuees even when their first guests had moved on.'

To encourage hosts, who were becoming tired of the permanent intrusion into their homes, and worried about food scarcity, the Somerset Guardian of 17 May 1940 announced that billeting allowances were to be increased from 31 May. The new rates were to be, for evacuees aged 10–14, 10/6 weekly; those 14–16, 12/6 weekly and those over 16, 15/-. Previously the rates had been: up to 14, 10/6 for a single child, or 8/6 weekly for each where more than one were billeted; over 14, 10/6 weekly each. (page 14). Presumably Bristol's weekly 21/- mentioned earlier, referred either to adults, or to children living in the elite Clifton area.

Attitudes to the evacuees

Elizabeth writes that 'Generally, evacuees were treated with a certain amount of suspicion. They had come from big cities and had very little knowledge of the country, and on the other hand, their hosts were very set in their ways and unwilling to allow for the fact that the children were used to a very different way of life. A lot of children came from poor homes, and did not have the social graces which some of their hosts took for granted.

'The press (Somerset Guardian March 8, 1940) also uncovered a further problem. "Husbands refuse maintenance" headlined an article about women having to sue their husbands for their upkeep. The husbands said they were only prepared to support them if they returned home, and this reflected badly on evacuees as a whole.' (pages 28 and 29.)

Evaluation of evacuation

'If lives saved is the criterion by which success can be judged, undoubtedly evacuation was successful . . . Financially, evacuation cannot have cost a great deal . . . But I must reiterate the most important contribution that evacuation made; that of promoting an awareness of the "plight of the urban poor".' It was this which prompted the following comment in The Economist on 1 May 1943.

'Evacuation was the most important subject in the social history of the war, because it revealed to the whole people the black spots in its social life.' In the long term, the country was forced to see the poverty which had been 'swept under the carpet' for so long, and as a result steps had to be taken to alleviate the resulting degradation.' (p 32).

From this general look at evacuation concerning our neighbours in Bristol, Pensford and Clutton, let us return specifically to the experience of a hostess at Chewton Keynsham.

Having evacuees at home farm was part of their war effort

Mr and Mrs Warren lived at Manor Farm, Chewton Keynsham, as working farmers, during World War II. Mrs Warren, Dorothy, mentioned to me that they gave the use of one wing of their farmhouse, with its separate entrance, to evacuees. At the outbreak of hostilities, they had billeted on them two Italian families, consisting of mothers and children.

Mrs Warren was quite happy to accommodate these evacuees from London, and regarded it as just part of her 'war effort,' in addition to her hard work on the farm. However, the evacuees were far from happy, and as Dorothy said, 'They thought it was terrible here. There was nothing to do or to see.'

Despite that, she commented that 'The children fled out of the farmhouse in panic on their first night here, when they had their initial encounter with certain creatures of the dark – harmless bats – which roosted there. Later there was excitement of a different kind when the local police arrived to evict one of the visiting Italian fathers who decided to stay with his family. That was simply not permitted.' Soon after that the families, presumably happily, returned to their London homes.

Later Mrs Warren had successive evacuees all the way from the severely blitzed city of – Bristol!

She recalled that one of our bombers crashed between Manor Farm and Upton Farm. 'The pilot fell to the ground in the field behind Exon's Dairy, opposite the parish church. Sadly, he was dead.' She thought that none of the crew had survived, though farmer Alfred Paget would know.

Dorothy recalled that 'German bombers making for Bristol flew along the Chew Valley, so we were bombed before Keynsham or Bristol. We were in bomb alley, and had many bombs fall harmlessly on our fields.'

We have looked at the local arrival of the first group of evacuees to Keynsham, and seen something of the wider aspects of the subject. Now we come to the 'ipsissima verba' of a boy who represents a later party of evacuees to Keynsham.

The wartime memories of Samuel Olive, an evacuee from London

'I was born in Stepney, London, on September 28, 1932' Mr Olive said. Stepney is 'a district at the heart of the East End, where tall blocks of flats have replaced most of the slums. The Highway, Stepney's main street, was once notorious for its seamen's drinking dens. Two picturesque 16th. Century inns are The Town of Ramsgate, close to which the infamous Judge Jefferies was arrested in 1688, and The Prospect of Whitby, an old smugglers' haunt. In pre-war days Stepney's Limehouse area was known as Chinatown because of its large Chinese population . . .' (AA Illustrated Guide to Britain, p 253.)

Samuel explained 'My father was named Samuel Olive, which was his father's name too. Living so near to the West India Docks, father was a docker to start with. Then he became a painter. He was working with a gang in a cradle high up on the side of a gasometer, when the support ropes broke and they all crashed to the ground. Only dad survived, and his jaw, his back and his legs and arms, were all broken. He was given £500 compensation, a fortune in those prewar days. Before the war he was in the territorials, so despite his earlier injuries, at the outbreak of war he tried to enlist with the colours, only to be rejected.'

After the evacuation of Dunkirk in May 1940, 'the large scale attacks on this country by German aircraft began on 10 July 1940, which is the generally accepted date of the beginning of the Battle of Britain.' (Mac Hawkins, Somerset at War, 1988, p 18). Young Samuel was then but a boy of eight, who during the Blitz, like thousands of fellow Londoners, went to the shelter of the London Underground Railway stations when the air-raid sirens wailed their frightening warning.

He recalled, 'We lived at 27 Knott Street, Stepney. One night we went down the shelter and when my mum and I went back the house had been flattened. The roof had gone and the front wall had gone and the bed was hanging through the ceiling. And of course, it was illegal to go into the house again once it had been bombed even though it was yours, wasn't it? All we got was a picture of me when I was a baby, a torch and some cutlery. That was all that we took. I remember that. They cordoned the area off, because of war claims. We were sent to Kensington, to a row of great big massive houses, with twenty rooms in them, where they said film stars used to live. We stayed there as a temporary measure, probably for a matter of weeks. Then we were moved to Keynsham'.

To a new life in the green village of Keynsham

It was in September 1940, just before his ninth birthday, that young Samuel came to Keynsham. He recalled, 'We came by train. There were hundreds of us children. Some went on to Bristol. There were probably about 80 kids got off here with around a dozen mothers. The station platform was packed with people. I remember seeing a large sign on the platform saying 'Keynsham Somerdale'.

'There were no teachers with us [schools having been closed earlier and the staff dispersed], but some ladies, possibly WVS workers, but without any uniforms, came down with us, and then returned to London.'

In answer to my questioning, he added, 'Now you mention it, we were given sandwiches before we left, but I can't remember any drinks. We had our gas masks with us in cardboard boxes, and our name tabs pinned to our coat lapels. We were met at the station by the WVS, with Mrs Margery Hickling in charge. We walked to the Church Rooms in Station Road, now no longer there, where we had tea and biscuits. Then various people came and collected 'their children'.

'Living in London, I had never seen a field, a cow or a pint of milk. All our milk was either condensed or evaporated from a tin. The sight of a field was like magic! In spite of this, I was home-sick for a while.

Local houses requisitioned

'Lots of houses had been requisitioned, hadn't they, and we were taken to Number 6, The Avenue. Three families lived there; the Fords were in the basement, we were on the ground floor and the Kilburns were upstairs. There were no evacuees on Priory Road; it was too posh. But at 8, Abbey Park were the Smiths, who came a year after us, the Throwers and the Sampsons. At Milward Lodge, opposite Cannock's Garage, were the Fergusons and the Fishers. At Milward House, opposite the church, were the Lerpinieres. Some families went to Saltford and Whitchurch. These houses were taken over completely by evacuee families.

'At first at No 6 there was no proper furniture. Gradually the locals gave us bits, and some came from the council. We had bare floorboards, which my mother, Mrs Kathleen Olive, or I scrubbed, till they came up white. Lino was a luxury. We slept on the floor on straw palliasses for a year or so before we were given beds. It was a beautiful house, but very cold. There were fireplaces in the bedrooms, but we only had coal for the living room. I slept in the attic and when later I told my dad I was cold, he just said, 'Put another coat on'.

'To start with, the only bathrooms and toilets were in the basement and the first floor, so we just had to share with the Ford's family of five and the Kilburn's six. We had no hot water, so when it was bath night, we heated water in a large boiler with a gas ring below it, used for the washing, in the big kitchen. We placed the large tin bath in front of the stove, to help keep the water hot. When mother got out, I got in, then my sisters got in, each in their turn after me. If you banged your leg on the side of the bath nearest the stove, you would get burned.'

25

Samuel recalled that many of the children from London had fleas, and remembered his mother using a special comb, 'which is why my hair is so thin today,' he laughed. 'In London I caught scabies from the shelters where so many different people slept on the floor. I went to the municipal baths where I had special mustard baths.'

For a year or so, the big brothers and dads were not permitted to join their families. From a sociological viewpoint, the three families of children at No 6 must have felt that in the Avenue they were a small surviving oasis of Londoners in the midst of the Keynsham desert of aliens. Hence we find Samuel saying, 'To start with, we and the local children resented each other, so we used to throw stones at any who came into our road.' They were but following a deeply instinctive national habit, centuries old.

'The neighbours weren't very pleased about us at first, which was quite understandable. We ruined the garden. We never had one in London. There our houses were back to back . . . Also we took the weights out of the bottom of the black out curtains. So it was 'those horrible kids from London,' but later they were very nice to us.

'There were two neighbours who were exceptionally nice who were maiden ladies, I believe, called Matthews. They lived at number 4, The Avenue. One was a nurse and the other a teacher. They come along with food and toys they had picked up and they laid on something from the Canadian Red Cross, clothes and toys, and a food parcel. A lot of the locals gave us furniture, because we just had the basics. They gave us tables and chairs, which were pretty old and we didn't think much of them at the time. Later we were given beds.

Another man I would like to mention is Dr Norman Gerrish, who was wonderful to my mother and family. She had rather a lot of children. I was the oldest, then came Iris, Lilian, and Christine who was a babe in arms when we arrived, and after dad came down and joined us, she had four more, Billy, Irene, Norma and Maureen. The Dr never charged us when he came or looked after the children. That was wonderful in those days. He was a nice man.'

In those days there were no Child Allowances, no Social Security payments and no free National Health Service. With a family of eight children, money was short. One understands why the kindness of the Doctor was so appreciated.

'Later my uncle came down but returned to London after a year or two. Grandad Samuel Olive also came to Keynsham and was on the gates at Frys, but he also went back. Dad came down a year after us. His sister Mary Ann Olive came down with us and stayed. Dad worked for the BAC, who during the war took over part of Fry's. When they later returned to Filton, he continued to work for them and commuted daily. We continued to live at No 6 till about 1952, a stay of over ten years.

When Bethesda Chapel became a school

'At first I went to school at the chapel in Temple Street [now a carpet shop] which was divided up by curtains into four classes grouped according to age. There were 50 children in my class, a mixture of Keynsham and London pupils. There were no London teachers with us there. In charge was our teacher, Miss Tidman, a little short lady who always seemed to have a hat on, even in class. I think she was the head teacher.

'You know how in those days, children used to draw swastikas on their hands with chalk, then slap other children on the back, leaving a mark. Well, one day I was falsely accused of doing this, and was horrified when Miss Tidman said I would have to undress in front of the class. [Presumably this was to reveal where he had hidden the chalk] Fortunately Freddy Kilburn, one of the boys I came down with, owned up that he had done it. I was so embarrassed.

'On another occasion, we were very frightened when we heard a plane come roaring low over our school. It crashed on the 'rec' between the chapel and where Hawthorns Home now is about a hundred yards away. A dozen of us boys dashed out of school up to the wreckage of this small German fighter. [Actually an English plane] It had exploded into bits of jagged metal, but it was not on fire. The pilot was still in it, dead. Tommy Ford said he picked up the pilot's glove, with part of his hand still in it. When we got back to class, we were all caned!

'The school had no playground. At the back outside were just the toilets . . .'

As a boy there, he felt he was quite quickly accepted by his class mates, but if he or his sisters put a foot wrong, the grown-ups would comment, 'They are only evacuees. What can you expect from them?' They were still 'foreigners'.

In his fourth and last year in primary school, Samuel attended Bath Hill School, though he thought that he was only there for a short time. The head teacher there was "Scratchy Mycock", who was a formidable man, a frightening man, who was always scratching himself.'

Broadlands Secondary Modern School

'I was there from 11 to 14. The head was Mr Connock, [who became the head in Feb. 1944 succeeding Mr. H.A. Baker, the first head, who was appointed in 1935] and lived at Whitchurch. His son was at the school then, and was held up to us as an example! [Poor boy. What a situation for him!] I enjoyed school there, particularly as they had playing fields, and as I enjoyed sports.

'One of my teachers was Mr Runnells, who took sport, carpentry and metal work, and encouraged me, and even made me a class prefect. As long as my work was up to date, I was allowed to pump up the footballs and mark out the pitch.

'In the summer I was allowed just a few days off in the month for haymaking, as long as I had worked hard at my lessons. This encouraged me to get on with my school work. I laboured in the fields towards Bitton, below Fry's [Sydenham Fields] for 4d an hour.

'While I was at Broadlands, I used to deliver papers for Hall's before school. After school I would deliver groceries for Mr Headley Chappell. Or I would clean the shop windows for Mr Boseley, who had a business next to the Fear Institute, for four shillings; and the windows and the glass on the tie drawers, for Mr Baker.' This young Londoner was not frightened of hard work!

Samuel said there were no gang fights between Keynsham boys and the evacuees. The newcomers really were becoming integrated into the community. But he recalled, 'There were fights between the Keynsham and the Brislington boys. About 9 of us would go to the Ritz Cinema there on Brislington Hill. After that we went to the local chip shop, where they started teasing us, and we would come to blows. But it was not premeditated, and never very serious. You never kicked anyone when he was down. You were far more frightened of the police, because if they came they would really thump you, so we would all run off.'

Life in post war Keynsham

It is difficult to work out just how many children from the different parts of London were cared for and accommodated in Keynsham, as they were dispersed among the local populace. With mother and family units it was easier to work out. Samuel said there were 8 Olive children, 4 Fords, 9 Kilburns, 4 Smiths ('the eldest became a navigator and was killed in the war'), and 4 Lerpinieres, making 30 in just five families.

According to Mr Olive, nearly all of these children remained in Keynsham after the cessation of hostilities and most married local people. 'I was still living in No 6, The Avenue, when in 1954 I left to marry Miss Drena Waller, a Keynsham girl. Four children were born to us, Robert John, Susan and the twins, Rosalynne and Christine.

'After the war, Fry's was still the greatest employer in the village. People came from Bristol to work there, and Bristol paid for houses to be built here to rehouse those bombed out in the city during the war. Also, if you worked for Fry's, it was easier for you to get a house locally.' Yet this Bristol overspill caused a lot of local controversy and bad feeling among the locals, as Keynsham people also needed houses, particularly with the addition of the London element.

The result was a postwar building boom in Keynsham. Houses in Cranmore Avenue were built and the Park Estate of Queens Road, Coronation Avenue, Caernarvon Road and the neighbouring streets all sprang up.

This links up with Mr Chris Wiggins' comments that when he took over the family firm after the war, 'You would only be granted a licence to build profitable private dwellings if you agreed to erect council houses, though we were in severe financial straits at the time and there was hardly any profit to be made from such building.' Yet one saw the pre-war firms of Wiggins, Willcox and Wiltshires again building and repairing houses. Hawkins and the Cooper Brothers also erected houses, but as Mr Wiggins said, 'As soon as the big contractors came in, we were all able to return to what we were best at, maintaining properties. We did not have enough staff to build houses.'

Today with so many new people living in this fast-growing dormitory town, it was only with the greatest difficulty that I was able to discover who had been evacuees in those distant war days fifty years ago. They are foreigners no longer.

And what happened to Mr Samuel Olive? With his family now grown up and married, still he lives happily on the Park Estate with his wife. And despite all the modernisation and consequent redundancy at Fry's/Cadbury's, he continues to work there as a skilled machine operator after 36 years at the factory.

Of his former home in beloved London, Sam commented rather sadly, 'I don't think that Knott Street exists today. The area is all flats now, though I haven't been up to see it.'

Endless evacuees endured

Mr Sydney F Holburn, Keynsham's first full-time official driver of the local fire engine during the war, lived with his wife Dora and their two children, Peter and Judith, at Number 1, Kelston Road. With spare rooms in their spacious house, they felt it their duty to open their home to evacuees from the capital city which they had been led to believe would be almost razed to the ground.

Mr Holburn recalled, 'There was a great cry throughout the county that all the cities were to be evacuated and that we were to accept evacuees from London. It came as a shock to a lot of Keynsham people to see the degraded condition in which a lot of Londoners were living. It just shook us. We just had to accept it. We were willing. We just handed over our prams, etc, to them. They had not got anything. There were all sorts of things that they needed, which they were just given. Their ability to handle just ordinary household articles was just an impossibility. They just weren't used to things like knives and forks. Some weren't even able to sleep on a bed. Some of the conditions of Londoners were terrible. We just had to accept what London sent. They arrived with their labels on and were allocated out to this and that house.

'We had a mother and two children if I remember rightly. Well, this had all been such a shock to the town that in the end we did not know what was going to happen. After a few days people began to think that perhaps the authorities had made a mistake in such big quantities being evacuated. There wasn't going to be the flattening of the city that they had expected.

'We went down the High Street one day, and there was our pram in front of the church, just parked in the road. The people had just gone back to London and left the pram. They never said a word to us . . . And they weren't the only ones. They were just gone, there was no goodbye. Just a moonlight flit sort of thing, that's all. And so we lost our evacuees. There had been a mother, and a child in the pram and one toddling, being about one and three. We were just grateful when we realised what had happened.'

Though the behaviour of the London lady was most discourteous to say the least, it clearly highlights just how wretched she must have felt, despite the many intended kindnesses of Sydney and Dora. The woman was completely out of her depth, through no fault of her own, or her hosts. There was just a great cultural gap between them, which must have caused her agony of mind, with no familiar faces and friends to confide in, and no husband for help. Utterly inadequate, flight was the only remedy for her.

Mr Holburn continued, 'So we were able to make accommodation for people that we could choose. We had a lady with two children, whose husband was in the army in Norway, as an undercover man. She was far better. She knew how to behave and accepted any courtesy that we put forward. We were much happier and could have gone on with her. She stayed quite a long while. Her husband then returned from Norway and was being given some training in England and she wanted to go to a town nearby to be with him. So off she went and we chose another.

'He was a Scottish gentleman from Edinburgh, with his wife and one boy. He was responsible for the tapestries for the Queen at Balmoral. His boy was about the same age as my younger child, Judith, and they got on very well together. We had very good associations there, so much so that we kept in touch with them after they left.'

I asked him, 'With regard to the evacuation of children, did Keynsham on the whole rise to the occasion and take the children to their hearts?' Sydney replied, 'Yes I would say very much so, and more so than a city like Bristol, or say Bedminster. They really put themselves out. There must have been hundreds of children, for they were coming two or three to a family in nearly every house.

Keynsham's first and last Roman Catholic school

'At the back of Victoria we had an old army hut, which we used as a Sunday School and which was occupied by the Catholics as a day school for Londoners of that persuasion. It was run by two or three Sisters wearing habits, who came down from London with their own church children, and gave them a sense of continuity. They were not meant to teach any of their doctrines. I went in there, say, when I was preparing my Sunday School lesson [Mr Holburn was the SS Superintendent] and I would not be quite sure that they were not teaching some of their Catholicism, but we didn't make any fuss about it.

'The nuns ran the day school by themselves, and had a cupboard in which to keep the children's and their own books . . . I imagine they went to the local homes sheltering evacuees, to make a list of those of their faith, and brought them down to their school. The school was full, and the hut held over fifty children or more . . . No, I don't remember what order the nuns belonged to. We let them just carry on there . . . No, there were no statues or anything like that, that I knew of. You see, they had to be honourable to our Methodist premises and not do anything contrary to Methodist teaching on our premises.

'They weren't there for the whole of the war, but they were there for some years . . . There was no conflict between the Catholic children and the Protestant children or with the local children. None to my knowledge. It was the war we wanted over,' Mr Sydney Holburn concluded.

One imagines that with a Junior School of around fifty pupils, the children there would be in year groups. From what Sydney said earlier, there would appear to have been a frequent turnover of school children as some returned to London, with possibly a core of more permanent evacuees.

My wife and I recall that when we arrived in Keynsham in 1964, and lived at 51, Charlton Road, once a week on a Tuesday morning, Roman Catholic children from nearby Kelston Road School would be withdrawn for Religious Education. Crocodile-wise they would pass our door and enter Number 49, the home of Mr and Mrs Knott, where a priest in his robes would also arrive to instruct them.

Though the legal right to withdraw children for sectarian instruction remains, Mrs P McGrath told me that she thought that today Roman Catholic children in Keynsham were no longer actually withdrawn.

St Dunstan's Roman Catholic Church, Keynsham

Let us digress from evacuees for a moment to ask just when was the Catholic church in Keynsham built, and why was it needed and why did Bishop Lee choose to dedicate it to St. Dunstan when one of the monks of Downside Abbey, who financed the project, suggested Richard Whiting, the last abbot of Glastonbury, who was put to death by Henry VIII?

'It was very fitting that the new church in Keynsham, Somerset, should be dedicated to a Somerset man who had been Abbot of Glastonbury and later Archbishop of Canterbury and who had crowned Edgar the first king of all England at Bath in 973,' [Extract from the commemorative brochure 'The Parish of St Dunstan's, Keynsham, Golden Jubilee 1935–1985'.]

One of the parishioners, Mrs Florence Henry, wrote of St Dunstan's that, 'Before it was built, Catholics in Keynsham had great difficulty in getting to mass, as there was no bus service on Sunday mornings, and people had to go by bicycle, car or hired taxi to Knowle or Bath.'

The brochure, edited by Professor P McGrath, declares 'The foundation stone of St Dunstan's Church was laid by the Bishop of Clifton on 16 March, 1935 and the first mass was celebrated on 20 October. Keynsham was at that time a small township with a population of about 5,000 . . . There is no means of knowing how many Catholics there were in Keynsham and Saltford in the mid-nineteen thirties, but mass attendance in the early days of the church seems to have been small. Some have put the figure as low as 20, but it seems to have gone up to over 50 as soon as the parish was established.

'Bishop Lee decided that there ought to be a church in Keynsham . . . Keynsham was fortunate in that the Bishop was able to make use of money which had been left in trust for building a new church in the diocese and which was being administered by the monks of Downside Abbey.

'The next step was to find a site in Keynsham. The original choice seems to have been for land on which the Charlton Cinema stood [today the Bingo Hall] but there was apparently opposition from the local residents. Fortunately another site became available, and . . . on 1 August 1934 the Bishop completed the purchase from Mrs Marian Crawford of the properties known as 20 Bristol Road (Mulberry Cottage) and 18 Bristol Road, together with the orchard and gardens.

'Mulberry Cottage was a fine building with eighteenth-century features but probably dating from the seventeenth century. [Its present owners regard it as older still than that]. It had a large mulberry tree near the kitchen of the present hall. Number 18 had once been a carpenter's shop and was a small

31

gabled cottage. The new church was to be built on the site of number 18 and its garden, and Mulberry Cottage was to be used as a presbytery. The price of all this property was £1,280. [page 5]

'And so St Dunstan's began its life as an independent parish. The congregation was small and it was a struggle . . . In 1936 there were only six children in the catechism class . . . next year the number rose to eight . . . Those who remember the parish in its early days speak of it as a small, active and happy community. Miss Oxford, who came in the spring of 1939, remembers the charming old-world garden with its wonderful roses, apples and Victoria plum trees and a lawn which Father Reidy made himself and of which he was very proud. There were May processions and Corpus Christi processions in the pleasant gardens. [page 7]

The arrival of the war time guests

'This quiet growth was shattered by the war, which brought large numbers of soldiers and children to Keynsham. The soldiers were billeted in the town, and four of them were in the Presbytery. The children were evacuated from London and were in the care of four Sisters of Charity of St Vincent de Paul whose strange headgear astonished the people of Keynsham, including some Catholics. There was no Catholic school for the children to attend, and the Methodists kindly lent their rooms to the nuns to use as a school. [page 7]

'During the war, a Mother and Baby Home was evacuated for a time to North Breach House, Corston, and there was a remarkable rise in the number of baptisms recorded in St Dunstan's Parish Register. The war years also brought to Corston the Poor Servants of the Mother of God who established themselves at St Teresa's and began the long association between Corston and Keynsham which continues to the present day.

'When the war was over, life slowly returned to normal. In due course, Keynsham and Saltford participated in the great expansion of housing . . . which meant a growth in the number of Catholics. . . . As the number of cars increased, the gardens and the orchard had to make way for a car park, and the great mulberry tree, in which altar servers and other boys often climbed, was cut down to make room for the kitchen of the new parish hall which had been erected in 1967.

'Canon Reidy's retirement in 1973 marked the end of a remarkable thirty-seven years in the life of the parish. . . . He had spent the later part of his time as parish priest living in the new presbytery which had been built by Mr Barrett in 1971. Various uses were found for Mulberry Cottage, but it presented problems. It was a listed building and an application to pull it down was refused. It was sold in 1983 for £18,500.' [page 9]

'Canon Reidy was succeeded by Fr Daniel O'Callaghan who was parish priest from 1973 to 1981. . . . He made determined efforts to set up a primary school. Attempts were made to find a suitable site and a census was taken to see how many children would use the school. By 1977 a primary school for St Dunstan's with a capacity for 150 pupils was third on the list of priorities for Catholic schools drawn up by Avon County Council, and it was thought the project might be realised within seven to ten years. Subsequent developments have made it unlikely that St Dunstan's will ever have its own primary school'. [page 11]

Mrs Sheila McGrath mentioned that one of the great drawbacks to the use of land behind St Dunstan's for a school was the extensive flooding experienced there from time to time. Older local residents remember the flood waters reaching the doors of the Crown Inn on Bristol Road. In 1990 the wide flooding of the area on both sides of the railway line extended to many acres and even saw the intrepid Doctor T Garrett windsurfing there.

'Naught for your comfort'

Returning to the subject of evacuees, Miss Joyce Knight remembers the arrival of the children from London at the outbreak of the war, commenting that 'they all came in one large group and I think it was on a Sunday. They were a rough lot. We were ready to have some but they didn't come for some reason. Mr Morgan, our neighbour next door in Station Road, had a young boy and a girl. But he was over 70 years old, with a housekeeper, and the children were just too much for them. He didn't actually complain, but it was just hard for them. In the end the mother came and took them away.'

This picture reinforces the description given by Mr Holburn of Londoners from the East End. One can understand the strain put upon elderly people who billeted, and the doubtful happiness endured by children who felt unwanted and rejected. In wartime there were many losers.

A Millwall family's refuge in Keynsham

Millwall is situated in the great U-bend of the Thames beyond and below Stepney, and enclosed the famous Millwall Docks, and the West India Docks. Its northern boundary was Poplar. 'The Thames east of Southwark is a working river, with shipping constantly moving in and out of the huge dock system . . . Eastwards, the districts on both river banks, badly damaged in the blitz, are a mixture of docks, industry, slums and experimental post-war housing developments . . . and much of the lively traditional character of the East End survives . . .'. (AA Illustrated Guide to Britain p 251.)

During WWI one of the Kaiser's Zeppelins had earlier passed over Millwall and there dropped some of the first bombs to fall on the city. A Londoner recalled that, 'I went up to North Street where I saw the distraught mothers digging with their hands among the rubble of a row of houses to rescue their children. Later, in Poplar Park they put up a large memorial to the children of North Street School who were killed.'

An inhabitant of Millwall declared that, 'We were really an island, with the water all the way around us. If we went shopping on a bus, we were often caught [stopped] by the swing bridges which allowed the boats through. If we were walking, we had little locks to go over . . . There was the East India Dock Road and the West India Dock Road . . . You could come through Blackwall Tunnel, then go up some spiral steps almost out into Millwall . . . The local people didn't like it being called 'The Isle of Dogs'. The legend is that Charles II kept his hounds there.

When war was declared in 1939, the Lerpiniere family from Millwall was split up. The two elder brothers were evacuated right away, and went off with a group of other Millwall boys to Oxford, accompanied by their teachers. Such was the confusion and speed of events, that Mrs Lerpiniere was uninformed as to where they had gone. Two days later she herself said farewell to her husband and set off with her three-year-old daughter Iris, in a carriage full of other mothers, for the West Country.

'I was among the 50 or so mothers who, with babies and toddlers, alighted at Keynsham, while the rest of the train full of evacuees went on to Bristol, then some to Weston and others to Cardiff.' She said that most of the London evacuees that she knew of came from Poplar, Stepney or Millwall. 'Nearly all the people from Millwall came here. One of the two Fisher families came from Stepney.

'However, we made our way to either the Drill Hall or the Bath Hill School. Billets had already been prepared for us by the WVS. All these women came and were looking everybody over and I saw all the women and children going out, and I thought, What's going to happen to Iris and myself? All of a sudden one lady came and said 'I think you're coming with me, you and your daughter.' All the time I worried where my boys were. I had no idea they were in Abingdon. Later my husband was informed, but he was still away in London. It was quite a while before I was told, and two months before I saw them again.'

Iris recalled, 'For the first few days we stayed with an elderly couple at the large white house at the bottom of Chandag Road. We were then moved to Green Lodge, the beautiful spacious home of Mr and Mrs Grosset.' Keynsham had its own paper mill in those days, and he was the manager of it. Later it was taken over by a number of different firms; lastly it belonged to DRG, before they too were bought out. 'We were there for two months in our two rooms, while mother looked for something larger to accommodate my two brothers when they would join us. Green Lodge had a lovely big garden that stretched down right across what is now the bypass, almost to the railway line. We were there from September to November.

'While there, mother went to the WVS lady and said that she was very worried about her boys and could she have them with her. She said that we couldn't have them with us at the Grossets as there was only one bedroom there. The official said mother would have to go to the Evacuees' Hostel, so we went into the Evacuees' Hostel, at 11, Bristol Road next to the old Manor House. The building has gone now and the site is St John's Court Housing Estate. Then one morning, without any warning, there were my two brothers just standing on the doorstep.

'Mother wasn't very happy there with the other evacuees, so she walked along the High Street, and looked up above Stokes's at Number 38, which seemed to have plenty of empty rooms. Mr Stokes was the Corn and Seed merchant with enormous sacks of grain and farming implements. It was next to the Victoria Methodist Church. He had a large premises, part of which today is the new wine shop. He sold mainly corn, potatoes, hay and a little coal.

'Mr Stokes said he didn't think he had any room, but asked mother who she was, why she wanted it and where she lived. However, soon afterward, his coalman called at the Hostel and asked mother 'Are you the lady who just called to see Mr Stokes? She said 'Yes' and he replied, 'Mr Stokes would like to see you.'

'Mr Stokes told mother she could have some rooms and showed them to her and said, 'You can move in when you like.' My father managed to send down some furniture left from the blitz. The docks had closed down, therefore he hadn't got a job, so he came down as well. That was January 1940 and we were all there together as a complete family, in a strange little house 2 down 1 up and a staircase in a cupboard.

'The Stokes' large garden at the back stretched down to The Hollies. There was a Dutch barn in front of it. It was a beautiful garden and contained 15 apple trees, 3 pears, 4 mays and one nut tree. It had chickens and hedgehogs in it. There was no Ashton Way then.'

'To get into the house you had to climb a wooden staircase, as if you were going into a barn. There was a great big room there, with another staircase up to the boys' room. Off the main room was another little one which was the kitchen. We were very happy there and the Stokes family was very kind.'

Iris explained that Mr Stokes' large three storey building contained, in effect, two long shops side by side. Next to the Methodist Church was his corn and seed business, while next door to that was a dairy with a courtyard behind it, at the rear of which were more buildings where the Lerpinieres lived. 'A wooden open staircase led to the cottage. An inside staircase was like a cupboard, and we used to sneak down the stairs to listen to ITMA.'

Next door again was the well known Hickling's ironmongers. 'The back of Stokes' has been destroyed', she concluded. Happily, the smart looking facade of Mr Stokes's premises is still there, a pleasure to look at from the High Street.

Then in 1942 they were offered a council flat at Milward House, which had been turned into flats,where they lived for 4–5 years. Then when Cranmore Avenue was built after the war, they were offered a house there.

The school for evacuees

Iris, though only three years old when she arrived at Keynsham, has inherited her parents' excellent memories. She recalls that, 'To start with, my two brothers and I, with all the younger evacuees, attended school at Bethesda chapel in Temple Street, which had been adapted into 'An Evacuees' School'. There were about 15 small infants together at the front of the building near the door. Then there was a space, a courtyard, then the rest of the building, where the big boys were. I remember being sent from the one building to the other with messages. Though I could already read, when they discovered my age, they sent me home.' Today, from Carpenter's Lane the two separate buildings are still discernible.

Later she returned to Bethesda for a while, then on to Temple Street School for a period, and finally to Bath Hill School, where she obtained a scholarship to 'Bath High' in Lansdown, a member of the Girls' Public Day Schools.

'A pitched battle'

Iris recalled there being some quite strong feeling against the London children, and remembered a vigorous snowball fight across the underground toilets at the junction of the High Street, Temple Street and Bath Hill. 'We had come out of Bethesda on the way home when we met the local children coming out of Bath Hill school, and there was a pitched snow fight between Keynsham and the evacuees. It was all of us against them,' she said.

'I can remember at Bethesda the teacher being a very large lady who always wore navy blue dresses with a fichu round the top. We seemed to spend a lot of time doing craft. I have a ghastly memory of rolls of sticky paper. Then I went to Temple Street where my teachers were Mrs Parsons and Mrs Breton . . . I can remember tremendous animosity against me as an evacuee because I won the scholarship at eleven. Earlier, my brother Bill was not allowed to sit a scholarship in Keynsham because he was a Londoner, and of course he could not go back to London to sit it.

'It was very much part of my childhood, the animosity between the Keynshamites and the evacuees. The children all had quite a war of their own going on. We all thought it was Hitler's fault that we were here in this dump. London was thought of as a paradise by the older ones, though of course, I couldn't remember it. As soon as the war was over, the older ones just rushed back, though the more thoughtful did not. My mother was quite adamant that we were staying here. In the end there were only seven or eight families that remained, the Kilburns, the Fords, the Olives, the Crouches and the Fishers. Janet Fisher also won a scholarship, and went to the City of Bath Girls.

'From Bath Hill we used to walk along Back Lane to the Baptist's Hall for school dinners. When I was in Mrs Parson's class, I was actually taught in the Baptist's Hall. When I was a third year junior, we were sent to Broadlands as there was no room for us . . . Once they decided to close the Evacuee School at Bethesda, we were all slotted in together, according to age groups.'

Her mother, with a rather different view point, recalled that when her sons were at Bath Hill School, they had their lunch, like many local shop workers, at the Womens' Institute in the large hut in the Park near the Drill Hall, run by the late Mrs Gwen Newman. Mrs Lerpiniere said, 'My lads got on very well with the local lads, and when we moved here to Cranmore Avenue, their friends from Broadlands school used to enjoy coming here, and some still call on us.'

Meanwhile Mrs Lerpiniere, who mainly met only local adults, recalled that they were very nice to her and treated the family well. There was no discrimination against any Londoners that she knew of. The Stokes family were very kind to them. Obviously it was in the world of the playground that the local feelings voiced themselves.

Iris was horrified when years later she attended a Women's Institute meeting, where a speaker described what marvellous things they had done for the evacuees during the war, who were described as 'filthy and lice ridden'. 'I was furious,' said Miss Lerpiniere. 'My mother was meticulously clean. She was proud that we were clean, polite and well bred. At Bath Hill the children lined up and had their heads examined by the school nurse. When it was my turn, she would say, 'There's no need to look at your head, Iris. I know it's always clean.'

Miss Lerpiniere recalled that a number of evacuees went back to London during the 'phoney war' period. She added that despite all that she had said, those who remained felt that Keynsham was a good place in which to live.

This is why Iris in 1984 took a leading part in opposing the proposed Gateway supermarket to be built on St John's Court. Lightheartedly she recalled how in 1989, an unknown elderly lady stopped her in the High Street and said, 'You have turned out well for an evacuee. Thank you for keeping the supermarket away,' and walked off.

Iris still doesn't know who she was, but she knew what she meant. Country people have long memories and some carry their grudges with them. Today Miss Lerpiniere, a former Chairman of the Civic Society, and now a town councillor, still uses her not inconsiderable abilities to preserve and care for her adopted town, despite her initial baptism of fire here. London would be proud of one of her own!

The Lerpiniere story reminds us that not all London evacuees were dirty and bad mannered.

'The London evacuee boy who lived with us'

'Lots of children came down from London because of the bombing. It was a very sad situation,' recalled Mrs Eunice Ollis. She was a most understanding lady, with clear memories of the war years that she shared with her elderly husband George Edward, a member of the well known local Ollis family, and known affectionately as 'Jim Ollis'.

We have examined some statistics and general aspects of evacuation, and then looked at the more specific experiences of a mother and daughter who came to Keynsham, and those of a boy who was sent here. We know how they felt about Keynsham, but how did the Keynsham people feel about them? In particular, how did the local 'hosts' regard their 'charges' and did the newcomers fit in with the other children in the homes?

Can you take this child?

Mrs Ollis continued, 'I had one little boy of my own, Clive Ollis and we were living at Number 11, St Anne's Avenue. People came along knocking at doors asking if you would take an evacuee child. Of course you hesitate at first off because you don't really know if you can fit one in and how it would turn out, or who they were going to be, so you don't immediately agree to it.

'But then you see these dear little children coming along, complete strangers, and you think, 'Look at that. If it was one of mine being pushed around . . . ! Well, to start off with , we didn't have anybody, then one day a lady came to the door with this boy. His name was Joe Burgess and Gwen Newman had his sister Alice Burgess. They came in and the lady said, 'Can you accommodate him?' Well, I looked at him and thought, 'Oh he's nice and clean and seems quite a nice boy and wasn't pushing,' so I thought, 'I suppose I could', so it was agreed upon.

A happy looking evacuee in Keynsham during World War Two

Left to right. Clive Ollis, aged 7 and his 6 month old sister Sylvia in her high chair, with Joe Burgess, the London boy who had come to live with them. The photo was taken in the garden of Mr Jim Ollis and his wife Eunice at 11, St Anne's Avenue, Keynsham, in August 1940. Joe was with them for five years.

'No, he didn't look forlorn. He just seemed at home. Being 11 he was a bit older than my boy but he fitted in well, and they played happily together. Well, he'd come from a big family; therefore he knew a certain amount of culture and he knew how to share, so things went on very well for a time and I grew to like him as one of my own, and he liked us. He was a very nice boy.

'Well, later when the doodlebugs [the VIs] started, his mother sent down to say how bad things were, and she said, Could she possibly come down just to have a little rest? Well, they were a big family. There was Bobby, Flossie, the Twins, and Freddy, but they weren't all coming. So I thought what a bad situation it was for them to be in, so they came for a few days to get away. Well, they came. She brought with her the twins, Bobby and Flossie, and Joe was already with me. Well, I thought this was getting a bit complicated all in together, and so this is what I did. I let them have my front rooms, that is, the sitting room and the bedroom above it. She could have all of them there together, and do her best. She would be quite safe and she could rest a little and recover from the terrible things she had been through. In the end, she stayed with me for months, and occasionally dad would come down too. He was a retired policeman, named George Burgess. They lived in the East End of London, at 20, Attlee Road, Bow, EC3.

'After a while things quietened down and she started getting restless and felt she ought to get back, specially when she thought of him up there all by himself. He used to write letters down and I expect they were a bit depressing, so it was agreed upon that she went back just for a visit by herself to see how things were. They had their own home. So she went, then came back, and arrangements were made for them to go back. I'm not sure if she went by herself first. Anyway, they all went, but Joe stayed back with me as he was one of the family.

To whom should a lad's earnings go?

'In the end, it came to school leaving time. While he was here, he was in the Scouts and quite happy. Then he had the chance of a job down at the Keynsham Paper Mills, which he took. But when it came to the chance of earning his living, and earning money, I thought it was time for his mother to get the benefit of his earning, not that it was much in those days. He thought about it for a while and being the sensible lad that he was, in the end he went back to his mother. Of course I did miss him for a long while and he missed being with us. It was like losing one of your own children. He got a good job and did well. He married but his wife doesn't have good health, and they have no family.

'However, every Christmas he sends me a card.' Mrs Ollis handed me the 1989 one, on which was written, 'To Eunice, Jim and Family. God bless. I always remember how good you were to me. Best wishes, Joe and Evelyn.' Sometimes on a Christmas morning he will phone me to wish us a Happy Christmas. His father died first, and then whenever he was on holiday in this area, he would call with his mother, to see us. His family was so genuine and honest. I appreciated this, and they appreciated what I had done for them. Joe knew my parents, of course, who used to help with the clothing, as people did for the evacuees.

'He was a very nice boy. I never regretted having him. I am always pleased to hear from him. He knew all my family here and of course his sister Alice was living with Gwen Newman in Steel Mills. She got on so well with Gwen that she was like a daughter. They always spoke well of each other. I think she stayed on with her after the war when Gwen moved to a bigger house in St Ladoc Road, till Alice too went back to London. Later she used to come and stay with Gwen for a week or a fortnight's holiday, when she would call in here to see how all the family were.

'I had four children and Sylvia was my second, born six years after Clive, so she was here at the same time as Joe. He loved her and used to take her out in the pram because he was that type and used to family life, you see. He used to play with her, and sit with her when she was in her high chair. She was the darling of the household, and so he grew up with her as well. She was very precious to him because she was like a sister.

'Joe was with us from about eleven to sixteen, five years, which was a long time . . . He didn't come to us at the beginning of the war, not until things started to get nasty on London [1940]. Before he came to me, he was evacuated to another lady who lived at Number 95, St Ladoc Road. She was very good to him, but she had never had any children, so her home was very smart with polished tables and so on, but he didn't have the freedom that he had been used to. The house was spick and span but there wasn't the feeling of home he'd been used to. Life was more regimented. There were times for this and that, with no exception, so they [the WVS] felt that it would be better for him to be in a family home, which was when I was approached. She was very nice to him and he said nothing against her; only that he felt lonely and wanted to be with a family, with children to play with.'

Nasty London children?

'I don't think anyone thought the children they took in were nasty children and a great nuisance. I would say, taking it on the whole, the little circle that I knew were quite happy to have them. Some weren't quite so well behaved as others . . . I wouldn't say they were forced on you. When they came you did have the opportunity to say no or yes. I mean you had to put yourself to a certain amount of trouble and inconvenience if you so wished to, but you did what you could in the circumstances, especially if you had children of your own and not knowing what you might be glad of one day.

'Quite a number of people took more than one. Then there was some sort of idea to keep a little family together. I can remember a family of two or three who went on the opposite side of me on St Anne's Avenue that went in there . . . Sometimes it cropped up that there were around the sort of parents who were glad that someone was looking after their children very nicely and giving them their freedom, like today some people put their elderly parents into a home and forget. I know that with this particular little family the parents weren't all that bothered about coming down to see them and all that sort of thing. The family that took them on were the Williams. He was a manual worker for the Council. Mrs Williams was a sick person; this is why it was such a big thing for her to take them on. She had heart trouble and had to spend quite a lot of time in bed. So her husband and her son and daughter had to take the burden of the extras. Mrs Williams had to have someone in to do her cleaning from time to time when she was laid up in bed.

'I had two more children, Lavender and Kevin. Sylvia is married and has three children. Lavender married David Waterman and they have a nice house in Hanham. Joe was average at school. He never said that any one picked on him at school or anything like that. But he spent most of his time at home here with us or with Clive. They both went to Temple Street, then Bath Hill, and Joe went on to Broadlands, and Clive to a Technical College.'

What, no fleas?

On the question of fleas on evacuees, Mrs Ollis declared about Joe, 'No, never. He was perfectly clean. Nothing like that whatever. Though he came from a large family and they were very poor, they were all thoroughly clean. And Joe having come to me from that other home, he was in lovely condition.

If someone came to you not clean, you would have to give a lot of thought to it.

'There were a lot of evacuee children here, mostly pretty young. The lot that came to us were the second lot. The first group came earlier, [September 1939] but these came as an emergency [Blitz 1940] and Joe's mother and her children came much later [1944]. To have a mother and her family join you was a complete change of life but in the circumstances you had to be rough and ready and get on as best you could.

'I expect I was paid something for having Joe but can't remember how much. It didn't make any difference where food was concerned because I would have shared it anyway, what we had. But I dare say that for some people who were not as comfortable as I was or had more expenses than us, things would not have been so easy. Money would have been tighter. My husband was working at Patchway, so we managed.

'We had a large rectangular iron Morrison shelter in our front room. It was a horrible looking thing. When we heard the German planes coming over, if we had gone to bed, which we tried to, we would get up and get in under it, though we were never damaged . . . I think most people had one of these shelters. You could if you wanted to. You asked and the authority provided it . . . It had an iron top and steel sides, with wire reinforcements inside the sides in case anything fell. No doubt Joe would have his own memories of the shelter.'

Mrs Ollis delved into a drawer and found the photo that years later Joe had sent her. Pleased, she handed it to me. Yes indeed, he had grown into a fine looking man, of whom she could be justly proud.

Sadly, Mrs. Eunice Ollis died during the eight years spent in researching, writing and revising this book. Her words provide an insight into the world of the evacuee; they also reveal her for what she was, a caring, conscientious, motherly soul.

Not only evacuees came

Lionel Wilson and his wife Hettie lived at 4, Avon Road, Keynsham. With a five bedroomed house they acted on the Pauline injunction that Christians should be 'given to hospitality.' Their daughter Charmian, now Mrs. H. Wakeling, recalls that they had staying with them a young mother and baby from one of the poorer parts of London.

'The mother used newspaper for nappies, and our neighbour at Number 2 complained at having dirty 'nappies' thrown over her wall. She had no idea how to wean her baby, so Mother taught her what to do. They were not with us long and soon returned to London during the 'phoney war' period.

'The mother of one local evacuee family was taken to task by a local woman, because the newcomer's children were not very clean. The Londoner's rapid riposte was that if she had had to carry a bucket of water up four flights of stairs, hers wouldn't be either.

'Mother was part of a team of ladies who by rota ran The Fear Institute Canteen, serving meals and beverages practically all day long. A teenage school girl, I used to help out on a Saturday morning and it was busy there. Mrs. Whittuck, (the wife of the solicitor Whittuck of W., Taylor and Caines) a lovely lady, seemed to be in charge and was a driving force there. She kept us on our toes.'

Harry Wakeling said, 'I used to go there from time to time for a cup of tea and a wad [any sort of cake] in the three years I was here. I suppose I went about fifty times. We only seemed to use one room at the front of the building, where food was served from the hatch. There was a dart board there, and some chairs and tables.'

Charmian commented 'In addition to British servicemen from the Army, the Navy and the Air Force, Allied troops from the Commonwealth would arrive, and at one time, American G.I.s as well. Officers had other accomodation.

'Mother, with a number of other ladies, had her name on a list held at the Fear Canteen, to which troops passing through could report, to find a bed for the night. Often we would get a call part way through the evening and a couple of servicemen would arrive. On one occasion it was two Canadians. And despite food rationing, Mother always managed to give them a meal. Throughout the whole war, there was hardly a time when there weren't other people staying with us.'

In addition to all the above duties, once a week Hettie would take her turn on the rota of ladies who cooked a meal for the many N.F.S. firemen who were on duty at the rear of the Lamb and Lark hotel.

'Sometimes, Officers' wives would stay with us to visit their husbands at Rockhill House. At other times, service wives would come to us for a hot bath.

'Mother was a member of the Women's Peace League, which assisted in getting Jews out of Europe before the war started. In 1938 Frau Löewy from near Prague, Czechoslovakia, was brought to stay with us. Later her husband was able to get away, and showed by sign language that he had been in prison there. After living with us for about a year, they found work as a married couple on an estate in South Somerset.

'After a day's work at Bristol, Father would be on duty as a member of the Special Constabulary. William Gibbons was in charge of the Specials, and Father was number two. Most nights he would report to the Police Station. His particular beat was the length of Wellsway, right up to Burnett Point.'

To return to the subject of evacuees, one wonders just how great was the influx of Londoners to this North Somerset country town?

Every one is counted

As we have seen, several quotations have referred to the large number of evacuees in the town here. Well, just how many juveniles did come to Keynsham in the war?

In answer to my letter to the Somerset Record Office at Taunton requesting information from the Keynsham UDC Minute Books, Miss S Berry, the Senior Archivist, kindly replied:

'The Minister of Health decided that the UDC should accommodate 2,200 evacuees of whatever description and 805 evacuees were received between 1 and 4 September 1939, divided as follows; 368 unaccompanied children including teachers and helpers, 434 accompanied children and 3 expectant mothers.'

Later in March 1990, Mr R J E Bush, Somerset's Deputy County Archivist, also searched the minutes of the Keynsham UDC. He wrote:

I have extended the search through the minutes of Keynsham UDC but have had to be very selective due to the limited time available.

In October 1939 Keynsham agreed to the transfer of 50 children, plus helpers and teachers, from Long Ashton. In the same month there were 2 cases of scarlet fever, one of diphtheria and several cases of impetigo among the children. There was complaint also of numerous cases of scabies and verminous heads and many households refused to take the evacuees until the infestations had been dealt with.

On 13 December 1939 it was agreed to accept one child from St Vincents RC School and seven from Smeed Road School for December 16 next. 19 others were refused.

The number of evacuees remaining in residence were:

Unaccompanied children	307
Accompanied children & mothers	45
Teachers and helpers	27
	379

On 16 March 1940 the council made a resolution that because of the proximity to Bristol Airport, Filton Aerodrome and Avonmouth Docks, application be made to the Ministry of Health to change the designation of Keynsham Urban District from reception to central area for evacuation purposes. This application was turned down so it was decided to approach Mrs Tate, MP for the division, for support. A deputation met Mr Titheley, Senior Regional Officer of the Ministry of Health, on 30 October 1940. He would not agree to change the designation but he did agree that the 230 evacuees still outstanding of the 650 allocation (420 had already been placed) would be waived. The council regarded this as 'a considerable achievement'.

On 7 May 1941 the number of evacuees remaining were:

Mothers, helpers & accompanied children	214
Unaccompanied children	121
Others	18
	353

On 11 June 1941 the figures were revised:

Unaccompanied children	136
Evacuated mothers	33
Accompanied children	81
Refugees (adult)	60
Refugees and homeless children	66
Teachers	12
Helpers	3
	391

This variation was due to withdrawal of billeting allowances in certain cases and an influx of refugees and homeless families from Portsmouth, Plymouth and Bristol.

Some sample figures from ensuing years are given below:

	26 June 1942	2 March 1943	2 Feb 1944
Mothers and children	124	108	96
Unaccompanied children	84	48	32
Teachers	7	} 3	} 2
Helpers	3	}	}
Others	54	23	9
	272	182	139

Summary

In round figures, in early September 1939 just over 800 evacuees arrived. Three months later, due to the 'phoney war', over half of these had left. Just under 400 remained in Keynsham into and through 1940, and 1941, the number falling, then rising. By June 1942 the total was reduced to 272, with only 182 in March 1943 and finally down to 139 in 1944.

Conclusions concerning the evacuees in Keynsham

Compulsory billeting. This does not seem to have been necessary in the town.

The welfare of the evacuees. The WVS monitored the welfare of the children for whom they were responsible by visiting them in their 'new homes'.

Fleas, lice, etc. There were undoubtedly a number of cases of this problem which was possibly quite widespread and which was understandably locally 'newsworthy'. However, there were also a number of cases of their complete absence, which of course, never made the 'news'.

The integration of two cultures. There are glaring examples of the conflict between the country children and the city newcomers. But against this, there is evidence of those who seem to have been readily accepted by, and quickly assimilated into, the local community of children.

Increased domestic duties. The acceptance of one, two or even three children, not to mention a mother and an occasionally visiting father, obviously caused a varying amount of reorganisation of the home, not to mention increased pressure on, and much more work for, the 'hostess'.

Keynsham mothers. If Mrs Ollis and Mrs Gwen Newman were typical of the many local mothers of fifty years ago – and there is little reason to doubt it – what a big hearted group of people they were, and still are! Many seem to have taken their 'charges' to their hearts and treated them like 'one of my own'. In some cases they forged life long links, and in a few cases sought to, and actually did, adopt their London child.

Well done the Mothers of Keynsham! London owes you a great debt of gratitude.

Chapter 4

Fry's factory in war time Keynsham

Since its arrival in Keynsham in 1922, Fry's has been the biggest employer in the town. When the 1939–45 war started, the factory made a considerable contribution to the war effort. In search of details of just what these were, I met Mr Brian Davies, who, among his many managerial responsibilities, cared for the firm's archives.

In his usual helpful manner, he brought out a heavy book containing many photographs of the war years at Somerdale. With the permission of Cadbury's, several of these are shown in this and another war section, which I acknowledge with gratitude.

Among the other material that the manager brought up, was the 1964 edition of the Somerdale Magazine, which featured the factory in the dark days of the war. Rather than attempting to put together an account of what happened 50 years ago, I have, with Mr Davies's permission, reproduced a copy of their own summary, illustrated by their photos.

SOMERDALE MAGAZINE

Vol 4, No 9.   **September, 1964**

1939 – THE BALLOON GOES UP

Twenty-five years ago the declaration of war with Germany was just a fortnight old. Although many people didn't know quite what to expect, the country was on the move. Already there were many men missing from factory work-benches and from office desks, the Reservists had been called up and the move to join the Forces had begun. In cities, towns and villages people were trying to accustom themselves to the strange, dim world of the blackout which was to last for six years.

1964 is a bumper year for commemorations. In August there was the 50th anniversary of the outbreak of World War I, followed in September by the 25th anniversary of World War II. And all this year exhibitions, dramatic productions and celebration dinners have been held to commemorate the 400th anniversary of Shakespeare's birth.

'Ploughing for kitchen gardens, March 1940,' is the Fry's caption. The photo faces North to the factory block, and the small leafless trees.

'Every endeavour must be made to . . . produce the greatest volume of food of which this fertile Island is capable,' said Mr Winston Churchill in The House of Commons, November 5, 1940.

The amount of literature produced in connection with these three anniversaries must be prodigious. Every Sunday newspaper worth its salt has carried features on both wars. In this issue, the Somerdale Magazine, too, makes its contribution. This article, however, has a more particular perspective, to show how the war affected Somerdale, its employees and production. The photographs are taken from the Firm's archives and illustrate how totally different a war-time Somerdale looks from the Somerdale of today.

THE WAR YEARS AT SOMERDALE

Mr Chamberlain's dreaded announcement on that Sunday morning of 3rd September, 1939, marked the end of an uneasy peace which had existed since his meeting with Hitler in Munich.

In that period, the country's re-armaments programme had been increased and volunteers were called for the many branches of Civil Defence and ARP (Air Raid Precautions).

Gas masks were assembled in our vacated Bristol factories and in the fortnight preceding the outbreak of war, many of our people who were Reservists and Territorials had been recalled to the Colours.

During the first couple of months of the war, measures for protecting Somerdale and the people working here went ahead with all speed. A great change came over Somerdale, that was to last for the next six years. The huge 'Somerdale' sign on the railway embankment was camouflaged and many walls were sand-bagged for protection. Blast walls were also erected. The railway siding was completely enclosed and blacked out and all the entrances of the air-raid shelters were made gas proof.

Only weeks after the war started, windows (said to comprise enough glass to cover a strip a yard wide and 56 miles long) had been made opaque by huge quantities of black-out paint. In addition, thousands of yards of material had been made up into curtains to darken rooms where, hitherto, daylight had been essential.

Throughout the eerie silence of that cold and bitter winter there was plenty of evidence to show that the country's overseas supplies were drying up. For instance, at Somerdale there was the constant withdrawal of lines whose ingredients came from the four corners of the earth – pistachio, banana, raisins, dates, nuts, candied peel, sugared rose and violet petals, to name but a few.

Then came spring and the fall of Holland, Denmark and Norway, and the fighting in France and Belgium.

The first of the daylight raids, in brilliant sunshine, the flock of raiders immediately over Somerdale and heading north; the crump of bombs in the distance; another raid two days later, being scattered by a handful of Hurricanes – all those helped to produce at Somerdale an atmosphere of war.

'Sheep may safely graze' even on Fry's precious playing fields, in war time, as seen here in April 1940. Beyond the field is Chandos Road.

Not only 'Dig for Victory' but 'Ploughing for kitchen gardens' is Fry's caption to the Fordson tractor turning the sward in March 1940.

In these conditions, the Firm's ARP organisation was born. Perched on 'C' Block roof and in constant touch with the ARP centre in the basement, the Spotters kept a sharp look-out, hour after hour, and when danger became imminent a system of bells warned all above ground to take cover. Here at Somerdale, alerts were registered. Of these, many developed into raids, of which nine were classified as 'major'.

Following the fall of France the LDV or Local Defence Volunteers – later called the Home Guard – were formed, with our own Company at Somerdale.

During the Blitz, Bristol, of course, received a battering and our showroom in Union Street served cocoa to workmen engaged in demolishing dangerous buildings and clearing roads. In Bristol and its outskirts, shelters were thronged nightly by thousands and our Shelter Service distributed to them free, hot cocoa. One van was also stationed at Portsmouth.

A Mobile Canteen, too, was built and this was available at a moment's notice to proceed to any incident. It provided valuable service. For instance, after the first heavy attack on Bath, which began at 11.00 pm on Saturday, 25th April, 1942, enemy raiders left behind, in addition to several large fires, a far greater proportion of HE bombs than were ever dropped during any blitz on Bristol.

The Mobile Canteen set out for Bath and the first distribution of cocoa took place at St Stephen's Church, where a large number of AFS (Auxiliary Fire Service) and Welch Guards were making strenuous efforts to put out an obstinate fire. The AFS had been on continuous duty without food or refreshment for nine hours and the drink was received with considerable enthusiasm. Cocoa was also given to the large numbers of homeless people who lived in the immediate vicinity.

The canteen then went to Twerton, where rows of small houses had suffered severely. Again troops and the public were given cocoa, as were the AFS who were fighting fires by the railway line. And so it went on – all in all during the week, the Mobile Canteen gave away 12,000 cups of cocoa.

Back at Somerdale, the large number of employees on war service was a considerable drain on manpower. It reached a stage where there were only a quarter of the men left and only a fifth of the girls. Yet output of the Factory was a third above the highest peace-time figure. The explanation for this lay largely in the change-over from assorted packing to 100% block chocolate. Furthermore, the reduction of output to five or six main lines allowed greater standardisation and longer runs.

However, chocolate wasn't the only thing being produced at Somerdale during the war. Enemy raids had at last immobilised a section of the Bristol Aeroplane Company's works at Filton and the late Lord Beaverbrook, then Minister of Supply, directed us to vacate 'C' and 'O' Blocks. The BAC Drawing Office and Engine Cowling Department moved in. The former, which occupied the whole of 'C' Block except the basements, was said to be the largest Drawing Office in Europe.

An odd note was the part our playing fields played in the war effort. Shipping losses were mounting, due to hostile submarine activity; yet the ever-increasing flow of arms and equipment produced overseas reduced cargo space for imports to the minimum. Meat was scarce, so flocks of sheep and lambs were put out to graze on the playing fields. We also did our best to support ourselves with vegetables.

It was hoped that the war would end in 1944, but these hopes were dashed late in the autumn of that year when the enemy broke through in the Ardennes.

However on 8th May, 1945, it was all over. The nation went mad – and if scenes at Somerdale were a little more restrained, such as machines being decked with flags, the relief was nevertheless just as sincere. The residents of Chandos Road held a celebration and, later, we welcomed back those who had been in the Forces or engaged on war work.

Finished were the days of gas masks and Home Guard; of ARP and Mobile Canteens; of alerts and hareing for shelter in the middle of the night. Perhaps, at long last, there would once again be 'blue birds over the white cliffs of Dover'.

* * *

The Fry's chocolate factory and their war effort

No one could accuse Frank Passco of being a new boy at the factory. The June 1977 issue of 'Somerdale Venturer' recorded how Mr Passco joined the company as a boy straight from school. His first job in the Union Street factory was on the La Font assortments. The work generally was quite difficult at that time and he was called upon to work in many departments of the factory. After three years he was engaged in making display dummies, which brought him into contact with the laboratory, to which eventually he transferred.

In 1933 the laboratory moved out to Keynsham and Frank continued his work on the analysis of materials. He attended night school at the Merchant Venturer's, and although not qualified, he became a junior analytical chemist. Part of his duties included the meteorological readings which he continued until he retired, although not on the original daily basis.

For six years he cycled daily to Fry's and back, until his marriage in 1939 to Flossie Short, when he bought 24, Avon Road, Keynsham, at the entrance to the old show ground. He was fortunate. Up to and during the war, hundreds of employees continued to cycle in from Bristol and the surrounding areas. There were fifteen cycle sheds to accommodate them. Today there is not a single cycle.

Though open to the public, the GWR laid on four trains specifically for Fry's Somerdale; they carried staff from Ashley Hill, Avonmouth, Bedminster Down and Bath. Coaches also brought employees in from the country. Pre-war there was far more day work than shift work, hence the work-force of some 6–7,000 people. The GWR trains brought the raw ingredients right into the factory, and also transported the finished products back on to the main lines, and thence on to their national and international destinations: some were reached by plane. However, the factory did have its own small steam driven shunting engine, with no carriages, to distribute the raw ingredients to the appropriate departments. This was still used during the war.

Today the chocolate arrives by tanker, already roasted and mixed, for the

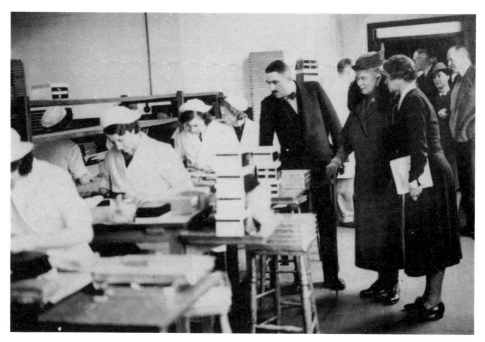

The visit of Queen Mary to Fry's Chocolate Factory at Somerdale, Keynsham, in January 19, 1940, to encourage the war effort.

'Fry's Shelter Vans' took urns of hot chocolate to civilians spending cold nights in communal shelters during the raids by the Luftwaffe.

final stage on the production line. Originally there were four main blocks. A block made the chocolate, B block was the moulding and cream section, and C and D blocks made special lines of products. The roasting of the cocoa bean was continuous by day and by night, according to demand. The smell was lovely, and local people could tell the direction of the wind by whether or not they could enjoy the enchanting elixir.

It was not only the homo sapiens that were attracted. Wasps were ever a threat, and were particularly partial to ginger when it was being cut up. Various measures were attempted to banish this pest. One was to place drums outside the factory building, filled with water, the lids having holes drilled in them. Syrup was smeared on the lids, which so attracted and inebriated the wasps that they fell through the holes and were drowned. Unfortunately, what attracted wasps also attracted bees. Loud complaints were voiced from Stockwood Vale, where one bee keeper lost the whole of his hive of bees.

By the River Avon, hungry rats also responded to the tempting smell. Being nocturnal, they were not often seen, but they were there, always a constant trouble, in their search for easy sustenance. Sundry measures were used to eliminate them. Fry's maintained a full time rat catcher, with his white haired terrier. Later he was known as the Rodent Officer, now upgraded to the Hygiene Officer. Today, dogs are not even allowed on the playing fields. And where there are rats, there are mice.

1939, the commencement of hostilities

For so large a complex of buildings, Fry's was fortunate in that it suffered very little from the bombing. Frank recalled, 'I know one bomb landed on the laboratory. It came through the roof, where it was slightly diverted and crashed through the concrete floor and landed in a load of paper on the floor below. Its soft landing probably stopped it going off. By the time that I went in next morning, the bomb disposal squad had already been and removed it. You could see the hole where it went through.

'When there was the big day-time raid on Filton, the entire Fry's work force of some 2–3000 people were ordered into the basement for the five hours duration. There we sat, talked and some knitted. Arrangements for such emergencies had been made long ago and there was even a canteen down there. Air raid and fire drills were practised regularly, and the factory even had its own siren mounted on the top of one of the blocks.'

During the war, the BAC had taken over the whole of the four floors of C block to manufacture aircraft parts (24 hours a day). Many local women worked there, in one of three shifts. Frank remembered, 'We were not allowed in there, and had to make a detour to pass the block.'

Two nights a week found Frank fire watching on the roof of U block, where the laboratory was. After a day's work he would go home for tea, then report back at eight o'clock in the evening. There, on a three hours on, three hours off rota, he would patrol the roofs, watching for incendiary bombs. He was fortunate. Some employees from Bristol went straight from their factory work to factory fire watching, and then back to work next morning, without going home at all. Obviously though, only the factory's employees could have access to the roof blocks. Their 'watching' was compulsory and unpaid: it was part of their war effort.

Up to a decade ago. Fry's had always had its own fire brigade. It had one fire engine and several trailers, and during the war its permanent staff was enlarged by additional employees, who all practised regularly.

Naturally they had proper uniforms and worked on a shift system. The factory possessed a loud fire alarm bell. Fry's owned the Chandos estate, and if

The thirty year old Private Frank Passco, RAOC, in 1943 when he was stationed at the massive army camp at Crookham, Herts. He recalled that at that time he was not feeling particularly happy as he had been parted from his young wife after just four years of marriage. The photo belongs to Mr F Passco.

you lived there, you were expected to join the brigade as there you would be able to hear the alarm bell.

'During the war the factory was never on fire. The brigade was incorporated into the National Fire Service, and so was probably called out to help in the blitz on Bristol and Bath. Mr Charles Vincent, the chief fire officer, was very efficient, and he was also a foreman at the factory,' recalled Frank.

The firm had a 'Gas Decontamination Unit' of specially trained men, who wore protective clothing, and went round testing for poisonous gases if something suspicious was discovered on the roofs. 'I was one of the men involved,' said Frank, who explained the necessity of special clothing. 'The clothes looked like being a lot of trouble, but gases could be serious if you were not properly clothed. Sometimes a poison could only affect you if you swallowed it. You could be contaminated without it affecting you. Mustard gas was really chlorine gas. We were on call night or day. Mr W B Walker was in charge of the unit, though in overall responsibility was the chemist, Mr A E Mills. Fortunately, our skills were never put into practice.'

Fry's took seriously the national slogan, 'Dig for victory'. Accordingly they ploughed up the land in and around where the car park now is, and farmed it to grow food for their canteen. If by the week-end there was produce over, employees could buy it. Additionally, the firm released land for workers' allotments on the slope down to the river, which were eagerly sought after and made most productive.

Little known is the fact that during the war, Fry's produced a special 'export line' of chocolate for Europe which contained additional B1 vitamins that the Continent lacked.

Back in the factory, there were periodic lunch hour concerts by visiting variety artists. Occasional film shows encouraged special efforts in the 'Salute the soldier' and the 'Wings for victory' weeks. At night time, black linen curtains hid the blocks from any prying Luftwaffe planes passing overhead. In strategic areas, high walls of sandbags offered some protection from bombs.

The Fry's platoon of the Home Guard

To further defend their factory, Fry's enlisted their employees in their own branch of the Home Guard. Once again, conscientious Frank joined. 'In 1939 you were looked upon to volunteer. I was given a uniform right away but there were no guns at first. We had regular Sunday morning training parades and two evening duties. Later, we fired rifles on the Cheddar range: none of us had ever fired a gun before.'

By 1940 a Platoon under Mr W Conn involved a 'Somerdale Section' and a 'SWR Section'. Major W S Scammell wrote in 'The Story of No 2 Company' that, 'In June 1940 the Somerdale Industrial Section became a Platoon [No 8] under the command of Mr Morris, who had previously served from the earliest date in No 3 Platoon, and later as No 13 (Fry's) Section commander.' (p 16.)

No 8 Platoon under Sergeant S Mills was to guard the factory gates and the factory roof. Sgt W Wicks guarded posts 2 and 3, Sgt S Newman posts 4 and 5 and Sgt W Stevens posts 6 and 7. One of the managers Lieutenant

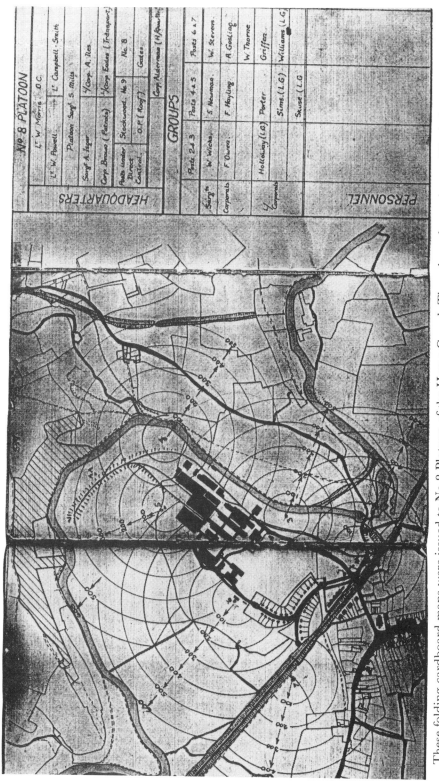

These folding cardboard maps were issued to No 8 Platoon of the Home Guard. They show the environs of Fry's factory, indicating the 8 posts for defending the complex. From each, 100 ft circles enabled the Home Guard to pinpoint accurately an attacker's position, and so set their weapons accordingly. Scale: 6 inches to the mile.

C W Morris from Stockwood, was in charge, aided by Lieuts W Powell and Campbell-Smith.

Frank still has a four page cardboard folding map of the factory, showing the position of the eight posts surrounding the firm. From every post, six circles, stretching outwards, each indicated a hundred feet distance, giving the rifleman the position of his enemy. The six groups of circles intersected each other, so that the whole of the surrounding fields of fire were covered and re-covered.

'A Factory Unit of the Bristol Aeroplane Company at Somerdale became attached to the Company, with Lieut Campbell-Smith as their immediate Commander, forming part of No 8 Platoon under Lieut Morris.' That was how Major W S Scammell recorded the integration in 1941 of the Fry's BAC section of the Home Guard into No 2 Company. But even in war time, only Fry's own men could legitimately occupy the factory's land, so naturally No 8 Platoon guarded Fry's.

As we have seen, in addition to his full time work in the laboratory, each week Frank spent two nights fire watching, and two nights on duty with the Home Guard and a Sunday morning too. Despite this, in 1942 he received his calling up papers. He was posted to the Royal Army Ordnance Corps, where as a corporal he became an 'ammunition examiner', deciding which shells were unstable or out of date. Most of the time he was stationed in Scotland, with a period at Ashley Down, Bathford. The corporal was demobilised in 1946, to return to his wife and home.

Frank returned to Fry's and the familiar laboratory, and worked there until he retired in 1977: by only six months he missed fifty years of service with the company. Additionally he served on the catering committee, was a union officer and a welfare officer and the secretary of the Medical Aid Fund. As the Somerdale Venturer concluded, 'We join with all his friends and colleagues in wishing Frank a long and happy retirement.'

Now, fifteen years later, he is hale and hearty, and as a good Methodist, still cares for people. Independent, he lives in his own home, where his daughters Avril and Lynne regularly visit him. Faithfully he served Fry's, which was and still is, the largest employer in Keynsham, despite its change of name to Cadbury's.

Chapter 5

The war over Keynsham,
a chronological account of events

'As a small boy I remember being taken to see a Royal Flying Corps plane which had made a forced landing in a field at the top of Charlton Road, during the 1914–18 war. Happily, the pilot was uninjured. Planes were few and far between over North Somerset in those days, and a large number of people flocked to see it,' wrote Mr W Sherer.

It was only 21 years after the end of the First World War, on September 3, 1939, that Chamberlain solemnly announced to the House of Commons that, once again, a state of war existed between Britain and Germany. In the war years that lay ahead, planes, and Luftwaffe planes at that, were to fly all too frequently over Keynsham and North Somerset.

Writing in the September 8, 1989, issue of the Keynsham Chronicle, Mr Brian Woodham wrote, 'Keynsham was an important landmark and "sky crossroad" for Allied and enemy aircraft'. Later he told me that that was why Lord Haw Haw had declared that St John's church would never be bombed.

1940

From his research into the diaries of both the Civil Defence and Air Raid Precaution's wardens and from the KUDC records of the war, Mr Ian James lists in an article in the Keynsham Chronicle of February 2, 1987, some of the following events. However, at the Somerset Record Office, Taunton, I was subsequently to research the 'Daily Summary Reports' (ref CD/Gen/3/19). These commenced with an overall picture of enemy activity during the previous 24 hours, followed by a succinct account of damage to the towns and villages of Gloucester, Somerset, Wiltshire, Devon and Cornwall. My additional quotations will all be in square brackets.

June 20. Keynsham's first air raid warning.

June 25. Incendiaries fell at Hicks Gate, and bombs dropped on Bristol city centre, Arnos Court and Brislington.

June 26/27. Major W S Scammell, who wrote 'The Story of No 2 Company of the . . . Home Guard', recorded that 'Our first reported bombs arrived on the night of the 27th June, 1940, when five fell close to the Marksbury Post. There was a great exodus of people from Bristol and Bath to look at the craters, which were something of a nine-days' wonder.' (p 13.)

June 29/30. Bombs landed in the locality of Perry's Quarry.

August 10. Sundry German leaflets were dropped by plane at Hunstrete, one entitled, 'A last appeal to reason'.

August 19/20. 'The peace of Keynsham was rudely disturbed by what was then a mammoth explosion near Keynsham Cricket Ground. In fact 14 bombs fell within one small field, and one crater was 40 ft in diameter and 10 ft deep.' (Scammell p 13). Mr James, recording the incident, wrote that 9 bombs fell in fields, 2 in Breeches Lane, Chandag, near the bungalow of a Mr Kendal and one did not explode. [Window damage]

Mr Les Whittock clearly recalls the occasion. 'I remember going to work at 6.00 next morning as I worked for Mr Payne, whose farm was by the Ashmead roundabout, and who then owned the bombed field. I rounded up the cows from next to the craters for milking. The field is now part of the Wellsway School complex, for Mr Payne owned all the land from his farmhouse up to the school.'

'There were four of us lads of around 14, including Jack Carpenter, to hand milk the herd of 40–50 cows. For one person to milk six an hour was good going. The bombing had upset the cows and the milk yield that day was down considerably.'

August 24. Oil bomb dropped on Keynsham High Street. This was the bombing incident described earlier by Edward Joll, the nine-year-old eye-witness.

Terror of night fire bomb raid

This is the title of the Keynsham Chronicle's article of March 20, 1987. It described how on the night of August 24/25, 1940, Number 59, High Street, received a direct hit from a 500lb petrol/oil bomb. It was the only house in Keynsham to be gutted by enemy action. Mr Geoffrey Carter, an Auxiliary Fire Serviceman who lived nearly next door, aided by a passing Australian soldier, rushed to bring out the heavy bed-ridden 80-year-old Mrs Wallace and her devoted middle-aged music-teacher daughter, Miss Beatrice Wallace. Mr Frank Bees, who also was in the AFS, said that this was the only time during the war that he used his fire axe.

The house was owned by Mrs Bertha Carter, who bought it for her elderly mother. Mrs Carter also owned the popular china shop that used to be opposite at Number 50 (now Mountstephens), and always had a hundred tea sets in stock.

The Keynsham building firm of Edward Wiggins had the contract to rebuild the inside of the house, and Mr Les Harding did much of the work. Their bill, 'to rebuild Number 59, High Street, after damage by explosive incendiary bomb, roofing, plastering and decorating and making all good' was £221 5s 4d. The Inland Revenue dealt with claims for war damage and in November 5, 1940, could offer only £172 9s 0d. A dissatisfied Mrs Carter took legal advice from solicitor W S Scammell and on Jan 15, 1942, the matter was still unresolved.

In 1987 when the property was renovated, scarred timbers were found. Mrs Carter's married daughter, 'Phyl' Clayfield, said, 'It does not surprise me that burn marks have been found, for if any beams or rafters of acceptable condition

The only building in Keynsham believed to be gutted by Nazi bombing

Left to right: Numbers 59 and 59a (Halliday's), High Street, Keynsham, as it was in 1939, before the bombing.

After the bombing of the night of August 24/25, 1940. Of the house and furniture, only the shell of the building remained.

were found after the bombing they would have been used, as new timber was hard to obtain. In fact the floor of the house was stone and to change it to timber we had to do with wooden blocks.'

Mrs Carter also owned the land between 59 and 61. (The latter was The Undertakers, now Fads, belonging to Mr John Carter, her father-in-law). A Mr and Mrs Halliday came to Keynsham around 1920 and as a friend, Mrs Carter had 59a built so that Mrs Halliday could there pursue her profession as a hairdresser. The builder was John Willcox, who constructed the house between April and September, 1923, for £198 5s 5d. Mrs Carter took out a mortgage on this 'two up, two down' house for £204.

After Mrs Halliday, one or two other people used it as a hairdressers, until Mrs Kathleen Beese took it over in 1953 and named it 'Jolyon's'. Years later, in the 1980s when the Oxfam shop was being rebuilt, they used both 59 and Jolyon's, with its quaint narrow winding staircase. Today the former 59 and 59a are quite unrecognisable. The 'New Look' has come indeed to Keynsham, sweeping away every vestige of that part of the old High Street, with its former charm.

Mrs Phyllis Clayfield's war-time memories

The daughter of Walter and Bertha Carter, 'Phyl', was born above the china shop at 50, the High Street, Keynsham. When her parents retired in 1938, she moved with them to 43, West View Road. A business-woman like her mother, Phyl worked in Bristol. She commented, 'During the war, after a heavy raid, it was very difficult to get to Bristol. Normally I went by train but on one occasion at St Anne's, we were told to get off as there were unexploded bombs ahead. An alternative rail link took us to Bedminster from where we walked. Then again a road could be closed off, with the notice, 'Unexploded bombs.' Sometimes there would be neither trains nor buses running. On Saturdays we worked until 1.00 pm. On one occasion I walked all the way to Bristol, arriving about 11.50 am The boss said, "Thank you for coming, but seeing it has taken you so long, you had better go home now", so then I walked all the way back to Keynsham.'

She said that people with children could have indoor Morrison shelters. There were very few outdoor Anderson shelters. 'One family in West View had a half-size billiard table, and used to get under it if things got too hot. We used the downstairs back room and put a heavy bookcase across the patio window which we taped up against a bomb attack. All four of us slept there.

'I was such a deep sleeper that, if there was a heavy raid, my parents would make tea, but I would sleep right through it. Mother's main moan was that if there was a heavy raid, Dad would put his hat and coat on and go outside to see what was happening. To be really honest, it was not too bad in Keynsham, unless you were a nervous person or on your own.

'In those days we were encouraged to keep our baths half full of water in case the mains were hit. In one West View home, an incendiary bomb landed right in the water-filled bath.

'I was a West View Road fire-watcher and when on call, I used to wear a pair of Dad's trousers. I was on duty every sixth night, but on many occasions

The remains of 59, The High Street. Phyllis Clayfield said that her cousin Jeffrey Carter and another fireman rescued the elderly Mrs. Wallace. Due to her ample proportions the men were unable to lift her by the arms. They were forced to drag her by her feet out of the downstairs rooms through the back garden and into the garden of Mrs Heal next door, where she was treated for shock. Mrs Kathleen Beese's photos.

_____ July _____ 1925

70

Mr Walter Carter

Dr. to JOHN WILLCOX & SONS,

Builders and General Contractors.

ESTIMATES AND PLANS PREPARED FOR ALL KIND OF WORK.

SANITARY WORK A SPECIALITY.

1923   Material A/c for Building Shop.

Week ending

			£ s d
April 7.	3 - 4" pipes 1- 4" x 4" splay. 1 4 x 4 junction 3 - 4 bends 5 cwt mortar		19 6
" 14th	1 ton 1 cwt mortar. 8 Bull nosed, ½ bg sand + ½ bg cement		1 . 6 . 0
" 21.	9 x 3 air grating. 3 yds 9" damp course, 2400 bricks. 1 cwt sand.		9 15 - 6
	½ cwt cement 1 ton 1 cwt 2 qrs mortar		1 . 1 . 5
" 28th	2 cement heads, 1 ton mortar. 2 Rolls Vulc. Felt + Vulcanite		3 . 5 . 0
	oil. 19 - 14" x 12" Tabling. 1000 bricks		4 19 0
May 5th	1 - 4" gullie. 1 - 4" x 4" junction 3 . 4" pipes 3. 4" bends 1 . 3" pipe		15 . 6
	3 . 3" bends . 1 ton Yellow gravel + haulage		1 : 6 . 6
" 12th	1 ton 1 cwt 2 qr mortar . 1 chimney bar 600 bricks. 1 4 x 4 splay junction		3 - 13 - 11
" 19	2 - 9" x 3" air gratings. 1 chimney pot . 1½ bg cement, 1½ bg sand.		
	3 cwt mortar 600 bricks .		3 - 11 . 0
" 26th	1 bag cement 2 tons 10 cwt (Plaster mortar)		2 = 18 = 0
29 to June 1st	1 ton 1 cwt 3 qrs (Plaster mortar)		1 . 2 0
may	Making + fixing stairs at Keynsham		12 : 9 . 6
	Taking particulars, making + fixing shop front including		
	cornice, facias, trusses, pilasters, door + frame with		
	fanlight + forming flat Roof over.		22 : 17 : 6
June 6 to 8	2 cwt mortar . 1 12" x 9" x 2" fire bar . 1 bkt cement .		5 . 0
" 14th	1 tub lime putty. 18th to 23rd 1 ton 11 cwt sand . 5 bags cement		4 . 0 = 0
	2 cwt gravel - 1 - 6 x 6" Iron grid. 28 ft. 6" V jointed M.B.		7 9
25th to 30th	10 cwt Pebbles 9 cwt sand. 4 cwt spar . 2 bags cement		2 . 10 . 6
	½ cwt lime. 28 ft 1½ x ½" batten 1 - 9 x 3" air grid . 2½ cwt lime putty		17 6
July 2 to 7	2½ bags cement . 5 cwt . gravel .		1 . 5 . 0
" 9 to 14	Petrol .14 lbs paint . ½ pt knotting . 7 tbs putty, ochre		
	umber 7 lbs white paint + glass paper		1 . 6 . 11

A fascinating invoice for building 'Hallidays', at 59, High Street in 1923.

KELSTON HOUSE, HIGH STREET,

KEYNSHAM, Oct 17th.1944 **194**

Mrs W.Carter. *72*

Dr. to EDWARD WIGGINS

CONTRACTS NET
(due on completion)
ESTIMATES FREE

Builder, Decorator and General Contractor.

1944							
		To Rebuilding No 59 High Street after damage					
		by explosive incendiary Bomb. Roofing, plastering					
		& decorating & making all good.					
Nov	28	G.E.Ollis, making string course for Roof 2½ hrs				5	5
		H.J.Box Rebuilding.	26 hrs	@ 2/2	2	16	4
		W.G.Viney "	24 "	@ 1/7	1	18	0
		W.G.Harvey "	2 hrs	" 1/4		2	0
		2/1		1/9			
		20 ft 1½" Batten	40 old Bricks			3	1
		10 cwt Mortar				8	4
Dec	5	G.E.Ollis 34½ hrs (Work on Roof)		@ 2/2	2	14	0
		H.J.Box Rebuilding 50½ hrs		"	5	9	4
		W.G.Viney " 43 hrs			3	8	1
		L.Harding helping with coping 1½hrs				3	3
		11/8	4/6				
		14 cwt Mortar 1 cwt Cement				16	2
		6/3	1/14/0				
		50 Bricks 2 Rolls Roofing felt			2	0	
		7/1	4/4½				
		10 yds Roofing felt 1 - 13 ft 3" x 2"				11	5
		1/3/4	6/8				
		5- 14 fts 3" x 2" 2- 15 fts 3" x 2"			1	9	0
		8/0	2/8				
		2 - 12 ft " 1- 8 ft ditto				10	8
		10/11½					
		7 - 15 fts 2" x ¾" 2 - 10 fts 2" x ¾"	2/1			13	0
		2/11	7/5½				
		7 lbs Nails 1- 17 ft 4" x 2"				10	4½
Dec	12	H.J.Box 44 hrs		@ 2/2	4	15	4
		L.Harding 1 hr (Journey for freestone)				3	0
		W.Crew 7½ (On Roof)				16	3
		G.E.Ollis 7 (studding Partitions)				15	2
		20 ft 3" x 2" p.p.d				6	11
		9/0	4/2				
		2 cwt Cement 5 cwt sand				13	2
		1/10	9/0				
		20 ft 1½" batten 6- 18" crease				10	10
		8/4	3/9				
		10 cwt Mortar ½ cwt White spar				12	1
		2 lbs nails 10d 6 ft 6" coping stone 15/6				16	4
		12 ft run of Freestone & 1-qoinstone			1	17	6
		Carried forward.			36	12	8½

The cost of rebuilding 'Halliday's in 1944. What wonderful prices!

there was not even an air-raid warning. One night was the exception, so I took shelter in the home of a neighbour, who was the organiser of fire-watching in our road. He said, 'You can't go out with all that noise', so his wife and I just sat and had a drink and some cigarettes till it was safe to go home.'

September 4. Between Manor Road and Courtenay Road, nine high explosives were dropped. The same night one landed at Queen Charlton. Padfield's Farm was hit by two oil bombs, and three incendiaries fell at Kelston. A delayed high explosive at Newton St. Loe exploded the following day at 10.30 am. At Keynsham a high explosive bomb was found in the Park's field.

Major Scammell recorded that occasional bombs and enemy activity persisted in the area during the month.

September 5. ['Enemy attacks developed shortly after 21.00 hrs and were more intense than on the previous night. Principal areas involved being Bristol, Gloucester and N Somerset where a large number of HE and IB (incendiary bombs) were dropped, causing extensive damage to private property and a number of casualties, some of which were fatal. A high proportion of unexploded bombs fell causing the evacuation of persons in threatened properties.

Keynsham. A number of boxes, 1½ in sq, containing 4 or 5 pills were found in the district this morning and are presumed to have been dropped by enemy planes last night. Twenty boxes are in the hands of the Police and one has been submitted to the Public Analyst, Bristol, who reports them to contain tapioca starch and to be quite harmless.']

September 6. At 10.30 pm two unexploded bombs were found at Wick Farm, Compton Dando. [At 01.55 hours, 7 HEs (high explosive bombs) in a field at Whitchurch]

Air battles over Bristol

Mac Hawkins in his excellent book, 'Somerset at War' (Dovecote Press, 1988) wrote that, 'Although not directly in the front line for the Battle of Britain itself, Somerset also suffered from the attentions of the Luftwaffe. The large scale attacks on this country by German aircraft began on 10 July 1940, which is the generally accepted date of the beginning of the Battle. Large numbers of bombs fell in woods, marshes and on farms, as well as on towns'.

'For Somerset the Battle of Britain reached its climax during the last week of September 1940, when the German Air Force intensified its attacks on the aircraft industry . . . The first of two large-scale attacks occurred on the 25th – the airfield and the works of the Bristol Aeroplane Company in Filton were the Luftwaffe's major objective.

The German planes consisted of over 58 Heinkel He 111 bombers, guarded by 40 Messerschmidt Bf 110 fighters. At 11.48 am precisely they passed over the three main BAC factory groups and released their bomb loads. 'The works suffered severely; 900 houses on the Filton area were also damaged . . . there were many casualties.' 160 died.

'Twelve Hurricane pilots of 238 Squadron were just too late on the scene and started their dive to attack . . . Fierce combat developed with the He 111s and the Me 110s . . . Damage had been inflicted on several Heinkels and the formation began to spread out. Further running fights ensued and the British fighters went for the stragglers.'

Mac Hawkins continued, 'Ivo Peters was at his factory [The Polysulphin], in Keynsham as the battle raged overhead;

'The sirens had gone so I instructed my staff to go down to the air raid shelter to take cover. I could hear there was a tremendous aerial battle going on – instead of going down to the shelter myself I went outside to look. It really was quite fantastic – one minute there was a terrific amount of noise with planes twisting and turning in the sky – the next minute it was all over and really very quiet. I noticed a Spitfire in trouble – plainly it was losing height and realising that it was about to come down, jumped in my car and made off towards Bath. I got to Newton St Loe and noticed the fighter in a field to the left of the main road between the GWR and the Midland Railway lines. I went over to speak to the pilot whom I found perfectly all right. I offered him assistance and he said he would be grateful for a lift to Colerne airfield, which I gladly gave him.' [page 29]

'September 27 . . . was the last occasion on which any comparable number of German aircraft crossed our coasts in daylight. There were in all four major attacks on southern England in which the enemy used a record number of aircraft; about 850, of which 57 were lost; the RAF losing 28. . . . In the morning the Germans sent 300 planes to bomb London and others to Bristol. The target at Bristol was to be the Parnell Aircraft Company, who manufactured Frazer-Nash gun turrets. The Germans thought they would meet little resistance and were unaware that No 504 Squadron had been moved to Filton the preceding day . . . Ten Messerschmidtt Bf 110 fighter bombers . . . each carrying two 500 kg. bombs, took off from their base in Cherbourg . . . with an escort of 89 fighters.

'Sirens sounded again in Bristol at 11.30 just as 504 Squadron were taking off in their Hurricanes from Filton.' They attacked and a 'melee of twisting and turning aircraft ensued, each vying for position. The dog fight was watched by hundreds of people on the ground and many clapped and cheered as the enemy scattered in all directions. Bullets, spent cartridge cases and shrapnel rained down on the streets below'. [page 36]

'Molly Wallbridge, a Somerset girl in the Bristol ARP, saw the air battle going on whilst fishing from Keynsham weir;

"I was standing in the middle of the weir fishing for roach. The noise of the water drowned out all sound, but something made me look up . . . the sky was full of planes. I watched our fighters climb up into a formation, scattering the Germans in all directions. Dangerous to be caught outside because of the falling shrapnel and debris, I splashed my way over the weir as quickly as I could back to the bank to the shelter of an old mill, where I stood in the doorway to watch the air battle going on. I still couldn't hear anything of it for water going over the weir. The sky was full of vapour trails – it was quite fantastic to watch." '

Mac Hawkins concludes his detailed research into the events of the 27th by recording that, 'The running battle continued, resulting in a complete route of the German force. The Hurricanes of 504 Squadron pursued their quarry to the south coast and shot down further aircraft . . . By mid-day the first returning Hurricanes landed back at Filton. Ten aircraft made it back there . . .' [page 38]

That was not the last that Bristol and Keynsham saw of the Luftwaffe. The night Blitz then began and in the first great attack on Bristol on the night of November 24th, 1940, 'Wine Street and Castle Street were entirely destroyed by fire, with 200 people dead and 689 injured.' December 2nd saw 270 people killed and on January 3rd 149 died. [page 44]

September 25. 'During the notorious daylight raid on Bristol Aeroplane Company's works at Filton, Squadron Leader P K Devvit's 152 Squadron Spitfire I, made a forced landing near the road/rail bridges on the Bath Road, not far from Newton St Loe having been hit by one of the attacking Heinkel He IIIs. Devvit was seen running to the nearest AA box.'

Mrs Doreen Wiltshire recalled that when her husband was away at night on Home Guard duty, 'I would be at home with our five children at 50, Temple Street. When the raids started, I would run with the children down to mother, Mrs Veale, at Number 72, where we would all shelter under the stairs. Sometimes we stayed there all night, and at other times we went home after the "all clear".' Later she obtained an all-metal Morrison table shelter. Thinking back to those days she said, 'The cottages that we lived in were lovely little places.'

October 15. [IB8 dropped on an area covering from Keynsham to Avonmouth] About 25 incendiaries fell in a straight line from Charlton Park to Hanham Woods at 19.40 hrs. All fell in open ground except one which slightly damaged 40, West View Road, the property of Mr Raines. [No casualties.]

November 19. Bombs fell at Kelston Park and Newton St Loe, a few days before Bristol suffered its most devastating blitz.

November 24. The fringe of this reached Keynsham between 7.30 and 10.30 pm when incendiaries fell at Hicks Gate and Queen Charlton. Eleven fell in Keynsham; in Charlton Road, Charlton Park (No 2 and 'Trencrom'), 57, Albert Road, 9 and 11, Handel Road, Roseland in Queens Road and at 66 and 98, Park Road. [A number of HEs fell in fields at Pensford at 19.20 hrs.]

Bombs fell in fields west of Kelston Road and there were hayrick fires at Durley Park and Stockwood. One high explosive landed near Grange Road, Saltford, two on Mr Brownsey's Broadlands Farm, Keynsham, two on Salmon's field and Mr Sweet's Lays Farm, Charlton Road. Several unexploded bombs were found in the area and an unexploded AA shell at 'Ashwick', Charlton Park. [20 HEs fell in the Keynsham area and 5 at Stockwoood.]

War-time memories of a school boy

William Down recalled that, 'A lot of incendiary bombs dropped around Cranmore Avenue and in the fields off Charlton Road towards Broadlands School. We boys picked up some that had not gone off. We should have handed them in to the air-raid wardens, but we didn't. One of the boys, now dead, knocked one as hard as he could against a manhole cover to make it go off. There was a very small explosion, and it then started burning and kept burning like phosphorus. We used to buy phosphorus and put it in a bottle with water, and screw the top on tightly. We would leave them on the grass or throw them into the water, to see them explode.

'There were loads of bombs round here dropped by the Germans on their way home after they had tried to destroy Bristol. From our door we could see the sky all lit up round Bristol and Avonmouth. I had no frightening moments, but it was quite exciting to hear the bombs going off in Bristol. We had quite a number of high explosive bombs round here but Keynsham was not targeted and they fell harmlessly into the fields. We used to collect the shrapnel.

'I remember looking up in the sky and seeing a dog fight between our planes and the German ones. You could see them diving and swooping but I didn't see any shot down or hear the sound of gun fire.

'At home we had a flat-topped Morrison shelter made of steel plates and thick girders, but I can't remember going into it. We didn't use it when the sirens went, but I suppose we would have done if bombs were falling near us.

'For protection, the houses in Temple Street had concrete blast walls about 8 ft tall in front of them on the edge of the pavements.'

Another Keynsham boy also had a lucky escape with a bomb. Mrs Charles Gurnsey's son, Tony, likewise found an unexploded incendiary bomb and took it home. He kept it in the shed where he and the other boys played with it and generally kicked it around. Then one bonfire night they threw it on the fire, and the result made it seem like daylight as it lit up the whole of Keynsham!

December, 2/3, 1940. Bristol's second blitz and both Keynsham and Saltford were affected. A house at Durley Park and a hayrick at Queen Charlton were hit by incendiaries, while others fell in fields south of the Bath Road. 'Avon Villa', Saltford's Post Office at the time, was hit and a lady outside handling one was hurt. [15 HEs in Keynsham – Queen Charlton area.]

A high explosive landed on the road at Saltford Hill near the railway station, another at 'Glen Cottage', while five, plus one that did not explode, fell across Saltford golf course. A 3 inch gas main was set on fire at the Glen.

During a raid on the 3rd, 'starfish' decoy fires, south and west of Bristol were lit, one being just north of Queen Charlton.

Mrs Ann Randall writes that, 'Decoy fires were lit in the fields between Keynsham and Queen Charlton, and into Stockwood Vale. Enemy aircraft thought they were incendiary fires started by the first wave of bombers and released bombs into the fields. I know by the craters we often found as children that quite a few bombs must have been dropped there which were intended for Bristol.

'We often made a collection of dry wood ready to be taken to the fields

68

by men in late evening, with cans of paraffin which would help to get the wood to light. A few ARP wardens would arrive on bicycles and carry the wood under their arms from where we had piled it at the end of St George's Road. Mother said it was dangerous them having paraffin . . . On one occasion father was called in to help get a cow out of a steep-sided crater into which it had fallen.'

1941

Jan 3/4. During Bristol's fourth blitz, a number of incendiaries fell in the Keynsham area where a bungalow was damaged and telephone lines brought down. [In addition to the IBs at 22.20 hours 4 HEs fell on Keynsham. 5 HEs at Queen Charlton damaged the water mains. 3 HEs at Saltford.]

January 16/17. Avonmouth was badly hit. Several high explosives fell at Compton Dando and a cottage was destroyed.

January 29. An aircraft, thought to be a Hurricane, crash landed at Stockwood Flats, and the pilot survived.

There was a searchlight at Compton Dando and another at Newton St Loe. In 1941 a gun site for four 3.7 in. AA Mobiles was established on the hill between Corston and Saltford.

Miss Mary Fairclough had heard that local children had collected brush wood for decoy fires. On the subject of bombing nearby she remembers, 'One night a German plane going home in a hurry jettisoned the whole of its load in half a field, at the lower end of where the Federated Homes are now, towards Dunster School [also not there then], at the back of Parkhouse Farm. The field stood on end.

'On another occasion there was a massive crater in those fields, big enough to put in a double decker bus. At one time, during a very wet winter, bombs caused heavy clay to come up in huge slabs, forming grotesque shapes like that of the Hartland coastline.

'Mr E Loxton, a Queen Charlton farmer, threatened that if there were any more unexploded bombs on his fields, he was going to give up farming, as already three or four of his cows had been killed, not to mention numberless chickens! Two very large walnut trees just clear of "Hembers" had been blown to smithereens.'

There was a feeling in Keynsham, according to Mr B Woodham, that some German pilots deliberately dropped their bombs in the fields surrounding the town. He explained this belief to be founded on the pattern of the bombing, which was not close enough to harm but was sufficiently close to be excused as a 'near miss' when the bombers photographed their handiwork. Mr Jack Smith said, 'I think Woodham was right, and that we were chosen not to be bombed. We were very lucky.'

However, Mr John Penny, the joint-founder of the Fishponds Local History Society, who devoted ten years to researching 'Air crashes in the County of Avon, 1919–1987', disagreed. 'A Target List drawn up in Germany in the early 1930s designated Fry's as the sole target in the area. Originally it was listed as "GB 8243, Keynsham, a steel rope manufacturing factory" and was only much later updated to "Keynsham's Fry's Chocolate Works". Bath was "GB 9935", with Foxhill being "GB 1467" and "GB 14115" being "Bath North Camp".' John said that most German pilots would not have known where Keynsham was, let alone tried to bomb it. 'Most of the Luftwaffe bombing was not very accurate, and they generally thought they were over Bristol. Any bombs dropped on Keynsham were just an overspill from Bristol or Bath.'

Air Raid Shelters

A number of houses in Keynsham had their own privately built air-raid shelters. Jack Smith, the licensee of the former London Inn in Temple Street, which backed onto the Chew, had one built partly below ground at the rear of the Inn, with benches on three sides of it. He and his wife used it, and some of their friends, until the raids were over. At 69, Charlton Road, my home for twelve years, a concrete shelter had been built in the garden adjoining the rear of the house, partly below ground. There were three steps down from garden level, then on the right was the small living quarters, behind a thick blast wall. The solid fuel Tortoise stove remained there in the corner, with the flue pipe still projecting through the wall. At the end of the shelter was an escape window – one did not wish to be buried alive. After the war it was used for coal.

Throughout Keynsham there were a number of indoor Morrison shelters. Quite different were the thick concrete blast walls, built for protection, in front of living room windows, to be found in Temple Street, Albert Road and Summerleaze, and at the Council houses in St Ladoc and St George's Road. The height of the walls depended on the height of the windows, the walls ranging from 6 to 8 ft. From these examples one can see that they were widely erected throughout the town.

Unlike the Morrison shelters' limited height of around 4 ft, Anderson shelters were about twice the height, arched and narrow like a Norman window, and made of corrugated steel. Usually they were sited in one's garden, away from the house. Miss Fairclough believes there must have been some in Keynsham, with possibly one or two in Charlton Park, though she could not recall having seen any.

In the town a number of the larger pre-Edwardian houses had cellars, which could be used as shelters. Mr Frank Bees recalls that the house opposite him in 8, Albert Road, possessed a cellar dug out at the rear of the house. Some families brought their beds down onto the ground floor. In his home, thick outside wooden shutters were put up at night over the living-room bay windows to prevent flying glass.

During heavy bombing, many families would take shelter in what they considered to be the safest place in the house, that is, under the stairs, well away from flying glass from broken windows, and from shrapnel. Mary remarks that she even knew of at least two babies being born 'below stairs'. There was no shelter at her home at 43, Charlton Road, so that during raids they would sit on the stairs, or go under them if the bombing was heavy.

Mr C Wiggins said that there was no shelter at his home in the High Street and though he was away much of the war on active service, he believed that the family would probably have gone under the stairs if it was necessary. But he added, 'Keynsham was never really attacked, so really the family just sat tight and hoped that all would be well.'

As a boy, John Baker lived at 9, Queens Road before and during the war. He recalled that in the 1930s, Queens Road was still an unmade up road, lined with large elm trees. There was a gateway into the fields on the left hand side going up.

He said, "Father built a shelter for us of galvanised iron and odd planks of wood. He was doing his own thing. Mr. Percival Pera senior, at Number 13, built a larger stronger shelter with concrete walls and floors, and a re-enforced roof. But as they were both built on clay, they were prone to flooding, and so were nearly useless as shelters. There were no bunks in ours and I never used it. However one night a stick of bombs were dropped in the nearby field, bringing up a lot of clay. One crater was exceptionally large. We were at Newton St. Loe that night. The Pera family, who were safely in their shelter, were much affected by the blast from the large bomb, which made breathing difficult for them for a while."

Gladys, one of the Pera children, recalled that her elder brother Percival, who was a builder, actually constructed the shelter. She said, 'I was a child during the war. Families from five of the eight houses there joined together to have built one large communal shelter. We all used it when from time to time there were raids. We were in it when Bath was blitzed, while the men stood outside watching. I think there were five sets of bunks in it and often we slept there all night. I can remember doing my homework in it."

Mrs Leslie Crowther remembers the war over Keynsham

Mr and Mrs Crowther kindly allowed me to talk to them about their war memories. Mrs Crowther, formerly Jean Stone of 13, Manor Road, had her own sharp memories of local events when the feared Luftwaffe made its appearance over Keynsham. Still slim, vivacious and full of joie de vivre, she told me how her father, Walter Stone, managed to obtain heavy railway sleepers to give added protection to a shelter in the garden that he dug out himself with his brother Bill's help. 'Later we had an indoor Morrison shelter,' she said.

Jean recalled the 3 September, 1939, the day that Neville Chamberlain announced that the country was at war with Germany. 'I remember I was sitting on the swing in the garden swinging high and low. The windows were open as it was a lovely early September day. I ran into the house when I heard mother crying in the kitchen. It was the first time I had seen an adult in tears.' Her mother Winifred was well aware of the might of Germany, and what war meant in terms of human suffering and tragedy. WWI had finished only 21 years earlier.

Leslie looked at Jean and prompted her memory with the one word, 'Bul-lets'. She remembered at once. 'Not far up Manor Road were the swings. One day I was playing there with my sisters when a small German aeroplane sud-denly appeared and machine-gunned us.' Happily no one was hit. Later, bullets were picked up near the swings. One can imagine the children's terror – and then the tears.

On the night of August 19, 1940, the sirens sounded, and from her shelter Jean could hear the whistle, then the scream, of approaching bombs, as a fleeing Luftwaffe bomb aimer jettisoned his cargo. The bombs landed nearby in the fields, making a colossal crater in the grounds of what is now Wellsway School. Some of the bombs failed to detonate.

At 11.45 am on September 25, 1940, 58 Heinkel bombers with an escort of 40 Messerschmitt fighters, as yet unchallenged by the RAF, unleashed their bombs on an unsuspecting Filton and the aircraft works was devastated with much loss of life. (Mac Hawkins p 25)

Jean recalled the events of September 27, 1941, when the Luftwaffe, with a force of 89 fighters to protect their 10 bombers, returned to Bristol. She was at Bath Hill School, where Mr Mycock was the headmaster. 'When the siren went, you could run home if you were near enough, or go to a friend's house. Arrangements had been made for us to go Mrs Smart's in Temple Street. At 11.30 am the siren went and my sister Lesley and I ran to Mrs Smart's, only to find she was out. We sheltered under the stone archway of the passage that led into Mrs Smart's back garden, where Kwik Save is now. From there I peered out and had a wonderful view of the German planes as they flew over the town.'

But this time the RAF was there, and the Luftwaffe received a hammering. As Jean said, 'I could see the dog-fights going on. I saw one German plane shot down and crash, and people coming down in parachutes.'

To children, war in the daytime could sometimes be exciting. But at night time, it could be frightening. As Jean said, 'I remember to this day the fear and apprehension experienced in the early hours of the morning when I awoke to hear the overpowering roar of aircraft engines, seeming to be almost in my bedroom. The next moment there was a terrific explosion. I saw what I thought was a mighty fireball overhead and thought our end had come.' That was at 1.45 am on August 26, 1944, when a Wellington bomber crashed just a few hundred yards up the road.

To ensure the equal sharing of the nation's limited resources, petrol, clothes and food were rationed, and coupons issued to obtain them. Jean wrote, 'I am sure other people will have told you about the excited buzz that went round if any oranges or bananas arrived in the shops. I can remember being sent down to join the queue to get our allowance, picking young nettles, too, to use as greens, and the constant walks with an old pram to collect logs or wood, as coal was rationed. I hated that.'

As we reminisced about our wartime memories, Leslie said that he and his family arrived at Twickenham, South London, just as the German offensive of the dreadful V1, commenced, the 'buzz bombs' as he called them. At home in Bromley we referred to them as 'doodlebugs', but we both remembered the experience of the pilotless planes with engines that would cut out over the city, before crashing into the helpless metropolis.

* * *

A Keynsham man was closely connected with the Bristol raids of September 25 & 27, 1940. Edward Cannock wrote, 'I was apprenticed at B.A.C. and was there at the time of the first raid on Wed. 25th. After the 'All Clear', we were sent home and told to report on Thurs. 26th. On arrival we were directed to a field in Gypsy Patch where we learned that an unexpected bomb had lodged below our workshop. Again we were sent home from where on the Friday I witnessed the shooting down of a Messerschmitt 110 which fell into Stapleton Rehabilitation grounds.

'Several other Keynsham men survived the first raid. I do not think there were any local casualties.'

An English plane crashes in Keynsham

February 1941. Mr Sherer recalled the day when an English trainer plane crashed in a field in Park Road by the Cameroons, killing the two crew members. 'The doomed plane narrowly missed houses in Albert Road.'

Mrs Minnie Bates, married in 1939 and then living at Dapps Hill, also recalled the occasion, though with certain differences.

'I was making a feed for my six-weeks-old son, Wilf, when a plane came low over the Workhouse and broke up. I saw a wing of it fly past my window. There was an explosion as the plane crashed in the field above the Workhouse, just a few hundred yards from my home. I could not leave Wilf but Elsie Miles rushed round to help. But it was too late. The plane was blazing furiously and she was told, 'Keep back'. Another witness told Minnie, 'The two men had fried like bacon in a pan'. Later, when the bodies were recovered,the matron from the Workhouse put a large apron over the bodies.'

At the bottom of Dapps Hill was the old gasometer building, used as a temporary morgue during the war. There the bodies were placed. The added twist to this tragedy was that one or both of the young men had girl friends in the town, and as so often happened, the airmen had notified them that they would be flying over Keynsham that day. Minnie was not sure if one couple were actually engaged, but 'Dr Claude' certainly administered a sedative to one of the girls.

William Down also recalls the event. 'I was in school at Broadlands when the German plane came down near Park Road. There was no siren, else we would not have been in our classes. We were even told to get under our desks. During the day we heard where it had come down, so as soon as school was over, we dashed up to look. It was exciting to us. The police kept us back. We looked for bullets, as they were useful for swapping at school.'

Though the London evacuee, Samuel Olive, also referred to this same crash as being that of a German plane, they were both incorrect. The hope,and then the belief, that a Luftwaffe plane had been brought down, appears to have been the product of uninformed patriotic school gossip. I contacted John Penny. He stated that German planes came down at Fishponds, Radstock, Portbury, Falfield, Weston-s-M., Failand and one at Lulsgate airdrome intact having run out of fuel, but none came down in Keynsham. Sadly the crashed plane that the evacuees saw was one of ours.

John said that official records show that it was a Blackburn Shark II, serial number K 8503. This biplane, similar to a large Tiger Moth, was only used by the Navy, and came from the No. I Air Gunnery School, The Fleet Air Arm, Worthy Down Airfield, Hampshire, known as 'HMS Kestrel'. It crashed in daytime at Cameroon's Paddock, Keynsham.

The plane was on a Wireless Exercise. Both men were aged twenty. The pilot, Sub-Lieutenant John Wm Ridler, was the son of Albert and Margaret Ridler of 158, North Road, Bishopston, Bristol. The Telegraphist Airgunner was Eric Wm E Burton, Naval Airman 2nd class. Their certificates of death are at the Registrar's Office, Bath. Their bodies now rest in cemeteries at Winchester and Derbyshire.

Many of the early Fleet Air Arm records were discarded before the end of the war, so the official cause of the crash is unobtainable. However, there is a rumour that the pilot was engaged in unauthorized aerobatics with the old biplane, which was unable to stand the strain. A similar accident occurred with a Shark II in northern England. The fact that the pilot came from Bishopston strengthens the story of a romance with a Keynsham girl.

The recollections of an Air Raid Precautions driver

A young man of thirty when war was declared, Mr Jack Smith, of the London Inn (whose father Reginald Smith was the licensee of the Lamb and Lark) was turned down by the army as medically unfit. So he joined the local ARP under the direction of the Chief Warden, Mr Alex Cunningham of Wellsway. Jack was in the First Aid wing of the ARP and as a driver he used his own car, a Standard 12. There were quite a large number of wardens, and their centre was at the gas works in Dapps Hill, where there was a large general room, a storeroom and a mortuary. His uniform was a dark blue serge battle dress top with matching trousers, a blue helmet and a gas mask. Later their base was at the School Room on Station Road, where Dr Claude Harrison and Dr Gerrish were members.

'We dealt with bodies, which we took to the mortuary, or did anything else required of us. Keynsham was not hit badly, but one night when Bristol was badly bombed, we were called into the city and sent to Muller's Orphanage and put on reserve. It was terrible driving through the Horsefair, with bombs falling and flames from the high buildings on fire were meeting overhead. I felt very sorry for the fire fighters. Actually we were not required and were sent home next morning. That was the only time we were called in.

'When the plane crashed at the Cameroons, my brother-in-law, Harry Ollis, and I were in Temple Street. We heard the crash and saw the smoke and ran very quickly to the site, and were the first people there. The plane was burning fiercely but at first you couldn't get near it as bullets were going off like the clappers. After they stopped, we were able to pull the two men out, poor devils. Both were still just alive. They were breathing, but their eyes were shut, they could not speak and made no movement. One had his leg cut to pieces with the muscles hanging out. Soon after this, nurses arrived and a vehicle took them to the local hospital, where they died. A small dark girl who lived in Albert Road was said to be connected with one of them.

'I sold the London Inn to H Ollis and started market gardening at

Stockwood Vale. So it was work by day and report to the School Room every night, where I slept unless required. We were fortunate at Keynsham and were not often called out as there was little loss of life. On one occasion I took a body from Whitchurch to the Dapps Hill morgue, and on another occasion a body from Brislington. One was a man, the other a woman.

'I remember the daytime attack on Parnell's Aircraft Factory, Yate. [September 27, 1940] The German planes [10 Messerschmitt Bf 110 fighter-bombers, with an initial escort of 89 fighters] came up the channel, swung inland, then approached Bristol via Keynsham. The planes were at no height at all and you could see the pilots quite easily but they made no attempt to bomb Keynsham. And right after them came our fighters. The wardens tried to get people under cover but they just wanted to stand and look. I was one of them. There was a loud noise of machine-gunning. I believe very few of the enemy planes escaped, and later our Spitfires came back and did victory rolls over Keynsham.

'Occasionally heavy German bombers would come over very low at night, where we could see them. We didn't go to the shelter, but got nosey and wanted to know what planes they were. It was a frightening experience.

'A number of unexploded bombs fell on the town, and the Americans dealt with them. They were young coloured boys who drove heavy khaki-coloured Chevrolet open trucks, some 35–40 hp, with 8 rear wheels and double drive, which were very strongly built, with metal sides but no reinforced front to protect the drivers. There is a bit of land at the end of Stockwood Vale, beyond what was Charley Minty's farm [now a fabulous house] where they detonated the bombs in the daytime. After a raid, the trucks would go backwards and forwards, maybe a dozen times, going like the clappers, with one big or several small bombs in the back. I never went too close to see.

'These Americans were as good as gold; they were wonderful people. We were glad to see them go by. One morning, after a raid, there was an HE bomb sticking out from one of my market garden fields, which they happily removed. On another occasion my tractor was stuck, so passing by, they gladly pulled me out and refused any payment. They were good lads. I think they were living in Nissen huts at Pixash Lane.

'Further still along the valley were decoy lights to lure the Luftwaffe away from Bristol. They were not very prominent. They were used much more on the Mendips.'

March 1941. This month brought many incidents, particularly in the first three weeks.

At this time, Chris Wiggins was on a seven day embarkation leave at the beginning of March, and left England on the 15th, 1941. While he was on leave, the siren went for a day time raid on Bristol, so accompanied by his brother Philip and one of his sisters, he drove up to the Queen Charlton quarry area to watch the action. While the planes and the bombs were not visible, they could see the flashes of the explosions.

The attack appeared to be north of Bristol, possibly at the BAC. He said they neither felt grief, anxiety or anger. 'We just accepted it. We had all expected a German blitz long ago since the declaration of war and so we just took it as it came. There was no special feeling of relief that it was not Keynsham.

While I was on duty at Brighton, in 1940, a lone German plane dropped two bombs and we watched them coming down, before diving for cover. We just accepted it. About this time, several small vessels arrived from Dunkirk bringing over mainly French troops, prior to the main evacuation. Again, we just accepted it.'

April 11. ['Keynsham, 1¾ mls NNE of, at 01.45, 3 HE. No damage or casualties.']

April 13. ['Keynsham. Whitchurch areas. Approximately 17 HEs and numerous IBs. Pensford. Numerous IBs.']

May 5. ['Keynsham. In field at Hicks' Gate Farm at 23.30 hrs. 1 HE. No damage or casualties.']

June 2. ['Clutton, 6 mls S of K'm at 00.52. 12 HEs. No damage or casualties. 3 cows killed.']

October 9, 1941. At about 15.30 hours a tragic accident took place over Saltford. Two Whirlwind twin-engined single-seat fighters from 263 Squadron, Charmy Down, collided in mid-air. P 6968 crashed into the weighbridge of Saltford station, killing the pilot, Flying Officer D J H Hoskins. The other plane, P6999, fell near Bath, and Flying Officer H J Coghlan bailed out.

1942

January 25. A Tiger Moth plane crashed into Tenett's field, Newton St Loe.

March 3. A Spitfire from 2 Ferry Pilots' Pool, crash-landed behind the Queen's Head at Willsbridge.

April 3. A bomb dropped near Somerdale, slightly hurting two boys. At 20.50 hrs a single enemy aircraft dropped four high explosives at Bitton, damaging the California Pumping Station of the West Goucestershire Water Company. Oldland Vicarage and Church were also damaged and about 105 houses needed attention in the area.

April 25. A house 'Guarlford' and a bungalow 'Elmleigh', both in Stockwood Vale, were damaged in the late afternoon. The house was subsequently deemed to be beyond repair.

April 27. A serviceman was seriously injured by a high explosive three quarters of a mile from the police station at Newton Park.

When the Luftwaffe finally found Bath

Sat. April 25, 1942. In 'Somerset at War' Mac Hawkins pointed out that many departments of the Admiralty had moved to Bath, making it an important military city, though it had no anti-aircraft guns for self defence as it was thought that it would never be attacked. He continued, 'However, 163 German bombers left N W France to attack the city.

'At 23.15 hrs enemy aircraft came in low over the lip of the hills . . . The flares were followed by thousands of incendiaries and Bath became a bowl of smoke and fire. Wave after wave of bombers roamed the skies above the city. Unopposed, the attackers were able to circle the amphitheatre at a few hundred feet, firing at will with machine guns at the Civil Defence workers and fire-fighters below to discourage their efforts.

'With the target now pinpointed by the stab of fires, the enemy began to drop HE bombs . . . Tremendous damage was caused. Following a lull lasting just a few hours, the attack was resumed . . . An estimated 40 or more bombers crossed the coast and reached Bath at 04.35 . . . In the small hours of the following morning, Monday 27, the enemy returned to Bath with 65 or more bombers. Flying at roof-top height, they added to the devastation of the previous night in a 90 minute raid of great intensity.' (pp 63 and 70.) 417 people were killed, 357 were seriously injured and 515 more slightly wounded. Over a thousand buildings were damaged beyond repair and 16,883 other buildings suffered damage.' (p 70)

Mr Brian Keeling said that he was only a small boy when war broke out. At the rear of his grandfather's house, 'The Shrubbery', in Wellsway, the garage was made into a family shelter by adding a further 6 in. layer of concrete to the roof and reinforcing the walls with stone, with a dog leg entrance. When bombing was heavy at Bristol or Bath, his family would leave their home just up the road at Number 43 and would sleep in the shelter.

He recalled that, 'Though it was said in those days that the Luftwaffe could not find Bath because it was in a dip surrounded by hills, when it was finally hit, I can remember standing in 'The Shrubbery' garden and seeing the city absolutely aglow with flames.'

Speaking of another occasion, he said, 'I can vaguely remember seeing some planes engaged in a dog fight going on in the sky. On another occasion some delayed action bombs were dropped in the fields roughly where Wellsway School was later built. The family went over to have a look at them, when they suddenly blew up, fortunately without hurting any one.

'My father was in the Observer Corps and they kept watch from a post on the hillside near the hospital. There used to be a mounted bofors gun near the Chewton Keynsham bridge. After the raids were over, shrapnel was to be found scattered around and on the roof of our factory. I also remember seeing what looked like strips of aluminium hanging from telephone poles and wires. It might have been to do with anti-radar devices.

'I recall that one night Father stepped back sharply into the shelter when a German plane machine-gunned Keynsham and continued up Wellsway.' [Gwen Newman also remembered this event, saying that a German plane, a fighter, she thought, strafed the High Street.] 'I can't remember bombs actually blowing up houses in Keynsham, but I recall there being a board put on a post by the Cricket Field, which was said to change its colour if there was a gas attack.'

Low flying planes

The September 8, 1989, issue of the Keynsham Chronicle records that Mrs Elsie Woodham, who was born in 66, Temple Street, remembered that during the war, RAF planes would fly down between the houses of old Temple Street. Apparently they did this for cover and to surprise enemy bombers whom they chased to destruction after breaking cover. 'One could see quite plainly the pilots at their controls as their planes screamed past. It reminded us that, though living in a small market town, as Keynsham was in those days, the war for us, like the people of Bath, Bristol and elsewhere, was just outside our front door.'

During raids, it was the AA guns from Whitchurch that made most of the frightening noise, recalled an octogenarian, adding that a large naval gun from Horfield, known as 'Purdown Percy', would send shells screaming into the night sky at the Luftwaffe.

1943

April 8. The only known incident was the crash of a Spitfire I, P 9541, from the 52 Operational Training Unit (OTU), at Newton St Loe after an engine fire.

The sewing brigade of the Women's Voluntary Service

A member of the local branch of the WVS, Miss Fairclough, said that their uniform consisted of a green greatcoat and a green hat, hence their not very flattering nickname of the 'old green trout'. Such uniform was only issued to the women without home ties, who were able to help in Bristol after the heavy raids. For others, 'uniform' was simply a green armband.

At the beginning of the war, the authorities made preparation for every contingency resulting from massive bombing. So among other social responsibilities that were to fall on the WVS was that of feeding hungry people. Mary recalls being instructed in 'Emergency Cooking', and how to construct an open air hearth, with a hole below for the fire, for preparing meals.

During the period of hostilities, the REME corps of the army was stationed at a camp off Wellsway, where, among other things, they repaired weapons and military vehicles. Their continuous heavy work meant that their overalls were often ripped and torn and badly in need of repair. An appeal went out from the corps, asking if it was possible for local ladies to repair them. The women of Keynsham magnificently rose to the occasion.

The WVS organised this, under the direction of Dr Sharman's wife, Jean. The Army delivered torn denims to Mrs Orr, the wife of the manager of the nearby ESA Robinson factory, at their home in Avon Mill Lane, [it being the residence of the former manager of the Brass Mill.] From the great pile of denims heaped up in the hall, scouts would take them to the homes of various WVS leaders, scattered throughout Keynsham.

These ladies would involve voluntary 'sewers' from their neighbouring roads, and supply them with khaki denims. Garments too torn for further use had their sleeves, pockets and suchlike cut off for patching overalls not so badly torn. Miss Fairclough had her own team from Charlton Road, Charlton Park, Park Road, West View Road and Westbourne Avenue. She had great respect for their competence, and claimed, 'They could patch galvanised iron with bailing wire if asked,' and felt that the older women were the tougher. 'When you're older, you are used to going on when you feel you can't.'

The REME camp below Uplands Farm

With the commencement of hostilities in 1939, The Royal Electrical and Mechanical Engineers, as a temporary measure, pitched six to eight bell tents at Burnett Knapps, on the left hand side of the brow of the hill, opposite the Munitions Dump. There the licensee Jack Smith found them, isolated and without provisions. He had access to cigarettes, drink and food, and daily used to supply them with the necessities of life. 'It was a wonderful time then when we all helped each other,' he reminisced.

Though at the beginning of the war the REME were billeted and worked at Burnett (and the RASC at Rockhill Farm), later the War Ministry hired from Mrs L Sherer, at a peppercorn rent, a six acres field between Courtenay Road and Uplands Farm. There several rows of black Nissen huts, some six huts to a row, totalling at least thirty in number, were erected, together with a canteen, kitchen and toilets, recalled Mrs Sherer's son, William Sherer.

He said that the field was oblong shaped and sloped towards Wellsway. 'One entrance to the camp was from Courtenay Road, next to their home at 'Smisby', but the main entrance was from Wellsway, opposite the haulage firm.

'A large tarmacked area fronted onto Courtenay Road and was regularly used for drill. The reveille call was not the tuneful note of the bugle but the rasping voice of the sergeant. The shouting of orders could be heard daily. Each morning some one hundred soldiers would line up in columns of four and march up to the Gypsy Lane site to repair vehicles. At lunch time they would march all the way back, only to return for the afternoon's work. Far from singing 'Tipperary', the men rather seemed fed up, and their long marches certainly held up the traffic that passed up and down the narrow Wellsway.

'On the brighter side, a contingent of some thirty ATS girls shared the site, and did the cooking for the Officers, and other duties. Normally a Captain was in charge, though on one occasion a Major was in command. My parents, like those of other Keynsham families, made the soldiers welcome at week-ends and in the evenings, and of course there was the Fear Institute for meals and relaxation. Unlike American soldiers in Keynsham at the same time, the British soldiers were neither well paid nor well supplied with tobacco and sweets.

'Different companies were stationed there. The soldiers, aged from twenty to forty, were all skilled men. One man was a plumber, while a few looked after the gardens. They were all decent chaps, and there was no trouble. Many of them could have been killed when in 1944 a bomber flew very low over the camp and crashed the other side of the road. Yet they were not involved in the tragedy; RAF personnel took charge.'

With the cessation of hostilities in 1945, the camp was then used by National Servicemen until it was finally closed in 1947. Today, the smart houses in Cadbury Road and Silbury Rise, built thirty five years ago, give no hint of the hundreds of servicemen to whom Nissen huts on this plot of land was for a while their war-time 'home'.

August 1943. Major Scammell recorded, 'It is worth mentioning that after three years church bells were returned to ecclesiastical use, and no longer were reserved as a national danger call.'

1944

March 24. ['Daily Summary No. 436. Period 12.00/27/3/44–12.00/28/3/44. Shortly before midnight a comparatively large force of enemy aircraft approached the S Coast of Devon with the appearance of attacking Plymouth. The attack on Plymouth did not materialise and the formation took a course N and E of the town, and later spread out over wide areas of Somerset, Gloucester, Wiltshire and beyond the region to South Wales and Oxfordshire.

A few bombs and IBs were dropped at widely separate points, chiefly in Somerset, causing slight damage and injuring a few persons.

Eight enemy aircraft were destroyed in the region.'

There were IBs at Taunton; 9 UXBs (unexploded bombs) at Weston; an HE at Winscombe with 1 person injured; fire damage to 2 small buildings at Highbridge; 1 HE at Cannington but no casualties; at Yeovil IBs caused a 10-pump fire, damage to hayrick and cottages, and a Home Guard ammunition dump involved. No casualties.]

The crash of the Wellington bomber

August 26. 'I was very frightened as a young boy when I was woken up by the terrific noise of an aircraft flying very low over our house. It was one of our planes and sadly it crashed just up the road in the field opposite Uplands Farm. Next day I went up to see it but we were not allowed to get near it. Later, bits of the scattered wreckage were handed in to the police station,' recalled Brian Keeling.

William Sherer is reported in the Keynsham Chronicle of February 18, 1983, as saying that the crashed bomber narrowly missed his old home in Courtenay Road and the nearby Army camp there, as it hurtled earthwards. 'I was the first on the scene after the crash. Uplands Wood was ablaze and machine gun bullets were exploding in the wood. A herd of cows were in the field but they escaped injury. Inspector Allen, then head of Keynsham Police, arrived shortly afterwards and took charge.'

The Chronicle of March 30, 1990, reprinted details of this tragic event. 'The Wellington bomber, [of 'Bomber Command Unit No. 12, OTU'] serial Number LN293, took off from Chipping Warden, Northants, at 22.09 hrs. on August 26, 1944, on a diversionary flight to be followed by a 'bulls-eye' exercise over Bristol at a height of 17,000 ft. The flight involved flying over the North

Sea and approaching Bristol from the north-east. The crew had been briefed to maintain radio silence except for a message when recrossing the English coast. This was duly carried out and the brief message, 'Crossing coast' was received at 0020 hrs. An hour and twenty-seven minutes later, the aircraft struck the ground almost vertically at a high speed at Uplands Farm.'

The weather conditions were good and the official accident report noted the wind 'as 2 mph W, visibility 4 miles, no cloud, icing negligible and a slight ground haze.' The pilot was W/O Harvey, who had 764 hours flying experience, 49 being in Wellington planes and 20 of these being night flying. The wreckage was gutted by fire and the engines were buried to a depth of twelve feet.

Various eyewitnesses reported that wreckage of the Wellington was scattered over a wide range in small pieces. At the point of impact, a small area remains barren: grass has never grown on the spot since the crash.

Four bodies were accounted for at the scene of the crash, where Dr Claude Harrison had the grisly task of picking up the human remains and placing them in an opened parachute.

The body of wireless operator Sergeant Hankin, with the unopened parachute attached, was found one and a half miles away. Mr Jim Ollis recalled that the body of this airman was found impaled on bean poles on the allotments where Cranmore Avenue is now. Mrs M. Bates said that Mr Exon, the dairyman, stopped Dr Claude and said, 'Look what I've found in the cabbage patch'. Though the airman was still just alive, by the time that the Doctor returned with his case from the surgery, the airman had died.

The body of bomb aimer Sergeant Martin, was later found three and a half miles away hanging in a tree at Hencliffe Woods, Hanham. His parachute

The night a Wellington came crashing back to earth.

A Wellington bomber similar to that which crashed mysteriously at Uplands Lane, Keynsham, in 1944.

The S W Aircraft Recovery Group at Uplands Farm circa 1985, hard at work in an archaeological dig for parts of the Wellington bomber that crashed here on August 26 1944. It weighed from 25–35 tons, and was flying at some 500 mph. It hit the ground almost vertically. G Morley's photo.

Later, Group Leader G T Morley, in the white shirt, discussed progress with a team member. Centre front: uncovered parts of the plane are piled up for cleaning, identification and recording. G Morley's photo.

had disintegrated and the canopy and rigging lines lay one mile north-east of his body. He was cut down by a Mr Williams and a Mr Irwin. For some years later, local people placed a wreath at the foot of the tree, and a few bulbs. Today, the tree is still there, but the bulbs have died and the act of remembrance is discontinued.

The Wellington had come down in a field with a steep slope and the National Fire Service had to use two pumps to bring water up from the River Chew. A precis of The Accident Investigation Report of November 17, 1944, stated that, 'The general destruction of the airframe was so extensive that no evidence relating to the pre-crash condition of the controls and control surfaces can be obtained. Only the port engine could be salvaged and this showed no signs of internal failure. Witnesses on the ground state that at 01.45 hrs. an aircraft was illuminated by searchlights for approximately two minutes. It then dropped two yellow flares and the lights were doused accordingly. It cannot be established whether the aircraft in question was LN293. The cause of this accident remains obscure.'

Mrs Mary Luke of Wellsway remembered the night of the crash. 'The noise of the descending plane woke me and my first thought was that the V2s had discovered how to get this far . . . Then there was a terrible crash. The sky turned a bright orange (I always had one curtain open) and then a ghastly silence. Within minutes ambulances and fire engines were roaring up the road and I understand that Dr Claude Harrison was the first doctor on the scene.' A fireman present at the scene said that rabbits, paralysed with fear, sat motionless.

The late Mrs Dorothy Warren and her husband, Ted, farmed the fields from Chewton Keynsham up to Uplands Farm. As the Chairman of the Milk Marketing Board he travelled extensively round the world, accompanied by his wife. Dorothy said that the morning following the crash, when she went across the field, her cows were all looking at the wreckage, for as she said, 'You know how inquisitive cows are.'

The crew of the Wellington bomber, LN293

Mrs Janet Snart's correspondence with the Ministry of Defence Air Historical Branch 3 (RAF), Great Scotland Yard, London, and with RAF Innsworth, Records, produced the following information concerning the crew.

Pilot Warrant Officer John R HARVEY, NZ412686. Born in Ponsonby, Auckland, New Zealand, he was buried in Carlisle Cemetery, Cumberland. A newspaper report says that 'Warrant Officer J Harvey, on attachment from the New Zealand Air Force, was just 22 and had been married six months earlier to his 19- year-old bride, Mary.'

Sergeant Donald M PATERSON, CAN/R206161, trainee navigator, from Toronto, Canada, was buried at Kingston-upon-Thames Cemetery, Surrey.

Sergeant Frank S MARTIN, 1398507, trainee bomb aimer, was born on 15 December, 1915, in Belvedere, Kent, and was buried at St Mary's Churchyard, Denham, Bucks. W/Officer R Brand stated that Frank's father, James

9ft down, a metal detector helps locate broken pieces of the plane. One of the plane's 12 gear shafts with its needle bearing still in situ, was recovered intact. The gears were made at the BAC factory in Bristol. The stainless steel bomb hook, which kept the HEs in place, was found in perfect condition. G Morley's photo.

Some of the plane's hundreds of bullets, recovered from their wooden boxes, were found fused together. D Dyson's photo.

Henry Martin, and his wife, Rosina, lived at 66, Perona Road, Belvedere, Kent. Frank left Belvedere to live and work in Denham, where he met his wife, Bertha.

He was a member of the local Territorial Army and enlisted at the outbreak of war, aged 24. In 1941 his wife lived in Oxford Street, Denham. From 12 January, 1940–23 January, 41, Frank was a corporal in the RASC. The Innsworth records state that 'Sergeant Martin was a temporary sergeant.' He was only 28 when he died in Hencliffe Woods.

Sergeant William E HANKIN, 1819276, trainee wireless operator, was born in Nottingham and was buried there in the Southern Cemetery Section. His body was found on allotments in Keynsham.

Sergeant David E EVANS, 3025155, trainee air-gunner, of Abercrave, Brecon, Wales, was buried at St Cynog Churchyard, Ystradgynlais.

Sergeant Elwin BLEWITT, trainee air-gunner, was born in Rhymney, Wales, and is buried at Rhymney Cemetery, Gelligaer, Glamorganshire.

Fifty years later, in connection with a proposed Memorial Service, attempts to contact the relatives of the crew were unsuccessful.

Of the actual crash itself, the unpunctuated report from RAF Innsworth declared, 'ROC observer states aircraft diving under power fired two yellows colour of the day then crashed and burned 2 crew baled out parachutes opened prematurely caught up in aircraft all crew killed.'

Of the plane itself a report in the Keynsham Chronicle of January 28, 1983, records that, 'Air Controller Mr John Dunford said that he had found a piece of aircraft in Lyndhurst Road, Keynsham, in about 1954 and it had been identified at Filton as part of a Bristol wartime engine. As Wellington bombers were fitted with Bristol Hercules engines, he thought it could well have been from the crash.'

About 1985, The South Western Aircraft Recovery Group, together with The Severnside Aviation Group, used a JCB to excavate the Uplands site of the crash. Group Leader George Morley's team, aided among others by Mr Doug Dyson, located parts of the starboard engine some 6–7 ft down, smashed to pieces. Several pieces were retrieved, together with ammunition boxes containing two thousand rounds of ammunition. The rest of the engine was so far down that it was simply covered over again.

As the crash occurred so quickly, George suggested that the cause could possibly have been due to faults with the controls. He thought that the chaffing found on the rigging lines of the parachute indicated that Sergeant Martin had pulled the release cord too soon, so that the lines were caught up with the plane's wheels. This could have caused the parachute to spin round, hence the chaffing, before it disintegrated. What a terrible ordeal for the airman, over three miles up in the middle of the night!

It was particularly tragic that such an awful crash should occur so near to the end of the war. Three months earlier in June, 1944, the Allies had landed in France. Though the V1s and V2s were still to inflict terrible damage on London, the crash virtually marked the end of 'the war over Keynsham'. As Mr V James said of it, 'Despite all the enemy activity recorded above, there were no deaths among the civilian population, and relatively little damage was caused, most bombs falling in open fields.'

The Memorial Service

The tragedy of the Wellington's crash was recalled half a century later, when on Friday August 26, 1994, at 2.00 pm, a Memorial Service was held on the hillside slope opposite Chewton Keynsham. It was a beautiful day with a few light clouds scurrying across the blue sky. A row of stones had recently been laid in the shape of a cross on the bare earth where the crash had occurred, and a few bunches of flowers had been laid on it. A crowd of nearly a hundred had gathered to pay their respects and gratitude to those so tragically killed in the defence of their country. These included Mr A R Warren, the farmer in whose fields they were, and Mr A and J Paget, who farmed nearby.

Above the rough circle of earth were three rows of baled straw, mainly occupied by the ladies, while the men, a number with cameras, stood behind them. Below the cross was a line of mixed ATC cadets from Keynsham led by their Commanding Officer, Flight Lieutenant F Ephgraves. From Acton, London, came Warrant Officer Rick Brand with some of his ATC cadets from 2370 (Denham) Squadron, the town from which the dead Bomb Aimer, Sergeant Frank Martin, came. Pilot Officer Murphy stood beside them. A bugler and detachment of eight members from RAF Locking, Weston-super-Mare, led by their Pilot Officer, formed a Guard of Honour and sounded the Last Post and Reveille.

Next to them was a band of Standard Bearers with their standards, being, mainly those of the Keynsham branch of the Royal British Legion, and that of the Royal Observer Corps, carried by Observer Officer Murray Whitcher. Other members of the Legion, and former members of the ROC, were present, proudly wearing their berets and medals. Former Observer Officer Doug Dyson of the ROC, replete with beret and medals, cast a professional eye at a low flying, unusual looking plane that passed over-head just before the service started, and identified it as an American Lockheed Electra. Wansdyke and Keynsham Councils were respectively represented by Mr B Organ, wearing his chain of office, and by Mr B Heaven (ex RAF), the former chairman.

The concept of the memorial service was that of Mrs Janet Snart, who, aided by Mr 'Bob' Dodd, President of the Keynsham branch of the Royal British Legion, organised the event. At the commencement of the service, she spoke of how she had heard of the airmen's deaths, and of her subsequent researches. She said, 'As we walk or drive in the valley below, we must stop and look up to this spot and tell our children, and they theirs, of what happened here; of the brave men who gave their lives in the cause of freedom and a decent life for everybody, lest we forget.'

Mr Dodd spoke of how an official enquiry by Bomber Command had been unable to establish the cause of the crash, and indicated that 'Grass has never grown on the spot where the plane crashed.' Two small boys placed posies of flowers bedside the cross, and a RAF cadet laid a wreath of poppies.

The Rev Simon Stevenette then conducted a short service of remembrance. After the singing, unaccompanied, of 'All people that on earth do dwell,' and

ATC cadets from Keynsham and Denham assemble for the Memorial Service, below the cross of stones. Among the cadets, Warrant Officer 'Rick' Brand in his peaked cap and blue jersey, holds his notes in front of him. Author's photo.

At the commencement of the service, Mrs Janet Snart and Mr 'Bob' Dodd, standing beside the minister, both spoke briefly about their research into the tragic crash and their planning of the service. Author's photo.

After the Memorial Service on August 26, 1994, former Observer 'Doug' Dyson was photographed holding part of the camshaft from one of the engines of the crashed Wellington. It had earlier been excavated by the S W Aircraft Recovery Group, in which Doug had been involved. Author's photo.

the reading of the Psalm 121 by Mrs Nellie Luke, he spoke of God's continued power to sustain people. Six ATC cadets then read aloud the names of the fallen. WO Rick Brand then spoke of how Sergeant Martin, 1398507, had moved from Belvedere, Kent, to live in Oxford Road, Denham, where he worked. There he met and married a local girl. 'When the balloon went up', he joined the RAF. So far they had been unable to trace his wife or any of his family.

'We have brought a plaque with us to be consecrated,' he said. The minister then blessed the commemorative plaque held by a cadet, which was to be taken back to Denham. The words of remembrance, 'They shall grow not old' were spoken by Squadron Leader J Evans, the Somerset County Chairman of the RBL, and then the Last Post and Reveille sounded. 'O God our help in ages past' was followed by the National Anthem and the Blessing.

After the service, refreshments were generously supplied at the delightful little Chewton Keynsham Church by a band of willing ladies. Stories were told and addresses exchanged. Rick's traditional walrus moustache was duly silently admired. What with the hearty laughter, the presence of so many young and older men in uniform, and the large number of medals sported, together with a sprinkling of officers, it really seemed like a war-time occasion. There was a real esprit de corps. Our dead comrades, never far from our thoughts, would surely have thoroughly approved of the gathering.

Rick showed me his file on Sergeant Frank Martin, with a photo of his headstone, sporting the RAF eagle, in St Mary's Church, Denham. He said that they had planted a tree in his memory, with four wooden posts surrounding it. The new plaque, bearing his name, number, and rank, would be brought out on parade night and held beside the standard. Rick finally departed for home, with a posy of flowers from the hillside cross, to be placed below Sergeant Martin's headstone.

Mrs Snart later wrote in the Parish Magazine, 'After the service was over, someone asked me, 'Why did you organise this service?' and I could not answer, but now perhaps I can. I did it for the man who said, "I have had a good and happy life thanks to men like these." For the woman who said, "My dad was in the RAF; it could have been him and I wouldn't have been born." And for the man who said, "I was 10 in 1944 and curious and I came the day after the crash to look. I regret being curious, but it gave me a reverence for life".'

Chapter 6

The Air Raid Precautions wardens' recollections

'The men and women of the Civil Defence began to train themselves in Air Raid Precaution duties at a time when 'appeasement' was the order of the day. When the inevitable war came, the nucleus of a comprehensive Air Raid Precaution service was fortunately in being, trained and capable of rapid expansion . . . Under the ARP Act of 1937 county councils became the responsible authorities and planning began on a wider basis. In June 1938 the administrative county was divided into eight areas, each with its own organiser and staff. Keynsham came under No 2 (Bathavon) Area, with Radstock, Midsomer Norton, Frome and the Rural Districts of Bathavon, Frome and Clutton . . . On 2 September, 1941, the ARP merged into the Civil Defence General Service.' (Mac Hawkins p. 179.)

In the possession of Mr E Cannock is the following newspaper report which appeared during the 1939–45 war. 'It was decided at the meeting of the KUDC, after discussion of the ARP personnel, to carry out an inspection of all the ARP service posts in the urban area . . . The General Purposes Committee reported it had fully investigated the position of the personnel, which comprises a total of 159, of which 23 were paid, giving a total wage bill weekly at £62.'

'Major P E Chappell, the area ARP officer, had met the committee, and had stressed the fact of the mutual assistance arrangement with Bristol whereby the Home Office required that a certain minimum number of personnel in respect of each service should be available throughout the 24 hours. In view of the difficulty of providing this 24 hour service with volunteers a certain number of persons had been put on wholetime paid service.'

Just what qualifications a warden possessed is revealed by the Recorder of Newbury, Mr E Terrell, himself a warden in London, who wrote in The Times, 'The function of a warden is purely defensive and protective. He has spent many months of spare time learning the evil nature and properties of high explosive and incendiary bombs and of gas, the nature of his duties to the public, and the risk he must run and those he should avoid in the event of raids. He attended lectures, practised with bombs, and even experimented in gas chambers. He attended and took part in rehearsals. He learnt his sectors and groups, and delicately investigated dangerous buildings. For his enthusiasm he received no kind of reward.

'During the first few days of war the public realized that a service was born for their special protection against raids. With this realization came confidence and a greater feeling of security.

'During war the warden advises upon the construction of shelters erected by private individuals, obtains and fits gas masks (and in particular baby masks), holds exercises against actual raids, advises upon the complicated rights of landlord and tenant concerning shelter costs, makes complete and careful inspection of vast bodies of flats and their safety devices against fire, explosion and gas. Every night, from 6.30 pm to the early hours of the morning, he is blacking out lights in co-operation with the police. He has to be tactful, courteous and sometimes stern. No one who has not worked on the black-out can appreciate the difficulty presented by the vast blocks of flats erected in London. In poor class districts the cost of black-out materials hits hard, and the warden has to help in overcoming this difficulty.

'For these services, a full time warden receives £3 a week and must be on duty for raids during the whole 24 hours. The part time warden receives nothing. Their cost of shoe leather alone is considerable.'

'Some ARP wardens behaved with consummate tact. In Belgravia, a friend

WILLIAM F. UPTON

Keynsham Accountancy and House Estate Agency

35 HIGH STREET, KEYNSHAM

TELEPHONE—KEYNSHAM 19

Local Agent for Daily Express Services and Tours by Saloon Coaches

BOOK YOUR SEATS IN ADVANCE TO COUNTRY AND SEASIDE

Bristol Tramways & Carriage Company Ltd. Greyhound and Associated Motors Express Services

---

COOPER & TANNER Lᴛᴅ.
F.A.I.

Auctioneers, Valuers, House and Estate Agents

AUCTION SALES of Live and Dead Farming Stock, Landed Estates, Residential and House Properties, Furniture, etc.

VALUATIONS of Tenant Right, Probate and Mortgage promptly carried out.

HOUSE AND ESTATE AGENCY. Lists of Properties for Sale or to Let always available on application.

Rent Collection and General Management of Estates undertaken.

Houses and Estates always required for applicants.

Offices :

BEECH HOUSE, KEYNSHAM Telephone 98
and at Frome, Glastonbury, Sparkford and Castle Cary

TELEPHONE 294

PRINTING LOCALLY

Let this be a **GUIDE** to your **Printing Requirements** Commercial and Private

Consult

Sᴛ. KEYNA PRESS

54 HIGH STREET, KEYNSHAM

Cheap, Efficient, Prompt

ADVICE AND ESTIMATES READILY GIVEN

26

Telephone: KEYNSHAM 99

HERBERT W. G. BELSTEN
(MEMBER OF B.U.A.)

Carpenter, Builder and Funeral Director

10 CHARLTON ROAD, KEYNSHAM, Nr. Bristol

29

These two pages are from the 1930 Keynsham Guide. In 1935 Upton was Clerk to the KUDC. The St Keyna Press, an old well-established firm, was during the war 'Sector CB4 Warden's Post'. Belsten's undertaker's business was later taken over by Leslie J Guyan, and succeeded by his son, Jim. Though the firm has changed hands, it still trades as Guyan L J and Son and is managed by Jim's son, Michael.

of one found slipped in his letter box, on a warden's buff-coloured report form, the following;

"As I passed by your window in the dark of the night,
It surprised me to notice a streak of bright light!
Now I really must warn you, it's my duty you know,
That unless you're more careful, you'll spoil the whole show." '

The Keynsham Urban District Council take a hand

Another cutting from the local paper records, 'Concern at the absence of air raid shelters in the area was expressed at a meeting of Keynsham Urban Council. The meeting adopted a resolution, moved by Mr George E Chappell, presiding, that representations be made to the County Education Authority to see that proper shelters were provided for the children attending the schools in the district.

'It also decided to make further representations to the county council for the provision of Anderson shelters for the inhabitants of the urban district in view of the fact that no provision was made in the district for the protection of the normal population, now considerably increased by the influx of evacuees.'

Another report states that, 'Captain Norman Kinnersley, MC, chief warden of Keynsham, presided at the first wardens' supper and social held at the Wingrove Hotel, Keynsham, and was supported by Captain Scammell and Mr Cannock, joint officers in charge of the Keynsham Report Centre, and by Dr W P Taylor and Mr G R Ashton, Clerk to the KUDC.'

According to official instructions, the first public duties of a warden commenced after an air raid warning signal has been given. While wardens might request that window lights be covered, they 'had no right to demand that a thing should be done.' Should the public disregard their warnings, the wardens would then report the matter to the police.

The Keynsham Report Centre

Mr E Cannock recalled that the Report Centre was in the Old Magistrate's Court at the rear of the former stone built Police Station on Bath Hill. He said that it was manned at all times by one of the three officers in charge, Captain Kinnersley, Captain Scammell and Mr E A Cannock. At their command desk, they received telephone reports from wardens of incidents, and had to evaluate the situation and to expeditiously determine what action to take and who and what organisations were to be detailed to deal with the bombs, the debris, the fire, the casualties and the accidents. Written reports from the wardens would follow.

Under the Civil Defence Organisation in 1941, the officers liaised with the National Fire Service, the Home Guard, the Police Force with its Special Constabulary, the Fire Guard ('Watchers'), the Women's Voluntary Service, Messengers, Rescue Squads, Gas Decontamination Squads, First Aid Parties, Bomb Disposal Units, and the ARP 'ambulances'. From the Civil Defence control room in a basement of County Hall, Taunton, in times of special needs such as the blitz, various units from Keynsham and the county, were sent to Bristol, Bath, Exeter, Plymouth and some, even to London.

Members of the ARP were issued with dark blue serge trousers and battle dress tunics and black tin helmets. To distinguish the officers, their helmets were a different colour, which Edward Cannock thought was white. Naturally all members carried the obligatory gas masks. On the occasions of the various national financial drives such as 'War Weapons' Week', the local members of the ARP, in full uniform, as a distinct unit, would join in the parades through the town.

When bombs landed or planes crashed, the wardens, in whose area it occurred, had to record the events on the official report forms, and hand them in at the Report Centre, where in due course the information was relayed to Regional HQ at Taunton. These reports constitute a guide to the possible record of the total number and types of bombs dropped in the No 2 Bathavon area. Mac Hawkins [p 183] enumerates them as, '1,177 HE; 5,177 IB [Incendiaries]; 8 Phosphorus; 2 Mines and 124 UXB' [unexploded bombs].

The three officers in charge at the Magistrate's Court were on duty in rotation, and at the height of the Bristol blitz, they even had their beds there.

As Edward said, the work of the officers and the part time wardens was unpaid and no payment was expected, possibly apart from any clerical staff. Major P Chappell, who lived at Bath, as the full time Area Officer, did receive a salary, as did full time wardens.

Not only were there individual street wardens, but over them were the Sector wardens, responsible for a whole area of streets, such as the Bath Road district and the centre of town. In the Gas Works building at Dapps Hill were situated the Decontamination Group, the Rescue Group's equipment and the mortuary.

Among Edward's many 'treasures' are two photos. The first was taken in 1944/45 at the rear of the Magistrate's Court, showing the Keynsham 'Special Constables'. On the seats at the front were the two regular Police Force Officers in uniform, then Mr E A Cannock in a suit, as Chairman of the Council, then lastly, but also in the uniform of a Police Officer, was Mr William Gibbons the officer in charge of the 'Specials.' Behind them stood the ten local constables in uniform, with their flat hats. Among those recognised were Arthur Church of 'Nicotine', his tobacco shop in the High Street; Councillor R A Harvey, from the Station Road newspaper and confectionery shop; Cyril Beale, a baker; Robert Hickling, ironmonger; and H Brett, ex-Army. Behind them, but not in uniform, stood a further thirty or so other Keynsham men.

His second photo is of the Civil Defence Corps. On the back of it, he has written, 'Mainly Report Centre Staff and Officers of the CD/ARP Personnel, at HQ behind the Keynsham Police Station, circa 1943/44.' Of the 41 members present, 15 were wearing WWI medals, with Captain Kinnersley proudly sporting his MC. Eight men on the front row, and one behind, were also wearing, on their sleeves, service chevrons signifying 5 years of service.

CIVIL DEFENCE

OFFICE OF THE REGIONAL COMMISSIONER.

hone No. : BRISTOL 23346
rams ~~SHARP~~, BRISTOL
*EMREGCOM

SOUTH WESTERN REGIONAL OFFICE,
19, WOODLAND ROAD,
BRISTOL, 8.

S E C R E T

1st August, 1940.

Dear Sir,

Daily Summary.

In order that Controllers may be kept informed of Major Damage etc. in the Region, it is proposed to issue a Daily Summary giving information available up to 1800 hours.

The Summary will follow the lines of the Situation Report and be in three parts.

Part 1 - General appreciation.

" 2 - Details of incidents.

" 3 - Supplementary information referring to previous summaries, and any points of special interest.

The Summary will be posted to each Controller personally. The particular secrecy of the information should be appreciated. Copies or extracts must not be made, but it is hoped that Controllers will find a value in a wider knowledge of events.

Yours faithfully,

Moore

Regional Officer.
No. 7 Region.

A.R.P. Controllers.

The 'Daily Summary' contained succinct accounts drawn from the Report Centres of the whole of the West of England.

Mainly the officers and staff of the CD/ARP HQ, Keynsham, 1943/44

Left to Right

TOP ROW   Kinder Stinchcombe * Mattick R Hall ?

3RD ROW   * Bailey P * * * * Johns W * * Wilding * *

2ND ROW   Fear ? Murphy Dawtry C E * * * * * Pope W * * Sinfield Button *

FRONT ROW   * * Bowden L, Scarman G B, Cannock E A, Capt N S Kinnersley, Crofts F, Belsten S, Stokes E, Turner R, Chappell P E.

Memories of a fire watcher, recalled by William Sherer

'In 1941 the Government passed a law requiring all men and women between the ages of 18 and 55 to register for fire watching duties. Women and children under 14 were exempted.

'Each street had its own quota of fire watchers. Their duties were to keep watch for fires caused by enemy action. Small fires caused by incendiary bombs were supposed to be extinguished by the watchers. Larger fires had, of course, to be dealt with by the Auxiliary Fire Service. Each fire watcher was supplied with a steel helmet and an armband bearing the initials FW. Each household, too, was supplied with a stirrup-pump, which had to be paid for, and cost £1 10 0 (£1.50), I believe.

'My experience of the ARP or Civil Defence as it was later called, was confined to Wellsway and Courtenay Road area. These were split into sections. Air raid wardens were appointed. These, nominated by residents of all areas, were responsible to see that fire watching duties were carried out. When the sirens sounded they were supposed to be the first out, ensuring that their neighbours who were supposed to be on duty that night were at their posts.

'Mr George Clothier, a well-known local shoe repairer who lived in the cottages opposite Uplands Farm, was warden for the upper Wellsway section. Mr Barker was warden for the lower section of Wellsway and Manor Road. Manor Road was not built over as it is now. It was just another lovely bit of Keynsham which fell victim to the developers! During the war I was running the farm at Smisby, and as this was a 'reserved occupation', I was exempt from war-service.

'The wardens were not paid, but issued with white helmets. The late Mr A Nicholls was the air raid warden for Courtenay Road. There were only four houses along that road, so the late Mr F H Hember and I had to take our turn in upper Wellsway. Mr Nicholls and another resident, the late Mr Cam, remained in Courtenay Road, as there were farm buildings there. Actually both gentlemen were volunteers, as they were just over age for compulsory service. Councillor Jack Jones of Manor Road was also a warden.

'In late 1941, after a heavy bombing raid on Bristol, which did enormous damage, and unhappily caused a heavy loss of life, Stones, a Bristol building firm, took over a four acre field owned by Mr Nicholls, where they stacked timber for safety away from the city. Timber was in very short supply in those days. Later, lorry-loads of salvaged timber from blitzed homes were brought out there. The unuseable timber was sold to locals at 10/-, or 50p, a cart load, which was a lot of money then. There was always a ready demand for this.

'Prisoners (or inmates as they are now called) were brought out from Horfield Prison about 8.30 am to 4.00 pm, to pull out nails for re-use. They were 'trusties', ranging from a struck-off lawyer or black marketeers to young men (mostly well-educated) who refused military service. If the prison guard was not too strict, it was possible to talk to them on the few day-time occasions I was there. When there was an execution at the prison, the body had to hang for an hour. An ex-Army sergeant was hanged for killing his illegitimate son, so the prisoners were kept locked up for that hour. This meant that the trusties did not arrive at the timber yard until 10.00 that morning. They were very sombre when they came.

'Mr Barker of Manor Road, who drove a GPO van in Bristol, was the senior warden for the Wellsway area. A very direct no-nonsense man, he was alright with me. In 1942 it was decided by the powers-that-be that Mr Bedford should be a paid official, in overall charge of Civil Defence in the Keynsham area. Apparently he decided that, at night, one fire watcher should be permanently placed at the timber depot. The choice fell on me, so when the sirens went I had to jump on my bicycle and ride to the field at the end of the lane. I had for company a night watchman who was once an Army officer, who claimed to have served under Lord Kitchener. He had a watchman's hut and a coke brazier to keep him warm. I was better off than most wardens as I was paid 30/-, £1.50, a month, but I was out nearly every night.

'There was a cattle drinking trough in the field filled up with water pumped from an adjacent well. Apart from that, there was only a bucket and a stirrup pump. Little chance of a fire watcher and an elderly night watchman extinguishing a fire at a large timber dump! There were no bombs of any description dropped in Courtenay Road, Wellsway, or the Manor Road area, throughout the war.

'When the shop in the High Street was hit and on fire, two passing Australian soldiers rescued the lady trapped upstairs. They then went off without giving their names, and were never traced. They were real heroes.'

The Conflagration in the High Street

Mrs Phyllis Clayfield also remembered the occasion when the old house and shop at 59 and 59a, High Street, where her grandparents had lived and which still belonged to her family, was on fire. She recalled that she had just come home by train from Warminster, before midnight. 'As I walked up the High Street, there was a barrier across the road, and much shouting and people running about. I could see the flames and the smoke and knew that something was on fire. There were a lot of other people looking on. Wardens prevented me from going further along the High Street, so I turned up Charlton Road to reach home in West View Road.

'The warden responsible for our road was Frank Cooper, a builder, who was very efficient. When the raids were on, my father, Walter Carter, would get up and go out to see what was happening. Mother used to get so annoyed with him. She would say, 'Your place is here at home. You should be here to protect us.' On one occasion he was outside Miss Webster's house on the corner of Rock Road and West View, (now a day nursery), while shrapnel was falling around him. He didn't even have a helmet on, but he survived.'

Sector patrols of wardens

The following map belonged to Mary's father, Mr Sydney Fairclough, of 43, Charlton Road. She explained that among others, the Civil Defence Corps consisted of the head warden, the sector wardens, local wardens, then leading fire watchers and ordinary fire watchers. Sydney was a leading fire watcher and the map indicates the extent of his jurisdiction, officially designated as

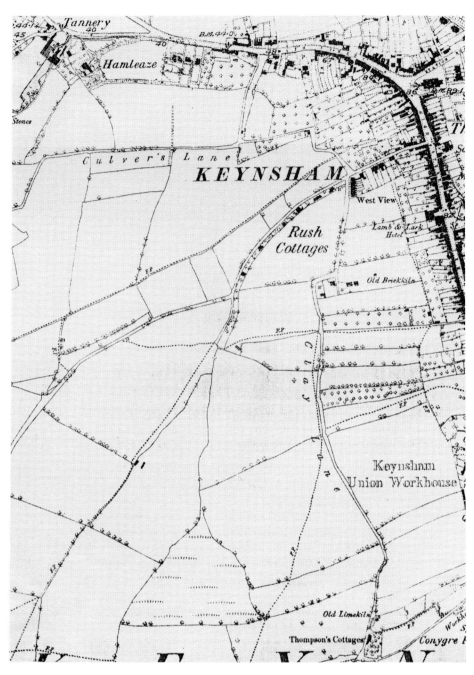

W G Hoskins in 'English Landscape' (p 59) speaks of a typical 16th century construction as 'a village strung out along a single street'. This O S map of 1884 shows that little had changed.

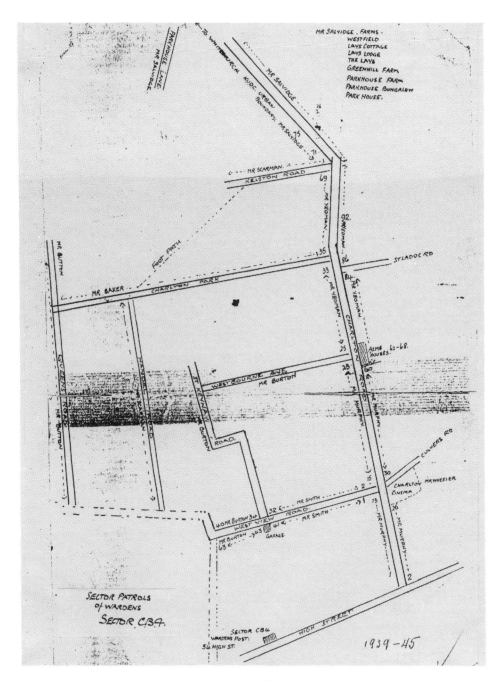

Sydney Fairclough's hand-drawn map of 1939 showing Charlton Road and the Civil Defence Sector CB4. He was responsible for the wardens of the area. Their names and the houses over which the fire wardens watched are clearly marked.

'Sector CB4' with its own CB4 warden's post at 54, The High Street (now Dunn & Co.).

It is interesting as it delineates the exact area that each watcher had to cover, and also because it lists the names of the personnel, all being men. The lower part of Charlton Road was cared for by Mr. Murphy, the central area by Mr Yeoman, which included the Almshouses. The top of Charlton Road came under Mr Salvidge, who also watched over the following sites listed as 'Farms'; Westfield, Lays Cottage, Lays Lodge, The Lays, Greenhill Farm, Parkhouse Farm, Parkhouse Bungalow and Park House.

West View was the responsibility of Mr Smith aided by Mr Burton, who also watched over St Keyna Road and Westbourne Avenue. Kelston Road and Handel Road came under Mr Scarman; Charlton Park was Mr Baker's responsibility, while Mr Button had Queens Road. The Charlton Cinema, today the Bingo Hall, was Mr Wheeler's sphere as a fire watcher.

Although the roads are not all as straight as the map might suggest, it is interesting to see just how far Keynsham had expanded by 1939. Perhaps it is ever more fascinating to note the roads and streets that did not exist at that time.

Other ARP Wardens

On September 13, 1994, my wife and I spent a day at the Somerset Record Office, Taunton, researching the Civil Defence records. Almost overcome by the vast amount of documentary material relating to WWII, we extracted from a card 'Index of ARP Wardens', Box 17, CD/Gen/4/48, the following abridged details of Keynsham members of the Civil Defence.

Bowyers – Alice Elizabeth, Miss; 53, Albert Road; born 1917; assistant nurse at nursing home; joined 3.11.41; Telephonist, Report Centre.

Buchan – Henrietta Mary, Mrs; 'Myles', Wellsway, housewife; born 1911; joined 19.1.42; telephonist.

Burnard – Lewis Patrick; 22, Manor Road; born 1876; retired; warden.

Callender – Dorothy Katherine, Miss; 3, St Keyna Road; born 1886; joined 17.3.40; First Aid Post.

Harding – Frank Ernest; 43, Park Road; born 1881; house painter; joined 9.11.39; Rescue party.

Hayman – Harold Paul; 23, St Ladoc Road; born 1899; joined 20.7.41; left 17.11.42.

[Hayman's niece, Mrs P Clayfield, said that he built the houses on the left hand side of Handel Road, going up. Chris Wiggins said his family built the block of four at the bottom on the right hand side, while Cooper constructed those further up that side, around 1937–38.]

Hurd – Herbert Sternson; 'St Gabriel's', 18, Albert Road; born 1884; clerk; joined 16.2.41; messenger, First Aid Post; terminated 15.11.44.

Mills – Edith May, Mrs; 37, High Street; born 1893; joined 3.9.39; Nurse in charge of First Aid Post.

Page – Alfred Charles, 15 or 57, Albert Road; born 1903; haulier; joined 14.7.1940; Rescue Party.

Patch – Alfred Frank; 'Cosycot', 8, Combe Road, Keynsham; born 1896; cabinet maker; joined 3.9.39; warden.

Raine – Thomas; 40, West View Road; born 1878; tobacconist; joined 16.6.40; 1st Aid Party.

Reynolds – Stanley Herbert; 59, West View Road; born 20.4.91; no employment; joined 26.1.41; telephonist clerk.

Turner – George Reginald; 3, Charlton Road; born 1890; joined 3.9.39; warden.

Turner – Allan Frederick; 33, Rock Road; born 1907; corn agent; joined 3.9.39; 1st Aid Party.

Wells – Charles Kenneth; Grange Nursing Home, Bath Road; born 1877; retired; joined 1.9.40; telephonist.

Whatley – Frederick; 58, Park Road; born 1893; labourer; joined 9.11.39; Rescue Party.

This list of war activities undertaken should more correctly be designated 'Civil Defence' rather than 'ARP Wardens'. Obviously this list is far from complete, for it does not even mention any of the wardens referred to earlier in this chapter. Possibly this is connected with the words of an Albert Road gentleman who recalled that 'they were always coming and going'.

From the list of the 16 'Defence' workers listed, in 1940 Mrs Bowyers was the youngest at 23 and Lewis Burnard the oldest at 64, with an average age of 47.

Victorian wardens

The list only designates 4 men as wardens, Lewis Burnard, Harold Haymen, Alf Patch and Geo Turner. In 1940 their average age was only 44, but this still meant that they were all Victorians. It's rather surprising.

Rescue parties

The list of men who comprised the Rescue Service is incomplete, as the group comprised 7 or 8 men. Mentioned are Fred Harding, Alf Page, Thomas Raine and Fred Whatley. Their average age in 1940 was 51, 3 of them also being Victorians! Unlike wardens and fire watchers, who were basically concerned with the roads in which they lived, the Rescue Service were at the battle's front. In Bath and Bristol their lives were constantly endangered as they sought to rescue people trapped in and under blitzed houses, which were likely to collapse further still if they were unwisely disturbed in the rescue operations. That is why people such as Frank Harding, who was connected with the building trade and who was familiar with the construction of houses, were involved.

Periodically during rescue operations on houses destroyed only hours earlier, quiet would be called for as everyone listened for the possible cries of buried people or their frantic knocking. William Sherer was told, 'You could hear the injured crying beneath the rubble.' The rescue teams were brave men indeed. Their leader was Reg Willey, who lived next door to Les Harding, both of whom worked for the builder, E Wiggins.

A Keynsham hero decorated

Mr Chris Wiggins said that after his father's untimely death, and during his own absence during the war in the army, 'Mother kept the family firm going with its 8–10 workmen, with the help of a foreman who was in reality the manager. He was Mr Reginald Willey, who was in the Rescue Service.' This comment reminded me of a reference to him in Mr Mac Hawkins book, 'Somerset at War' concerning his activities at Bath during the terrible raids there.

It recorded, 'There were many awards for bravery; Mr R N Willey of Keynsham, the leader of the 2/6 Rescue Squad, received the George Medal for his outstanding work at the Circus Tavern. Willey had constantly put himself at risk by tunnelling his way to victims that had been buried under the table, when their house had collapsed on them.' [page 68]

Chris described Reginald as, 'A quiet man, 5 ft 7 in. tall and of medium build, who had been father's carpenter before the war. During it he did a tremendous amount of heavy rescue, mostly in Bath and Bristol, as it wasn't needed in Keynsham. He worked by day and dug people out by night.

'He left the family business around 1947/48 when I took over the firm, and he set up on his own, first in Keynsham, then in Brislington. He was married with three daughters, who are all married.'

Mr Leslie Harding served a five year apprenticeship with Mr E Wiggins junior, and stayed with the firm until he was called to the colours in 1940. He described 'Wiggins' as, 'The biggest building firm in Keynsham'.

Obviously he knew Willey well. 'He was the son of a carpenter on one of the Queen Charlton estates. We were the best of pals. I was his driver. In our spare time we built the houses that we both lived in, Numbers 11 and 13, Albert Road, in 1934. On Mr E Wiggins's early death, his widow decided to carry on the firm, and appointed Reg as foreman on condition that I helped him in connection with the public.

'He was made leader of the 'Heavy Rescue' as he was a builder and understood the structure of houses. He had a team of 7 or 8 men, who were not fit enough, or too old, to enlist. They had a depot at the bottom of Dapps Hill at the Gas Works, with a medium sized lorry equipped with ladders, planks, ropes and that sort of thing. They wore black tin hats and overalls. Normally they would be on standby duty about two evenings a week, unless additionally called out. When a raid was imminent, a red message warned them to report and await orders. Then they could be sent anywhere from Avonmouth to Bath.

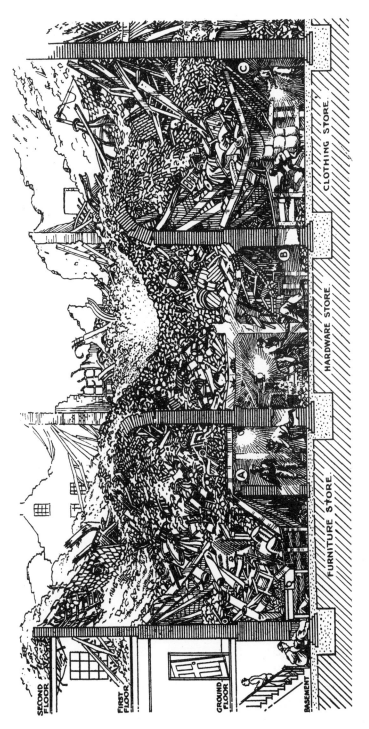

This picture is from the ARP Training Manual No 3, Rescue Service Manual, by HMSO, 1942, p 98, price 1/6 [9p.].

Fig 71   Rescue from Basement by breaking through the Division Wall from some Accessible Adjoining Basement. Where applicable, this is usually a fairly safe and expeditious method. From the basement on the left of the diagram access is gained by cutting walls and debris tunnels until A, B and C are successively reached.

'Next morning he would turn up for work as usual, though looking rather tired.'

Just why leaders looked so tired is best explained by the Rescue Manual's account of their nights' work. 'Most rescue operations have to be conducted under conditions of great difficulty and confusion, often made worse by darkness . . . On first approach to a large rescue incident, even the best leaders tend to be overwhelmed by the appalling confusion, and by the magnitude and apparent impossibility of the job . . . And it is at such times that a leader requires all his qualities of coolness, perseverance and courage, and to make full use of the knowledge gained in his previous experience and training . . . No rules can be devised to give leaders sure guidance as to how to tackle every job.' [page 81]

Yet Les continued, 'As he was only one member of the Rescue team, there was a lot of jealousy and strong feeling during the war among the local people when alone he was decorated.

'After the war, Reg had his own one man business, doing general repairs. Sadly he's dead now. Two of his daughters are widowed, and one still comes to see me every few months.'

Regrettably, Les himself is no longer with us. He died suddenly in his Albert Road home in June 1991, aged 82. He was a lovely man.

After the war

It is interesting to see on the 1939–45 War Memorial roll in the St John's Church the entries, 'Warden W H Belsten, Civil Defence' and also, 'Senior Warden R Hunt, Civil Defence.' This is a little misleading to newcomers to the town. Mr Belsten was the well-known Charlton Road undertaker who was succeeded by Mr Guyan. Mr Hunt was the highly respected Anglican lay

KEYNSHAM URBAN DISTRICT COUNCIL IN SESSION An 'Evening World' photograph of the monthly meeting of the Keynsham Council. In the picture Mrs M Hickling is seen discussing the demolition of Keynsham's blast walls and static water tanks. Other councillors are, left to right, Councillors E A Cannock (chairman), Col S H G Dainton (vice-chairman), H M Argile (surveyor), Mrs F C Smith, Mrs H A Downton, Mrs Hickling and Mr R A Harvey.

reader who ran the only boy's club in the town at the church hall in Station Road. Two worthy men indeed, but neither were actually killed on duty as wardens.

An Evening World newspaper photograph of May 8, 1947, two years after the cessation of hostilities, carries the caption, 'KUDC in session. At the monthly meeting of the Council, Mrs M Hickling is seen discussing the demolition of Keynsham's blast walls and static water tanks. Other councillors are E A Cannock, (chairman), Col S H G Dainton (vice-chairman), Mr H M Argile (surveyor), Mrs F C N Smith, Mrs H A Downton, Mrs Hickling and Mr R A Harvey.'

In retrospect

Mac Hawkins comments that 'compared with other parts of the country, Somerset suffered comparatively little damage and proportionately few casualties from enemy raids.' Though this is obviously true of Keynsham itself, it in no way lessens the dedication of all those connected with the Keynsham Civil Defence Organisation, who after a hard day's work, consistently and unstintingly gave their time and their services for the good of the community.

Chapter 7

The Royal Observer Corps in Keynsham

Origins

'On the night of May 31, 1915, Hauptmann Linnarz in the 536 ft. long military airship LZ 38 penetrated to the East End of London. He dropped 3,000 lb of bombs, which killed seven people, injured 35 and caused an estimated £18,000-worth of damage. There had been seven previous raids on Britain, but these were close to the coast and only ten people died. Now Linnarz had brought the war right to the capital of the Empire and the shock was to have repercussions which would reach forward to the Second World War.' ('Attack Warning Red', by Derek Wood, 1976, p 9.)

In the late 1930s, with the rise of Hitler's Luftwaffe and the record of their merciless bombing, Britain increasingly took steps to protect its citizens.

Referring to the expansion of the Observer Corps in 1936, T E Winslow in 'Forewarned is Forearmed' (1948, Wm Hodge and Co) wrote, 'It is of interest to notice at this point in our story how intimately the expansion of the O C was connected with the RAF programme of expansion and with the development of the Air Raid Warning System. The latter depended, to a large extent, for its operation, on the efficiency of the Corps and on the area which the organisation covered, while the RAF, for the control of its fighters overland, also depended on Observer Corps information as it was received at the various RAF Operations Rooms.' (p 38)' The categorical statement was, in fact, made that without an Observation organisation, it would be quite impossible to operate a warning system. (p 39)

'In 1938 expansion, recruitment and training at maximum speed was ordered ... [By 1939] the radar system and the Filter Room at Fighter Command were in operation (p 52) ... The Observer Corps was called out on 24th August, 1939, and from that date until 'Stand-down' six years later no Centre or Post was unmanned ... At all times unspectacular, to an outsider even dull ... their work was indispensable, though for some posts during the war, their principal enemy was the weather. (p 55.)

'Remuneration in 1939 was 1/3 an hour, with a maximum of £3 a week, with an opportunity of applying for employment on a full-time basis of a 48 hour week, or of accepting part-time employment.

'At the outbreak of war, the Observers were not required to recognise various aircraft, but this was soon rectified in September 1939 with the publication of silhouettes of all foreign aircraft.

'Tracking by night was, naturally, largely by sound, and Observers became increasingly proficient at this branch of their work ... and were able to estimate the height and strength and direction of the enemy with a degree of accuracy that made this information worth having.

'During the second and third weeks in August, 1940, the scale of attacks increased both by day and by night . . . This was particularly true of Bristol . . . On the accuracy and speed of the Observers' reporting depend the measures taken by the Air Raid Warning Officers; also the action taken by the RAF to intercept the raiders, if possible on their way to their objective, but failing that, on the homeward journey . . . In those two intensive weeks, sorties by the German Air Force totalled some 8,000 aircraft in the fourteen days of raids, while by night there were seldom less than 200 enemy aircraft over the country.' (p 64.)

The unseen work of the Observers was appreciated by those in command. After the heavy attack on Bristol and Clifton in November 1940, when in two days enemy planes dropped 2,000 incendiary bombs together with a number of high explosives in the area, though by no means one of the heaviest of raids, and only one of many – the Air Officer Commander-in-Chief said, 'I have heard with great satisfaction of the excellent work carried out by the personnel of Number 23 Observer Group Centre (Bristol) on the night of the 24/25 November. Please convey my congratulations to the Controllers and Crews of the Centre on their performance and spirit of determination. That members reported at the Centre in spite of extreme difficulties, and in several cases when they had sustained material loss, is particularly noteworthy.' (Forew'd p 72.)

'Towards the end of 1940 the number of unnecessary losses of our aircraft and particularly of returning bombers, led to experiments . . . to organise assistance for aircraft in distress . . . That work was, to a large extent, dependent on the Corps and its Posts and Centres. In this case a report was passed by the Bristol Centre that an aircraft, apparently lost, was circling some twenty miles south of Bristol. The Flying Control Liaison Officer initiated searchlight homing to Colerne, which was the nearest airfield, and the aircraft, following the directing beams, landed safely. But the sequel is of interest, as the pilot rang the FCLO to thank him for his searchlights and said that he had been flying from Netheravon circuits and bumps (practice landings) and that, after flying in cloud, he completely lost his airfield lights.

'Being totally inexperienced in night flying, he had decided to bale out after flying around for one and a half hours. He had not, at that time, known about searchlight homing, but when he saw the beams he had decided that they must mean something, so he followed them until he saw the airfield lights at Colerne, where he was given the 'green' to land. He was mystified and was surprised to know that the ROC was continually on the look-out for (in his own words) "blokes like me" '.

'Between January 1942 and January 1945, there are 131 recorded instances of information from ROC sources in the No 10 Fighter Group Area, which helped distressed aircraft to a safe landing.' ('Forewarned', pp 241/242.)

Changing the subject somewhat, 'The Distribution of National Air Raid Warning Districts Amongst ROC Centres, 1943 to 1945,' indicates that the Bristol ROC Centre was responsible for Warnings in Bath, Bristol, Dursley, Swindon and Salisbury. ('Attack Warning Red', p 261.)

107

PHILADELPHIA. 1876

PHILADELPHIA, 1876, Chicago 1893, Paris 1895, Franco-British 1909, Brussels 1910, Wembley 1924-25.

The above dates represent the wanderings of the Stand which is occupied by K1, Group 23. *KEYNSHAM*

Thanks to the generosity of Fry's, the famous Chocolate House, the Post became the possessors of an octagonal stand with a diameter of 8 ft. The earliest photographic record of the Stand is 1876, but it is quite possible it was in use some years before and it ultimately finished its display life in a small exhibition in 1933.

Has any other Post a stand with such an interesting record ?

This is truly an historic pair of photographs. Entitled, 'Fry's Look In' in 1876, the stand became K1's 'Look Out' in 1942. They are taken from a copy of the ROC's monthly journal. In 1876 the stand left Bristol for the USA and in due course for Europe. Then years later, until April 1942, it was used as the post of the Keynsham ROC situated in the Cameroon's field just off Park Road. An observer's head, with the post, is just visible. Today the fields have become a housing estate.

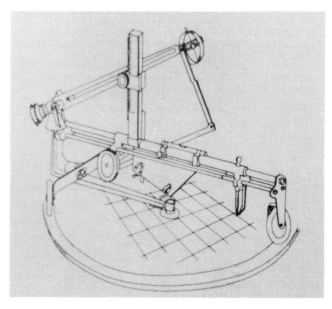

The vital post instrument, which enabled the observer accurately to plot the position and height of an enemy plane.

Chief Observer Alfred C Thomas

Mr William Thomas, of 'Gould, Thomas', who owned and ran the Albert Logwood Mill at Dapps Hill, had four children. The eldest, Rose Eleanor Mary, was born in 1877, Alfred in 1885, and then came Hilda and lastly Arthur. Rose was an accomplished pianist and won the All England Erhard Scholarship to the Royal College of Music, only to be tragically turned down on health grounds. The composer Edward Parry was very sorry that she had been rejected. She continued to play and was in great demand as a concert pianist. Later she married Mr Sydney N Fairclough, and Mary is their daughter, and the source of information for this section.

Alfred ran the family business at the mill, and was disappointed at not being accepted for military service in 1914 because of his essential work. As Mary said, 'He had to remain at the mill, to his extreme wrath and pain.' Accordingly, when in 1937 he was offered the responsibility of being in charge of the local branch of the Observer Corps, he was thrilled to accept. Not a young man, he felt that he was still doing something worthwhile for his country, after his disappointment in 1914.

Arthur went to India as a civil engineer, and in 1914 joined the 2nd. Battn. of 'Queen Victoria's Own Sappers and Miners' and, sadly, was killed on active service at Baghdad.

Speaking of her uncle's activities as the Chief Observer, Mary said, 'Fred was not much given to talking, but I gather they had their hairy moments on night duty. They were a close knit bunch. Their post was in the grounds of the old Cameroon's Farm, in the Dunster Road area. Fred was still running the mill, so his ROC work was done mainly at night.

'We were living in Charlton Road at the time, and mother used to frequently visit him at St Augustine's in Station Road. Fred was a man of few words, but in any case, as the wartime slogan declared, 'Careless talk costs lives', so they would not have discussed war-time activities.

'In 1942 Fred was 57. In the past he had suffered a number of serious illnesses which had aged him, not to mention the considerable strain imposed on him as Chief Observer during the heavy raids on Bath and Bristol. Accordingly, with considerable reluctance, he stepped down from the Corps. Immediately after the war he retired from 'Gould, Thomas' and sold the business to his nephews Robert and Keith Thomas.'

Mary mentioned that Tom Williams, who was the chauffeur-gardener for many years for Fred and before that for his father William, 'was a faithful standby as an observer if needed.' Tom's daughter Audrey said, 'He quite enjoyed it. During the day time, if he was doing a double shift and was unable to come home for dinner, my brother Raymond and I would cycle up Park Road, and take him some food and a flask of hot soup.'

Ivo Peters recalls the local Observer Corps

'For nearly six years the Royal Observer Corps maintained a constant watch upon the skies of Britain. They were the 'Eyes and Ears' of the Royal Air Force. The organisation was also essential for the efficient working of the air-raid warning system throughout the country. There were 29 observer posts in Somerset . . . The network of posts covering the whole of Britain was completed just in time for the opening phases of the Battle of Britain,' writes Mac Hawkins in 'Somerset at War', pages 169–170.

'There was at first no uniform and observers wore the same striped armlets as are usually worn by the Police, but with the words 'Observer Corps' superimposed on it in red letters. In April 1941 the valuable services of the corps were officially recognised by the grant of the title 'Royal'. In 1943 there was a complete reorganisation when official ranks were introduced for the first time, but the ROC remained unique: being composed of civilians, paid by the Air Ministry, and controlled by Fighter Command. The arrangement under which some of the personnel were full-time and others part-time volunteers continued.

'Uniforms began to be issued in 1941 . . . The function of the corps was to identify and report all aircraft, whether friendly or hostile. Each post was manned by two observers at a time; the full establishment for a Post was 21, including a Chief and Leading Observer . . . Posts, grouped in clusters of three or four, were connected together and to the operations room at observer centres by 'open' telephone lines', each Group consisting of some 36–40 posts.

'There were ten observer posts in the northern part of the county. They formed part of No 23 Group with headquarters at Bristol . . . The Somerset posts of this group were located at Winscombe, West Harptree, Keynsham, Westbury-sub-Mendip, Clevedon, Radstock, Weston-super-Mare, Shepton Mallet, Long Ashton and Frome.

'Outstanding events for the Observer Corps in Somerset were the engagements during the Battle of Britain, followed by the blitz raids on Bristol and on Somerset towns. Large numbers of enemy aircraft passed over the county during the German raids on Northern, Midland and South Wales cities, often for continuous periods of 12 or 13 hours . . . There was also the ever-increasing activity of our own aircraft going out to attack and returning in the early hours of the morning. The culmination was reached on D Day when thousands of British and American aircraft crossed the Somerset skies.'

Ivo Peters was in the ROC for many years and was awarded the BEM in recognition of his services to the Corps. In the latter part of the war he was Chief Observer of the ROC post at Keynsham. 'Our post was K1 (King I) and came under 23 Group, whose HQ was in Bristol . . . "King" cluster of posts were spread around the city; KI at Keynsham; K2 at West Harptree; K3 at Avonmouth; and K4 north of Filton. All four were linked by continuous telephone circuit and also the operations room.

'For medical reasons, at first I had difficulty in being accepted for service in the ROC, but eventually joined the Corps on January 1, 1942; they were well organised by then . . . The posts also varied in efficiency. I had a wonderful selection of people at K1. Two of my best observers were a Methodist parson and a farmhand. We had every type – from all walks of life and social classes.

'They were normally only two on duty at the post at any one time; No 1 was in charge and No 2 acted as telephonist and plotter. Many of us had to do a day's work and could only do evenings, nights or early mornings, except at weekends, but the Methodist parson was ideal for weekdays, as were retired people. We were expected to do a certain number of hours duty, and I tried to do at least 24 a week.'

To Mac Hawkins' masterly outline of the service, let a little more local detail be added. Mr A Paget said there was an observation post at Burnett Point, manned by Keynsham and Saltford personnel. They were to record the types, numbers, height, speed and direction of aircraft. He mentioned Jack Hickling, of the fine ironmonger's shop in the High Street, and Kenneth Gibbons (who had his own accountant's business in Bristol) as observers.

Mr Gibbons' son, Jonathan, remembered that his father's uniform amounted solely to an armband and a tin hat. He recalled, 'Father used to get up in the wee hours of the morning to go on duty, and would then go to work in the morning. . . . Mr A C Thomas, of Station Road, was in charge when the local Corps was formed and was later succeeded by I Peters.

'The Observation Post was down Park Road, which was all farms and fields in those days, through a gate, down the footpath and turn right. It consisted of a built up hillock, with a hut for when off duty. The site was sandbagged and binoculars were supplied, with height and direction finding equipment.

'Martin and his brother, Charles Gibbons, were both Observers. Charles, who had bought 'Sunnymede' in the late 1930s, resigned from the ROC. Martin soldiered on, until he was called up for the Royal Corps of Signals.'

It is worthy of note that, as a young man in WWI, Lieutenant Charles Gibbons was one of the first men to drive a tank, and was decorated for rescuing a fellow driver from his burning tank.

Other observers that Jonathan remembered were Mr Townsend, Wally Vowles and J Harvey, deceased, of Charlton Road. Obviously there were many more, not to mention the Methodist minister, the Rev William A Underwood. Mrs Randall recalls that Mr Tom Williams, of St George's Road, was an Observer, as mentioned earlier by Mary.

Ann Randall wrote, 'My father took me to the site during the war years and I do remember a dug-out with sand bags around it. The observers stood in the trench and leaned on sandbags to spot the aircraft through their binoculars. There was also a fair-sized hut on the site and on the inside walls were various charts showing aircraft from all angles for identification. There must have been items of comfort in the huts, but I expect I missed them as I was so fascinated by the charts.'

The Observer Post at Keynsham

'Opened January 1938 [at grid ref] T 653679, [site designated] 23/K I; resited to T 669659 April 1942; [redesignated when under Frome] 9/CI November 1953; underground December 1957; closed October 1968.' ('Attack WR', p 309)

From this concise statement, it would seem that Chief Observer A Thomas took command in January 1938, over a year before war was declared. It was over four years later, after plotting the squadrons of German aircraft in their punishing Battle of Britain blitz on Bristol, that the post was reallocated to

Chief Observer Ivo Peters in May 1954 at the K1 (Keynsham) post at Burnett, after its move from its original Park Road site. Captain Applegate, in an Auster 6, provides practice for the observers. An ROC Journal photograph.

The ROC post at Burnett went 'Underground December 1957 and closed October 1968.' Inside the man-made mound was the concrete 'observation' post with its sophisticated nuclear detection and measurement equipment, and a telephone. Now 24 years later, in these safer times, nature truly has taken over.

Burnett Point, at the Ministry supply base. Possibly this move coincided with Mr Thomas stepping down. When one turns off Gypsy Lane down the drive to the base, there is a steep bank some 20 feet high on the left hand side. That was where the post went 'underground' in 1957 for another ten years of service.

The Bristol No 23 Group

'Formed 1937 as No 23 Group.   Redesignated No 12 Group, 1953

GHQ Locations:

Little King Street, Bristol, (rear of Library), 1937–1943;
Worcester Terrace, Bristol,l 1943–1945; Kings Square Avenue, Bristol, 1947–1958.
Lansdown, Bath, 1958 – in use. Protected Accommodation opened August 29, 1959. Emergency Centre, Kings Square Avenue, Bristol. ('Attack WR' p 268)

Group Commandants:

Observer Commander F C Lockyer,   1943–1945
Observer Commander C H Davey, MBE   1945–1970
Observer Commander R G Pitt   1970
Stand-Down Caretaker; Observer Lieutenant H F Tarring. ('Attack WR', p 268.)

Group Officer Douglas Dyson

I am most grateful to Mr D Dyson for his valuable help in connection with my research into the ROC. To the warmth of his personality (He was York-shire born) is added a love for the 'Corps' and a willingness to share its history and his experiences. He lent me three books on the subject to read, which comprised over 1,000 pages! Quotations from these will follow later.

Doug joined the ROC as a post observer at K4, Almondsbury, in 1943 and served at various locations within the Bristol group during his 43 years service. He later became a Group Officer responsible for the training and administration of four posts within the Bristol group. Compulsory age retirement at 60 reduced him to the ranks, through which he again rose to become a Chief Observer until he finally stood down at 65.

He said of his war-time observing, 'Sometimes I did a 12 hour shift from 7 pm to 7 am, and then went to work at The Bristol Aeroplane Company Ltd. It was very interesting, for there were many aircraft about, especially near Filton, and the sky was full of aircraft of all types. We had nearby, in Gloucester, the Gloucester Aircraft Company, and were surrounded by airfields such as Moreton Valence, Leighterton, Colerne, Charmy Down, Lulsgate and Whitchurch. It was from Whitchurch that Leslie Howard took off on his fatal journey to Lisbon over the Bay of Biscay where the aircraft in which he was a passenger was shot down. Churchill also flew from Whitchurch, on occasions, it is rumoured.

'We wore ordinary battledress of RAF blue, with silver buttons emblazoned with the figure of an Elizabethan beacon lighter, with a brevet with the RAF eagle surrounded by the words 'ROYAL OBSERVER CORPS' worn on the chest. After the war the uniforms became standard RAF issue, with our own insignia.

'Some observers were full-time and others part-time. There was a complete mixture of types and occupations.

'The Observer Posts were all of a basic construction. Some were circular, others square. Some were sited on the top of high buildings, others on a local high point of land [Burnett]. All were sandbagged to shoulder height. Every post was issued with a rifle and ammunition for the defence of the post.'

The main piece of equipment was the circular chart table at shoulder height, with a grid map on it, indicating rivers, local landmarks and the positions of other nearby posts. Attached to the table was the all-important height and position plotting instrument. 'The post instrument was the basis of Observer Corps plotting for 25 years following its introduction in 1935. The estimated height of an aircraft was set up on the vertical height bar. The aircraft was then kept in view through the sighting arm, the movement of which caused the pointer to indicate the correct position on the black and white map of 10 mile radius. The second pointer formed part of the later Micklethwaite height-correction attachment for use when two posts were viewing the same aircraft. A telescope was often fitted up the sighting arm and a torch was fixed in the two clips to show the grid position at night.' ('Attack Warning Red', p 43.)

Doug continued, 'The instrument was relatively simple to use. One observer would estimate the plane's height and identify it, and the other would use the post instrument, looking through the eye piece and adjusting the view finder to ascertain the aircraft's position and height. With a telephone head set, the observer would read the details of height, position and number of craft to the plotter at the ROCHQ at Bristol.

'Posts were linked into clusters of three or four, with telephone communication to each other, and all three connected to the same operation's room plotter, giving independent but corroborative evidence for the claims of one post's report of tracking an aircraft.

'The information displayed on the plotting table was passed on to the various military and civil organisations, that is, the searchlight and ack ack batteries, and the air raid warning posts, for them to take appropriate action. The plotters were aware of the whole picture of attacks building up from the information given by individual posts. The Royal Observer Corps Liaison Officer, a serving RAF Officer referred to as 'ROCLO', was there to decide what course of action to take. He would pass on the relevant information to No 12 Group RAF Sector Command at Rudloe Manor, Box, where details from radar scans were also received. The Deputy Controller at ROCHQ, Bristol, was Mr H F Tarring of Wellsway, Keynsham. [He was an accomplished draughtsman, photographer and organiser.]

'The Observer Posts sometimes had searchlights in the next field and ack ack guns in the next, so if at night a fighter dived down the searchlight to immobilize it, observers could also be at the receiving end.

'When the Corps took on the nuclear reporting role the posts were sited underground in purpose-built bunkers equipped with instruments designed to record the position, height and power of a nuclear weapon, and the subsequent radio-active 'fall out' from such weapons. Warnings of attack and 'fall out' were also given from these posts.'

Moments of excitement, fear, joy and sadness

A young man when the war commenced, Doug was able to do a full day's work at the Patchway BAC, and then put in a full night as an observer. 'We all did 8-hour shifts. We were normally both on look-out, but there was a bunk, so if it was quiet, one rested while the other watched with ear phones on. When a warning came that 'hostiles' were about, you woke up your fellow observer, or if you heard aircraft about.

'A Bull's Eye' training exercise, when we plotted the aircraft's course, involved the whole of the defence chain, the searchlight and the ack ack being involved. On other occasions it could be a quiet night with nothing happening. We had to keep a log of everything we reported and of every visitor, and the chief observer would sign it when he came on duty.

'At night it was a case of 'sound plotting'. You could only estimate the height and number of aircraft, and their general direction. At times it was very difficult. Normally we would be warned if hostiles were approaching. Some enemy planes came over in small numbers; others singly. We also plotted all our own aircraft. In particular I remember the practice for the attack on Arnhem. They were coming in squadrons, and planes, towing gliders, just kept going and going for a long, long while.

'The RAF had floating targets in the River Severn below Aust Ferry [by the Severn Bridge], and down would come single low-flying Typhoons from Gloucester to shoot them to shreds. Our post, which was plotting them, was almost opposite the targets. We could hear the canon fire; and they used live ammunition. That was exciting.

'It was rather frightening when you heard a stick of bombs coming down, getting closer and closer. You heard the whistle of the distant ones, but as they got closer they sounded like an express train. One observer, when on duty, on hearing a bomb coming down, said to his fellow observer Ted Foote, 'I think that was near your house'. He replied, 'No, it was further away'. However, he was wrong. It hit the cesspit outside Ted's house at Patchway, so you can imagine the state of his home!

'On another occasion, after a bomb had been dropped near the Almondsbury hall, a military lorry drove into the crater. The driver shouted, 'You need lights on that hole,' and the reply came back, 'They don't drop bombs with lights on them round here'.

'We had a battery of four 3.7 in. ack ack guns and one searchlight in the field next to our post, almost in the grounds of Almondsbury Hospital. A driver of a mobile Bofors gun said to me, 'We're not getting near them, but we're giving you moral support'. One night Gerry straffed the master searchlight (radar controlled). You could see the bullets in the beam of the searchlight, followed by a stick of bombs. That was the night they hit the Filton Aircraft Works and a number of people were killed in a private house in Station Road.

'On 25 September, 1940, at 11.48 am, Filton was attacked by 58 Heinkel bombers and many people were killed and hurt [149 killed and more injured]. We were not allowed back in to the factory because of a number of unexploded bombs. As I walked to my home two miles away, I passed homes destroyed and cars on fire. Marching down the A38 by the airfield had been twelve soldiers, when a bomb landed in the middle of them and killed them all. As I passed by, their bodies were all laid out in a row at the side of the road. They were from the Royal Berkshire's.

'When I turned into our road, two houses were on fire. Ours had its tiles blown off and the windows blown out but Mum was alright in her Anderson shelter. A little girl was missing. My elder brother, a first aider, found her dead under a hedge. This brought home to me the futility of war. On another occasion, a night attack on Filton, just after a small bomb fell between a house and an 'Anderson' in the garden, causing some damage, and injuring the owners in their shelter, we saw a thief stealing from the house. We gave chase but he got away. If I had caught him . . . !

'In the first attack on the BAC at Filton on September 25, there were insufficient fighters to defend us. So next day 504 Squadron of 17 Hurricanes were brought up from Hendon. On Friday, September 27, the enemy set out to attack the Parnell Aircraft Company at Yate, and was intercepted by our fighters over the centre of Bristol. I was thrilled when the first of their Messerschmitt fighters, a ME 110, was hit and came straight down, exploding some 50 feet above Stapelton Institution (now Manor Park), and crashed in the grounds. The running battle continued, resulting in a complete rout of the German force. Kenneth Wakefield in his excellent book 'Luftwaffe Encore' (pub. 1979 by Redwood Burn Ltd.) gives a fascinating blow by blow and minute by minute account of the flight of the German planes in their two attacks on Filton, and of the counter-attack on them by our fighters.

'In 1944 we received secret intelligence from the powers-that-be that the Germans had targeted Bristol with V1 rockets from Cherbourg. The code name for them was 'diver'. If the word 'diver, diver, diver' came over the headphones, you knew what was coming. So I got my only sister, Kathleen, evacuated to my uncle's home in Barnoldswick. Fortunately, with the invasion of Europe, Cherbourg was captured by Allied troops just in time before any of the rockets were launched.

'From the Almondsbury Observation Post in 1944, I saw the trail of a V2 rocket, which had been launched from Holland, going up almost vertically as it reached a height of 60 miles, but I didn't see it descend on London. It was such a clear day that you'd never see it again. Our post reported it and it was plotted right down the chain, and it was verified that it was a V2.'

The Royal Observer Corps Club

This club covered the whole of the United Kingdom and its monthly Journal contained many articles on aircraft construction and recognition, together with reports from the different branches. The Bristol Branch was Number 124, and the issue of September 1941 records that the secretary was, 'H C Harvey, 50, Charlton Road, Keynsham, nr. Bristol.'

He was present at the AGM of the Western Area of the ROC held at Bristol, May 9, 1942.

'A very successful meeting was held on Sunday October 26, 1941, at 15.00 to hear a very instructive lecture on 'Balloon Barrage' by Squadron Leader Aubrey. 12 members passed their Third Grade Test and 8 their Intermediate Test [in aircraft recognition].

'Despite bad weather nearly 250 members of the ROC assembled at the Bridewell Police Station, Bristol, on November 14 to hear a lecture by Mr Peter Masefield on 'The Advance of Aviation.'. . . He was introduced by Air Commodore E Masterman, while Major-General G A Lindsay moved a vote of thanks . . . coupled with his thanks . . . was that of Deputy Controller of the Centre, Mr H F Tarring.

'Wing Commander Dolton proved a most entertaining visitor to the meeting held in February 1942 . . . On February 5 a further meeting took place at Keynsham, when K1 played the part of host to the Centre and other K posts.

'At the meeting held on August 21, 1942, Mr V G McAdams was elected Chairman of the Branch on account of Mr M F Gibbons joining HM Forces . . . Mr Hawkett of K3 gave a detailed talk on 'The Evolution of Wings and Tail planes.' '

Stand-Down 1945

'So it was that when VE-Day came on May 8, 1945, posts and centres viewed their celebrations with some misgivings. It was not until four days later that the ROC was at last allowed to stand down. Messages of congratulations flowed in from the Government and the RAF and these were passed down the lines along with more personal messages from area and group commandants.' [Attack Warning Red, p 181.]

'Finally, on May 12, 1945, posts completed their last plots and centre recorders filled in their last sheets. At 17.00 the great network of telephone lines and teleprinters fell silent, and the sinews of the air-defence network ceased to function.'

However, with the later threat from Russia, the ROC was re-formed in 1947. Years later in 'January 1968 the Labour Government, in the midst of an economic crisis, decided on massive cuts in home defence . . . The Auxiliary Fire Service, the Civil Defence Corps and the TAVR III were disbanded . . . On February 19, 1968, 680 ROC posts were to close. The corps was to be reduced from 25,000 to 12,500. Final meetings were held at most posts on which closure notices had been served. Typical are the last logbook entries of 9/C1, Keynsham, Somerset, a very enterprising and efficient post.

'April 5, 1968. 19.15. In the recent re-organisation of the ROC, our post was declared redundant and ceased to be operational as from last Monday, April 1, 1968. As the personnel on the post 9/C1 are to be dispersed as soon as possible, it has been decided to assemble at our post site this evening at the start of what will probably be our last post meeting, to say farewell to 'Charlie Wun'. Both the protected post and the observation post are open.

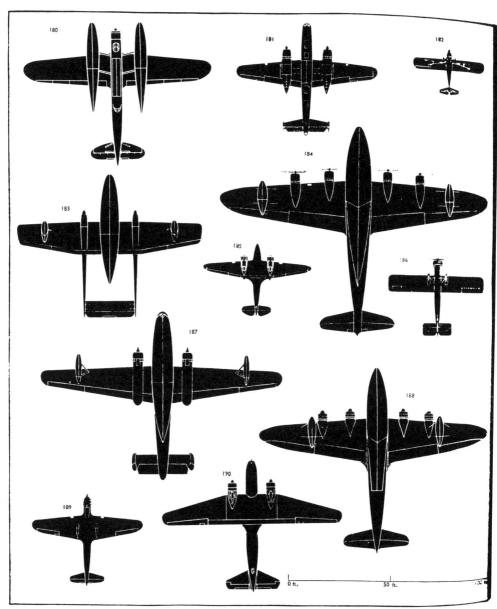

'Silhouettes to Scale' [December 1942] was a regular feature in the monthly ROC 'Journal'. Another series, 'Compare and Beware' showed photos of very similar British and German planes taken from identical angles.

118

'20.00 Both posts closed for the last time. Ivo Peters.' ('Attack WR', p 247.)

Doug Dyson carried on with his ROC work, overseeing and co-ordinating the training of new post members. Then on August 9, 1991 came a letter from Group Commandant J Morris, stating that because of 'the momentous changes in East/West relations . . . on 30 September, 1991, the ROC is once again to be stood-down.'

Awards presented to the Royal Observer Corps, 1945

These are listed in Appendix 1 and 2, pages 279–281, of 'Forewarned is Forearmed.' Only those relating to the Bristol/Keynsham area are listed here.

BEM

Observer Commander	N F Lockyer	(23)
Chief Observer	E S Harris	(23/K3.)
Chief Observer	C D Lock	(23/J2.)
Chief Observer	W E King	(23/H2.)

List of Officers in the ROC at Stand-Down 1945.

Observer Commander.

F C Lockyer	Group Commandant	Bristol
H F Tarring	Deputy Group Commandant	Bristol

Observer Lieutenant.

G P Dodge	Group Officer	Bristol.
A F Atteridge	DC (full time.)	Bristol.
J B Bretton	Group Officer.	Bristol.
J E Evans	DC (part time.)	Bristol.
J W Ewens	DC (full time.)	Bristol
T A Perks	Group Officer	Bristol.
C W R Walker	Group Adjutant	Bristol.
G B W Weldon	DC (part time.)	Bristol.
C A Westcott	DC (full time.)	Bristol.

'As the Royal Observer Corps moves into its second half-century of active life, its role is vastly different to that of 1925. The task may have changed but the spirit remains the same.' ('Attack WR' p 252.)

Keynsham's nuclear recording post

As has been mentioned earlier in this chapter, the ROC's post at the Cameroons near Park Road was in April 1942 transferred to a new site at Gypsy Lane, just above the Ministry Supply Base. From this 'vantage point' there is a magnificent view over the surrounding countryside. It was an ideal spot for Home Guard signallers, let alone plane spotters.

The post went underground in 1957 until they were finally 'Closed down April 1968.' Just what did 'underground' signify?

This indicated an underground recording post with special equipment to monitor the bearing, power and height of an atomic explosion, and the direction of the fall out, to alert the authorities in that area.

Flight Officer Doug Dyson paid courtesy calls to Burnett underground post. He described it as being, 'Some 6 ft wide by 10 ft long, and 7 ft high. It was made of reinforced concrete to combat radiation. Access was via a vertical iron ladder set in a square shaped shaft, which projected above ground some four feet, with an iron shutter at the top which bolted from the inside. A little further along was the ventilation shaft, with iron shutters against radiation. Some 2–3 ft of earth covered the concrete bunker.

'As there was no heating in the post, floor matting helped to keep the cold out. There was a table attached to the wall for maps, paper work, various instruments and a loud speaker telephone receiver. There were two bunk beds with blankets, and two chairs. To a ration of water was added self heating tins of food. There was a strip of fluorescent lighting, simply run off batteries. Three men, all part-timers, would be on duty at any one time, often for a 12 hr shift.'

Their special equipment was able to calculate the necessary information regarding nuclear fall out. The day of plotting the height and number of aeroplanes had quite gone. The new threat required new recording equipment, as the maxim 'forewarned is forearmed' still applied.

Today this narrow hundred metre long, man-made mound, after the closure of its post 24 years ago, has reverted to nature. Tall spindly trees grow through the undergrowth, but in winter it is just possible to see the two circular areas where once the iron door and the ventilation shaft originally stood.

Chapter 8

The National Fire Service in Keynsham

Here our source of information is Mr Sydney F Holburn, who had the privilege of being brought up 'a son of the manse'. The sixth and final child of a Wesleyan Methodist minister, William Holburn and his wife Madeline, Sydney was born at Navenby, south of Lincoln, in 1905.

During the 1914–18 War, the Rev W E Holburn was in the North Riding of Yorkshire circuit. So it was in Middlesborough that young Sydney watched in horror as a German Zeppelin, hit by British gunfire, caught fire and split into two halves, which dipped downwards. As blazing objects fell from them, his sister exclaimed in horror, 'Oh, how awful! They are German airmen burning.'

Later, in the field next to the school, Sydney could see camping soldiers, with rows of horses tied up near the playground, where during the evening each horse had one of its front legs tied to its thigh, so that they spent all night on three legs, their heads being tied to the ground. Even more disturbing were the rows of metal tripods, from which hung life-sized sacks of straw. In front of them were rows of soldiers with their rifles, who were being ordered by a sergeant, in a loud coarse voice, to more vigorously carry out their bayonet practice. 'If the sacks had been Germans, I would have been sorry for them', thought this sensitive ten-year-old. The two events planted in his mind the germ of pacificism.

Sydney Holburn recalled that, during the 1914–18 war, German warships fired on several areas of North East England, from Middlesborough up to Hartlepool.

Referring to attacks on England, Philip Clark wrote that, 'Zeppelins were sent on bombing raids over London from 1915. About 500 people were killed in Britain during the Zeppelin raids. British aircraft struck back by bombing German factories. Gradually the British improved their anti-aircraft defences, shooting down more and more of the slow-moving Zeppelins. Eventually they were replaced by aeroplanes'. [World War I, Granada Publishing, 1984, p 31.]

An undated cutting from The Keynsham Chronicle, from an unnamed elderly Keynsham resident, referred to an airship which was over Bath in 1916. He wrote, 'I have vivid memories of standing, as a small boy, in a meadow overlooking Keynsham, and watching the airship fly over Lansdown towards Keynsham. The Zeppelin raids over London were taking place at that time. This was the first airship seen in Somerset and consternation, even alarm, was caused by the airship's appearance, until reassurance came by the reading of the markings. It hovered over The Hams for a short time before flying off in a north-easterly direction. I remember, too, having a fine view of the ill-fated R33 in the early twenties. She hovered for quite a while over the Chewton Keynsham area one summer afternoon. Shortly afterwards she plunged to her doom in the Humber.'

Keynsham in the 1920s

Of that period Sydney Holburn wrote, 'It was round 1920 when six days a week a stream of people hurried round the church corner of Station Road, Keynsham, to catch the 7.58 am train to Bristol. In the city, Victoria Street led them to many varieties of work. Retailing folk had a Wednesday afternoon free. Industry in Keynsham seemed diminished and factories stood idle. The war was well over and the city absorbed its menfolk. Shops sought their earnings by lavish pavement displays such as gent's clothier Joll [Edward Joll's grandfather] stressing his bowler hats for 3/6 each in Victoria Street.

'In Keynsham, arguments and discussions resulted in green fields being taken over and dug for large areas of factory and even rows of houses with gardens for staff. This was Fry's following the example of the Cadbury's works in Birmingham. Of many names put forward, Somerdale was chosen and cut out and implanted in white stones on the railway embankment, probably fifteen feet high. So now the red bricks of street and factory stand established with sports fields, recreation halls and all the supplements of today.

'For many years work was done with brass and metals in buildings round the Rivers Avon and the Chew, but after the First World War, more and more buildings became unused and workers found other work.' Sydney Holburn recalled that when in 1923 Fry's finally transferred from Bristol to Keynsham, though many of its elder employees came with them, it was mainly new and younger local people that were employed.

He said of the town that some pavements in the High Street were then from 18 to 24 inches high, and most difficult to cross at night. He referred to the 'Drill Hall' on Bath Hill by its earlier name, 'The Territorial's Hall', where the soldiers had trained earlier prior, to the 1920s.

'Drivers wanted'

In 1939 Sydney was living in Keynsham with his wife Dora, (nee Hubbard), and their two children. His wife's uncle, with a partner, had started a wholesale china and glass business in Bristol, trading as 'Hubbard Hardware, Bristol, Ltd.' The outbreak of hostilities in World War II virtually closed down the family business, for which Sydney had worked for some years.

Sydney Holburn now takes up the story, 'I volunteered for work in the fire service, part-time to start with, but when the service asked for full-time firemen, I volunteered at Keynsham. The engine that we had at that time was most amusing, as we had to pull it out of the station and then get the ladder out and put it on top of the fire engine, because it would not fit into the station. We had just one engine in the beginning there, and one just did what one could.

'I was a driver. What happened was that there was a demand in Keynsham for a driver, and they couldn't get one, as men were not available. So the chief said to me, 'Why don't you apply, for you're driving all the time', so I went up to the Council Offices and applied for the job as a driver of their one engine. Apparently there was only one other applicant, and he wasn't what they wanted, so they simply appointed me. So I became the full time official driver and was the only full-time driver on the station.

'Later there were a number of drivers at Keynsham station, including the chief, which was necessary with the shift work. I had taught myself to drive and had earlier driven the firm's van. So basically I taught myself to drive the fire engine. Staff were kitted out with steel helmets, and axes, which were very rarely used, and heavy coats. At one time there were water-proof macs, which they later withdrew. They found that they were holding the moisture in so much that wearers were wet through with sweat, as the moisture could not escape.

My first job when I went on duty was to check all the engines. There was then a total of nine different engines that had to be tested, to see that their petrol was alright, that they were capable of starting, and that everything was in order to get them going if need be. By that time the brigade had obtained a yard next to the Lamb and Lark hotel on ground that had earlier been used for horse-drawn coaches and waggonettes in times past. Behind the hotel was a hall built for the Freemasons that was taken over by the fire service. Beds were put in it for a dozen men. We had 24 hours on duty there, and some of this would be spent in bed, almost fully dressed, so that at a moment's notice one could just run across the road to join the engines.

'The station had been re-formed and a station master appointed who knew what he was doing rather than those who did not know. The new man was Mr Smithson. All this was arranged by the Somerset or Keynsham UDC Council, who appointed him in line with national policy. The extra fire engines were at the Lamb and Lark, with their trailers, and extra pumps. You wouldn't recognise the trailers as fire engines but they were that just the same. They were drawn in from commandeered vehicles from this and that purpose, so these engines were very Heath Robinson. The actual engine that I am thinking of was an eight cylinder job that was very powerful for pumping. A lorry was used simply for pulling the pumper.

'On one occasion the pumper was on top of a local hill on the way to Bristol where it had been putting a haystack fire out, when orders came to come away from the fire. This was a curious thing, because the raid was still on and other fires were alight near Bristol. The only thing that we could think was that the authorities were putting a ring of firestacks around Bristol to draw German planes away. That was the night of the first raid on Bath. So we were recalled to the station.

'Personnel wise, there was a number of regular firemen, with the numbers made up with part-timers who came on about twice a week. There were about a dozen full-timers, with over twenty helpers. There were four telephonists, with two on, two off. They were at the station in the High Street. In the end we had about 20 full-timers on 24 hour shifts. There was no intention of aiming for rank or anything like that, until the country was taken over and we were organised on a national basis. Then the Bristol authorities came and organised us and controlled this area.

123

'We were told and encouraged to apply for promotion, for on the station was now some very expensive equipment, so we did apply. I remember going before a board of officers and feeling utterly foolish, and I think they too felt utterly foolish seeing me. It was really a farce. They had made up their minds beforehand, I learned afterwards, and knew who they were going to appoint and that was that. I was given the job of two stripes, as a semi officer sort of thing, and called a leading fireman.

'The station officer had two leading fire officers, one on duty and one off. There were changes in the ranks from time to time. The big change in personnel came with the invasion of France in 1940, and then firemen were moved from the North of England down to the South, to be within easy reach of the south coast, where there might be considerable raiding from Germany bringing fire in the South of England. So the South of England was covered from this station and further north. This meant we had more full-time firemen here, so that we were probably fifty strong.

'My responsibility was to have all the engines ready and running correctly and be able to get out immediately on call. Coming almost to the very last week of duty, I went down to start my shift at 9.00 in the morning, from my home at 1, Kelston Road. When I got to the station I said, "You're going to get a call in a moment," as on my way I had seen some smoke in West View Road and I knew it must be fire. A minute later the call came through, so I got my equipment on. By this time we had a very fine Leyland fire engine, and when we had gone to the raids in Bristol on it, it was the most up-to-date engine there of its type. We were very proud of it. So off we went to West View Road and found the house, where an electrical fault had set fire to the rafters, and the fire had crept down to a corner wardrobe, and set the curtain on fire. But they had found the fire before there was any serious damage. And they got the baby down safely. I went in and made thoroughly sure that those rafters were out.

'On duty there were camp beds to sleep on, and there were at least a dozen for those on their 24 hour duty. There was a canteen there, too, and a kitchen and toilets at the hall behind the hotel. I became the catering manager of the company. So I had to see that the food was brought properly, and we had a cook, a lady who came in from Bristol. The biggest problem was doing the returns, giving details of what had been done with the money, as I was allowed a shilling per person per 24 hour shift. I arranged to collect a shilling from each person which gave them two shillings per person per shift, which we handed over to the lady who prepared the food bought. She was paid by the Council and the extra one shilling each went on buying extra food, so that we could eat better. Rationing was such a thing in those days. Nowadays people cannot understand what it was like. To get sufficient food for working personnel was quite a serious job. Our allocation at the station was independent of the family's ration at home.

'As fire fighters, we were there for the raids, and that was our chief object. We weren't quite sure where the boundary of the raids on Bristol had been, so after one raid, some of us went up to the local fields at Queen Charlton and walked across them to find fires that might have been developing, to keep everything from being alight. This applied to an old shed or a stack on fire.

It was a case of 'Keep that light out'. We had already been out, but we were making sure that nothing was alight on our patch.

'At night time, one would hear the enemy bombers coming, so we would all be kitted out all ready. I remember the night they hit Coventry. We were in the High Street ready to go, but they just kept going. It was extraordinary. The planes just kept going over galore, without dropping a single bomb. We knew they were hitting somewhere. I chatted to a local air raid warden on his rounds, and he couldn't tell me where they were going.

'We were called out the first night they hit Bristol, and went to Durley Hill to a small fire. While there, I was very concerned, for there had been bombs dropped in the Charlton Road fields just above us, so I said at Durley Hill that I was rather concerned about my wife, and was it possible to phone her up on our equipment? So I did and found that she and the children were quite safe and was able to assure her that I was also alright.

'Yes, we did go into Bristol to the big fires. On the first night out there, we went to the centre of the city. The raid was over but the fires were still burning and we stayed there all day in the Baldwin Street area. It was hair-raising.. The fires just burned and burned. You never knew what was going to happen next. I never went to the Bath fires; I was off duty. One of our engines coming back saw a tall house that had been sliced in half, and there on the top floor was a man still asleep in his bed. I expect our engine phoned the information back. We certainly did not have a turntable engine with extending ladders.

'Sometimes we were very busy, and at other times it was just a case of filling in time with routine duties. Before disbanding, we all had a month's training and I had mine at Plymouth. The Keynsham station stayed open until there were just four of us full-timers, two on and two off. I remember that on Armistice night we were told that there was a haystack at Saltford almost burnt out. We decided to go and deal with it, after checking it out with Bristol, in case we were needed for a serious fire. When we got there, it was almost out, so we just let it go and checked around it.

'Mr Joll's father was a full-time fireman, while Mr Bill Robbins was part-time. Geoff Carter was my full-time number on the opposite shift, who lived in the High Street next to the fire station. We did a play organised by Miss Cooksley, with full dress, for a few days in the Drill Hall, as a Christmas event for charity.

'We started a pig club, as next to the Lamb and Lark hotel was a big garden with a shed suitable for keeping a pig. We started with a Large White, and then we kept two together. We bought them at eight weeks old, towards the end of the war. They were owned by eighteen members of the fire brigade. The country was glad of the meat, so we were able to keep half a pig, or one if we had two, to eat ourselves. The members of the club shared the preparations of the rations of bran, etc., so as full-timers, we had the responsibility to feed the pigs at regular intervals, to such comments as, "It's too early yet, we'll go up in half an hour's time." It was all part of the 24 hour duty. The pigs were killed by a local butcher from the High Street, who had a shop two or three doors away from the fire station, and whose assistant was a part-time fireman, who still lives in Keynsham today. He would kill them with a stun gun in the shed and hang them from the rafters, to be cut up.'

Mr Frank Bees recalled that Sydney was preaching at the old Zion Methodist church when Bristol was first bombed. Everybody dispersed under the pews when bombs were heard coming down, while Sydney later went home, collected his uniform and reported for duty.

Help for blazing Plymouth

'It was in 1941 that the towns on the South Coast, particularly Plymouth, were being bombed nightly by German planes from occupied France. Five of us, Geoff Carter (in command), Frank Batsdown, (whose father was a baker at Saltford), Charles Webb, (an RC who lived in Charlton Road) and another, with me at the wheel, set off at night for Plymouth. We were posted there, not knowing for how long.

'We arrived at 5 am and found ourselves on standby, with many other crews from towns from the West Country. We reported to HQ next to a hospital, where my brother Eric was responsible for the finance. Having a few minutes to spare, I was given permission to look in the hospital to see if he was around. And there he was, with some of his colleagues, exhausted after caring for their patients during the night's bombing, asleep on the floor of his office. We were delighted to see each other.

'Plymouth was ablaze in parts, here a church, there a row of houses. Later we were sent to a road shut off from the public, to dampen down the fires there. In other areas, fires were still blazing fiercely. Our mission completed, we were sent to a girls' school, empty of pupils of course, where food was provided for us, and a blanket for sleeping on the floor there.

'After a few hours' rest, we were told that another raid was imminent, and were told to be ready for redeployment back at the Plymouth HQ. However, Geoff Carter, acting on his own initiative, decided that we should drive to the outskirts of the city, for we would be no use if we stayed in the city centre and were killed. Events that night proved how wise he had been. On the outskirts we met stationary buses with their crews, with one particularly terrified conductress, whom I invited to shelter with me under a hedge, which somehow comforted her, though we could hear the bombs dropping and the shrapnel from our shells hitting the ground near us. All I could do was to pull my tin hat on more firmly, giving a small sense of security.

'When the bombing was over, it was back to the city to help fight the fires for the rest of the night and through the morning. At mid-day we returned to HQ, starving. I went to see my brother and explained we had not eaten all day. He went to the hospital chef, who was about to throw the leftovers from lunch away. How we enjoyed that welcome meal!'

Firewoman Mrs Delia Pillinger (nee Wiggins) on duty

In 1940, with her father dead and her brothers in the services, young Delia lived in the family home in the High Street where she helped her mother to run the home and the building business. Almost directly across the road was the old fire station. Acting on impulse, she joined the Keynsham Fire Service, and was one of the six full-time girls, who, with a number of other local part-time

Outside a Plymouth hospital, circa 1941, Driver Holburn with his then modern, high powered Leyland fire engine.

girls, manned the telephones and dealt with sundry returns. In a room above the fire station the girls worked eight hour shifts, usually with two, or even three, on duty together. She looked very smart in her full uniform, as later she attended an Officer's Training College at Saltdean, Brighton.

The fire station's telephone was an old fashioned instrument, with a hand winding mechanism. To phone the firemen's quarters behind the Lamb and Lark for an ordinary call, the mechanism was wound only a few times; if there was a fire, 'You'd wind the bell like mad and when the man answered, you'd tell them where the fire was. The Keynsham Brigade was ordered in to Bristol on fire fighting duty on the night of the first big raid there. Our "Chief" was Gordon Smithson of Durley Hill House.'

'I used to be on duty with Betty Brown. It could be frightening when the sirens went and overhead the drone of German planes could be heard, punctuated by the penetrating noise of our ack-ack guns. Then we had the lighter moments when we prepared for and put on the Christmas pantomimes. With home commitments, I did not try for a commission. I finally left the service in 1946 after the war was over. There were no medals for a telephonist firewoman; just the satisfaction of having done one's best for the country in its hour of need.'

Sydney, Frank and Delia represent the many full- and part-time fire fighters of Keynsham, who would each have his, or her, own story to tell of those years, of how they did their duty, overcame their natural fear, and bravely played their part for the 'village' and the people they loved.

The Saltford 'Action Station'

Through the war years, the thoughtful unassuming Mr Frank Bees was the manager of the Co-operative Stores' grocery department at Saltford. Like a number of other Keynsham men, he was a part-time member of the Keynsham Fire Service, and attended routine duty and training sessions during the week. However, whenever the siren sounded its chilling warning, he had to report for duty, even if he was at work.

Frank explained, 'Saltford alone of the neighbouring villages was an outpost of the Keynsham Fire Brigade, referred to as an Action Station. It comprised a team of six men. To the left of the The Crown Inn is its stable–outhouse building, which was pretty Spartan. We kitted it out with two bunk beds, a few chairs, and a telephone. Whenever we went out from the station, we always left one man behind to man the phone.

'Our transport was an old 18 hp Morris car, to which was hitched a pump and hoses, mounted on two wheels.' As the Leading Fireman in that group, when the siren sounded, he was responsible for driving his appliance to the Crown to await instructions, in an area he knew well.

'I remember the hedges at the top of Charlton Road being on fire after a heavy raid of incendiary bombs, and was present too at the fire in the High Street when we rescued the piano player from her home. That was the only time we used our fire axes.

'On one occasion when I was on duty with Jeff Carter going up Sherwood Road we could see through a dormer window that a fire had been started by

The photograph of one shift of the Keynsham National Fire Service

In Frank Bees' opinion, this photo comprises one shift of the full-time and part-time members of the Brigade on duty, taken around 1944 in the yard of the Lamb and Lark Hotel.

a bomb in the semi-detached houses of 64 and 66, Park Road. There was no one in, so we had to force an entry from the rear, and carried upstairs our two gallon canvas buckets of water, and the stirrup pump. The fine spray from it quickly deprived the bomb of oxygen and we soon had the blaze under control.'

Chapter 9

The Keynsham Home Guard, 1940–1944

From its inception, Keynsham was the Head Quarters of the No 2 Company of the 7th Somerset Battalion of the Home Guard. In addition to its headquarter's staff, the signallers and dispatch riders' unit and the stretcher bearers' section, there were nine platoons, each with its own officers and other ranks. Battalion HQ was at Flax Bourton.

Local Defence Volunteers

'On May 14, 1940, Anthon Eden broadcast an appeal, "We want large numbers of men to come forward and offer their services. The name of the new force will be "The Local Defence Volunteers." When on duty you will form part of the Armed Sevices and your period of service will be for the duration of the war." He had hardly finished his appeal before the first volunteers began to gather at police stations. Volunteers who responded to the call early on the following morning hoping to be among the first to enrol found themselves well down the list. Within a few days the numbers went into hundreds of thousands,' wrote Mac Hawkins in "Somerset at War." (Dovecot Press, 1988, p. 126)

Sir Charles Miles, Bart, of Clevedon, was entrusted by the Somerset Territorial Army Association to raise a Company in the Long Ashton Police Divisional Area. He convened a meeting of some local leaders at the Petty Sessional Court at Flax Bourton on May 21, 1940. The plan explained was that enrolled members should be formed into five platoons, one in each of the five Police Districts in the Long Ashton Police Division, and Platoon Commanders were appointed accordingly as follows:

1. Flax Bourton,   under Dr Wallace.
2. Keynsham,   under Captain Scammell.
3. Temple Cloud, under Captain Eshelby.
4. Portishead,   under Mr. Clements.
5. Clevedon,   under Mr. Christie.

The Company, as soon as formed, would pass under the command of Admiral Sir Hugh J Tweedie, KCB, of Wraxall House.

'The main ideas were to form village sections for observations, and mobile sections for fighting any enemy that might arrive: to select good observation posts to be manned from dusk to dawn: and to prepare positions and ambushes – all on a voluntary basis of six hours per man per week. Anyhow, off we all went to try and get something working' wrote Major W S Scammell, MC, in his fascinating 83 page book, "The Story of No 2 Company of the

7th Battn., Somerset Home Guard", published privately in late 1944. He continued, 'There were no enrolment forms, no rifles, no ammunition – in fact, no anything! Only a great determination that no enemy should set foot here without being seen and reported, and that he should be hit on the head with anything handy at the earliest possible moment he could be reached by a British hand and arm. The official instruction was that every volunteer should have an axe or loaded stick, to be provided by himself. The enthusiasm was tremendous and people were already asking what the indefinite "they" were going to do for the Home Guard in the way of weapons, training, drill, instructions and, in fact, soldiering complete in a week: but of course nothing happened in this way for months. Any how, that was a start.'

Early organisation

Later, on May 24, 1940, there was a meeting at the Keynsham Police Court of provisional leaders, when a rough procedure was agreed on for the enrolment of volunteers on a home-drawn form, and plans for observation posts and duties and communications were explained and laid on. The extensive knowledge of the locality and the marvellously accurate assessment of the qualities of individual leaders in the rural area were put at their disposal by the Police.

The area of the Keynsham Platoon, as No 2 Company was then called, covered fifty square miles and included twelve parishes, and substantially covered all the area between the cities of Bristol and Bath on the south side of the River Avon and about seven miles southwards from it. Fourteen Observation Posts were established in carefully-chosen positions uniting the points of observation, bearing in mind means of communication and accessibility for volunteers to man them.

The first record of the organisation set up was dated 26th June, 1940, and it shows the establishment of thirteen sections in the Keynsham area, each with their leader and HQ, their Observation Post and Communications from it.

Many more men than anticipated joined the LDV, so that on July 9, 1940, with a fighting force of 2,500 men, the Long Ashton Company became a battalion, and platoons became companies. So Keynsham progressed from a platoon to No 2 Company, commanded by Captain Scammell. Burnett, Chewton Keynsham, Corston, Saltford, Whitchurch, Pensford, Stanton Drew, Norton Malreward, Marksbury, Hunstrete and Compton Dando all came under Keynsham No 2 Company. Major F W Tennant was second in command. In August 1940 the title of Local Defence Volunteers was changed to The Home Guard.

'Late in April, 1940, I had returned from taking and bringing back convoys across the Atlantic. I had learnt from the Admiralty that I should not be required again immediately, so when Colonel Gibbs of Barrow Court asked me if I could help with the force locally, I was able to say yes, subject to further calls from the Admiralty.'

That was how Admiral Hugh J Tweedie came to be the Battalion Commander of the 7th Battalion of the Home Guard, from its inception, with the rank of Lt. Colonel conferred later. Prior to the cessation of hostilities in 1945, he wrote an excellent seventy page "History of the 7th Battalion of the Home Guard", for private circulation, from which the above introductory paragraph is taken.

'The Battalion HQ made Flax Bourton its Battle HQ, the administration being done at the Battalion Commander's home at Wraxwall House. Later, Battle HQ was the Long Ashton Research Station.' From here the Admiral, for over four and a half years, sought to train and prepare more than 3,000 officers and men to fight for their homes and their country against the hated invader.

Uniforms and weapons

The uniform first consisted of armlets, two per section, which were proudly exchanged by the observers as they came on and went off OP duty, bearing the magic letters, 'LDV'.

At this period, Miss M Fairclough recalls seeing two LDV members in tin hats cycling up Charlton Road to their 'post', while a mound of hardened tarmac at the end of Lockingwell Road became a 'defence post' with a stock of home made 'Molotov cocktails' at hand.

Mr Leonard Dunn, a trained carpenter, wheelwright and builder of buses, came to Keynsham from Swindon in 1930. In 1957 he opened 'The Handyman's Shop'. Earlier, in 1940 when the call came for volunteers, willingly he joined the force, despite his poor health. 'At first I had no uniform at all, just an armband and my weapon was a heavy walking stick which was all I could get hold of.'

'Flight Lieutenant Grossett, ex RAF, was our Platoon Commander at first. He was also the manager at the local paper mill. He hated walking, so when it was his turn to be on duty at Burnett Point, he would call up a lorry from the mill to take us there and back.' [Cpl L Whittock wrote that the lorry was usually driven by Pte F Balcombe as that was his job at the mill, the lorry being a three wheel articulated unit] Unfortunately, though, some two years later F Lt Grossett was taken ill, and was replaced by Lieut Cornick.'

'The men who faced Hitler' was the headline of the Keynsham Chronicle's article in its 25 Aug 1985 edition. It continued, 'Apart from local shotguns and an odd revolver or two, there were no weapons initially. Axes, heavy sticks and farm implements were recommended as weapons should the enemy appear. There was to be no indiscriminate or 'excited' shooting. If fewer than five parachutists were seen they could be reckoned as British. If more than that, they should be assumed to be the enemy – even if in British uniforms – in which case one had to act accordingly.'

A Home Guard record stated, 'The volunteer force is a fighting force and every means in our power must be used to kill and disable the enemy should he appear.'

Oral history is invaluable in supplementing documentary statistics, but the drawback is, that in recalling events that happened fifty years ago, understandably some differences occur in people's recollections. Mr Fred Balcombe, born in Fairlight, near Hastings, came to Keynsham in 1936 and worked at Robinson's Paper Mill. When the call for volunteers came, he reported to the Old Police Station in Bath Hill, where he said he was issued with an arm-band and a rifle.

'Flight Lieut Grosset was our officer and was a very good bloke. There was discipline of course, but not like the regular army. We were all civilians, so we were all like one big family; they were all nice chaps.'

As I tried to coax recollections out of him, he remembered guard duty at Burnett Point. 'I used to be on duty there with Leonard Dunn. We would have to cycle there, with our rifles across our backs. There was no army transport. At the Dump, there was a small hut just big enough to shelter in from the rain. It had no telephone. Our three hour stretch of duty was to patrol, as a pair, from the junction with Wellsway along to the cross-road toward Corston, nearly a mile away.

'There we would walk up and down, wrapped later in army greatcoats, complaining about the weather, but keeping our eyes open on the countryside during the night patrol. We each had five rounds of live ammunition. During the watch, the officer would come round to see us. When we were relieved, we got on our bikes and went home, ready for work next day. Sometimes during the raids on Bristol, we could hear shrapnel falling around us. Then we were glad to be wearing tin helmets.'

Fred was in the Home Guard during the whole of its existence, and reluctantly agreed that therefore he had received the Defence Medal, though protesting with modesty, 'We had a good time, but nothing outstanding happend to us.'

He recalled that the local railway goods yard, now the site of a stone carving firm, was still very active during the war. There used to be a lot of moving ammunition from there to Burnett Point Depot, and of army vehicles for repair to Rockhill Farm. And of course, there was a line from the goods station linking it to Fry's own railway siding.' He thought the goods yard closed down between 1950 and 1960.

The Admiral wrote that, 'During the autumn of 1940 we were gradually issued with Denim overalls, useful as producing some sort of uniformity, but useless as protection against wet and cold. Had the enemy struck at this country in 1940, '41, or '42, they would at least have been faced with a motley crew with many different kinds of weapons, from the sporting gun and rifle to the pitch fork.

'For a long time the question of arming the men was an insoluble question. The attack, if it came, might come any day. The problem, therefore, was not only the weapons we had, but how best they should be distributed. Should there be weakness everywhere, or should some details be comparatively strong and others entirely denuded?

'We started with 800 .303 rifles and some one hundred shot-guns, besides an unknown number of the latter in the hands of individual Home Guards. The hundred odd shot-guns distributed were those picked out from a much larger number handed in to the Flax Bourton Police Station in response to a public appeal. The guns had to be got out. The attack might come that night or next week: no one knew. There was no clerical staff, no labour and no transport. Luckily I owned a Ford utility van, and this van, in the course of four years, was to carry many tons of Home Guard equipment and clothing. I was the

No. 2 Platoon of No. 2 Company of the 7th Somerset Battalion of the Home Guard, possibly taken in 1942. Mr. E.J. Cannock provides the photo (taken by A. Scoins), and the following names:

Front row, left to right:
1. Pte. A.R. Norton; 3. Cpl., later Lieut. A.J. Membry; 5. Lieut. Gavin Fray; 8. Sgt. F.S. Condon; 9. Cpl. K.O. 'Rex' Harris; 10. Pte. 'Bill' J. Ryan.

Middle row:
1. Pte. Philip C. Minty; 3. Pte. 'Ken' R. Baber; 4. Pte. E.T. Fox; 6. Pte. David Jack; 10. Pte. later Cpl. D.H. Thorne; 11. Pte. G.G. Brearley; 12. Pte. J.D. Buttle.

Rear row:
3. Pte. John Pope; 8. Pte. 'Stan' G. Price.

driver and also supplied the labour . . .

'No sooner had the allowance of .303 rifles been distributed than a thousand .300 American rifles arrived. These were to replace the .303s. Nos 2 and 3 Companies (Keynsham and Temple Cloud) were each approximately 500 strong, and as it was not expedient to mix the two types of rifles, the whole of the arms of the two companies were withdrawn and they were reissued with the American rifles, 500 each, a matter of considerable labour and transport.

'Closely following the issue of American rifles came a supply of Tommy guns, no sooner distributed than withdrawn and replaced by Sten guns, the latter a splendid Home Guard weapon, and in such good supply as eventually to provide every man with a personal weapon, our rifle strength sticking at 1,800.

'During the autumn of 1940 and 1941, Lewis machine guns came along in fair numbers and served to bolster up the Companies who were short of rifles. These guns were withdrawn from aircraft. They turned out to be very useful and reliable weapons for our purposes.'

Reorganisation of Keynsham LDV from a platoon to a company

When orders were received that the Keynsham Platoon was to become a Company, the following details were notified:

Company Headquarters

Commanding Commander . . .   Captain WS Scammell, MC.
Second-in-Command   . . .   Major FW Tennant.

Assistant Officer and H.Q.
Platoon Commander   . . .   Mr. G.F. Clark.

The existing Sections were to be grouped into Platoons with Platoon Commanders, as follows:

No. 1. Platoon.

Platoon Commander – Mr. W.H. Conn.

Section No. 1. . . .	Keynsham and Part Mobile.
Somerdale Section . . .	Industrial.
G.W. Railway Section . . .	Industrial,

No. 2 Platoon.

Platoon Commander – Mr. P. Grosset, D.F.C.

Section No. 2. . . .	Keynsham.
Section No. 11 . . .	Burnett and Chewton.
Section No. 4 . . .	Saltford.

No. 3 Platoon.

Platoon Commander – Mr. F.W. Partington.

Section No. 3. . . .	Keynsham, Queen Charlton and Stockwood.

No. 4. Platoon.

Platoon Commander – Mr. F.A. Venn.

Section No. 5 .   . . .   Whitchurch.

No. 5. Platoon.

Platoon Commander – Mr. H.A.H. Fraser.

Section No. 8.   . . .   Pensford.
Section No. 9.   . . .   Stanton Drew.
Section No. 10.   . . .   Norton Malreward.

No. 6. Platoon.

Platoon Commander – Mr. C.W. Trussler.

Section No. 6.   . . .   Marksbury.
Section No. 7.   . . .   Hunstrete and Compton Dando.
Section No. 12.   . . .   Stanton Prior.

Section No. 12, Priston, to remain a separate section under Mr. J. Derriman.

By this time, the Corston Parish had been added to the Company's Area, and very shortly afterwards Saltford was withdrawn from No. 2 Platoon and, with Corston, formed a new Platoon known as No. 7 – under Mr. H.P. Gray. Also in June 1940, the Somerdale Industrial Section became a Platoon under the command of Mr Morris, who had previously served from the earliest date in No 3 Platoon, and later as No 13 (Fry's) Section Commander.

Early training

Major Scammell wrote that at first, with lack of uniform and weapons, little military training could be done, but they learned from the very start about Observation and Communications, Patrol Reports, Road Blocks, Ambushes and Scouting. The minimum of drill was done. A few rifles were obtained and as early as June 1940, squads were taken to Yoxter Range, on the Mendips, for firing practice and the foundation of range discipline, plus fire orders and control, was well and truly laid.

On July 1, 1940, ten rifles arrived and few days later a hundred more came, and later, more still. Denim overalls also started to arrive for No 2 Company. The Admiral indeed had been active.

One of the earliest members of the LDV was Private Jim Ollis. All through the war he worked for Siddeley Hawker, the engine makers at Patchway, Bristol. His military training would only begin after his arduous day's work. He said, 'I used to cycle to work in all forms of wind and weather, leaving home at 6.15 am for a 7.30 am start. At home, whenever the siren went, you got into uniform and reported to the Drill Hall. It could always be the start of the invasion.'

In addition to Yoxter, there was a firing range on Charlton Bottom, towards Queen Charlton, with the river on the right. 'We used to go there for Lee

137

Reporting for duty at Fry's in the summer of 1940, in the early days of the Home Guard, when there was more enthusiasm than uniforms and weapons. They were to follow.

At Fry's again, probably in August 1944 before 'Stand down' in Nov 1944. The Officers of No 8 Platoon and the BAC Section, (lt to rt). Lieut A Campbell-Smith, Lieut W Morris and Lieut AW Powell.

Enfield rifle practice about every six weeks. The targets were set up about a hundred yards away. I could at least hit the target (if not the bull). Some couldn't even hit the target, though most could.'

After a Sunday parade, some members would patronize The Talbot or the Druid's Arms, but not Jim. 'I don't go to pubs or smoke and I take plenty of exercise. That's the answer to long life.' He had cause to say that. He was born 23 December, 1912.

The son of one of the above Platoon Commanders mentioned that on one auspicious occasion when the Home Guard were engaged in rifle practice at the Charlton Bottom range, a certain anonymous marksman among them managed to put a bullet in the weather cock on the tower of the Queen Charlton church. Whether or not it was intentional, who the culprit was, and whether or not there was a local court martial, is not recorded in the Company Commander's 'History'. This is an example of oral local history, known among those connected with the Home Guard, and passed on with a chuckle!

'During the winter of 1940–41, really amazing progress was made in elementary training as well as the siting of positions, and at least a rough construction of defences and road blocks. It resulted in every road of any importance being covered in a good tactical spot in the Company's area,' recorded Major Scammell.

Miss Gwendolene Bennett wrote, "The Home Guard had a coach sited at the top of Charlton Road where the road goes on to Woollard. It was in the field on the left as you go up. I believe it was fitted with some bunks, and the group of men took turns to rest between their look-out patrols. I think there were six or eight men there at a time. If they spotted anything they had to cycle to a phone in Queen Charlton! They also patrolled the cinema – very spooky in the dark, according to my father, Henry Bennett."

Leaving the Home Guard aside for a moment, Gwen recorded that during the war, "Everybody in the same street had to have the same coal delivery firm and the same milkman, to save fuel and labour. It probably applied to bread too I suppose."

A High Street house ablaze, August 24, 1940.

Private Jim Ollis said, 'I remember the night when the petrol bomb was dropped in the High Street. One of their planes dropped it as he was being chased by our fighters. We thought it was the start of a big attack. That was over fifty years ago.'

The irony of an incident connected with this bombing is remembered by Jeff Whittock, then just a lad in the Army Cadets. 'The house hit by the incendiary bomb was burning brightly, when a nearby neighbour inadvertently put on the light without first drawing the curtains. At this, the local air raid warden, using the much quoted phrase, shouted, "Put that light out".'

Even in tragedy there can be humour. Mrs R Gyles remembered that night when the war arrived in the town in such a visual manner. During the night, the Home Guard were called in to safeguard the public from any falling masonry. Two uniformed men, armed with their rifles, resolutely stood guard outside the damaged house. Eventually these two local men, who had never had such an experience before, and who were embarrassed by the gazing crowd of neighbours and townspeople across the road, were given the order, 'Guard, dismiss.' At this, the two privates, one tall, one short, should both have turned right and marched smartly away. Unfortunately, one turned right but the other turned left, so that Tall and Short ended up facing each other. The onlookers loved it, and burst into loud laughter. But as they say in the army, 'No names, no packdrill'.

The first Company exercise was held on 13 October, 1940, when emphasis was laid on the use of cover and communications. The log book contained the sentence, 'The movement seemed good and revealed a surprising standard of training and undoubted keenness of all hands.'

Yoxter Range was being used with fair regularity and after the first 160 men fired there on 23 June, 1940, range firing practice continued at intervals. The Browning Automatic Rifle had appeared by October, and was fired at Yoxter on 20th October, 1940.

The Company's despatch riders

'From the very start the Company's despatch riders had been regarded as precious, and they always proved invaluable in sheep-dog work for lorries and all kinds of improvised transport that always bolted down the wrong lanes, it seemed, and never could reach Yoxter without the sheep-dog despatch riders to bark them back into the right way,' wrote Major Scammell.

The Battalion Commander's aim was that the Battalion should build up a strong group of despatch riders on motor-cycles with a real knowledge of how to get about the country in all weather, in daylight and dark. 'There were plenty of machines but, it soon transpired, not many riders who could find their way about. Mostly these machines were owned by men who went daily to work and back by one route, or if they went on holiday went out of the district altogether. They all had to be taught to read a map and to get through to their object by alternative routes if necessary. To do this, a bi-weekly service was organised that took the routine correspondence backwards and forwards between Battalion and Company HQs. However, due to the War Office's refusal to pay £5 for a minor accident, and most riders being young men dependent on their machines for work but only able to afford third party risk, other means of communications had to be explored,' the Admiral recorded.

However, Major Scammell firmly believed that at that time, no Home Guard Unit, and indeed few Regular Units, had anything to compare with the DRs of his Company for interest, local knowledge, and communications. They delivered their mail even when posts and roads were interfered with and blocked by enemy bombing.

Years later, Lieut A Pagett recalled that towards the end of the war, DRs were not used very much. 'We only had one in Keynsham, Frank Baxter, a man of mature years and small of stature, on a huge Triumph machine.'

Regarding 'Pigeon Post' he said that people used their own private lofts, for there were a number of pigeon fanciers. Messages were tied to the birds' legs, and it worked. But of course these could only be used at the week-ends and during daylight, as birds don't fly at night.

Corporal Les Whittock wrote that the DRs used their own motor cycles, for which they were given a petrol allowance. He said that the local pigeons used would have been supplied by Sergeant George Perry of Albert Road, who kept many pigeons.

'Some heavy air raids in Bristol occurred during this winter, and the men stood up to it well, and quite a few received commendations officially for their assistance in this connection', recorded Major Scammell.

1941.   Not civilians but uniformed soldiers

'In January the first issue of serge battledress arrived and caused quite an impression.

'In February, military commissions and ranks were issued and twenty Home Guard leaders accepted commissions. Platoon Commanders became Lieutenants and the Deputies, 2nd Lieutenants. Mr Clark became the voluntary Adjutant, with the rank of Lieutenant, and was a pillar of strength as well as a healthy critic throughout. Lt Fraser became Operational Second-in-Command with the rank of Captain, and was succeeded by Lt Bewley in command of No 5 Platoon. Major Tennant continued in the work of Administration and QM Section. G E James and D Kirkwood became stalwarts on Company office staff.

'Previously much help had been given by various lady volunteers, but in 1941 Mrs Mason took charge of them, and bundles of correspondence ceased to be a nightmare. She earned the title of "Chief Ferret". Company HQ Messengers were laid on, and an excellent working staff, which never looked back, was formed.

'Training continued, with a course of instruction on the modern way of killing in a scientific manner. Lectures included strategy, tactics, guerrilla warfare, weapons, and a striking lecture on 'Reaction to Fear', which was an outstanding psychological contribution. Other courses multiplied, in addition to the regular Platoon exercises and parades.

'June 1941 saw the Company emerge from its training grounds to startle the populace with ceremonial work in connection with "War Weapons Week", and the steadiness of the men on parade was notable,' recorded Major Scammell. Defence Committees were set up to co-ordinate the work of the Home Guard with the Military and Local Government. Invasion was still a constant probability.

A corporal remembers

Mr Les Whittock joined the Home Guard in 1941, aged 16. By that time he could say, 'I went straight into full uniform. It was a few months before I was allowed to keep my rifle and bayonet and take them home. None of us were allowed to take ammunition home. When the regular army had all the guns that they needed, we received a few of the short Sten guns, and then Piat grenades or mortar firing rifles for use against motorised vehicles, say at first one, then three, per platoon. We had no machine guns.

'Corporal G Camm lived at 17, Wellsway, [later the home of Professor and Mrs McGrath] and had an orchard at the rear of his house. He had a bunker there that locked securely, in which we stored our No 2 Platoon's ammunition, both blanks and live. His home constituted our Platoon HQ with our Lieutenant Cornick living almost opposite the Corporal. We used to train in the orchard, doing rifle drill, throwing dummy grenades, and crawling on our stomachs among the trees. For bayonet practice, which was great fun, we had hessian sacks tightly packed with straw and hung from the fruit trees. We trained on Sunday mornings from 10.00 to 12.00 am.

'At Hunstrete was the HQ's "Commando Unit". They had some tough nuts there. Mr C W Trussler, the head keeper at Chelwood House, who obviously knew the countryside well, was in charge of the unit, aided by his two sons. We were taught how to camouflage and stalk. All the local sections went to the unit for training. Occasionally on exercises, live ammunition was used, by experts, either side of you, fired by your own picked men. You would be warned of it!

'Sometimes during the week there would be night maneuvers on the hill top at Norton Malreward against a Bristol section in mock battles. At other times we would go to Dundry for the week-end, being on guard duty or training. Some men were so well camouflaged that you would walk straight past them, and then they would shoot you in the back. We used to throw thunderflashes at 'the enemy', but no one burnt themselves seriously.

'Every 2–3 months we would go for a whole Sunday to the Yoxter range on the Mendips and practice with live ammunition, using .303 Lee Enfield rifles, Sten guns and Piats. This was supervised by the regular army, who would set up the targets of cards of decreasing circles at 100 yards distance, and collect unexploded ammunition. The RASC lorries would transport us there and back.

'On one occasion when there were night manoeuvres between Chewton Keynsham and Compton Dando, I was responsible for taking tea round for our men, who were spread out there. I had the Lieutenant's car, but I could not find the light switch, so I had to travel round all night along the twisting road in the pitch black.'

The Drill Hall

With the formation of the Home Guard, the Drill Hall reverted to its original military function, after being used for such purposes as light opera. From the building, dummy grenades were taken for practice throwing in the nearby park. At one end of the hall was a small canteen for those on duty all night. The hall was large enough for the whole Company to be on parade at one time.

Corporal L Whittock took his section for drill, with and without arms, and for weapons training. He attended a week's Weapons Course in Hampshire for Home Guard Warrant Officers.

He said, 'Discipline was "quite good". The men were pretty obedient. Few were told to stand up straight. It was not a difficult job really. But when

Nov 1939. Fry's Decontamination Group, with their instructor, complete with tin helmets, gloves, wellingtons and gasmasks.

'OFFICERS of No 2 COMPANY, 7th Battalion of THE SOMERSET HOME GUARD, at Dec 31st 1944.' The photograph, taken by Veale and Co Bristol, belongs to former Captain AJC Paget, of Burnett.

on duty, every one had to conform to proper army discipline. There was no mucking about. You were addressed according to your rank. When you were in uniform, all Officers were saluted, not only those of your own Company in the Drill Hall, but whenever you met any of the numerous regular RASC Officers in the High Street.'

Guard duty

The procedure was that the night guard came on parade under its NCO, who took charge and inspected his guard, who then loaded their rifles and fixed bayonets. Double sentries were posted and relieved every two hours. Everyone had to sleep with his uniform, boots and full equipment on when off duty and no intoxicating liquor was allowed. The 'History of No 2 Company', written at the time, states that, 'This latter order was observed to the letter, despite grateful members of the public who tried to show their gratitude in liquid form. Never at any time did any NCO fail in the loyal discharge of their duties, which is high tribute to their progress as commanders and administrators of their men.'

Fifty years later, Corporal Whittock recalled that parades were held every Sunday and one or two evenings each week, depending on the demands of the men's main wartime work. One was on duty for the whole of the night once a fortnight. Outside the Drill Hall, where the railings had been taken away for the war effort [but now replaced], was a proper sentry box like those outside Buckingham Palace, facing the road, where one Home Guard member, with his rifle, would stand guard, two hours on duty, four hours off. Leslie thought the guard might have had five rounds of ammunition, but was rather doubtful, 'as some of the boys were prone to shooting off.'

Another site for night guard duty for the Keynsham Platoons was the vitally important and extensive ammunition store at Burnett Point, where eight to ten men spent the night in the guard hut and took turns to be on duty in the sentry box. They were situated just outside the perimeter ring of the barbed wire, inside which the regular army were also on guard. RASC lorries would transport the men there and back. Les recalls that one night on duty at that lonely spot, 'Private George Bees put a live bullet through the roof of the hut.' Yes, certainly up there they were issued with live ammunition.

Live ammunition, Communications, and the Signallers

Ammunition was scarce but the Company kept going and shot at various ranges: Portbury, Clevedon and Yoxter. Defence against gas was kept in the fore front and the issue of the service type of respirators was made.

August 1941 was another land-mark with the start of a grenade range at Perry's Quarry, where the throwing of live Mills No 36 grenades started in earnest. Northover Projectors appeared and the famous Molotov Cocktail in use by hand since the earliest days became our first type of artillery delivered with quite occasional accuracy through the Northovers. The experimental work of Corporal O Hopkins of No 2 Platoon in making the first Molotov cocktail, was highly commended.

'Another very important feature was progress in communication', wrote Major Scammell. 'In this period is to be found the commencement of the Signals Squad as such, and the Despatch Riders put on a firm basis; pigeons, land lines, signalling lamps of various types, were all brought into practical use, and although there were many disappointments an excellent system of communication was started, with Maes Knoll as a vital point. The most notable feature of that district was its foggy and wet nature, and generally a gale, with the rain blowing parallel to the ground, whenever the Signallers tried to storm the slopes and practice with their lamps, which increased their vocabulary and produced higher determination from them.

'The Signallers and the DR's started regular night duties at Company HQ from which great service they never looked back, and from March 20, 1941, until the end of Night Duties at Company HQ in August 31, 1944, the little band of Signallers and DR's, with very few exceptions, always took their duties at Company HQ each night.' Major Scammell paid a great tribute to their work, inspired, led and wisely governed throughout by Lieutenant Clark.

'Telephone wire was at a premium and instruments more so. Eventually in 1944, they actually had a certain amount of land line provided for them, and connected up the signal stations at Storm Point, Dundry and Maes Knoll and back to Filwood Farm and thence to Bristol Garrison Command.

'So to back up the GPO telephone they had despatch riders, signal stations, a certain amount of land lines and a very efficient pigeon service under the control of Mr Read, whose main loft was at Long Ashton within a few yards of Battalion Battle HQ.'

Private Ernest Wiltshire, of the former well-known building and decorating firm, was initially in No 2 Platoon and performed his share of guard duty at Burnett Point. However, with his interest in radio, he volunteered for the signal section when it was formed, and was accepted. He said, 'Most of my time was spent at Maes Knoll. I was just an ordinary signaller, so I was given one stripe. There were at least six of us there. Lieut G F Clark of Fry's was in charge and he used to pick us up by car and drive to the old farm at Maes Knoll, and we would walk up the last part.

'Our post was a wooden hut, specially erected for us, with a dug-out beside it. There was a field telephone there, but we did our morse signalling by use of lamps. Most of my time up there was spent in contacting other signal posts such as Knoll Hill, near Camerton, a post at Hanham and even one at Fry's. We had straight-forward conversations. Then it was work next morning. At a week-end, one could be there all night in connection with manoeuvres, as the exercises could take place over a very large distance.'

Councillor Ken Bye kindly called to tell me about his father, Private Jesse W Bye. At the outbreak of war, Jesse was a signalman at Uphill Junction, working for the GWR. He joined the LDV at the nearby village of Weedon and was only given an armband with LDV on it. Thus 'equipped', he patrolled the nearby hills, watching for the invader.

1943 saw promotion to a signal box at Fox's Wood, this side of the long tunnel into Bristol. Eventually he found lodgings with Mr and Mrs Carey at 19, Bristol Road, opposite St Dunstan's Church. He was transferred to the local branch of the Home Guard, who at that time were looking for members with

SOME OF THE OFFICERS, NCO's AND MEMBERS OF THE KEYNSHAM HOME GUARD

Taken in Keynsham Park late 1944, just prior to disbandment

Front Row – Left to Right: Corporal G CAMM; Corporal LJ WHITTOCK; Corporal JW OWEN; Lieut AJ MEMBRY; Major WS SCAMMELL, CO; Lieut RE CORNICK; Lieut FC SMAILES; Sgt KO HARRIS and Corporal AE TAYLOR

Middle Row: Privates CJ LYONS; IL STABBINS; JM WHITTOCK; NE BROOKMAN?; WH STABBINS; F RYAN; WE THOMAS; DL PRICE?; EE VOWLES

Rear Row: Privates THACKWAY; ET FOX; DH WHITE; GG BREARLEY; FJ BALCOMBE; E WIGGINS; CE JENKINS

specific skills. So being competent at morse and semaphore, he was recruited into the Signallers and Despatch Riders' Unit of 31 members.

Ken said that the Headquarter's group of the Home Guard used to meet most frequently at the Old Church Hall in Station Road. Occasionally military business was conducted at the nearby Pioneer, or in the function room of the more prestigious Wingrove at the top of the Bristol Road.

The Battalion on Parade

May 11, 1941, saw the first Battalion Ceremonial Parade, held on Clifton College Playing Fields, where they were reviewed by Field-Marshall Lord Birdwood, when seventeen Officers and two hundred and sixty-three other ranks paraded in conjunction with all the other Companies of the Battalion. Back in Keynsham, occasional church parades, and infrequently other ceremonial parades, were held.

A Factory Unit of the Bristol Aeroplace Company at Somerdale became attached to the Company, with Lieut Campbell-Smith as their immediate commander, forming part of No 8 Platoon under Lieut Morris.

'There was a demonstration by the RAF on Burnett Ridge when two Whirlwinds dive-bombed them 'by request' and still more impressive was their climbing performance', wrote Major Scammmell.

'On the Administrative side, Company HQ was squeezed from two rooms at the Old Police Station into one, where identity cards for members of the force were stamped, with hundreds more waiting, and the issue of emergency rations and supplies given. Relief came on October 20, 1941, when Company HQ was transferred to the ground floor premises of the Keynsham Urban District Council at the Public Library [now demolished]. At last HQ had efficient accommodation, with an Officer's Room and an ante-room, telephones of their own and a hundred and one other benefits'.

The formation of the Medical Squad

'In the summer of 1941, Dr N D Gerrish, MB, accepted the position of Company Medical Officer, with the rank of Captain, and from then on gave freely of his time and skill to the efficient organisation of first-aid services, and never failed to do anything asked of him for the good of the Company in operational and administrative arrangements with the utmost goodwill and success'.

Private L A Dunn, under L Corporal H T Bennett, was one of the seven men comprising the Stretcher Bearers Section. He said, 'Due to my poor health, I had to give up the military wing of the Home Guard. So Dr Gerrish recruited me into his band of men who constituted the Ambulance wing of the Home Guard. We trained at his surgery, under his instruction. We were quite separate from the civil ambulance service. Again, for uniform, we simply had an arm band. When the men were out on manoeuvres, we would go out with the MO in one of our own cars, to be at hand in case of injuries, not that I can remember any serious ones'.

In the years when our Country

was in mortal danger

LEONARD ERNEST GEORGE

who served from 4.7.40 to 31.12.44.

gave generously of his time and

powers to make himself ready

for her defence by force of arms

and with his life if need be.

George R.I.

THE HOME GUARD

A Certificate of Recognition and Appreciation by His Majesty King George VI, for the willingness of members of the Home Guard to die in the defence of their homes and their country. This testimonial is the proud possession of Private LE George's daughter, Mary George.

The Mobile Platoon – Observations of a Platoon Commander

'Lieutenant Cornick's men were called "the silent squad" being good at the field craft of camouflage and creeping up on one unobserved', said Private Jim Ollis. Lieut A Paget recalled that the Keynsham platoons all worked closely together and were well disciplined. 'They had a super-efficient platoon that in their training did all sorts of mad things. They were drawn from Nos 1 and 2 Platoons under Lieut W H Conn. On one occasion they broke through the security at Colerne Aerodrome and there they white-washed some planes, and escaped undetected. There was a great uproar about this.'

In his book on the history of the battalion, Lt Colonel Tweedie included a section on 'The mobile platoon, the observations of a platoon commander'. The above Ollis-Paget quotes, supported by what Major Scammell wrote of Lieut Conn, more than indicate that the Battalion Commander was referring to No 2 Company and the platoons mentioned above. The 'observations' then, were written by Lieut Conn himself.

'X Platoon of our Company was to be our Mobile Platoon. The men were largely picked at random . . . Quickly a pride in X Platoon grew. This feeling urged NCOs and men to undertake the most arduous training, with one object in view; to beat the enemy on our ground however well armed he might be.

'To do this, first class discipline must be maintained; if any member did not conform, out he went . . . The ages were from 31 to 57. During prolonged training it was surprising to find that the older men (45–52) were tougher and harder than the men in their twenties who joined us later.

'Early in 1941 night training began in earnest; this commenced with night cross country movement on a compass course. The first lesson we learned was that a squad of ten or twelve men could only manage one mile an hour if the movement was properly and silently done, keeping touch and control. We found how unfamiliar our own country could be in the dark away from roads and especially in fog and mist, and we were pleased to think of what the enemy would make of it if he tried to move off the roads.

'The men of the night learned how to handle high explosives, lay booby traps and so on. It became a regular thing to take part, with special troops, on their night attacks, which often took them afield into other counties. On these trips men wore denim overalls, blacked their faces, wore jersey caps and carried no rifles. The job was to lay explosives and get out undetected.

'We were always successful in getting into aerodromes, however well protected. We were amazed to find how easy it is to crawl through Dannert wire . . . The night squad became very keen on this kind of training, pitting their wits and training against other units; and they became very good at it. On one occasion it was a matter of dispute, some days later, whether we had in fact penetrated a certain strong point. We were able to hand the Commanding Officer a knife and sheath taken from the Sergeant in command of the strong point, having stalked him in the dark, leaving him ignorant of his loss.'

1942

The New Year opened with a steady continuance of winter training, and the arrival of new types of weapons: Thompson sub-machine guns, EY Rifles, being discharger cups fitted to some of their own rifles for projection of Mills no 36 and grenades no 68 (anti-tank), and later, Sten guns and Blacker Bombards. Every new weapon had to be worked out and understood and gradually taught down to Officers, NCOs and men. 2nd Lieut Fray proved himself both mentally and physically agile and a clear instructor.

Range practice continued steadily at Yoxter, Portbury and Clevedon, with some 250 men on parade for these events. Memorable was the first touch of battle inoculation at Clevedon on March 15, when victims, under cover of the sea wall, were joyfully fired at by selected Officers and NCOs with rifles, Browning automatic rifles, tommy guns, Northovers and detonators, very close to them. Major Scammell concluded that it was noticeable that the men appreciated the training in taking cover!

On a more sombre note, Corporal Whittock can still remember in 1942 the death, from consumption he thought, of Tom MacMahon in his section, who lived in Bath Road beyond Ellsbridge House. All the Home Guard members who could be released from work attended his funeral, in which Les was one of the escort of six men who marched from his home to Durley Hill Chapel, where the Officers formed a guard of honour.

Under Military Law, and Compulsory Enrolments

In January Major-General Lord Bridgeman explained that from February 16, 1942, the Home Guard would become part of the Armed Forces of the Crown on an unpaid basis and subject to Military Law and the Army Act when mustered to resist invasion. Attendances for training parades and duties became compulsory under penalty of prosecution in a Civil Curt. The maximum number of hours per month was 48, but regard had to be made to the men's civil employment and other circumstances. Resignations were accepted up to 16 February. Only ten men resigned, being less than 2%.

Training films arrived, and the owners of the Keynsham Cinema patriotically gave the free use of their premises and equipment.

Another important event was the introduction of compulsory enrolment, from June 1942, and the Company obtained quite a number of good recruits, some being quite outstanding.

Outside the Company there were interesting and 'alive' events: co-operation with the Royal Observer Corps and the formation of an Army Cadet Corps, under Mr C K Godwin, who received a commission in the Home Guard. He worked in close touch with both the Home Guard and the Cadets and provided a valuable touch and help with messengers and runners on many occasions.

A Young Soldier

Private Jeffrey Whittock was born in 1928 in Temple Street in the cottage next to Bethesda Chapel, and later moved to the tall houses at the top of Bath

Hill West, whose gardens reached back to the present Town Hall. He left school at fourteen and joined the Home Guard at the end of 1942.

'I was given full uniform, and a .303 Lee Enfield rifle which was quite accurate, which I kept at home with the eighteen inch bayonet. We were all responsible for our own weapons, as there were only just enough. We did quite a lot of square bashing in the Drill Hall. I enjoyed the drill. The elder men were helpful and there was a good esprit de corps. I felt I was a man doing his bit for the country. We had a specialized mortar team for the two inch mortars. At Kenn, Clevedon, we were able to fire live ammunition harmlessly against targets set up on the shore with the sea behind them.

'There was a supply of live grenades and ammunition at the Drill Hall, though we only practised with live grenades at the range at Kenn. You could throw grenades quite accurately up to thirty yards, and there was only a five to seven seconds fuse after you had thrown them. When there was throwing competitions, I always seemed to win', he added modestly.

The ARP Service

Lieut D Kirkwood worked with the Company Commander since September 1938, following the Munich Conference, in ARP warden's duties and the organisation of the ARP service in Keynsham Report Centre. When the LDV was formed, both men transferred their allegiance to the fighting force. Major Scammell recorded that the Lieutenant, "from then throughout proved an efficient chief administrative officer through all the murky doubtful times when nobody was anybody and everybody was somebody. He helped to unravel the many problems. In May 1942, having been previously commissioned with the other officers of the Company, he was promoted to the rank of Lieutenant, but was only on very rare occasions induced to don his uniform".

Not according to Army Regulations

Among those belonging to No 9 Platoon, under Lieut W Morris, was Private Frank Passco, who enlisted in 1939, prior to being called up in 1943. He explained that the Fry's Platoon for security reasons had to consist only of men employed by the company, as at night they patrolled the roofs and the grounds around the factory, and obviously had access to all the main buildings.

Frank did his Home Guard night duty on the roof of Block C where he worked, doing three hours on and three hours off. He considered himself fortunate because he lived in Keynsham, so that he had time after a day's work, to return home for a break before reporting at eight in the evening. However, many of the Bristol workers, with their bicycles, did not have time to go home before reporting for night duty, so they worked through the day, were on unpaid guard during the night, and then back to work next morning.

One Sunday morning training parade remains firmly fixed in Frank's memory. A section of Sergeant T Mill's Platoon at the Roman villa site, were receiving instruction on the firing of the Spigott Mortar (Blacker Bombard), which fired a 2 ft long 14 lb anti-personnel shell or a 20 lb anti-tank projectile. The ammunition was labelled 'drill' but when fired it turned out to be a 'practice' round. Private Passco said it missed him by inches, and fortunately also missed people on the old County Bridge, before hitting the wall of the White Hart Inn (the Lock Keeper), knocking plaster off its wall. Had it been a live shell, he said, it could have demolished the building! The Company's 'History' neither records the incident nor what Major Scammell said about it.

There is a somewhat humorous happening also not recorded elsewhere. An eighteen inch bayonet in the hands of an intoxicated private was a lethal weapon. Consequently, as the wife of a man from 'Brick Town' told me laughingly years later, "On a Saturday night we would hide his bayonet as he could be dangerous when he came home the worse for drink – when he could get it."

A Company Ceremonial Parade

To celebrate the completion of the Company's first two years of service, a ceremonial parade was held on May 31 1942 at Mr Warren's field at Wick Farm, Hunstrete. After an inspection by the Battalion Commander, there was a March Past, followed by a Church Parade Service, conducted by the Rev J W Tunwell of Corston, who had accepted the position of Chaplain to the Company shortly before, and who gave an excellent address. All units marched to the ground and likewise returned afterwards. An excellent band

The Home Guard in defensive positions in a slit trench at Fry's, then in full uniform with rifles, circa 1942/3.

152

from the 12th Batt. of Glouc. Home Guard attended and valuable service was given by the WVS canteen under Mrs Partington.

The British Long Jump Champion

Lieut W Morris was a Cambridge graduate, who held the British Long Jump Record, until in World War I, a German bullet went through his foot. He was the Production Manager for cocoa at Fry's. Major Scammell wrote of the supreme difficulties he had to overcome. 'He had to train No 8 Platoon, which comprised factory defence as well as normal Company life, and it was found necessary to reduce the BAC section which, by reason of their constant industrial changes, had grown too large on paper, and few know of the tact and skill displayed by Lieut Morris in this difficult period. There emerged a leader in Lieut Campbell-Smith in the BAC Section who proved a tower of strength as well as being an outstanding shot, and always Lieut Powell was on the spot, and No 8 Platoon became a more than useful fighting force within the Company.

'A number of other officers received new appointments. Lieut Grosset vacated the command of No 2 Platoon and was attached to East Group HQ; Lieut Cornick succeeded him in command of No 2 Platoon and proved a great success. Lieut Gillard was withdrawn from No 3 Platoon and was attached to West Group; and Lieut Fray was appointed to command No 3 Platoon and led them with great verve and dash. Lieut Gray of No 7 Platoon was seriously ill and was succeeded by Lieut Sutton, who proved a wise and excellent Platoon Commander. Captain HA Frazer, the second in command, was promoted to be the Company Commander of No 3 Company, a great loss to No 2 Company. Lieut Venn, OC No 4 Platoon, was promoted to Captain, to command the West Group of platoons.'

A further encouragement was the commissioning of Corporal H G Thomas and his appointment as the Company's first Intelligence Officer. Corporal H E Learoyd was also commissioned and appointed Platoon Commander of No 4 Platoon at Whitchurch, to replace Lieut Weir who was seconded to assist Captain Venn at West Group. By this time Company strength had reached 591 men, though the highest figure was 656.

November 1942 was an important month for Keynsham as a town, when, as Major Scammell recorded, "we first officially met representatives of the US Army when Col Parke spoke to us at the Drill Hall on the co-operation his Force so much desired with us, and how we could best achieve it".

1943

The Second Battalion Ceremonial Parade

This was held at Clevedon on May 16 1943, when the largest attendance of the Company was achieved, its strength on parade being 31 officers and 377 other ranks, 408 in total. The Battalion Commander inspected and addressed the Battalion and took the salute at a march past along Green Beach. High reports were heard of the apparent strength and business-like appearance of

Sketches by Major FW Tennant, in the possession of Mr CD Gerrish, captioned 'Reminiscences of Dogs in the Field.'

The second caption declares, 'The Home Guards' Midsummer's Day Dream.'

the 7th Somerset Battalion, equipped and steady and obviously purposeful.

Operational duties for the summer of 1943 continued with the Keynsham Drill Hall Home Guard, the Orderly Platoons and the nightly HQ Company duties all being fulfilled. However, because of the competing claims of agriculture, food production, factory production and colliery work, all at this time matters of national interest, training parades were reduced to just one per unit per week, and that one to be compulsory.

May 24 was a sad occasion for Major F W Tennant, who after three years of arduous and valuable service as the Quartermaster and Administrative Officer, was compelled to stand down from active service due to ill-health. Major Scammell wrote of him, "It is impossible to over-estimate the value of his work to this Company in particular, and we venture to think also in the realm of the Home Guard. His duties had been many and varied, his cheerfulness and courtesy limitless, and he achieved the respect and affection of all ranks. His work and attainments were deservedly recognised by the award of the British Empire Medal in the King's Honours List in December 1944".

2nd Lieut Briggs took over the duties of QM, while Lieut Gillard assumed the responsibility of the other administrative work.

The growing strength of the Stretcher Bearers' Section enabled them to combine in Platoon Exercises, particularly on June 12 1943. No 1 and 3 Platoon were engaged in a wood clearing exercise, and deputed their heaviest member to become a casualty, at the farthest point from the collecting base, to test the ability of the stretcher bearers. Corporal Thorne gracefully reclined on the stretcher, while the stretcher bearers groaned and grunted.

Hunstrete Camp

A series of week-end camps proved to be one of the high spots of the Company's history. These were held near Hunstrete Lake by the kind permission of Mr H Leyborne Popham, on June 19th and the following three weekends. Much work and planning by the Company Officers was involved, with training sessions commencing Saturday evening, and continuing through Sunday, though there was a short Church Parade led by the Chaplain before breakfast. Battlecraft and Battle Drill were applied in tactical exercises, with several platoons working and inter-communicating smoothly, reflecting the high standard of training attained.

'On 29 August Lieut Conn with his Platoon gave the Company a demonstration on fieldcraft and camouflage. He seemed, like a conjuror, to produce live human beings and burly Home Guards at that, from positions underneath one's feet and immediate touch, whose presence could not be detected until they moved.' (Major Scammell)

1944

No 2 Company was naturally greatly upset when over sixty men of all ranks were compulsorily transferred to the No 103 Gloucestershire Home Guard 'X' Ack Ack Battery. However, the Company soon achieved a firm friendship with the AA Units concerned and there was 100% attendance on the AA parades by the No 2 Company representatives, and one of them, Corporal J R Jenkins, was awarded a commission in the AA. No 3 Platoon suffered the greatest reduction in its strength, and most reluctantly was disbanded and integrated with No 2 Platoon.

The No 103 Gloucester Home Guard 'Z' Rocket Battery, 'C' Troop

'I had recently joined the Home Guard and on one exercise was in charge of a Browning Automatic Rifle, a "BAR," wrote Edward Cannock. He continued. 'Then I was one of the members of the Keynsham Home Guard transferred to the Anti-Aircraft Unit sited at the Knowle Golf Course which was equipped with rocket projectors. We were a mixed battery, consisting of some regular soldiers, some ATS girls and us Home Guards. I was on duty with Gunners Amesbury, M. Kent, Robert Rowcliffe, and Davidson Smith from Scotland.

'We reported for duty every sixth evening, to fulfil the required 48 hours every month. We were on duty from 10 pm to 6 am. We would have a meal, then sleep, fully dressed, on straw mattresses. If the warning sounded, we were up immediately. There were constant drill exercise alerts to keep us on our toes, though actually, we were never called on to fire the rockets.

'I was chosen to represent the unit at the final Stand Down Parade on

Rear row, left to right, Gunners Amesbury and D. Smith.
Front row, left to right, Gunners E. Cannock, M. Kent and R. Rowcliffe.

157

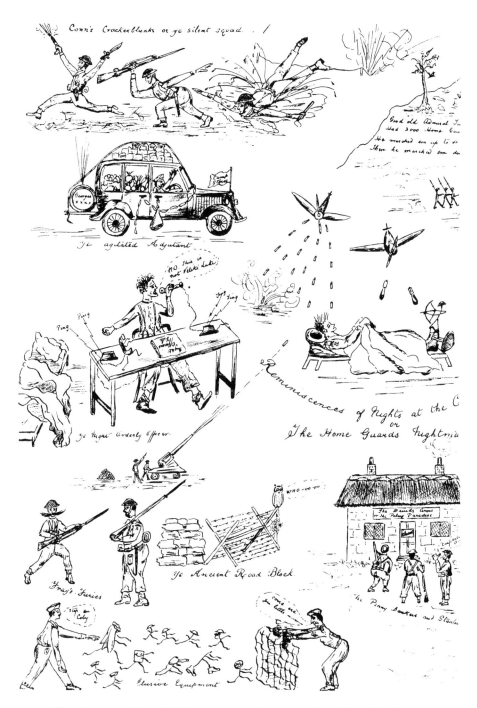

Sketches by Major FW Tennant, in the possession of Mr CD Gerrish.

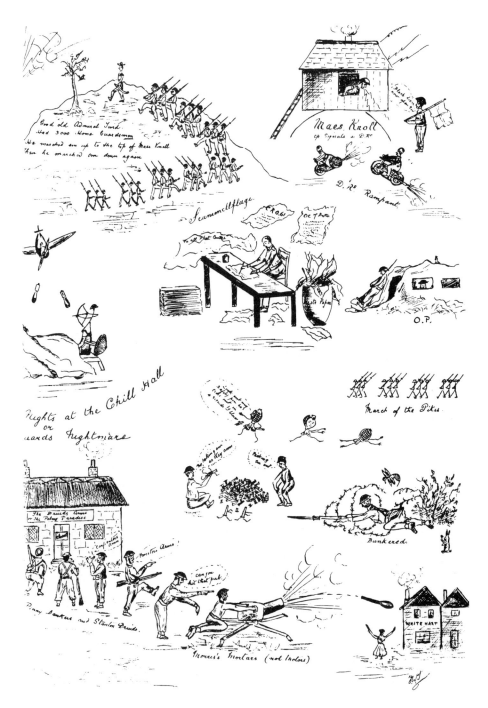

'Reminiscences of Nights . . . at the Chill Hall,' or, 'The Home Guards Nightmare.'

December 3. 1944, at Hyde Park, London. Units came from all over Britain and the salute was taken by King George VI. The Albert Hall was completely filled on the Saturday night by Home Guard representatives attending a special concert sponsored (in appreciation) by the Daily Mail.'

2nd Lieut A J Paget had acted as Company Weapons Training Officer for a time, but on being relieved by Lieut Bond, he was posted to No 6 Platoon under Lieut Blain. Sadly, Lieut G Weir and Lieut P Grosset were forced to resign their commissions on medical grounds.

'Bombing practices went on steadily in the new bombing range constructed by Captain Richards near Burnett, and battle inoculation plus live grenade throwing were really practical training, and valuable. Training twice a week was conducted by Lieut Conn, with some fifty NCOs at each session, which included a demonstration of 75's, Toggle Ropes over the River Chew, games useful in training, and a closing address. Major Scammell recalled that "We retain a vivid memory of some of the heaviest who had not followed the instructor's advice to empty their pockets, hanging upside down on a toggle rope over the Chew, shedding various personal articles to the fish, whilst a running commentary was supplied by the other victims, the most voluble being those who had already done it".

'Salute the Soldier' Week

In support of 'Salute the Soldier Week' a Ceremonial Parade and Inspection on the Keynsham Cricket Ground was held, when His Grace, the Duke of Beaufort, PC, KG, GCVO, inspected No 2 Company and congratulated all ranks on their turn out and steadiness on parade. The following day, Sunday April 16, a tactical display was given to the public in the fields off Wellsway, near Conygre Farm, of live weapon firing and an attack. Captain Richards, assisted by Lieut Bond and other officers, had planned and prepared the event, and the operational units were provided by Platoons 1, 2, 7 and 8, and an initial Guard of Honour was provided by No 4 Platoon.

Major Scammell wrote, 'The main points brought out were: concealment, and the value of camouflage for offensive purposes; the support of the heavier weapons in an infantry attack; the accuracy and power of covering fire by supporting squads; and control of the final assault made under cover of smoke. Lieut Fray was ubiquitous with noises off and explosives and battle noises, and the whole show was very realistic because the public could see the disintegration of the flower pots and other targets by the supporting fire; not only so, but an admirably sustained commentary by Captain Richards, with field amplification, made the points clear for the public to follow. The Battalion Commander, in his capacity as an Admiral, was received by the Guard of Honour, and Mrs Mavis Tate, MP, also attended, and both made very apt and most interesting speeches.'

In a subsequent letter of congratulation from the Battalion Commander, he wrote, "I think all those who saw the demonstration were impressed, and I only wish we could organise a larger public to appreciate all the work you and your officers have accomplished".

The following Wednesday and Thursday an exhibition at the Drill Hall displayed many aspects of Home Guard training. These included the exhibition of many types of weapons and how they worked; the signal unit with their popular pigeon post and DR deliveries; anti-gas equipment; field kitchen; miniature rifle range; medical exhibition; and an intelligence stall with maps, contours, etc; an event in which all ranks were able to participate.

A No 2 Company Officer remembers

The Paget family of farmers arrived at Burnett in 1755 and their descendants still live there at Elm Farm. Mr 'Alf' Paget said his grandfather used to farm land around Steel Mills,Manor Road and Wellsway. At the outbreak of hostilities Mr Paget was farming at Wincanton, where he joined the Home Guard and was appointed a 2nd Lieut. and Second in Command of the Wincanton branch. In 1943 he returned to his beloved Burnett, which his father had been farming, and transferred to No 2 Company. In 1952 he was promoted Captain when Churchill revived the Home Guard during the 'cold war'.

I was delighted to meet an Officer of No 2 Company who was still alive, and was glad to have the opportunity of questioning him about events of some fifty years earlier. Lieut Paget described Major Scammell as 'A great man. There is no doubt that he was very efficient. But he did not suffer fools gladly; then nor do I. We had a happy team here'.

He said that some men were less disciplined than others, particularly those in the loosely-grouped village platoons. Keynsham's platoons all worked closely together and were well disciplined.

"There was a 'Special Transport Services' unit, a suicide squad, which if we were overrun would have gone to the underground shelter at Common Wood, Hunstrete. This was fully supplied with rations and weapons, from which to carry out guerrilla tactics. Lieut Trussler was responsible for this. The men were handpicked from the local areas such as Clutton and Pensford. There is a book in the library about this, called 'The Last Ditch' [D Lampe, 1968, London, Cassell]".

Of the soldier-officer relationship, the Lieutenant said, "We all mixed in very well. We had to." Of the officers' uniform he commented. "There were no Sam Browne belts or anything like that. We had the same uniforms as the men, with just a shirt and tie added. Saluting was cut to a bare minimum. At Stand Down, weapons were handed in, but we were allowed to keep our uniforms, which by then were well worn.

"The massive Burnett Point Stores were also used for refurbishing guns and reboring barrels. There were extensive bunkers for storing shells and so on. ATS girls were camped at Courtenay Road and soldiers at Rockhill Farm. Some 30–40 of them marched up to the camp and back every day.

"There was a detachment of the Bomb Disposal Squad from the Regular Army stationed at the end of Stockwood Vale, who were very brave men. On the approach of enemy planes, they lit up the decoy lights to get them to drop their bombs. All the houses in Stockwood Vale were given really heavily re-enforced shelters, as the troops had. . . The air-raid wardens were centred on the Police Station.

"A number of men were transferred to the Anti-Aircraft batteries, and were picked up by coaches. These batteries were sited all around Bristol, but the Home Guards were not very pleased at having to do that work. There was a battery at Corston, and a searchlight at Compton Dando, driven by powerful generators and manned by regulars.

"The Observer Posts at Winsbury Hill, Burnett, Stantonbury and the Queen Charlton quarries, were all windy exposed places for night duty.

"The average age of the Home Guards was forty or more. There were more than twelve battalions in Somerset alone, because I was in the 12th Battalion at Wincanton." Mac Hawkins in 'Somerset at War', lists 15 Somerset Battalions (p. 130–135); of these, at stand down, the local 7th Somerset (Long Ashton) Battalion, with its complement of 2,507 officers and men, possessed by far the greatest numerical strength.

The civilian occupations of the Home Guards

With a Company over six hundred strong, there was obviously a considerable range of occupations. The Officer Corps, over thirty strong, not unnaturally included a number of professional men, starting with Major W S Scammell, MC, LLB, of 9 Priory Road, who was a practising solicitor in the town. Major RW Tennant, of 17 Station Road, was retired from the Regular Army. Captain FW Partington is believed to have been a lecturer at Bristol University, while Captain GE Richards, VC, was a nurseryman at Willsbridge. Engaged in agriculture was Lieut AJ Paget at Burnet, Lieut JI Derriman at Priston, while Lieut CW Trussler was the estate manager at Hunstrete House.

Lieut RE Cornick was an insurance manager, and Lieut FC Smailes of Bath Road was also in insurance. Lieut P Grosset, DFC, of Bath Road was the manager of the ES and A Robinson paper factory. Lieut GH Blain worked at W and HO Wills and Lieut WM Bond was with a Metal Agencies Company at Bristol. Lieut RH Gillard of Charlton Park was the Managing Director of a department store. Lieut GC Fray was alone in being the licensee of the Horse Shoe Inn, in Temple Street. Lieuts CK Godwin and AJ Membry worked in Bristol.

Lieut GF Clark was the manager of the Westminster Bank, while L/Cpl AW Thackway was the manager of Lloyds. Captain ND Gerrish, the MO, was in practice in Station Road. Lieut W Morris was a manager at Fry's where Lieut AW Powell and Lieut HF Dominey also worked. On the same site, at the BAC section, was Lieut A Campbell-Smith.

Sergt G Camm, like Major Scammell a warrior from WWI, was retired, and tragically, his son Gordon who was in the army, was captured by the Germans, and later, trying to escape, became entangled on the barbed wire and was shot and killed. Sergt Jack Harris, of Park Road was in the rag trade, while Sergt Jack Owen was the estate mason, and a master bell ringer, at Burnett. Corporal LJ Whittock, and his brother Jeff worked on local farms, as did Pts W Scabbings and C Lyons. LCpl AG Hembrow worked at Robinson's, where he sadly lost an arm, had a hook fitted, and carried on serving in the Home Guard.

Miss Mary George kindly phoned me to say that her deceased father, Pte LE George, of No 8 Platoon, lived in Chandos Road a few doors away from his fellow Private, WJ Goodwin. Only a child at the time and the youngest of three, she gathered that "Being in the Home Guard was hard work but father enjoyed it. He had full uniform and a rifle and ammunition, and was on parade through the town. He was also on duty as a 'fire watcher' on the

```
SUBJECT:  Ceremonial Parade Home Guard, Hyde Park, London.
          December 3rd, 1944.


To   Sgt. W.E. Blake, AA/146.
     Gnr. E.J. Cannock, AA/3525.

From O.C.,
          103 Glos. H.G. Rocket A.A.Bttry.


Reference above, you have been selected to represent 103 Battery
at the above parade on December 3rd.

As no doubt you are aware, selection has been based on your
past H.G. record and your keenness and correct military bearing
at all times during your service.    It is assumed therefore
you will accept this honour and agree to be present on the
above date.

Unfortunately owing to short notice, names had to be submitted
by return to higher authority with the result that there was
insufficient time to consult you, before forwarding your
names.

I shall be obliged if you will confirm by return to this H.Q.
your agreement to represent the  Battery.

No expense will be incurred, as you will be issued with return
railway warrants and out-of-pocket expenses for the journey.

Further instructions, times, etc., will be forwarded at a later
date, and on confirmation from you.

                              Capt. R.A.,
                   for O.C., 103 Glos. H.G. Rocket A.A.
                              Battery.

19 Mayfield Park,
Fishponds, Bristol.
14th November 1944.
```

During WW2, Mr E Cannock joined the local Home Guard, but was later directed into the 'HG Rocket Anti-Aircraft Battery'. Following the eventual 'Stand Down' of the Home Guard, Gunner EJ Cannock was one of about a dozen men chosen to represent the area at a special Ceremonial Parade in Hyde Park on Dec 3, 1944. There the salute was to be taken by HM King George VI, to honour the work of the Home Guard. This letter constituted his invitation, which he happily accepted and thoroughly enjoyed.

roof of Fry's." All 62 members of No 8 Platoon did, of course, work at Fry's, plus 12 more in the BAC Section there.

At Pensford a number of Home Guards were coal miners. I am grateful to Lieut Paget and Corporal Whittock for this information.

Stand Down

The final night duty, on 31 August 1944, at Company HQ was taken and conducted by Lieut James on 31st August. So ended a long series of unbroken service by all concerned since June 1940. The last Drill Hall Guard to take resident duty was on September 3, when No 2 Platoon hauled down the Company flag.

The War Office instructed them to stop compulsory drills and training on 11 September. The black-out ended on Sunday 17 September. The 'Smoking Concert' celebrations which followed on Saturday, September 21st, were held at the Drill Hall, for which Captain Partington and a small committee workd hard and with great success. About three hundred attended and spent four happy hours at ease. The programme, entitled 'Operation Relax', would be hard to beat for wit and pith, and the occasion was well supplied with food and drink. At the end of this chapter there is a copy of the four page programme 'Operation Relax', which belongs to Lieutenant Paget.

The Third Battalion Parade

On 28th October the order to 'Stand Down' was received, to be effective from 1st November. A third and final Battalion Parade was held at Ashton Park on December 3rd. This was to be followed by a dinner for the officers of No 2 Company on 9th December.

But for the expense of transport and the difficulty of providing it, the Battalion Commander would have liked to have held a Battalion Parade every six months, to stimulate rivalry between the Companies. However, in connection with the last Battalion Parade, the Battalion Commander wrote, "Finally on 3rd December, a Parade was held at Ashton Park following a Parade March through Long Ashton village, to mark the end of the useful life of the Home Guard – a day not without regrets for most of us, for if our training through four and a half years of our existence had been hard, it had not been without considerable interest, and it had brought together all manner of men in a common cause. In this final parade, there were 1,250 men present, and a representative number of the women who gave such valuable help to the Battalion and Companies".

Private J Whittock remembers the occasion. "There was a special parade, with a number of speeches, in which we were thanked for our services. After that we handed in our uniforms and weapons at the Drill Hall".

The photograph of the Officers of No 2 Company (belonging to Lieut Paget) was taken at 'Stand Down' in the Keynsham Memorial Park, sited roughly where the band stand was erected later.

Mr Charles Gerrish, the son of Captain Gerrish, MB, found among his father's possessions two large sheets of paper, containing light hearted sketches of the Home Guard on duty, drawn by the Company's Adjutant, Major FW Tennant and signed 'FWT'.

The final event was the Officer's Dinner on Saturday, December 9th, 1944. The programme for this event, (also belonging to Lieut Paget) was, unfortunately, printed on thick yellow paper, a colour very difficult to photostat. The front page, like that of Operation Relax, showed the Somerset Light Infantry cap badge. Below it, it read,

"Officer's Dinner – On the Occasion of the Standing Down of the Home Guard from active duties, November 1, 1944, and to Commemorate Voluntary Service in Home Defence from May 16, 1940 [dated] Sat Dec 9 1944".

The Menu list consisted of soup, braised tongue, roast turkey, sausages, vegetables, plum pudding, mince pies and coffee, with an extensive wine list.

The 'Toast List' was,

His Majesty the King	– Major Scammell, MC.
Our Guests	– Captain Partington;
The Company Commander	– Lieutenant Conn;
Toast Master	– Captain Richards, MC.

Then came the heading 'Autographs', of which Lieut Paget collected forty-one, including that of Lt Colonel Tweedie and Major Scammell. With so many signatures of so many Officers mentioned by name in 'The History of No 2 Company' for their outstanding work in the Home Guard, and with so many of them being now in the Battalions of Heaven, this mere programme itself constitutes an historic document.

Final letters

The Defence Medal was given to those who were in the Home Guard all thorough its existence. Others who served for a lesser period received a letter of appreciation from His Majesty, King George VI.

Mrs L Harrison, whose husband was in the Home Guard, values the valedictory letter sent to him in December 1944 from the Battalion Commander, on thin yellowish tissue-like paper so widely used in the war years. It starts,

'To all Officers and Other Ranks, 7th Somerset HQ

Best wishes to you for Christmas and may the New Year be the forerunner to many which bring you and yours much happiness and prosperity.

Our special charge as Home Guards has passed, but the War is not over and maybe the hardest fight still lies ahead.

Penang, Singapore and Hong Kong, all cities more familiar to me even than Bristol, represent millions of people who for generations had implicit faith in Security and Peace under the Union Jack. When the challenge came, we failed them rather ignominiously and we owe it to ourselves and to them to do all in our power to help our forces to utterly destroy the enemy and vindicate once more "Faith in the British Empire".

Wraxall House, Long Ashton. Hugh J Tweedie.'

A further letter, this time from the Company Commander, sent at the same time, reads,

'To: All Officers, Non-Commissioned Officers and Other Ranks at No 2 Company, 7th Battalion, Somerset Home Guard,

STAND DOWN MESSAGE

Everyone of you has given valuable and voluntary service in the Home Guard. You did not actually come to grips with the enemy but you did all in your power to be ready and fit to deal with him if he came, and to defend your area to the uttermost.

Your service and effort has received the recognition and thanks of His Majesty the King and the whole country. Please allow me to express and tender to each of you personally my own sincere admiration for your long and devoted work, my pride in having had the privilege of being your Company Commander from first to last, and my gratitude for your constant and loyal support in our united and joint endeavours.

A Happy Christmas. May a Peaceful Future Year and Good Luck be to you always.

WS Scammell, Major,
OC No 2 Company, 7th Batt Somerset Home Guard, Keynsham. 1944.'

Conclusion

It was the view of the Commanding Officer that, 'The Home Guard in general, the 7th Battalion of the Somerset Home Guard in particular, and (casting modesty aside) the No 2 Company of that Battalion in the very particular, can claim to have deserved success, however indifferently it may have achieved such an elusive end.

All ranks displayed grit and determination, self sacrifice, kindly co-operation, and a great team spirit in a superhuman effort to uphold and preserve the highest principles of human life. What more can be said? Just that we hope our beloved Prime Minister [W Churchill] was right as usual when he said, in 1940, that for a thousand years and more men will say of this country, at this time, that it was their finest hour. To this the Home Guard made its small but sincere contribution.'

* * *

So ended the 20th Century war episode in which if North Somerset had been invaded by the Germans, or 'if the balloon had gone up', the phrase used in those days, Keynsham, at an hour's notice, could have put over six hundred soldiers, disciplined and trained in the use of modern weapons, on the field, determined to defend their homes and loved ones in a Herculean manner, or die in the attempt.

Perhaps there was initially a small element of the 'Dad's Army' about the Company, though even this is highly debatable. A few were 'Old Contemptibles' from World War I and some others little more than boys. Yet it was the WWI men who possessed valuable battle experience. So with enthusiasm and dedication the Home Guard became a force that would have given a first class account of themselves to any aggressor. We will never know how many saboteurs snooping around the highly valuable ammunition depot at Burnett Point, were deterred from planting bombs by the presence on duty there of the Keynsham Home Guard.

Appendices

'The Story of No 2 Company' concludes with Appendix I, on the Organisation of the LDV in June 1940. Appendix II lists Commendations . . . Honours and Awards'. Appendix III is a 'Nominal Roll of All Ranks Serving in No 2 Company', by Platoon, at 'Stand Down' on Nov 1, 1944. Though these appendices extend to five pages, they are given in full as they constitute, in effect, a roll of honour and a recognition of who these men were, who comprised this well trained fighting force, to whom we owe so much.

7TH BATTN. SOMERSET HOME GUARD

APPENDIX I

LOCAL DEFENCE VOLUNTEERS—KEYNSHAM DISTRICT

PARTICULARS OF ORGANISATION, 26th June, 1940

Platoon Headquarters:
Police Station, Keynsham

Platoon Commander:
W. S. SCAMMELL

Second-in-Command:
F. W. TENNANT

Assistant and Group Section Leader for Keynsham Parish:
G. F. CLARK

County H.Q. Area Organisers ·
Col. GIBBS—Major LYON
Territorial Hall, Taunton

Company Headquarters:
Police Station, Flax Bourton

Company Commander:
Admiral Sir HUGH J. TWEEDIE, K.C.B.,
Wraxall House, nr. Bristol

PARISHES	SECTION	SECTION LEADER	POST
Keynsham	No. 1 (Part Mobile)	W. H. CONN	H.Q. Guard
Keynsham, Burnett and Chewton	No. 2 Section / No. 11 Section	P. GROSSET / C. STOKES	Burnett
Keynsham and Queen Charlton	No. 3 Section	F. W. PARTINGTON	Perry's Quarry
Saltford	No. 4 Section	H. P. GRAY	Saltford Golf Course
Whitchurch	No. 5 Section	F. A. VENN	Whitewood Farm / Hursley Hill
Marksbury	No. 6 Section	W. WILLIS	Marksbury Road
Hunstrete and Compton Dando	No. 7 Section	C. W. TRUSSLER	Hunstrete Hill, Compton Dando
Publow, Woollard and Pensford	No. 8 Section	E. W. KING	Pen-y-banc, Pensford
Stanton Drew & Stanton Wick	No. 9 Section	A. FRASER	Bromley Colliery
Norton Malreward and Norton Hawkfield	No. 10 Section	H. T. LANE	Maes Knoll Farm
Priston and Stanton Prior	No. 12 Section	J. I. DERRIMAN	Wilmington Hill

Industrial Sections :
Fry's .. Somerdale .. W. MORRIS .. A. and C. Roofs, Somerdale

Headquarters and Miscellaneous Services :
M.C. Despatch Riders, Messengers, Office Staff, Signallers .. *Volunteer i/c* W. F. BAXTER
Armourer .. .. .. W. H. OLLIS
Keynsham Church Bells.. .. C. J. FORD, also H. NEWMAN

167

APPENDIX II

NAMES OF MEMBERS OF NO. 2 COMPANY WHO RECEIVED OFFICIAL COMMENDATION FOR GOOD WORK IN ENEMY AIR RAIDS AND OTHER BRANCHES OF HOME GUARD WORK

Work in Air Raids :

Capt. FREDERICK ARTHUR VENN
Section Commander HUGH WILLIAM STEVENSON BRADWELL
Pte. JOSEPH JOSHUA SMART
Pte. WILLIAM ALAN HEMBROW
Cpl. EDWARD ALFRED MOUNTAIN
Pte. DONALD REAKES

HONOURS AND AWARDS

British Empire Medal (Military Division) :

Major F. W. TENNANT

Certificates of Good Service. (Mentions in the Honours Lists) :

Lieut. WILLIAM MITCHELL BOND
Sergt. SIDNEY THOMAS MILLS
Sergt. NORMAN WALTER TOVEY
Lieut. WILLIAM HENRY CONN (awarded January 1945)

APPENDIX III

NOMINAL ROLL OF ALL RANKS SERVING IN NO. 2 COMPANY AT THE TIME OF
THE "STAND DOWN" ON 1ST NOVEMBER, 1944

Company Headquarters:

Major	W. S. SCAMMELL, M.C.	Capt.	N. D. GERRISH
Capt.	F. W. PARTINGTON	Lieut.	G. C. FRAY
,,	G. E. A. RICHARDS, M.C.	,,	J. P. T. BRIGGS
,,	F. A. VENN	C.S.M.	O. H. SYKES
Lieut.	G. E. JAMES	Major	F. W. TENNANT, B.E.M.
,,	G. F. CLARK	Cpl.	F. S. CONDON
,,	W. M. BOND	Pte.	W. H. OLLIS
,,	R. H. GILLARD	Sergt.	S. COBERN
,,	H. G. S. THOMAS	Cpl.	L. W. UPTON
,,	H. P. GRAY	Pte.	R. STEWART
,,	D. KIRKWOOD	Cpl.	D. A. RICHARDS
,,	C. K. GODWIN		

Signallers and D.R.'s:

Sergt.	W. H. BONE	L/Cpl.	R. T. WEATHERSTONE
Pte.	J. W. BYE	,,	H. G. WICKINGTON
Cpl.	L. CAVENDER	,,	E. G. WILTSHIRE
,,	A. G. COOK	Pte.	R. W. YOUNG
Pte.	R. O. COOPER	,,	K. F. BRINE
L/Cpl.	P. DEVONSHIRE	,,	A. COOPER
Pte.	R. A. FIELDING	,,	D. A. FRY
L/Cpl.	H. J. MANN	,,	N. A. GULLIS
Cpl.	W. J. MATTHEWS	,,	F. H. LEONARD
Cpl.	A. MACKENZIE	Cpl.	L. F. LINDSEY
Pte.	E. J. PESTER	Pte.	W. N. MARTIN
,,	B. G. PETERS	Cpl.	H. P. T. OCOCK
,,	H. J. STEVENS	Sergt.	W. G. PERRY
,,	R. O. TAYLER	Pte.	F. J. WHEELER
Sergt.	H. F. WARE	,,	T. G. WILLOUGHBY
Pte.	B. V. WATSON		

Stretcher Bearers Section:

L/Cpl.	H. T. BENNETT	Pte.	L. A. POWELL
Pte.	L. A. DUNN	,,	S. SHAW
,,	H. EDOUARD	,,	W. G. SIXSMITH
,,	G. K. FOSTER		

No. 1 Platoon:

Lieut.	W. H. CONN	L/Cpl.	G. T. FISHER
,,	H. F. DOMINEY	Pte.	C. J. FORD
Pte.	I. H. BROOKMAN	Sergt.	D. HAM
,,	R. BURT	Pte.	W. J. HATHWAY
,,	R. H. COLE	,,	F. R. JAMES
,,	L. G. COOK	Sergt.	R. LEAR
,,	W. F. COOPER	Pte.	T. W. OLLIS
,,	H. W. CROOK	,,	E. J. PEARCE
,,	L. E. DAVIS	,,	W. G. RAYSON
,,	S. G. DAVIS	,,	S. G. ROADNIGHT
Cpl.	E. G. DOMINEY	Cpl.	E. R. SHEPHERD
Pte.	A. S. DOOLEY	Pte.	W. E. THOMAS
,,	H. L. ELMER	Sergt.	H. G. TYRRELL
Cpl.	W. A. L. FRANCIS	L/Cpl.	A. E. WARE

No. 2 Platoon:

Lieut.	R. E. CORNICK	Cpl.	J. W. OWEN
,,	A. J. MEMBRY	Pte.	D. L. PRICE
2nd-Lieut.	F. C. SMAILES	,,	S. G. PRICE
L/Cpl.	K. R. BABER	,,	C. L. ROSE
Pte.	W. BAILEY	,,	W. J. RYAN
,,	F. J. BALCOMBE	,,	F. J. SMITH
,,	G. G. BREARLEY	,,	I. L. STABBINS
,,	N. E. BROOKMAN	,,	W. H. STABBINS
,,	J. D. BUTTLE	,,	W. W. STRONG
Cpl.	G. CAMM	,,	T. STEPHENS
Pte.	F. G. DAVIS	,,	W. H. STUCKEY
,,	R. ELLIOT	Cpl.	A. E. TAYLOR
L/Cpl.	N. S. EMMERSON	L/Cpl.	A. W. THACKWAY
Pte.	P. E. FORD	Cpl.	D. H. THORNE
,,	E. T. FOX	Pte.	P. G. J. TURVILLE
,,	W. H. GREENSLADE	,,	E. E. VOWLES
Sergt.	K. J. GRIMES	,,	D. H. WHITE
,,	K. O. HARRIS	,,	G. R. WHITE
L/Cpl.	A. G. HEMBROW	,,	E. C. WIGGINS
Pte.	C. E. JENKINS	,,	H. W. WILKINSON
,,	C. J. LYONS	,,	E. G. WILLIS
,,	P. C. MINTY	,,	J. M. WHITTOCK
,,	W. T. NICHOLLS	Cpl.	L. J. WHITTOCK
,,	A. R. NORTON	Pte.	A. J. WOODHAM

No. 4 Platoon :

Lieut.	H. E. LEAROYD	Pte.	T. B. JAMES
,,	W. J. FROST	,,	A. E. JEFFS
Sergt.	E. V. BAKER	,,	W. H. KING
Pte.	H. C. BARNES	,,	J. E. KING
,,	B. J. BARRETT	,,	W. K. LANE
,,	R. S. BEECHAM	,,	W. H. LEWIS
,,	C. BISHOP	,,	W. G. LLEWELLYN
,,	R. BOWDEN	,,	G. H. MATTHEWS
L/Cpl.	A. E. BOWER	,,	E. P. MURPHY
Pte.	J. BOWRING	,,	C. E. ORCHARD
,,	N. A. CHARD	,,	T. H. PARSONS
L/Cpl.	B. J. CLARK	,,	D. B. PUDDY
Pte.	T. J. COLES	Cpl.	A. P. RAMSAY
Sergt.	J. E. COLSTON	Pte.	R. F. REAKES
Pte.	T. W. COX	Sergt.	G. E. SADLER
,,	W. H. DAVIS	Pte.	F. G. SAGE
,,	G. W. DURSLEY	Sergt.	GILBERT SAGE
,,	H. M. EDGELL	Pte.	R. J. SHORT
,,	A. H. S. EDWARDS	,,	W. W. SMEDHURST
,,	L. W. EDWARDS	Sergt.	A. H. TARRANT
,,	J. EVANS	Pte.	R. A. VENN
,,	N. W. FIDDAMENT	,,	A. VINER
,,	W. F. GILES	,,	G. W. VINER
L/Cpl.	A. W. HAYES	,,	B. G. VOWLES
Pte.	H. B. HILLIER	Cpl.	W. B. WEAVER
L/Cpl.	F. W. HOPSON	Pte.	S. C. WILLIAMS
Pte.	F. A. JAMES		

No. 5 Platoon :

Lieut.	H. F. PALMER	Pte.	E. W. BEACHAM
,,	A. PYM	Sergt.	W. BISHOP
,,	G. PALMER	Cpl.	J. H. BOURNE
Pte.	E. J. V. ASHLEY	Cpl.	A. G. BOWN
,,	W. C. ASHLEY	Pte.	J. H. BOWEN
Cpl.	E. ATKINS	,,	D. BRIDGES
Pte.	W. BABER	,,	E. R. BRIMBLE
Cpl.	E. I. BAKER	,,	S. BRIMBLE
Pte.	W. J. BAILEY	Cpl.	M. W. BROWN
,,	J. BALL	Pte.	A. J. BURGE
,,	W. E. BALL	Cpl.	R. CATHCART
,,	J. BARNES	Pte.	E. W. CHIVERS
,,	R. J. BARNES	,,	M. COLES
,,	A. S. BATES	,,	G. H. COOK

L/Cpl. R. DAGGER
,, W. DAY
Pte. S. H. DUCKETT
,, J. EVELY
,, H. F. FILER
,, F. J. GILES
,, D. H. GILL
L/Cpl. H. GILL
Pte. H. J. GILL
Sergt. C. N. GROOM
Cpl. R. J. HARVEY
Pte. A. HAWKINS
,, K. G. HAWKINS
,, H. J. HEWISH
,, C. C. HOD'DINOTT
,, P. HOWE
,, E. C. HUDSON
,, H. T. HUDSON
,, G. T. C. HUGHES
,, E. W. KING
L/Cpl. D. L. LEECH
Ptc. C. H. CORP

Pte. R. H. McMAHON
,, H. W. MORRIS
,, A. J. PENNEY
,, D. S. PENNEY
,, W. POWER
,, L. A. PRICE
Sergt. A. E. PURNELL
Cpl. B. S. SIMNETT
Pte. G. W. SMART
,, J. SPERRING
,, F. J. SPILLER
,, H. F. STEVENS
,, A. E. SULLY
,, V. H. THOMPSON
,, W. E. THOMPSON
Sergt. N. W. TOVEY
Pte. W. G. TOVEY
,, E. G. WHITE
,, E. J. WINSTONE
,, C. C. YORK
,, N. DRAPER

No. 6 Platoon :

Lieut. G. H. BLAIN
,, J. I. DERRIMAN
2nd-Lieut. A. J. C. PAGET
Pte. S. M. ALLWARD
,, C. E. W. ALLWARD
,, T. W. F. ALLWARD
,, F. BAILEY
,, H. C. G. BAILEY
,, L. BAILEY
,, C. E. BAKER
L/Cpl. N. BAKER
Pte. S. BATES
,, G. F. BEAUCHAMP
,, F. BIGGS
,, A. BIGGS
,, W. H. BOX
,, A. F. BRIDGES
,, J. BRIMBLE
,, W. G. BUCKINGHAM
,, F. A. J. CLARK

Pte. H. F. CLARK
,, L. S. COLES
,, S. COLES
,, J. W. COOK
Cpl. I. F. J. COOMBES
,, C. J. DEACON
Pte. A. J. DEACON
,, W. DYER
L/Cpl. J. FRY
Cpl. F. A. GAGE
Pte. F. G. GARRETT
,, A. L. GARRETT
,, F. C. GARRETT
L/Cpl. G. R. GODFREY
Pte. R. G. HARRIS
,, C. HARVEY
,, C. HATCHER
Sergt. L. M. HAWKER
Pte. H. O. HEUSTON
,, W. E. HILLIER

172

Pte.	W. E. HODDINOTT	Pte.	J. PRIOR
„	H. HUTTON	„	G. RADFORD
„	S. HUTTON	„	A. RAWLINGS
Sergt.	C. JAMES	„	W. RAWLINGS
Cpl.	C. C. LATHAM	„	C. SAMMAN
Pte.	F. J. LIGHT	L/Cpl.	L. R. READ
„	W. LITTEN	Sergt.	E. C. SMITH
„	W. J. LITTEN	Pte.	V. W. G. TANNER
„	H. V. MAGGS	„	S. TAYLOR
Cpl.	G. MILLEN	„	R. L. TIBBOTTS
Pte.	C. NOKES	Cpl.	E. F. WHIPPIE
Sergt.	G. R. PALMER	L/Cpl.	R. T. WHITWHAN
Pte.	A. W. PARSONS	Pte.	H. T. YOUNG
„	A. E. POCOCK	„	J. YOUNG
„	T. H. POCOCK	„	W. J. YOUNG
„	B. POPLE		

No. 7 Platoon:

Lieut.	N. G. SUTTON, M.C.	Pte.	H. W. LAPHAM
Lieut.	L. J. C. BUNKER	Cpl.	C. H. W. LASPER
Cpl.	P. M. BLACK	Pte.	W. F. LITHERLAND
Pte.	A. J. BRAIN	Pte.	A. B. G. LLOYD
L/Cpl.	W. T. BRAY	Cpl.	E. A. MOUNTAIN
Sergt.	R. R. R. DAVIS	Sergt.	J. M. MURRAY
Pte.	L. B. FORD	Pte.	J. H. NASH
L/Cpl.	R. T. FORD	„	J. NICHOLLS
Pte.	E. J. GILLINGHAM	„	D. W. OLIVER
L/Cpl.	H. N. HARPER	Sergt.	W. H. PATTERSON
Pte.	G. R. HAWKER	Pte.	E. W. J. PARSONS
„	H. H. HEAD	„	R. J. PRIOR
„	R. S. HOLLAND	Cpl.	F. W. ROGERS
L/Cpl.	L. C. JAGO	Pte.	P. B. ROWAN
Pte.	F. C. JAMES	Cpl.	A. G. SHORE
„	I. L. JONES	Pte.	D. L. TABRAHAM
Sergt.	S. G. KING	„	W. H. TAYLOR
Pte.	R. H. LANGFORD	„	C. H. WEBB
„	E. W. P. LAPHAM	„	F. C. S. WEYMOUTH

No. 8 Platoon :

Lieut.	W. MORRIS	Pte.	A. H. BOYCE
„	A. W. POWELL	„	H. J. BRADY
Pte.	G. ALLSOPP	„	S. T. BRODERICK
Cpl.	L. E. ALDERMAN	„	F. BRYANT
Pte.	A. N. O. BATHE-TAYLOR	„	D. E. BUNDY
„	C. BOWDEN	„	S. C. COOPER

Pte.	C. R. Cox	Sergt.	S. T. Mills
,,	F. J. Darney	Cpl.	F. A. Owen
L/Cpl.	J. R. Eade	Pte.	E. H. Parsons
Pte.	H. L. Dennis	,,	E. W. Philpot
Pte.	G. Evans	L/Cpl.	J. Porter
L/Cpl.	A. E. Feltham	Pte.	A. Portman
Pte.	P. F. W. Floyd	,,	A. T. Pruett
,,	S. Garland	,,	F. G. Purse
,,	L. E. George	,,	A. Reed
,,	W. J. Goodwin	,,	J. Ricketts
Cpl.	B. Gosling	,,	W. Rogers
Pte.	E. J. Greenslade	,,	R. Ryan
,,	R. W. Gregory	,,	A. C. Sage
Cpl.	A. E. Griffin	,,	J. Strutt
,,	F. H. Hayling	,,	C. L. Thomas
,,	E. A. Iles	,,	A. Walker
Sergt.	H. H. Isgar	,,	H. M. Watts
Pte.	F. W. Jenkins	,,	C. A. Webley
,,	G. Jenkins	,,	H. F. White
,,	R. H. King	Sergt.	W. T. Wicks
,,	G. C. Lear	Pte.	J. Williams
,,	F. R. Lewis	Cpl.	W. Williams
,,	R. E. Light	Pte.	J. J. Wilson
,,	E. J. Maggs	,,	G. H. Young
,,	B. F. Marsh		

B.A.C. Section :

Lieut.	A. Campbell-Smith	Pte.	I. MacMulkin
Pte.	J. Harper	,,	T. J. Mills
L/Cpl.	R. A. Harris	,,	L. R. Milton
Pte.	D. N. Higgs	L/Cpl.	S. R. Skuse
L/Cpl.	C. A. Holloway	Pte.	F. W. Webb
Cpl.	G. V. G. Holloway	,,	J. White

No. 9 Platoon :

Lieut.	F. HARDING, D.C.M.	Pte.	H. T. LANE
Pte.	A. E. BELL	,,	I. W. LANE
Cpl.	H. O. BURTON	Sergt.	F. W. LEAT
Sergt.	R. J. CARTER	Pte.	A. G. LOCK
L/Cpl.	C. J. CLARK	L/Cpl.	V. C. LOCK
Pte.	W. H. CLARK	Pte.	E. H. G. MACKARKNESS
,,	R. W. Corbett	L/Cpl.	B. K. MARDON
L/Cpl.	H. A. FEAR	Pte.	C. MARCHANT
Pte.	H. W. FLOWER	Cpl.	C. McKINNON
,,	G. W. GILPIN	Pte.	S. W. PITMAN
,,	C. I. GEORGE	,,	S. ROBERTSON
,,	H. R. GOODMAN	Sergt.	G. E. ROACH
,,	R. H. GOODMAN	Pte.	R. J. RUDD'
,,	D. B. HASELL	,,	V. J. SINGER
,,	A. J. HASELL	,,	W. S. TAYLOR
,,	V. W. HOWE	L/Cpl.	M. C. THOMPSON
,,	W. M. HOWE	Pte.	S. G. TUCKER

The Home Guard was re-formed in 1952 and put on reserve in 1956.

Keynsham and surrounding areas were covered by E Company of 3rd/4th Somerset (Bath) Home Guard Battalion.

E Company was commanded by:-
Major G Thompson
Captain AJC Paget 2 I/C

The Battalion Commander, Lt Colonel Sir HJ Tweedie, concludes his History of the '7th Somerset Bn Home Guard,' firstly with an appendix recording that Pte G Lovell, No 1 Company, was 'Killed by Enemy Action While on Duty' and 'Sgt Les Tripp, No 4 Company, [was] Killed by Enemy Action.' Of those, 'Wounded by Enemy Action,' in No 2 Company, were Pte AE Norris and L/Cpl. Alfred E Feltham. He then lists the HQ Officers, and lastly records the names of all the Officers of the 9 Companies. Space forbids the full lists; No 2 Company shows the format followed.

7TH SOMERSET BATTN. HOME GUARD

LIST OF OFFICERS WHO HAVE SERVED IN No. 2 COMPANY

COMPANY COMMANDER
Major W. S. Scammell, M.C.

SECONDS IN COMMAND
Capt. H. A. H. Fraser   Capt. F. W. Partington

OFFICERS COMMANDING GROUPS OF PLATOONS
Capt. G. E. A. Richards, M.C.   Capt. F. A. Venn

PLATOON COMMANDERS

Lieut. H. J. Bewley	Lieut. W. Morris
Lieut. G. H. Blain	Lieut. H. E. Learoyd
Lieut. W. H. Conn	Lieut. H. F. Palmer
Lieut. R. E. Cornick	Lieut. N. G. Sutton, M.C., Croix de Guerre
Lieut. R. H. Gillard	
Lieut. H. P. Gray	Lieut. C. W. Trussler
Lieut. P. Grossett, D.F.C.	Lieut. F. A. Venn
Lieut. F. Harding, D.C.M.	

OTHER OFFICERS

F. W. Tennant, B.E.M. (Major, retired)	Lieut. A. J. Membry
	Lieut. A. G. C. Paget
Capt. N. D. Gerrish (M.O.)	Lieut. A. W. Powell
Lieut. W. M. Bond	Lieut. A. Pym
Lieut. L. J. C. Bunker	Lieut. H. G. S. Thomas
Lieut. A. Campbell-Smith	2nd-Lieut. J. P. T. Briggs
Lieut. G. F. Clark	2nd-Lieut. M. E. Brodie
Lieut. J. I. Derriman	2nd-Lieut. W. J. Frost
Lieut. H. F. Dominey	2nd-Lieut. C. J. Horlick
Lieut. G. C. Fray	2nd-Lieut. G. Palmer
Lieut. C. K. Godwin	2nd-Lieut. F. C. Smailes
Lieut. G. E. James	2nd-Lieut. G. M. Weir
Lieut. D. Kirkwood	

Chapter 10

When the Americans came to Keynsham

It was in the summer of 1943 when Keynsham awoke to find that the American Army had arrived. Unlike World War I when muleteers were billeted on the local populace, the local Americans had their own barracks in Pixash Lane, one for white soldiers and another for black troops. Other detachments were billeted around the Bristol area, in the Tickenham and Ashton Gate areas and between Warmley and Staplehill.

They were in England as part of the build-up of forces prior to D Day, June 6, 1944, and the Invasion of Europe. They were involved in the transporting of weapons and ammunition from the Keynsham goods yard to the massive arsenal near Burnett Point, together with guard duty there.

'We used to see the glow of the landing lights when they were full on at Colerne airdrome, set against the blackness of the night sky, at the approach of the USA aircraft. We felt that here at last was the extra help that we needed. At the actual time, the Americans were great company and gave us the feeling that someone could and would give us a hand', recalled Miss M Fairclough.

'I vaguely remember them going round in their large army lorries. I used to cycle past their big camp near Warmley on my way to work at Patchway, where they were camped in large tents for sleeping and eating', recalled Mr Jim Ollis. He continued: 'I recall white Americans walking down the High Street with their arms round our local girls. They used to go to the Lamb and Lark Hotel a lot for drinks. As Americans go, the soldiers looked reasonably smart. A couple of girls married "GIs", one being from St Anne's Avenue and still in the States. She was Ada Down, whose brother William still lives in St Anne's Avenue. The girls were about 19–20 years old, and are happily married and my daughter corresponds with one of them.'

I discussed the subject with various Keynsham ladies. One of them said, 'A number of Americans were to be seen in the Fear Institute but no coloured ones; it was mainly the REME who used the Institute. The Americans used to come in from the huge Ashton Gate camp. They were quite popular and well accepted by the town's people. I never heard anything against them. They were 'hot stuff' and the younger local girls ran after them. They were not often seen in the local shops as they were so well provided for with confectionery and tobacco: for them it was more window shopping as they walked out with our girls. A number of local families entertained them.'

Another lady confirmed that there were a number of local romances, but she had no photographs to show, as films had been difficult to obtain in war time. She said that the Americans were not a common sight here, 'as they were mainly just passing through'. However she added, 'They attended the local dances at the Drill Hall, which were accompanied by a small band of three or four musicians. Mother would give a bed to American or Canadian soldiers who were just passing through, as part of her war effort. They would arrive on a Saturday morning and sometimes would help me with my homework'.

A third lady recalled that as children 'We thought the Americans' speech was rather peculiar and that they were not really real, as we had only seen them in the past in the cinema. There was a little mimicking of how they spoke, from "Hello" to "Hi". Among themselves elderly residents mocked their accent and manner of speech. There was certainly ample evidence for the accusation that the Americans were "Over paid, over sexed and over here." Their riposte was that the British were "underfed, underpaid, undersexed and under Eisenhower".

One lady mentioned that there were a number of coloured soldiers in the town. 'There used to be a bakery where "Alder King" is now. On one occasion the lady behind the counter was quite frightened when for the first time in her life, a large black American soldier in uniform appeared and seemed to tower over her as he waited to be served. The lady whispered to another customer, "Please don't go until he's gone". She need not have worried. . . .' But the "Hole in the Wall" restaurant in Bath, much used by our overseas visitors, acquired a notorious reputation.

Mrs Ann Randall has kindly contributed the following fascinating article entitled,

'The United States Army invasion of Keynsham'

'It must have been 1943 when they came. They were in temporary camps, some under canvas, mostly at Burnett, and I believe they were also in billets in some homes.

The High Street was full of them in the evenings and at week ends.

At that time I attended the Baptist Church in Keynsham and many of them came to the services and were then taken home by members of the congregation to dinner or tea.

As children, (I was 13 at that time), we were invited to attend the 'ball game' (baseball) at the Frank Taylor Memorial Ground, Wellsway, in the summer. Cricket was not played there then as most of the local team were in the forces, except for Dr Claude Harrison (related to Dr WG Grace). When my father asked Dr Claude about this game the Americans were playing on the cricket ground, his reply was, "It's only the children's game of rounders, Harry" so my father was not impressed, especially thinking that they might destroy the cricket pitch for ever! We had to buy a six penny (old money) savings stamp for entrance. I remember going on several Saturday afternoons with my brother.

They had put up temporary stands for us to sit in. We were given sweets the like of which we had never seen before. There was almost a one to one American friend beside us who would tell us about the game as it progressed. We then understood the words of the game, the "mound" where the pitcher stood, and "wound up" to throw the ball, we hoping the batsman would hit it out of the ground and go for a "home run". They made it all sound very exciting, but in effect it was just as Dr Claude had said – "a children's game".

Music was played over a loudspeaker during the interval and we were introduced to popcorn and the sound of Glenn Miller.

The JN Fear Institute was used by US Forces as a canteen/club. I am sure many a young lady at that time learned to "jitterbug" at the dances held in the old Drill Hall.

We found the Americans very friendly. They were taken aback by our Spartan way of life and when they saw our "rations" they truly thought we were starving. The local cinema in Charlton Road was always full to overflowing at every performance but I dare say many of them went to Bristol or Bath for what entertainment there might have been available at that time.

In 1944 as suddenly as they came, they went and as the war in Europe drew to a close they were sent either for a tour of duty to Europe or back to the United States.'

Ann mentioned that while the Americans were here, it was almost impossible to walk down the High Street at the week-end as there were so many soldiers about and people spilling over into the road. There were many more white than black Americans present. At such times there would be both jeeps and lorries around.

Marriages of American soldiers to Keynsham girls

There were certainly a number of matrimonial alliances between soldiers and local girls. To ascertain the exact number, both the register of civil marriages and those in the Free Churches would need to be consulted. The Marriage Register at St John the Baptist, Keynsham, contains a few such entries. Three of these were dated 1945, the last year of the war, and are as follows:

'17 Feb 1945. Harold Fay OTT, 22, bachelor, Private, USA Army, 2 Wick House Cottages, Bath Road. Father – Harrison OTT, farmer, [to] Jocelyn Marie LEWIS, 19, spinster, cost clerk, 2, Wick Hs Cott, Bath Road, Keynsham. Father, George James LEWIS, clerk'.

'25 Feb 1945. Lake MARTIN, 24, bachelor, Private, USA Army, 13, St George's Road, Keynsham. Father, Lake MARTIN, deceased, farmer. [to] Fay Medora HODDINOTT, 21, spinster, typist, 13, St George's Road, Keynsham'. Father – Reginald H HODDINOTT, traveller. By licence. Minister, V Shaw. The two young Americans, presumably stationed in Keynsham and both with farming backgrounds and possibly friends, found love and solace here, before participating in the invasion of Europe in 1944, and later, marriage.

'10 Oct 1945. James Proctor DENNISON, 36, bachelor, T/5 US Army, 91 Linden Avenue, Bloomsfield, New Jersey, father – Harry Clark DENNISON, retired, [to] Margaret READ, 31, spinster, stenographer, 22 Bristol Road, father – Albert G READ, accountant.'

Ann Randall remembered the celebrations at the wedding of Fay Hoddinott. 'In spite of the food rationing we had a street party in the road at St George's where she lived. I saw her leave the house dressed in white. Neighbours brought their drinks out and there was dancing in the

179

street to music. The party took our minds off what was happening around us. They now live in America.'

She added that Fay had two brothers. During the war Robert H Hoddinott was in the Royal Navy and, sadly, was lost at sea. His name is on the local Memorial Roll. The other brother saw service in Germany and is believed to be living there with his German wife.

Mr J Ollis was correct when he spoke of the marriage of Ada Down but it was fifteen years after the war. The Register at St John's states,

'3 Dec 1960. Raymond Wilmer CLEWLEY, 23, bachelor, RAF Station, Fairford, Glouc. Father – Adelbert CLEWLEY, labourer, [to] Ada Eleanor DOWN, 20, spinster, factory worker, 5 St Anne's Avenue, Keynsham. Father – William John DOWN, deceased, labourer.'

Ada's brother William of St Anne's Avenue said that Raymond, a ser-

The wedding reception of Sergeant Raymond CLEWLEY, of the United States Air Force, to Miss Ada Eleanor DOWN, on 3 December 1960. They were married at St John's Church, Keynsham, and the reception was held at the then Co-operative Store's Hall, used now by the Jehovah's Witnesses. Due to distance, none of Raymond's family or fellow servicemen attended, though the church was well full. Ada was not worried about marrying an American, being only nervous of flying there. Soon after arriving in the USA her mother arrived for a six months' holiday, her sons financing the flight. Ada's brothers said they would bring her back if she was unhappy! Fortunately, this proved to be unnecessary. Today Raymond, as chief mechanic, is in charge of Maine University's transport.

geant, was a mechanic attached to the RAF at Fairford. A party of 3 or 4 Americans frequented the Fox and Hounds public house, where they met Ada and her friend Rosie Tucker. Subsequently the two girls married two of the Americans. After the wedding, Raymond had to complete two further years of duty. Today, happily married, Ada lives in Bangor, Maine, USA, with their two children, Shaun and Peter.

An octogenarian remembers

"During the war we had a Morrison shelter in our Dapps Hill home. We were very glad to have it, for we were frightened to death during the raids. With my husband away in the army, we felt safe in there with the children and sometimes we slept there all night, or at least until the siren sounded the 'all clear'. Towards the end of the war when things had died down, we didn't use it, and as the children kept hitting themselves against it, Dr Claude had it removed for us," recalled Mrs Minnie Bates.

"There were a lot of Americans in Keynsham passing through. They were very nice people and very polite, though there were too many of them. The coloured ones were few and far between. The soldiers were billeted at Pixash Lane and they used the accommodation long after the war, as late as 1960. Yes, some of our girls did become 'GI Brides'.

"I used to visit my parents in Bristol, where the bombing was very severe. One day I was coming back to Keynsham on a bus when an American soldier got on. He looked at Wilf and said, 'What a nice little lad' and taking a packet of gum from his pocket, he asked, 'Am I allowed to give him this?' When we got to the bus stop by St John's church, he lifted him off the bus, kissed him, and said, 'He's going to grow up to be a little general'. He was only a young man and I thought how nice he was. I never saw him again."

In conclusion, turning from Minnie's delightful story, and the talk of old Keynsham families, to the departure of the Americans in 1944 for the invasion of France, Ann Randall (then Ann Stevens) commented, 'When the Americans left, some people were gratified. There was a general sigh of relief, for the town had been sinking under the weight of the people. As a small town we weren't used to that.'

Chapter 11

Memories from the Home Front
The autobiography of Jean Williams, a wartime wife and mother

My husband's father, Henry Williams, was already dead when I met Bill, but his mother Edith (always Mam to her sons) was a marvellous woman with a quiet sense of humour which Bill inherited, as did most of her five children, Dorothy, John, Percy, William and Joan.

When I knew her first in the mid 1930's she was about 56 and I look back in wonder at the difference in dress between her and me, now in my 70's. She and her sisters, Thirza and Nell, were always dressed in black or navy blue, black wool or lisle stockings and, to go out, a black hat, with their long hair done in a bun held in place with hair pins.

The house at 1, Rock Road was always spick and span, with shining brass on the doorstep and in the living room. Everyone had to help as she went out to work almost to the last year of her life and took in washing, in the days when it was done in a coal boiler – later a gas one – with a huge wooden mangle under cover in the tiny garden, to get the worst of the wet out.

Amongst other places they worked at the Vicarage – where Vicarage Green now stands – for the Vicar's wife, and always did the cleaning of the Parish Church of which Thirza was the Verger until about two years before she died, and that cleaning was mainly scrubbing.

Like myself in later years, Bill's mother had a husband away at war and later, when he died from the ravages of malaria, had to bring up five children alone.

There were no special allowances for one parent families in those days, no Family Allowances or Housing Benefits! Just a widow's pension and what you were able to earn, and that went on all her life; but when she died all her grandchildren had had their half-crown's for their birthdays for that year and she owed no one any money!!

Bill was like his father in that he always looked stern and forbidding until you knew him and then he was a different person. He was as solid as a rock, with a great sense of humour; a loving husband and a devoted father to our three children, Valerie, Colin and Geoffrey. Bill was a strict disciplinarian, insofar as everyone knew to what limits they could go, and the children were smacked hard when they were naughty.

After the war ended Bill moved to Oxford, where he worked for a milk company as manager at one of their large branches. After his mother died Bill moved back to Keynsham, with all our belongings and the family, complete with fish tank, in the back of the furniture removal lorry. As we drove at last up Bath Hill he said, "Home at last and it's raining". For the next 20 years he worked as a Factory Records Clerk at Fry's, Somerdale. Sadly he had to

DESCRIPTION OF MAN

Age 25 yr 18 days   Height 5 ft. 7¼ ins.

Colour of eyes Grey   Colour of hair Dk brown

If this Certificate is lost or mislaid, the fact must be at once reported.

The finder should send it to the nearest Local Office of the Ministry of Labour and National Service.

[75996] 30128/5836 750m 9/39 M&C Ltd. 706

The 'Description' of 25-year-old William when he joined up in 1940 was that he had 'grey eyes' and 'dark brown hair', and was 5 feet 7 inches tall.

DISCHARGE CERTIFICATE.

If this Certificate is lost no duplicate can be obtained.

1. Army No.	2. Surname
5385913	WILLIAMS

3. First Names WILLIAM GEORGE.

4. Effective Date of Discharge	5. Corps from which Discharged	6. Rank on Discharge
25 OCTOBER, 1948	ROYAL ENGINEERS	SAPPER

7. Service with the Colours	8. Service on Class A.T. Reserve	9. Total Service
5 Years 339 Days	2 Years 161 Days	8 Years 185 Days

10. Cause of Discharge

11. Campaigns and Service Abroad

N.W. EUROPE 6.6.44 To 28.2.46

12. Medals	13. Military Conduct
1939-45 STAR; FRANCE & GERMAN STAR; DEFENCE MEDAL; WAR MEDAL 1939-45.	Exemplary

Signature and Rank, Officer i/c Records.

Date 16 FEBRUARY, 1949   Place BRIGHTON

[S.11638] 250,000
Bw. 1/47 G.9999

3037507

When he finally resigned from the Army Reserve on 16 February, 1949, it was recorded that his 'Military Conduct' had been 'Exemplary'.

183

be medically retired and throughout his 9 years' illness he remained a man of great character and courage.

We had been married for nearly 45 years when he died in 1981 and our family lost its anchorage and a man dearly loved, a man who did not want to leave his family and fought so hard for his life, refusing to be an invalid.

Now for the years 1939–1946 as we women knew it, especially the young wives left alone. My sister's husband, Bill Taylor, was in North Africa in the Air Force. My mother's husband, Jim Douglas, my stepfather, was in the Middle East, having been recalled to the army at 43 years of age on his last month of 12 years service in the Army Reserve, and was a survivor of Dunkirk. Nowhere in the family did we have a man at home.

So the first years dragged on with rationing, blackout and air raids; with little money – 15/- (shillings) a week for a wife and two children and part of that stopped from the man's pay. My sister Sylvia and I and our four children ended up living in my Mother's old rambling house in Frampton Cotterell, Gloucestershire, only reached by two lanes, between plum and apple orchards, with a bucket lavatory at the bottom of a huge garden.

We pooled the rations, making food easier. My mother kept chickens and so we had fresh eggs and poultry to eat for Christmas. We grew all our own vegetables and of course, in season, we had to pick the fruit in the orchards and from that we made jams and preserved a certain amount.

My mother is still alive today; at 89 years old, living in Keynsham on her own. [Sadly, no longer with us] In those days of war she thought nothing of going out and killing a chicken for our dinners or a rabbit. We used to pick hundreds of pounds of plums in season and the market men would pick them up each day and pay us one old penny a pound.

We had severe winters when we would be snowed in, sometimes for six weeks without a bus; trees would be blown down across the lanes and we would have to saw our way out. Luckily there was no shortage of firewood then.

When you needed a bath you had to walk around the side of the two-winged house to fetch buckets of water to fill the boiler and of course you did not dare to let the fire go out even in the hottest or bitterest of weather. What a difference from today's living standards with bathrooms, hot and cold water and indoor toilets! That was the only way to get hot water.

Clothes were a problem with clothing coupons and little money. I learned from my mother how to dressmake and made all the children's clothes, boys and girls, mostly from other people's cast-offs. The three boys were so proud when I learned how to put proper pockets into their trousers: they do not remember anything about it now.

Eventually my sister and I both took part-time work; me tailoring with Watham and Gardiner, and Sylvia at an aircraft factory, which was bombed by stray bombers several times at Yate. We each gave mother half of our wages for looking after the children. Our lives were all work, but it was just as well, as we missed our menfolk so much and I remember thinking at 25 that the war would never end, or that when it did we would no longer be young or ever carefree again. How right I was; we were all different people by the time peace came.

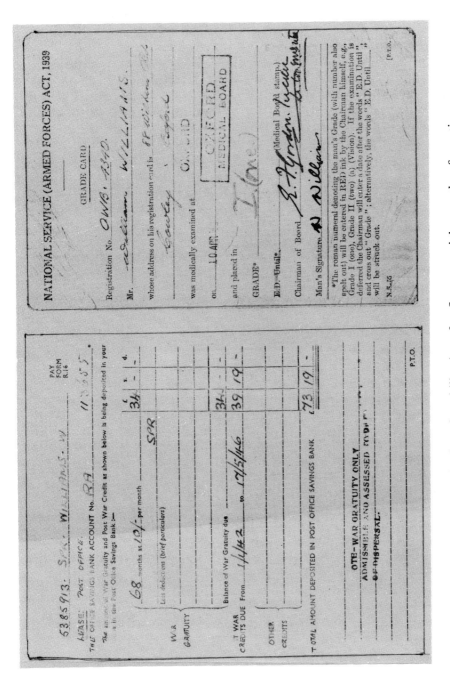

What a soldier received on demobilization after five years eight months of war-time service.

During these years the bombing of the area went on: bombs in Keynsham High Street luckily did little damage. Frampton Cotterell was also bombed by stray bombers and you could always see the barrage balloons. We watched the dog fights in the summer sky of 1940 when the aircraft factory at Filton was attacked two days running, with our fighter aircraft so high waiting to pounce on them.

We stood in the bedroom looking out of the window at 1, Rock Road, Keynsham, in November 1940 and saw Bristol burning. Bill's mother and youngest daughter were crying and terrified. To this day my whole being jumps at the sound of a siren and my mind still can see the miles of firemen's hoses and the "Danger – Unexploded Bomb" notices all through the city and the bombed trains of Temple Meads Station.

From autumn 1940 to the following Easter, the siren seemed to go every evening at dusk and the all-clear would not sound till daybreak. One night over the German radio, Lord Haw Haw boasted that the Luftwaffe were going to raze Castle Street, Bristol, to the ground, which they did the following Sunday night. One night in November 1940, Bill's mother's brother, Archie Newman, and his wife Dollie were killed in a raid at Brislington, where they lived near the King's Head. They were among 70 people buried in a large communal grave.

There were not many purpose-built shelters. Most people sheltered under a strong table or below the stairs. My daughter Valerie recalls that at Rock Road during the bombing, 'we cuddled together on a mattress all night, frightened to death, under the stairs'.

Our children had never seen a banana or an orange; they had no sweets, and only home-made toys, but it is very true that what you have never had you never miss, and so they were content. Even the big rugs on the flagstone floors in my mother's house were hand-made on a huge wooden frame, from good sacks and cut-up rags. Everybody helped and nothing was wasted, and I think that that idea has stayed with my generation all our lives.

In Keynsham during the war, part of the famous chocolate factory at Fry's (now Cadbury's) was taken over by the Bristol Aeroplane Company. There many local girls and wives, who had earlier only been engaged in domestic service or possibly had never worked at all, gladly entered into their war service, making parts for planes.

On cycling home from work one day in May 1945 I heard that the war in Europe was over. A non-smoker and a teetotaller I bought a small bottle of whisky and a packet of cigarettes, and to my mother's disgust my sister and I sat and smoked the cigarettes and drank the whisky, not able to cope with the anti-climax in our lives.

It was nearly another year before Bill came home from Hamburg. At my daughter Valerie's school in Oxford a special letter from the King was passed to the children of that school whose fathers were still away on VJ day. Out of all the pupils in the school, there were only three men away on active service, Bill being one of them. Six of the best years of our lives had been spent lonely and apart. No one can know what it was like, unless they had lived through those years.

My jealousy of women of my age (25–30) whose husbands were in reserved occupations, when I saw them together, was quite terrible. More so as I have never been a jealous or envious person, but the years of 1940 to 1946 seemed so utterly wasted, with no husband in my life. Thousands of women must have felt the same, my mother and my sister among them, but we never spoke of these things. A tight veneer was kept on our lives until the end of the war.

I can remember when Bill came home. We were back in Oxford as we had had a chance of renting a house there. I went there with my two children on VJ day, in an altogether strange part of Oxford. We went up the Iffley Road by bus and then walked, passing VJ parties being held in the streets. With all the effort to get there, we had quite forgotten that it was VJ day. It must have been August 14 1945.

Bill came home from Hamburg in March 1946. The army wanted him to stay on, but he'd had enough. He wanted to be back with his family. I met him at Oxford railway station, with Valerie and Colin. We were overjoyed. It was wonderful to have him home. We intended never to be parted again. Later, in 1954, we finally came home to live in Keynsham again, for good.

PART TWO

AT THE BATTLE FRONT

Chapter 12

William ('Bill') George Williams, 1915–1981
'I was there'

The auto-biography of a Keynsham soldier, posthumously assembled by his widow, Mrs Jean Williams, from her husband's lengthy record of his war service.

* * *

My mother's family, the Newmans, and my grandmother's, the Ollises, have lived in Keynsham for centuries, the Newmans going back to the 11th Century and one of them always being associated with the Parish Church of St John the Baptist. The Ollis family, as is well known, came originally from Holland or Germany.

I was born on 21 March 1915 at 1, Rock Road, Keynsham, in the County of Somerset, the third son and fourth child of my parents, Edith and Henry (Harry) Williams, whilst my father was in India on Active Service with the Somerset Light Infantry. He had met my mother when he came to Keynsham as Recruiting Colour Sergeant for the Somerset Light Infantry. A Londoner – born in Bow – he was always known as 'Cockney' Williams to the local people, and was a founder member of Keynsham Silver Band, playing the Double-Bass. In later years my brother Percival played the euphonium and I played the cornet. When Keynsham Cinema was built, the opening was a big occasion, and I played cornet solo, it being the only time that my mother went to the Cinema.

In those days we were comfortably off financially until my father was invalided out of the Regular Army due to malaria. He took the job as part-time caretaker of the Drill Hall on Bath Hill and life was quite good for those years, until he died when I was nine years old in 1926. Some older local people still remember his funeral, the biggest they had ever seen in Keynsham, with full military honours.

Then followed years of poverty, and my mother had to go out to work and take in other people's washing. I remember the house was always filled with wet washing or ironing. I have the postcard that mother sent me when I was about twelve in 1929 saying, 'You must get a loaf of bread and ask Louie (my aunt) if she will lend me ½ penny to go with this one for your dinner (of chips only). Could you scrape some potatoes after you light the fire tonight'.

I tried to join the Army and the Police Force several times as there was terrible unemployment in the country, but was always refused because I did not quite reach the 5' 9" minimum height.

191

NATIONAL SERVICE (ARMED FORCES) ACT, 1939

ENLISTMENT NOTICE

MINISTRY OF LABOUR AND NATIONAL SERVICE
EMPLOYMENT EXCHANGE,

Date .... **5 JUN 1940**

Mr. W. Williams,

83, Wilkins Road,

Cowley, Oxford.

Registration No. ON.B.4340

DEAR SIR,

In accordance with the National Service (Armed Forces) Act, 1939, you are called

upon for service in the .... TERRITORIAL ARMY .... and are required to present yourself
between 9 a.m. and 12 noon
on ..Thursday........ 13 JUN 1940 ...... 19......., at 10 a.m., or as early
as possible thereafter on that day, to :—

INFANTRY

OXFORD & BUCKS. LIGHT INFANTRY, COWLEY BARRACKS, OXFORD,

OXFORD

.... (nearest railway station).

A Travelling Warrant for your journey is enclosed. Before starting your journey you
must exchange the warrant for a ticket at the booking office named on the warrant. If
possible, this should be done a day or two before you are due to travel.

A Postal Order for 4s. in respect of advance of service pay, is also enclosed. Uniform
and personal kit will be issued to you after joining H.M. Forces. Any kit that you take with
you should not exceed an overcoat, change of clothes, stout pair of boots, and personal kit,
such as razor, hair brush, tooth brush, soap and towel.

Immediately on receipt of this notice, you should inform your employer of the date
upon which you are required to report for service.

Yours faithfully, J. W. ALGAR

Delete
if not
applicable

N.S. 12   (4884) Wt. 27800—8813 9/39 B.W. 677

William's 'Calling up' papers, dreaded by many.

T47-245.   Date as postmark.

My address until further notice will be :—

Number (if any) and Rank 5385913 SAPPER.

Name in BLOCK letters WILLIAMS. W.G.

Squadron, Battery, Company } No. 5. E.S.O.D.
or R.A.F. Unit

Battalion, Regiment, etc. } R.E.
or R.A.F. Formation

FORCE, APO No. or Place Name B.W.E.F

Signature W. G. Williams

INSTRUCTIONS.—Use this card to notify a change in your address. Fill
in the particulars above and send it to (A) your relatives and friends and
(B) to your O.C. Unit to enable him to redirect your correspondence.

Later, an official card giving but a brief address. 'Careless talk (or writing) costs lives'
was the motto in those days.

Oxford 1940
Private W.G. Williams, of the
Oxford and Buckinghamshire
Light Infantry

During this time I married my wife in Keynsham Parish Church and much against my wishes I found employment in the Pressed Steel Works at Cowley in Oxford and moved there to live, understanding that it would be a reserved occupation if the rumours of war should come to anything.

On 3 September, 1939, a beautiful summer Sunday, I heard Neville Chamberlain's broadcast saying we were at war with Germany, not realising how all our lives would change, and that we would live a lifetime in the next six years.

On 10 April, 1940, I was called before a medical board in Oxford and passed Grade I for military service (my height no longer mattered). Then came the evacuation on the beaches of Dunkirk. Within a week my papers came to report to Cowley Barracks and the Oxford and Buckinghamshire Light Infantry, six weeks of injections and intensive training – I certainly knew I was there! – and we marched out of Oxford behind the Regimental Band, people lining the streets to watch us go – where we did not know.

It turned out to be Northern Ireland and soon after we arrived there we heard that Pearl Harbour had been attacked and America was in the war. I was there as we marched all over Northern Ireland, as we went out on training schemes that kept us out for weeks, route marches that ended in our Company being lost, and always it rained! We lived with our ground sheets on our backs. After one such march I went before a medical board; was regraded to B2 and back to Cowley Barracks in Oxford as not fit for a front-line regiment. My posting came and I was amazed that it was to Corsham, near Bath, with the Suffolk Regiment.

I was there when the Luftwaffe bombed Bath, helping to dig a communal grave and lay to rest approximately 60 coffins, with King George VI and his Queen, Elizabeth, looking on, amid all the destruction.

Then came another posting to the Military Police at Bulford on Salisbury Plain. I certainly knew I was there!! Life was hell and the pay only a shilling a day. I had just finished my training with them and received another posting – to the Royal Engineers at Preston. No wonder we took so long to win the war if everyone was moved about as I was! I was in London on an electricians' course when the Duke of Kent was killed in a plane crash and was one of the 24 hour guard at the lying in state in Westminster Abbey.

Now things were really hotting up. 1944 and I was in a huge camp in Horley, Surrey, confined to barracks and not allowed to write home. The tension was electrical as we boarded a ship at Newhaven on 31 May and went round and round in rough seas apparently going nowhere until the night of 5 June 1944 when we knew we were going to invade France (the Second Front that those who did not have to be there had been demanding for months).

Now serving under General Montgomery, there was no time to think of the dreadful sea-sickness that bugged us all. In the early hours of 6 June 1944 all hell was let loose. We were about 3 miles off the coast of France when we were ordered down the scrambling nets into the landing craft and then from the landing craft into the sea with ships' guns, bombers, anti-aircraft guns, all making a nightmare so that now I have a job to believe it ever happened, but I *was* there on that day, on that beach, amidst all the death and carnage.

Our job was to clear a way through the mined beach and we came into the

The message of General D.D. Eisenhower, Supreme Commander of Allied Armies of Liberation in Europe, prior to the 'D Day' landing in France on June 6, 1944.

SUPREME HEADQUARTERS
ALLIED EXPEDITIONARY FORCE

Soldiers, Sailors and Airmen of the Allied Expeditionary Force!

You are about to embark upon the Great Crusade, toward which we have striven these many months. The eyes of the world are upon you. The hopes and prayers of liberty-loving people everywhere march with you. In company with our brave Allies and brothers-in-arms on other Fronts, you will bring about the destruction of the German war machine, the elimination of Nazi tyranny over the oppressed peoples of Europe, and security for ourselves in a free world.

Your task will not be an easy one. Your enemy is well trained, well equipped and battle-hardened. He will fight savagely.

But this is the year 1944! Much has happened since the Nazi triumphs of 1940-41. The United Nations have inflicted upon the Germans great defeats, in open battle, man-to-man. Our air offensive has seriously reduced their strength in the air and their capacity to wage war on the ground. Our Home Fronts have given us an overwhelming superiority in weapons and munitions of war, and placed at our disposal great reserves of trained fighting men. The tide has turned! The free men of the world are marching together to Victory!

I have full confidence in your courage, devotion to duty and skill in battle. We will accept nothing less than full Victory!

Good Luck! And let us all beseech the blessing of Almighty God upon this great and noble undertaking.

Dwight D Eisenhower

'While British and American airborne troops landed on the Normandy coast, 4,000 ships were being used to transport vast armies on a great all-out assault on Hitler's Fortress of Europe. Fleets of aircraft silenced the enemy batteries and attacked his troops whose beach positions were pulverised from air and sea'. (Newnes Pictorial Knowledge, vol. 2, p 254)

village of Ver Sur Mer, 5 or 6 miles from Bayeaux. We were issued with 40 francs invasion money, a tin Tommy cooker that used methylated tablets, 7 cigarettes, 7 boiled sweets, compo packs to make tea and meals and a big biscuit, the rations for a week unless you could find a cow to milk. We had field service cards issued to let wife or mother know that you were still alive, nothing more.

We never stopped until we were trying to take Caen and then we were given a rest from the front and taken the few miles to Bayeaux. My Pass for Bayeaux reads 1000–2200 hours, so on 28 July 1944 I was there – in beautiful Bayeux Cathedral, the first time we had been rested from the minefields, the noise, the carnage that is war for a few hours since 6 June. From Bayeaux to Caen, from Caen to Falaise, with terrible sights all around us, our job just to clear minefields, roads and bridges so that all reserves could be brought up to consolidate our gains. After Falaise it was go, go, go. Two hours in Rouen and Amiens. Was I really there? All my souvenirs prove yes, I was there.

Then came the race to Antwerp and the docks. The need was to get our supplies in by sea. The enemy was going backwards all the time, except for one big hiccup in the bitter winter of 1944, when the American Army was pushed back into a huge bulge, the Ardennes Gap. There we lived, ate and slept in trenches full of snow until reinforcements arrived, with General Montogomery once more in control.

After Paris was liberated I was one of the lucky ones to win a two day Paris leave, and to stay in the Hotel Ambassador from '1400 hours 16 Nov. to 1400 hours 18 Nov. 1944.' There I enjoyed the Follies Bergere and the things in Paris that had not been subject to bombers, but above all, running hot water, a bathroom and a lavatory.

Then it was back to the front. After the peace of Helmond in Holland where I made good friends, the race was on for Berlin. It was building bridges and crossing rivers until we reached Hamburg. I was there in the ruins of that city when Germany surrendered and the plight of the ordinary German and especially the children tore at your heart. I had the Thanksgiving Service from Luneburg Heath, but I was still not able to believe it was over. That nightmare I had lived through was finished.

I had fourteen days home leave in June 1945. On the boat I met my brother John quite by chance for the first time in five years as our leaves had never coincided. He was with the Royal Artillery so we had both been in the hell, not the glory, they call war; the horrors of finding the Concentration Camps and all their victims afterwards. Insanity?

Then back to Hamburg again to work on the cleaning up and helping to restore water, sewers, lights and above all food to our enemies. I was in Germany until March 1946, when I came home with the France and German Star, the 1939–45 Star, The Defence Medal, The War Medal 1939–45, a sports coat and trousers, a Trilby hat, clothing coupons, a Ration Book and a magnificent War Gratuity of £73.19s.0p to compensate for six of the best years of my life being taken away from my wife and children and my dear mother.

I have passed over the tragedies; the heartbreaking separation from my family; the knowledge that 'Home' was being mercilessly bombed; that my uncle and his family at Brislington died in one of those raids in a specially

<u>LANDING CARD.</u>

NAME OF UNIT:................No. 5 Engineer Stores (Base) Depot

YOU BELONG TO:..............................ARMY GROUP TPS.

YOU WILL COME UNDER COMMAND OF: HQ 11 L of C Area

IMMEDIATELY ON LANDING GO TO: (a) PERSONNEL TRANSIT AREA   )
) of the
           (b) WHEELED VEH TRANSIT AREA) Beach
) on which
           (c) TRACKED VEH TRANSIT AREA) you land

FROM HERE YOU WILL BE DIRECTED TO: ARMY GROUP TROOPS Section of

ASSEMBLY AREA.

      Code Names for these Assembly Areas are:-

       1 KIPLING   )
       2 SWINBURNE) According to which beach you
       3 DICKENS   ) land on.
       4 DEFOE   )

     11 L of C Area Report Centre established in
    Assembly Area will tell Offr or NCO IC of your
    party what to do or where to go next.

REMEMBER if you lose this card that you belong to ARMY GROUP
TROOPS.

3 weeks after 'D Day', a brief card to say that he was still alive.

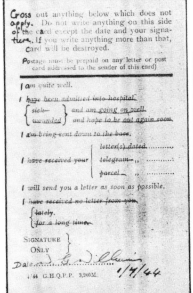

197

Hamburg 1946.
On the right, Sapper W. G. Williams,
with a fellow member of the Royal Engineers.
Notice how the area just behind them has
been completely flattened, presumably by the RAF.

reinforced cellar while their own house stood untouched; seeing my best mates blown to pieces with booby trap mines or in some cases shot by themselves because they could not stand the life.

You could not think of these things and keep your sanity. Usually you were too tired, cold and wet to think of anything else but the present. Whatever we had been as civilians, undergraduates or labourers, we had no choice but to obey. 'Ours not to reason why, ours just to do and die'.

I pray to God that my children and grandchildren will be spared from the horrors of my generation and my father's generation.

[Bill died in 1981 after a long illness borne with great courage.]

Chapter 13

Major Harry Wakeling, recalls his posting in 1939, as a teenage Territorial, to Keynsham.

In November 1939 I was one of twenty-six unhappy soldiers who arrived in Keynsham after a long train journey from Sheffield. Unhappy because we had been posted from the TA unit we had joined in Hull in early 1939. The unit was part of 1st Cavalry Division (still horse mounted) and was going to Palestine. As we were not nineteen years old we could not go and so we were leaving many friends and a unit of which we were very proud and instead of a journey to Palestine – which sounded very glamorous in those early days of the War – we had landed up in a very small place called 'KEENSHAM' which we were told was near Bristol.

The unit we were joining in Keynsham was a Bristol TA unit (915 AA Coy R.A.S.C.) and apart from us 'foreigners' from Hull and about thirty young Welshmen who had been sent from 53rd Welsh Division because they too were under nineteen, all the rest of the unit were from the Bristol area. The unit was based in Rockhill House, Wellsway, and was commanded by Major Stuart Evans – a Bristol solicitor.

For two or three weeks or so we recent arrivals slept on the floor of the Drill Hall on Bath Hill. We were issued with three blankets and a canvas palliasse which we stuffed with straw. Toilet and ablution arrangements were rudimentary to say the least. We marched to Rockhill House for all our meals – the cookhouse there being in a stable later occupied by Mike Williams' Garage.

Sometime in December we moved into the Rockhill House camp and slept on the upper floor of the large stable block opposite the House. The winter of 1939/40 was very cold. There was no form of heating whatsoever in the barn and sleeping on the floor with just three blankets and a straw palliasse was extremely uncomfortable. The remainder of the unit was accommodated in wooden huts and more were being built but it was some months later before we were able to move into one and given a bed on which to sleep. There were no baths or showers in the camp. Once a week we were issued with clean laundry and taken into Bristol where we had a hot bath in the 'Slipper Baths'. Otherwise it was cold water for washing and shaving unless one had a contact in the cookhouse from whom one could scrounge a mug of hot water for shaving.

In Rockhill House itself was Company HQ and the Officers' and Sergeants' Messes. The unit was a Transport Company responsible for delivering food, petrol and ammunition to the various anti-aircraft units (gun batteries, searchlight units, etc.) in the Bristol area.

When I arrived there were very few 'proper' army vehicles – the majority were requisitioned vehicles still bearing their civilian markings, a motley collection of bakers' vans, removal vans and so on. We new arrivals, none of whom had ever been behind the wheel of a motorised vehicle in our lives, were taught to drive on these vehicles after the most rudimentary theoretical lectures on driving procedures. There were no small vehicles on which to practise, no practice area – four or five of us would go out with an NCO instructor, one driving the vehicle whilst the rest of us shivered, freezing to death in the back of the vehicle awaiting our own turn to crash the gears (no synchro-mesh in those days), stall the engine every five minutes or so and weave our way around the minor roads around Keynsham, a menace to anything and everything on the road at the same time. Fortunately in those days there was very little traffic on the roads. Gradually the civilian vehicles were replaced by War Department three ton lorries, petrol tankers and ambulances.

On Friday nights there was an exodus from the camp. Apart from those on duty and the fifty or so of us who were 'foreigners' most of the rest of the unit went home for the weekend.

I was one of the fortunate ones who found a 'home from home' in Keynsham. On the first Sunday morning after we arrived, the whole unit was marched to the parish church. The Roman Catholics 'fell out' and went along to St. Dunstan's, whilst three of us 'Nonconformists' as we were called, went to Victoria Methodist church. Sitting in the pew in front of us were a couple with their two young daughters – one with long pigtails aged about eleven and the other about five years old. After the service the lady from the pew in front asked if we would like to go to tea that afternoon. I did so and the young girl in pigtails and I were married in the same church some eight years later in May 1947.

The lady who invited me to tea that Sunday morning was Mrs Hettie Wilson and the house to which I went was No. 4 Avon Road. Living next door were Mrs Wilson's parents, Martin and Mary Scears. Behind the two houses were 'the grounds' in which there was a hard tennis court immediately beyond the gardens of the houses, and behind that a large orchard, four grass tennis courts, a bowling green, a croquet lawn and a small disused quarry. The sport facilities were run by the St. Keyna Sports Club and were still in use in the summer of 1940.

The old quarry was approximately one hundred yards long, twenty yards wide and sixty to seventy feet deep. The face of the east side was very steep but it was very easy to scramble down into from the west edge. There were many ammonites to be found.

In later years I often joked with my father-in-law, Lionel Wilson, that the only reason I had been invited to tea in November 1939 was so that I could help him dig out and construct a very large and deep air raid shelter in the orchard. It took many, many hours of back-breaking work. It contained four bunk beds and room for three or four others to sit on chairs and was frequently used during the raids in 1940. It was situated approximately where the acacia tree now is in Dragons Hill Gardens.

Keynsham in 1939/40 was a very small, quiet place in which it seemed to us as ex-city dwellers, that everyone knew everyone else. For entertainment there were the pubs, the canteen in the Fear Institute, the Charlton cinema (two different films a week) and a dance in the Drill Hall every Saturday night. As we had to be back in camp by 2230 hours it was not possible to go into Bath or Bristol except on Saturdays when we had the afternoon off. Perhaps this was just as well as my pay was two shillings per day of which I sent five shillings and threepence per week home – leaving me with eight shillings and ninepence (44p) per week. Although one was supposed to be back in camp by 2230 it was very easy to avoid this by not 'booking out' at the Guard Room and sneaking back into Rockhill House by crossing the cricket ground and crawling under the barbed wire between the ground and Rockhill camp. There was always a helpful sentry who would help by holding up the wire.

In the early days sentries were 'armed' with pick axe helves – no rifles being available. In July 1940, however, when invasion appeared imminent, we received boxes of .300 rifles which had been shipped from America. They had been in store since the 14–18 War and were smothered in thick grease which we laboriously removed with paraffin. Apart from rifles all that the unit had to stem any invasion, had it occurred, were a few Boyes anti-tank rifles – about which all I can remember is that they were fired from the shoulder and had the most vicious recoil. All of us suffered from very bruised shoulders after our first lessons on firing them. We were also taught how to make 'Molotov Cocktails' which were bottles filled with petrol with a fuse attached. The theory was that on the approach of an enemy tank one would light the fuse, leap out of cover and throw the bottle of petrol on to the tank – a theory which thank goodness was never put to the test.

During the heavy air raids on Bristol in 1940/41 members of the unit were called out of pubs and the cinema to return to camp. Every vehicle was sent to the ammunition dump at Burnett, loaded with ammunition which was then delivered to anti-aircraft batteries around Bristol – Pill, Portishead, Pilning, Purdown, Avonmouth, Whitchurch are some of the names which spring to mind. I well remember driving down Rownham Hill after one of the raids and seeing the centre of Bristol a mass of raging fires – a horrifying yet awe-inspiring sight.

I left Keynsham in 1942 and went abroad. On my first leave to UK in late 1945 I thought I would spend a couple of days revisiting Keynsham and looking up the Wilsons. I knew the elder daughter had removed her pigtails because I received a lock from them (which I still have) in a letter I received in Sicily in 1943. What I hadn't suspected was the vast difference between a young girl of fourteen and a young lady of almost eighteen. The couple of days extended to a week and as I have said we were married some eighteen months later. I often thank my lucky stars that I went to Victoria Methodist Church that Sunday morning in November 1939.

Postscript

In 1942 Harry attended an Officers' training course (O.C.T.U.) and as a commissioned officer in the Royal Army Service Corps was posted to North Africa. It is said that, 'Napoleon's armies always used to march on their stomachs', and it was the responsibility of the R.A.S.C. to ensure that the vital supplies of food and of weapons kept up with the Allies' advancing troops.

With the defeat of Rommel in North Africa, Lieutenant Wakeling was for a year engaged in the Italian Campaign. Later, still with the R.A.S.C., he saw service in France, then in Germany, where he was when hostilities ceased.

Since his retirement in 1959 after 20 years service as an officer in the regular Army, he has made his home in Keynsham, though the town is now very different from that which it was when he was here in the hectic days of 1939–42.

Chapter 14

A Keynsham soldier on the Japanese 'Death Railway', Thailand, 1942–45.

The autobiography of Private Leonard Hall, R.A.S.C.

The Godfrey family of Temple Street was an old and respected Keynsham family, to whom many local families are proud to be related. They claim that the Godfreys were originally farmers, whose cow sheds were against the high walls at the rear of the car panel-beaters premises in Temple Street. The late Mr L Ellis explained that in the late Victorian era, Mr Jonas Godfrey would bring his cows down from what is now the Manor Road playing fields to drink from the river at Dapps Hill, then on to Temple Street to be milked. He owned a 5 acre field by the turning into Coronation Road, not then built, where he grazed his horses.

From the front section of this extensive Temple Street building, old Mr J Godfrey also ran a coal business, using his horses to collect coal from Pensford and Timsbury, to be sold in 'the village'. Next door, at today's Kasbah', his younger son, Thomas, lived with his wife, and ran a Second Hand business, in addition to being responsible for buildings and stock at the rear of his father's premises. While there were some cow sheds there, and even pig sties, the main buildings were horse stables, though Mr Ellis has a photo of a fine bull there!

When Jonas died, his elder son James ('Jim') and Tom started the lucrative family business, as 'J and T Godfrey, Hauliers'. After the 1914–18 war, the brothers bought two old chain-driven lorries with solid rubber tyres, which, as business increased, they replaced with a number of more modern lorries, which were kept at the front of the premises. Above the cobbled floor (now covered over with cement) some 12–14 feet was a ceiling, with beams above it, and reached by a vertical wooden ladder. In this loft area, which they referred to as 'the tally', hay used to be stored for the horses and other live-stock.

Years later, the firm was sold to Russetts, who in their turn were bought out around 1950 by Tucker, the panel beater. Inside the building, just off Temple Street, was an old-fashioned petrol pump which the Godfrey brothes had used only for their own vehicles.

If one stands just inside the building, it can be seen that at one time the Kasbah and Tina's were quite separate and unconnected houses, possibly built in the 18th century. At a later date heavy iron girders were placed from the taller Kasbah to Tina's, and the total area covered over. Miss M Fairclough vaguely remembers walking along Temple Street around 1920 and noticing that the haulway from the street to the cattle sheds had been covered over. Unfortunately Mr Ellis rather disputed the date, saying that he could never remember the building being other than covered. But he did recall that at one time the cattle shed area at the rear was covered over, until it was burnt down in Mr Tucker's time, never to be rebuilt.

Jim and Tom had a sister, Ethel Sarah Jane Godfrey.

The Weekly Chronicle of Saturday May 23, 1964, refers to a 'Mr Z W Hall', and records that 'Mr Hall's family was for many generations connected with the Cornish tin mines. Mr Hall senior was manager of the famous Redruth mines. When the tin industry was crippled by the abundance of imported metal, the Hall family moved to Keynsham. That was in 1891. Mr Hall remembered the long journey from Cornwall, when foot-warmers were put into the carriages at every stop. Whenever he was asked his Christian name, he always replied, 'Zachariah, spelt the Bible way'.

Grandson Hubert Hall adds to the story that, 'Mr Z W Hall's son, Rosewell Z Hall, was only five when he arrived in Keynsham. He was educated at Bath Hill school where Mr Wheeler was the headmaster. For a while the family moved to Bristol, where he attended Merrywood Grammar School'.

When the family returned to Keynsham, Rosewell met Miss Ethel Godfrey; romance followed, and later they were married. They were blessed with five children, William, Leonard, Herbert, Norman and a daughter who lived only a short time. They lived at 9, Rock Road, the last of a terrace of four stone houses. Next door lived the Wiltshire family. Sadly, 7 and 9 were later demolished to make a wide rear entrance to Temple Street, and to Tucker's premises.

'Hall's the Newsagents'

Employed locally, Rosewell was a wire-drawer, reputedly able to stretch a small piece of wire to a remarkable length. Later, in the First World War, he worked on 'munitions' at Torrance's at Bitton. Then came a period at Robertson's Jam Factory, until he took the plunge and went into business on his own as 'Halls the Newsagents', in the High Street, helped by his sons. As Leonard (born December 15, 1915) said, 'We could rightly say that we were the largest newsagents in Keynsham, though among others, Harvey's of Station Road also sold papers'.

The Chronicle recorded that, 'He started his newsagent's business in 1932 and his trade increased rapidly. He says it is a business he loves and his three sons are now in partnership with him'.

'We were in business until 1965, when Dad sold out to Menzies,' Leonard recalled, who had helped in the shop, selling papers, sweets and tobacco. He was a tall young man of 6 ft who, when he went to the local railway station daily to collect the evening papers, would there jump on to the weighing machine which always registered '150 lbs', that is, 10 stone 10 lbs.

When war was declared in 1939, (as he recalled fifty years later), 'I was dragged into the army. Aged 24, I knew that I would have to go and I just accepted it. I was the first of the family to go.' Now we come to Mr L Hall's own written account of those days.

'1940 sees the call to serve, so off to Bulford Camp I go. Did I say camp? It was still in the course of construction. The fields were absolute mud and slush. The drill command was not 'Left, right', but 'Slip, slop' through the mud.

Training finished, I was posted to a unit in Scotland, and was immediately sent home on embarkation leave. However, events delayed this deployment.

'I was in the Royal Army Service Corps and for the next few months there were, more or less, just routine marches etc. until Easter 1941, when the whole Division moved to the Manchester area. Again it was more routine exercises, and I was, in fact, on an exercise on Salisbury racecourse, when I was recalled to my unit to be sent home on embarkation leave once again, but this time it was for real.

Guests of the United States Navy

'It was now October 1941 and we set sail from Liverpool on the 'Warwick Castle' in a convoy of six troopships with but one destroyer for protection against German U Boats. We were just one day away from the British shores when we met a large merchant convoy far better protected than we were. Anyway, the escorts changed round and our one destroyer brought the merchant ships back to England, while we went on to Nova Scotia. The interesting thing was that our powerful escort of a battleship, an aircraft carrier and destroyers, were all USA ships, at a time when the 'States' was not officially in the war.

'At Nova Scotia we transferred to the American troopship 'The Orizable', where, with other troopships, we were protected heavily by American warships, including 'The West Point' and 'Mount Vernon', two of their most prized ships. We hugged the East coast of America to Trinidad, and further south we crossed the South Atlantic to Bombay via Capetown and Mombasa. By this time the 'States' was officially in the war.

'While in India, our destination was changed to Singapore. We were the 54 Brigade of the 18th Division, and the 53 and 55 Brigade were already there. We sailed from India in the Free French ship, 'The Felix Rouscell' with 'The Empress of Asia', protected by just one destroyer. When the Irish crew of the 'Empress' knew we were going to Singapore, they refused to stoke the engines, and the troops had to do the stoking. This delayed our arrival at Singapore, so instead of arriving under the cover of darkness, we arrived in broad daylight, and became subject to an air attack.

'We were unable to manoeuvre as we were amongst the minefields, but we were lucky on our ship, though our boat had a dummy funnel, and the Japanese managed to drop a bomb down it, which killed some of our men. But 'The Empress' was set alight and the ship was abandoned. We were so unprepared for attack that our only defence was to tie machine guns to the ship's railings. However, it was a pleasure to see the speed and skill with which the Royal Navy's destroyer swung round in a very short distance and how she gave such a good account of herself.

The Royal Army Service Corps

'Our duty as the RASCW was that of transport. We supplied the fighting troops with ammunition, food, petrol, etc. The term a 'break in the lines of communications' meant that, in effect, no supplies were getting through. We did one job as the RASC and took the Norfolk Regiment to the front line at

Singapore, where we were under rifle fire before we left. We returned to our base at another part of that large island complex, at Tekok Woods. There we were given ammunition, and told to go and ourselves fight. That was the end of us as the RASC.'

More than once our Keynsham boy was offered promotion, but turned the stripes down. In the NCO's mess he would have to contribute to the mess funds, and as a good Methodist teetotaller, he objected to subsidising other's drinks. In any case, just one stripe made you 'the dishcloth' and when Leonard asked about the chance of a second stripe, he was told vaguely that you never knew what might turn up. As 'the dishcloth' he would lose his proficiency pay of sixpence a day, though at Singapore, he was for ten glorious days on 'Colonial Pay.'

The Battle for Singapore

Singapore was not just a city, but an extensive island. Private L Hall continued, 'It is now February 6, 1942, my fiancee's birthday, which is why I can remember the date. I began to write to her, but the call came to go to our battle lines. We crawled up the malaria drains and dug ourselves in on a certain hill, on the south of the island, behind the Indian infantry. Our trench was about four foot deep with additional height given by the earth that we dug up being thrown in front of us. There were some twenty of us in our trench, armed only with rifles. One of the worse experiences there were the Chinese crackers that went snapping off behind us, as if we were surrounded.

'Defending Singapore were the Norfolk, the Suffolk, and the Leicestershire Regiments plus the Northumberland Fusiliers, whose officers taught us bayonet fighting on the ship coming over. That was very nasty and I am glad that we never had to do it in reality.

'The 18th Division alone was 20,000 strong. There were also Dutch and Indonesian troops present. There were possibly up to 80,000 Allied troops there.

'For ten days the battle raged but we were very much unprepared, as the island had been armed to expect an attack from the sea, and our failure to make a complete destruction of the causeway from Malaya allowed the Japanese almost free passage to capture the water reservoir on Friday, February 13. Our troops tried in vain to recapture it. We went from Friday to Sunday without a drink, in that climate.

'Then on Sunday February 15, we saw our General with other senior officers going forward towards the Japanese, flying the white flag. Upon seeing this, our section discussed trying to get away, but by a majority decided against it. I was one of the 'anti' but I think that if I had known what was to come, I would have been 'pro'. We assumed, rightly I think, that the Japs had command of the sea, so that really we could not escape.

'A senior British General in Burma said that all soldiers say they will fight to the death, but only the Japanese do it! I never left Singapore as a fighting soldier, as the Japs were almost on the island by the time that we arrived.

The Internment of the Prisoners of War

'The word for Japanese, in their language, is Nippons, though we called them 'Yellow baskets'. The Nips instructed us to march to the Changi area of Singapore by February 19. From then until early June we saw very little of the Japs, but food was extremely short and our clothes began to rot, mainly due to perspiration. Our footwear needed repairing, but there was nothing there for this purpose.

'There was a special Chinese area in the city, but the Nips so hated them that they escorted all the Chinese soldiers down to the beach, and made them wade out into the sea. There they were mowed down by machine gun fire, and left for the tide to sweep their bodies out to sea. You can't believe how cruel the Japanese could be. We wondered what was going to happen to us.

'About the middle of June the Japs demanded 2,000 men and I was one of them. We were marched to Singapore railway station and were put into steel cattle trucks, 30 men per truck, for 4 days and 5 nights as we were transported to Thailand. What a journey in the heat of the day! We were near suffocation. We alighted from the train at Bam Pong and marched to Nong Pladuk. Oh my, what a meal was prepared for us! Large pans of scrambled eggs? But no, it only looked like scrambled eggs. It was rice that had been treated with calcium. Did we have heart burn that night!

'Nong Pladuk became the starting point of what is now known as 'Death Railway', rightly named in my humble opinion.'

Geoffrey P Adams in his brief history, 'The Thailand to Burma Railway' (1976) wrote, 'Burma was best supplied by the sea route via Singapore, Malacca Straits to Rangoon and Moulmein, but the Japanese planners appreciated that Allied seapower would try to cut this vital maritime link. Imperial General Headquarters (IGHQ) thus decided to build a new railway to connect Bangkok, Singora and Singapore to the established Burma Railways via Moulmein Ye and Rangoon. Other engineers had surveyed routes to cross the jungle-covered mountains between the Gulf of Siam and the Indian Ocean; all had rejected the project as uneconomic to operate and too costly to construct in such difficult terrain. But economic gives way to necessity in war-time. IGHQ therefore planned the railway early in 1942 and in the official orders issued in June it was clear that it would be built immediately regardless of costs in money and human life.

'The Imperial Japanese Army (IJA) captured tens of thousands of prisoners of war in those early battles in South East Asia, Indonesia and the Java Seas. These British, Australian, Dutch and American prisoners would be the labour force handed over to the special railway regiments of the IJA. Together POW and IJA would build what the world came to know as 'The Death Railway', wrote Adams. 'Too many of the Japanese and Korean soldiers were cruel, sadistic and inhuman. . . . Japan had not signed the POW section of the Geneva Convention' (p.2)

208

The Camp of The Prisoners of War

Private Hall recalled that the huts were made mainly of bamboo, which grew around them in great profusion, and up to six inches in diameter. The steeply sloped roof of the one storey hut was made of 'attap', being large palm type leaves stretched over a bamboo frame. The side walls were similarly constructed. There were doorways but no doors.

'We slept on split bamboo canes, which stretched the whole length of the hut, some 3–400 feet long, without a break in them. You could not fall out of bed. You had above 18 inches to lie on, which just about gave you room to turn. There were about 500 men in the hut, on the two rows of beds either side.

'The place was alive with bugs. When you awoke in the morning, your body would be like pebble-dashed ceiling paper from these blood suckers. You slept right through it as you were so dead beat. There were also fleas, but worst of all were the big lice, up to three-eighths of an inch long. If you had bugs in your clothes, you could put them out in the sun, which would hatch out the eggs, and then kill the young, but not so with the lice. The only way to get rid of them was to boil them, but wood was so restricted. I was lucky enough to get a three quarter size blanket from the Red Cross, but after two days it was so full of lice that I sold it to a Thai peasant and was able to buy some bananas while the Nips were not looking. Then it was back to sacking, which was so loosely woven that the lice would not stay in it.

'There was great variety in our three meals a day. At breakfast it was rice and stew, for lunch it was stew and rice and for tea it was rice stewed tea. We had our own words for a number of events. Reveille was,

'Come and get your rice and stew,
Nippons say it's good for you.'

'The rice was of very poor quality, but if you picked the maggots out, there was very little rice left. After all, maggots are a delicacy!

'Their time was two hours ahead of Thai time, so they brought in Japanese time. The idea was that we should be at work by 8.00 am, so reveille would have been about 7.00 am.'

'The day temperatures in Bangkok range from 31 degrees C in December to 35 degrees C in April.' (Adams.)

'The only clothing that the Nips gave us was a loin cloth, about 18 in by 9 in, and two lengths of cord to tie it round our waist. We were ordered to have our heads completely shaved, which our own barbers did. As we had no hats, in that tough equatorial climate, we took it as just another form of Nippon cruelty. We nicknamed the cloth, 'a Jap–happy.'

The Punishment Block

'The recent television series, 'Tenko' was quite accurate. Our guard house stood on stilts, below which was the punishment block. Sited there were wooden cages, in which there was just room for you to sit with your knees doubled up, almost touching your chin. If you wanted food, there was only rice, and that heavily laced with salt, and without any form of drink. You could be punished by being imprisoned there for 24, 48 or 72 hours.

'However dreadful you felt, you just must not give in. Though things got so bad that you just didn't value your life, you had to keep going, and try and make light of the hardships. You couldn't give the Nips the satisfaction that they had you beaten.

PRIVATE LEONARD HALL, Royal Army Service Corps, 1940.

'Another form of the harsh treatment that our captor's subjected us to was to make us stand to attention, with a board placed across our hands, and a football placed on the board. Remembering the heat of the sun, and that we were near enough naked and hairless, if the football fell, you were in for the most severe punishment.

'The Nips would kick and hit you with a crowbar or anything that came to hand, for very little provocation. On one occasion we rebelled. The whole camp had been fallen in for reveille and duly counted, but when the Nips gave our CO, Major Sykes (from Liverpool), the order to dismiss us for work sections, he refused to give the order. The Major was removed and held in a compound, together with a Lt Colonel, with a circle of soldiers with their cocked rifles pointing at them, but he still refused to give the necessary order, as a protest at the ill treatment of his men.

'Meanwhile the camp's some 2,000 POWs stood rigidly to attention, wearing only Jap–happies, in the baking sun, for what must have been at least four hours, surrounded by belligerent Nip soldiers, who had sent for reinforcements. If a comrade fainted, you simply held him up. You urinated just where you were. Dicing with death, the Major held out and refused to give the order, 'Dismiss for work sections.' In the end the Nips gave in and gave him a written undertaking that his men would be treated better. But it was not worth the paper that it was written on.'

Medical supplies

Leonard declared that Thailand was a very beautiful land, and wrote that, 'I have always held the Thai people in high esteem. Throughout the 3½ years of captivity, the people of Thailand managed to pass a few medical supplies to various camps along the railway line.'

He recalled that there was a bamboo fence round the edge of the camp, and prisoners were not allowed within 4 yards of it, though in any case it was meant to be escape-proof. Obviously escaping was forbidden. However, at night prisoners did risk getting out through it for essential medical supplies for their fellows. One night a prisoner was spotted disappearing through the fence. The whole camp was immediately ordered to parade and, when counted, a soldier was missing. They doubled the guard but still the Englishman returned without being caught.

At roll call next morning, every one of the hundreds of POWs was present. Unable to discover the culprit, mass punishment was threatened unless the guilty party owned up. Obviously he had to do the honourable thing. The Nips ordered him to show them where and how he escaped, after which they took him outside the camp and shot him dead as an escapee. But as Len pointed out, as he had returned he was not trying to escape.

GP Adams summed up the situation when he wrote further that, 'The Japanese made few plans for the reception of the POWs, and neglected the provision of adequate food, medical stores and accommodation . . . Malnutrition, tropical diseases, cholera, worm infestation and a multiplicity of other ailments took a high toll of POW life. POW doctors toiled to save life and limb,

211

but the IJA refused to provide necessary medical stores and drugs.' (Pages 2 & 5).

'You can't reason with them.'

Private Hall recalled that the fanatical IJA engineers and guards decided just how much work was to be completed each day, and detailed the necessary work force. If 100 men were required, 100 men had to go to the railway construction line, even if ten of them were on stretchers, and had to lie there all day in the sun and possibly die. It was no good 90 men offering to do the work of 100 to let their friends stay in camp. You could not reason with them. They just would not listen.

Len fell foul of the guards on one occasion, as he said, for trying to be clever. As all conversations with the Nips had to be in Japanese, and speaking English forbidden, he was instructed to do a certain job. Pretending not to understand, he declined to do the work and received a blow. Reeling, he asked by his actions, 'Why did you do that?'. The guard said in English, 'You understand English, don't you?', to which Lenard unthinkingly answered 'Yes,' for which he received a further blow for speaking in the forbidden language.

'My worst moment was back at camp. We had nicknames for the guards and we called one 'the undertaker' and we were making fun of his name amongst ourselves, when he finally realised what we were doing. Then he stopped, put a bullet in his rifle and pointed it straight at us. I thought I was going to die. We all bobbed down, but he did not fire.'

The death railway

Adams records that 'The first 55 km from Nong Pladuk to Kanchanaburi, over flat lands, was easy to construct, but at Tha Makham lay the main natural obstacle of the River Kwae-Yai. To cross this barrier the IJA brought from Indonesia, in sections, a steel bridge of eleven spans, each of 22 metres; it was placed on the banks of the Kwae-Yai at Tha Makham. By October 1942, POWs were constructing a great wooden bridge which was completed in Feb 1943 and took its first train. The steel bridge, constructed entirely by manpower, using a few pulleys, derricks and cement mixers, was finished by May 1943 midst great rejoicing by the Japanese'.

'Many POWs and Asian labourers were force-marched to the camps scattered along the 415 km of railroad. Many died and were buried or cremated where they fell. The camps were often mere shelters. The monsoons made movement and work more arduous. When the schedule fell even further behind, thousands of sick and ill-prepared POWs came up from Singapore to perish by the thousand around Nikhe, or even later after their return to Singapore.

'It is estimated that more than 100,000 died. Official British records indicate that 30,000 British, 13,000 Australians, 18,000 Dutch and 700 Americans worked on the railway. Some estimates state that 18,000 POWs died during construction, while thousands more suffered life disablement. Many IJA men were later executed or imprisoned for their infamous crimes, unique in railway history.' (Op cit, pages 4 & 6.)

After the Railway

Looking back, Leonard wrote, 'I consider myself to be very lucky to survive, having been involved with the construction of the railway from June 1942 until Jan 1945. Then we moved to a place called Ubon close to the French Indo-China border. Here we were preparing a landing strip for aircraft.

'On the morning of Aug 15, roll call was just over, and we were all prepared for another day's work, when the Japanese Major in charge appeared. With the usual ceremony when he wished to make an announcement, one table was placed at the highest point available, covered with a white tablecloth. Then bowing to the sun, he announced that the war was over. Some one called out and asked who had won, but this was unanswered.

'That was it. We went back to our huts and celebrated. That night a party of us marched up to and through the guard house, where the Nips, thinking we had come for them, leapt out of the windows. Then we split up and came back beside the outside of the huts, and the Nips jumped back in through the windows.

'We had no special parade as our officers had earlier all been taken from us. Next day or so, one or two men arrived, who identified themselves as British Intelligence Officers, who had been working on the railway line, dressed as Siamese, so that they could report on Japanese activities. One of the officers then returned a shirt to a soldier who had earlier sold it to the 'peasant' for a few coins with which to buy food.

'The officers took our names, and passed the information on. Our planes came and dropped parcels of some food but mainly cigarettes. Too much food, after our poor diet, would have been bad for us. A few weeks after the Japanese surrender, we crossed a wide river, and went by train to Bangkok. At every village we passed through, the Thai people gave us a tremendous wave off, including drinks of rice whisky. Arriving at Bangkok really early in the morning, we slept by the railway line, and used the rails as pillows.

'We were flown to Rangoon, where we were re-kitted, prior to returning by boat to Liverpool late on Friday afternoon. At Hoyton camp the Army did a marvellous job in providing us all with a pay book, a ration book, X-raying us, providing leave passes and travelling documents. I was home in Keynsham by 3.00 Saturday afternoon.'

Ex-POW Hall concludes his biography, 'On reflection, I can never forgive them for the lack of medical supplies, for the lack of sanitation, which was non-existent, and for the lack of sufficient food. But also, I feel that as a nation we are rightfully trading, and friendly towards them, and that my dislike for them must die with me.'

With regard to the atom bombs dropped on Japan, he had 'Not one bit of sympathy for them. Otherwise, we would all have been doomed in the jungle. How many more of our men would have died? It was total war. It was better that a million Japanese died than one more of our men.'

Almost an octogenarian, tall and upright, a father and grandfather, Leonard, still lives in Keynsham. He attended the 37th Annual Reunion Service of Remembrance of the Far East Prisoner-of-War Association (1941–1945) at the Barbican Hall on Sept 8, 1989. It was conducted by

213

'Bishop Richard Derby, formerly Hong-Kong Volunteer Force.'
   The Lesson was the wonderful words of Isaiah, Chapter 40,

'Comfort ye, comfort ye my people, saith your God.
Speak ye comfortably to Jerusalem and cry to her, that her warfare is accomplished . . .'

   The hymn at the end of the service was,

'The day thou gavest, Lord is ended,
The darkness falls at Thy behest.'

   After Reveille, the Bishop led the assembly in the FE POWs Prayer.

The FE POWs Prayer

'And we that are left grow old with the years.
Remembering the heart ache, the pain and the tears.
Hoping and praying that never again,
Man will sink to such sorrow and shame.
The price that was paid we will always remember.
Every day, every month, not just in November.
We will remember them.'

Chapter 15

'Dunkirk, May–June 1940'
by Major B J Robe, RA

In September 1939 when war was declared, I was a Gunner-Surveyor in the Survey Battery of the 3rd Survey Regiment, Royal Artillery, a Bristol-based Territorial Unit. Our job in Survey Battery was to provide the field information to establish the exact position for all guns of the Army Corps' artillery so that their fire could be acurately co-ordinated on to specific targets. For this we used precision-built and costly theodolites, surveying instruments mounted on tripods, to measure horizontal angles between trigonometrical points in degrees, minutes and seconds.

On 1st April 1940 we crossed the English Channel from Southampton to Le Havre and then spent the latter days of the 'phoney war' on the France/Belgium border (unprotected by the Maginot Line!) based on the small French town of Laventie. Incidentally, we were Corps troops and our Corps Commander was General Adam; so appropriately, our Corps sign was a green fig leaf.

In May, when the German thrust into Belgium came, we advanced North through Ypres almost to Brussels until the speed of the German tank-led advance forced us to withdraw to prepare surveyed gun bases for our artillery regiments to fall back to.

Then, one evening, amid much uncertainty as to the tactical situation, we bivouacked near the village of Lys in Belgium some miles North-East of Dunkirk. At about 1 a.m. we were roused and mustered with our vehicles, with orders that we were to proceed immediately to the Dunkirk area to arrive before daybreak and the 'buzz' was that we might be withdrawing to England – tactically of course. There was no moon and the night journey in convoy through narrow, Continental, country roads in pitch blackness without lights or signposts was difficult and hazardous, especially when encountering French convoys of horse-drawn vehicles travelling in the opposite direction.

We had hoped to reach Dunkirk before daybreak but progress was slow and dawn found us on a road beside a wide canal when the first wave of Jerry bombers came over. Its bombs straddled the road we were on, the canal and fields adjoining, setting a number of our lorries on fire, causing many casualties, showering muck, stones and bomb splinters around us and into the canal, and stunning to death, it would seem, a herd of grazing cows, frozen motionless upon their feet, a most eerie sight. With the road impassable, vehicles had to be immobilised and abandoned. But we salvaged our heavy but valuable theodolites and covered the remaining 15–20 miles to Dunkirk on foot, heading for the docks area, the while being subjected to frequent attacks of bombing and machine-gunning raids. It didn't help our morale that we saw no Allied planes – though we now know the reason why.

I remember sheltering in boats in the docks (a strange and stupid choice) and then in the cellars of dockside buildings, watching the trickles of dust fall from the stone walls under the concussion of exploding near-miss bombs. I had filled my water bottle with fresh water; many others had filled theirs with liqueurs and spirits from abandoned estaminets, including Jock Gallagher, a 'Regular' member of our battery and a noted tippler whom I last saw sitting on a pile of rubble, firing his Lee-Enfield rifle at the low flying bombers passing overhead and swearing at them in Gaelic.

Somehow I became separated from my comrades and when night fell, something, I know not what, impelled me to walk out of the docks area and across the town. I was confronted by a large town-square, its buildings totally ablaze on all four sides the victims of fire bombs. There were no people. With no knowledge of the town's street pattern, I crossed this square and eventually came up to a steel-girdered bridge over a wide water-way. The bridge had been heavily bombed but sufficient of it remained to enable me to cross, climbing through girders. I continued my apparently aimless walk until I reached a sea shore with sand dunes behind it, where, with other groups of soldiers, I spent the rest of the night. With daybreak came the view of the peacefully calm Straights of Dover with the masts and funnels of sunken ships lying a few hundred yards off-shore. The long stretch of golden sand was littered with debris, abandoned kit and equipment, stores and even weapons. All too soon, with daylight, came the sorties of low-flying German fighters, strafing the Allied troops on the beach with machine-gun fire. There was a certain amount of cover among the sand dunes from the machine gunning and their aim must have been poorly directed, for there appeared to be few casualties though many near-misses.

So the morning passed. For sustenance I had my hard-ration of chocolate-cake, never previously tried, and my precious bottle of water which I shared with others – with careful rationing (French liqueurs can create insatiable burning throats). We waited, hopefully, scanning the sea for some form of sea-transport to take us off; away to the South-West a huge, billowing cloud of black smoke from the blazing Dunkirk oil installations blotted the horizon, in marked contrast to the clear skies above us. At some point, an officer appeared among us on the beach ordering everyone to abandon whatever they were carrying and pick up a rifle. Since it seemed likely that we should shortly be fighting a landward German assault with our backs to the sea and my sole personal weapon was a .38 revolver, for which I had been issued precisely 5 bullets, this struck me as a reasonable thing to do. So I demolished and left my fine theodolite I had carried so long so far and found a Lee-Enfield rifle, without any ammunition – not even a bayonet.

Again, without any noticeable reason, I was drawn to move a distance along the beach to a long breakwater formed from enormous blocks of rock, pushing out from the shore into the sea. Here I found there was a queue of weary, low-spirited soldiers moving very slowly towards the sea where there was a deeper water. I discovered our queue was being marshalled by a Royal Naval officer who warned us to keep our heads down and keep still from time to time as the now somewhat less frequent flights of German fighters came over.

Gunner 'Len' Brewer.

1906–1940

The uncle of Howard Jeffery, Len lived in St. George's Road. Before the war he enlisted in the Royal Artillery as a regular soldier. He was 27 when he married Maud Hine in Keynsham in 1933. Their marriage was blessed with two children, Pauline and Keith. A fine man and a good friend, husband and father, sadly, he was killed at Dunkirk. His late wife received a telegram saying, "Missing believed killed; no known grave." He was only 34.

I remember that whenever these 'heads-down' halts came, I was so tired that I slept, at least momentarily. I heard a rumour, much later, that the naval officer on our breakwater had been killed. I do hope it wasn't true, for he was a great inspiration for us.

And then the unbelievable happened. A British destroyer came into view and headed straight for our rocky breakwater. It drew alongside so close to the jagged rocks that it was a feat of seamanship even in a calm sea; with any sort of rougher sea it would have been impossible. We were able to clamber aboard her somehow or other, I can't remember how, and we had the wonderful reassurance of having the deck of a British destroyer manned by British sailors under our feet, or rather our bottoms as we sat in the most restful positions we could find. The loading was quickly accomplished, for everyone was aware of the peril of a naval ship on such a hostile shore and we were away out into the Straits, to start a long zigzagging course for the coast of England. I unbuttoned my artillery mounted greatcoat which I had kept with me in case of need (I still have it) and unlaced my heavy army boots so that I would be free to discard them if something unpleasant were to attack our 'saviour'. Happily none did and we sailed into Dover harbour unscathed. But as we came to the quayside a German bomber appeared out of the blue and scored a direct hit on a cargo-boat in another part of the harbour.

But we were safe on English soil, thanks to the Royal Navy, and fortified with mugs of tea and 'wads', thanks to welcoming ladies who must have been the foundation of the WVS. With commendable speed and organisation we were marshalled into a waiting train in the dock station and, by a meandering route which I am sure defies identification, passed through beautiful English June countryside. Several hours later, bursting for a loo, we were delivered to a newly-built camp at Barton Stacey near Andover in Hampshire. And then I discovered for the first time that my feet were covered with blisters and I could hardly walk on them.

So, with many thousands of other British troops we were rescued from the burning to fight again in other fields, in Burma, but this time with 25 pounders, 'screw guns' and 3 inch mortars of a Jungle Field Regiment.

I still remember every year at 11 am on 11th November with many others who were my friends, Gordon Camm of Wellsway, a giant forward of Keynsham RFC, who never returned from Dunkirk, and Captain RJC (Bob) Smith, RA, of Rock Road, another rugby club member, who died fighting the Japanese in the jungle around Imphal and Kohima.

10th Nov 1994

* * *

In Volume II of 'The Second World War' (p 90) Churchill lists the composition of the 861 rescuing vessels of May 28–June 4. Of the 243 ships sunk, 19 were from the 39 destroyers involved. 98,671 troops were rescued from the beaches, and 239,555 from Dunkirk harbour, totalling 338,226 British and allied troops rescued (p 102).

Chapter 16

An old soldier remembers a different Keynsham in another age

The recollections of Lance Bombardier Leslie Harding, R.A.

Mr Leslie Harding was born in Rock Road, in 1908. Soon afterwards, the family moved to 31, The High Street, next to 33, 'Longton House School'. Actually Leslie went to the free school in Temple Street until he was 8, then to 'Bath Hill', at the end of Mr Wheeler's headship, and the 'reign' of Mr Mansey. 'At least I enjoyed the company of other children there', he said.

'We boys wore long black stockings, which my mother, Beatrice, who came from Blagdon, knitted. They were thigh length, held up with garters, and we pulled our knee length trousers over them. But they were a blessed nuisance. You were always pulling them up. If you ran across the playground, they would slip down.

'I can't remember much about the First World War, apart from seeing a few men in army and navy uniform on leave about the village, but no airmen.

'I recall looking out of the back window of 31, and seeing an airship going past. It was not very high, and was cigar shaped, with a suspension carriage underneath. It seemed very big as we never saw anything else in the sky! It was moving slowly and I saw it for about five minutes. My parents said it was a Zeppelin but I think it must have been one of ours, being so far over this country.

The veterinary surgeon and the blacksmith

'When I was a boy, if my metal hoop broke, I used to take it to the black-smith across the road to repair, which he did for a penny. This was before Fry's came in 1922. There were two of them, Mr Beck and Mr Ruck, whose son, Ronald, was a postman. They were strong hefty men, who worked with bare arms and wore aprons. They would pump the bellows with one hand and belt the iron with a hammer in the other. Though cheerful and helpful, you only entered when there was something to be done. Mostly they were busy shoeing horses, which probably came by appointment.

'Their forge was the building that stands by itself just through the arch-way next to the wine bar. The bar used to be the Westminster Bank. Before that, around the period of World War I, it belonged to two vets, Barrell and Bath, for whom Beck and Ruck originally worked. Then the vets left and the blacksmiths worked for themselves. They were there till about 1920. They used to lead the horses right into their smithy to shoe them. Mr Trott was the blacksmith at the other end of the town, by The New Inn. After Beck and

Ruck finished, the site became my boss's [E Wiggins] new builder's yard after leaving the Halifax building.'

Electricity

One of Leslie's joys 70 years ago, in 1920, was to slip down the High Street to the rear of the Railway Tavern, by St John's Church, to see electricity being generated. He said, 'Electricity was first produced at Chewton Mill, by the river, then behind The Railway Tavern, and for a while both sources were producing electricity at the same time. We were the first town to have it in the High Street.

'As a boy I looked in to the plant in the evening to watch the one boilerman putting coal on the fire to heat the water, to drive the steam engine that generated the electricity. His name was Ben Mutlow. At first the electricity was used to light the High Street and the homes, but not for cooking. It probably wasn't strong enough for that. That came later. My house in Albert Road, built in 1934, was the first all electric house in the town.'

The book, 'Around Keynsham and Saltford' by B Lowe and T Brown, reminds us that, 'The Parfitt Brothers pioneered street electric lighting in Keynsham in the 1880s. By 1923, Bristol Corporation Electricity Dept had come into being.' [page 153]

Gas Lighting

Leslie recalled that earlier there had been gas lighting in his High Street home. 'There was a gas pipe across the ceiling that ended in the middle and disappeared into a wooden rose, but we didn't have gas. We just used light from the coal fire and paraffin lamps. Really we lived in one room. If you went anywhere else, you took a candle, on a holder to catch the drips. At other times you used your hand or jacket to stop the candle being blown out.

'Sometimes we used father's postman's paraffin lamp. It was a metal container, about 6 in tall and 4 in wide, and known as a 'bulls-eye' because of the thick round glass at the front.

'It burnt paraffin oil, and had to be kept upright. It had a hook which crooked into father's button hole. All postmen had one. They were not heavy and we used it to go to the outside toilet at night. So there was no gas or electricity in the house till I grew up and put in the electricity, and the gas company put in a cooker around 1925.'

'Keynsham in old picture postcards', by Barbara Lowe, records that 'The Keynsham Gas Company Ltd was formed in 1857 and went into voluntary liquidation in 1928. In the years 1891–1892, the cost to the ratepayers for lighting fifty street lamps in Keynsham was £98 17s 6d.' [photo 73]

'Built into the Pia's-limestone wall on the East side of Avon Road between Dragon's Hill and 'Sunnymede' were two iron lamp standards, about 10 feet high. They were very old when I was a boy, and had no 'cage' at the top, neither were they connected to a gas main. I suspect they were oil lamp standards provided by the brass mill owners to light their vehicles and workers along Avon Mill Lane', wrote Bert Robe.

The last local gas jet? I found this old gas mantle with its gas pipes in place, at the rear of the shop next to Oxfam, which was using the premises while the charity shop was being rebuilt in the mid 1980s. Soon afterwards this shop too was completely rebuilt and extended at the back, making yet another long thin Keynsham shop, and the gas jet gone! (Author's photos)

The hanging tree

'If you go up Wellsway and turn right to Chewton Keynsham,' Leslie said, 'at the top of the hill on the right hand side just a little way down, there used to be an old medium sized tree. It had one thick branch that jutted out over the field and was believed by the older Keynsham people to be the local hanging tree. I remember that part-way along the branch was a deep circle that went right round the branch, as if a thick rope had been tied there, and restricted the branch's growth at that point, but not beyond. There was no rope there when I knew it. But of course, hanging had been a widespread punishment for many years. The tree has gone now.'

However, Miss M Fairclough commented that, 'The tree was a pine and I have a drawing of it. I rather doubt if it had been a general 'hanging tree', but my great grandfather, 'Old Robin Thomas' is supposed to have come up from Chewton one morning and found a man hanging there, which seems to have been accepted as suicide; the shape and position of the tree would have made this easy, as there was a ten foot drop below the branch.'

Two generations of postmen

Leslie recalled that his father Herbert, (1875–1950), with four children, and his grandfather, James [with ten children, who lived at 87, Albert Road] were both Keynsham men, and had been postmen here. 'Father used to push a red PO handcart to meet the 6.0 a.m. train from Bristol with the mail and parcels (nothing came by road) and then push the cart back to the Post Office to sort and deliver them. On the way back he would empty the letter and wall boxes, and then sort those. He only delivered in Keynsham, but their area included Queen Charlton, Chewton Keynsham and Stockwood, where deliveries were made by bicycle.' Fortunately for Herbert's early start, he lived almost next to the Post Office.

'At one time postmen wore a pill box hat with a pointed rim and at another time had a hat with a similar rim at the back as well. The Post Office provided the full uniform of tunic, trousers and hat.' The 1887 Jubilee photo of the four postmen outside the PO showed a tunic that buttoned almost to the throat, with six brass buttons. A large canvas bag at the waist hung from a single strap over the shoulder.

Leslie described his father as 'Easy going and hard working. He was a postman all his life, as I think his father was too. He died in 1958, aged 83', he said.

Leslie explained that, 'At the end of the First Great War, the owners of the old PO building refused to renew the lease, so Mrs Gray, the new postmistress, opened a new PO building opposite the church, at the site of the last shop before Milward House. The subsequent photo of her, with her eight postmen, was taken in the garden of the new premises.'

Just to remind you, and to put the subject into perspective, 'The first inland post for public use was established in 1635 by Royal proclamation, but not until 1710 was a general post office created for the three Kingdoms and the colonies under the control of a Postmaster General. The famous mail-coach

Taken outside the Postmans Shelter at Nordrach Upon Mendip Charterhouse Aug 23 - 1903

This photograph, belonging to the late Mr Leslie Harding, shows his father, Herbert Harding, 'Taken outside the Postman's shelter, at Nordrack Upon Mendip, Charterhouse, Aug. 23, 1903.' Herbert (1875–1958), a postman all his life, started his career on the Blagdon postal area. Leslie claimed that the shelters were erected specifically by the Post Office for their postmen, whose deliveries were made on foot in that exposed area.

[which later came through the High Street] came into being in 1784, roads were improved [the loop of Bristol Road straightened out and Bath Hill dug out and the road widened] and the postal service vastly enlarged . . . The big postal reform whereby penny postage came into operation throughout the Kingdom began in January 1840 and became a great success when the railways became established. Then came prepayment by means of the adhesive postage stamps instead of collection on delivery.' [Newnes Pictorial Knowledge, Vol 10, page 327.]

The indefatigable Mrs Connie Smith, the first secretary of the Keynsham and Saltford Local History Society, in a well-researched lecture given to members in Dec 1967, on 'The Royal Mail', pointed out that the early mail coaches went from Bristol to Bath via Bitton, not Keynsham.

'Misdemeanours were severely dealt with as can be judged from a case before the Brislington Magistrates in 1829, when the driver of the mail from Bristol to Calne was fined £5 with 1s 5d costs for allowing an outside passenger to drive the coach. This happened between Keynsham and Bath, and this is the first direct record I have yet found of any mail coach travelling through our parish.

'Our Postmaster in 1830 was Stephen Whippie . . . George Rickets was Postmaster in 1870 . . . he was succeeded a year later by Miss Annabella Coleman. Miss Rachel Spiller was appointed in 1875 and this very capable young woman held the position for practically the next 40 years, and married one of her postmen, Mr Albert Harvey, in 1894 or 1895.

'Miss ME Ford became Post Mistress after the war, followed by Mrs Turner in 1915. Her husband operated the telephone exchange in Rock Road. Mrs Gray became the next post mistress in 1917 and continued for the next 30 years. There were five postmen at first and this number grew to 10 or 12 to cope with the mail as the population grew . . . The new PO on the site of Tredegar House was opened in 1960,' Mrs Smith concluded.

Miss J Cannam worked for the Post Office after the war, for the first seven years at Willsbridge 'which was a country office in a shop there', she said. 'Then for fourteen years I was at Keynsham, which was a Crown office. To start with I was the only woman among fifteen men. I used to start at five in the morning, and delivered mail throughout Keynsham, Chewton Keynsham and Burnett. Most of the time I cycled, and we worked from a large hut behind the PO opposite the church. I enjoyed the work very much'.

Leslie recalled that for a while his father had been a postman on the Blagdon post area, delivering and collecting letters from outlying hamlets, hence the charming photo of 'the Postman's Shelter', to aid him on his Mendip rounds.

Both Leslie and his younger sister recall that as children living at 31, High Street, Keynsham, they witnessed the arrival of the Royal Mail coach at the Post Office practically next door, as a regular event. He said, 'I can remember once a week the Royal Mail coach from Bristol to London would stop almost outside, at the PO. We would be in bed and would hear Mum and Dad say, 'Here comes the Royal Mail coach'. We could hear the horses' hooves and the noise of the coach. We would look out of our bedroom window and see the top of the coach. There were no passengers on it. Dad, of course, was on duty to

The Post Office in 1887. L to r: Jim Ford, Henry Grenut, Jimmy Harding and Albert Harvey. Extreme left, the pump at 'Pump Court'. Note the uniform of brass buttoned tunics and peaked pill box hats. The caption over the door reads, 'Postal Telegram Office'.

Bath Hill West, circa 1935. This just shows the arches of the bridge. Right, the Ollis home, 'Spring Cottage', on its two levels, with its fruit trees, later all demolished to straighten the road. Far right, the W.W.I. building. The road sweeper has a flat-bottomed hand cart.

225

Long service medals for two generations of Keynsham postmen, circa 1935. Lt to rt,
Fred Harvey, his father, Albert Harvey, Colonel Daynton (lived opposite the Bird in
Hand, S'ford), James Harding and his son Herbert.

The rear of the 'New P.O.' c. 1935, in the High St. opposite the church. Lt. to rt., standing, Mr Townsend, Jack Ollis, Fred Parsons, Mr Burridge, Ronald Ruck and Mr
McMahon. Seated, Mr H Harding, Mrs Gray the Postmistress, and Mr F Harvey.

receive and hand over the mail. I think the coach then called in at the Talbot for food.'

The Imperial Service Medal

Leslie proudly unfolded the single ancient page from an old PO journal, and handed it to me. Among the items of news recorded was one entitled, 'Unique.' It recorded, 'Presentations of Imperial Service Medals are not infrequent, but a recent little ceremony at Keynsham (Bristol) was perhaps unique. The recipient was Mr FW Harvey, who retired on November 5 after 44½ years. He was accompanied by his father, Mr CA Harvey, who retired from the Service 25 years ago after 44 years' service at Keynsham; while there were also present Mr H Harding, who received the SM on 30 April of this year after 43 years' service, and Mr Harding's father, Mr J Harding, who retired 28 years ago after 35 years' service at Keynsham. All four were born in Keynsham.'

The Keynsham Fire Brigade

'Assembled in the yard of the 'Lamb and Lark Hotel' is Keynsham's Fire Brigade of the early 1900s. This shows the horse-drawn appliance which replaced the hand-drawn one kept in the church porch,' declares the caption to the fascinating photograph, Number 49, in 'Keynsham in old picture postcards.'

Ronald Headington, of Spring Cottage, Bath Hill, said that his grandfather Ollis was responsible for providing the horse to pull the engine when the fire bell was pulled.

Leslie recalled that the next fire station had been in Charlton Road, just a little way up, on the right hand side, through double doors into a stone outhouse sited at the end of Mr JR Fear's garden. He was the town clerk. 'It had a bell above the doors which was loudly pulled by anyone on the outbreak of a fire, to summon the part-time firemen.'

Leslie knew something about fire fighting as he was one of the eleven members of the local brigade from 1929 to 1940, accompanied by his two brothers, Clifford and Philip. By then they had pukka uniforms, with impressive tall shining helmets, to go with their relatively modern fire-engine. Leslie had a fine photo of the three brothers in uniform, having won the local award for efficiency in the brigade.

Ex-fireman L Harding commented that, 'There were few fires in the town between the wars, as Keynsham was such a small place and the fire station in the High Street was in the centre of the town and all of the men lived nearby. Sometimes I was called out at night individually as people feared to call the brigade out as it was expensive, so if there was a small fire in one room, they sent down the road and called out the nearest firemen. Often members put out a small fire without the brigade being called, and everyone was pleased, including the Council.'

'We never used a lot of water, as fires were caught before they became big. Everyone had buckets in those days for collecting water from wells and pumps. To call out the Brigade, you smashed the glass outside the station,

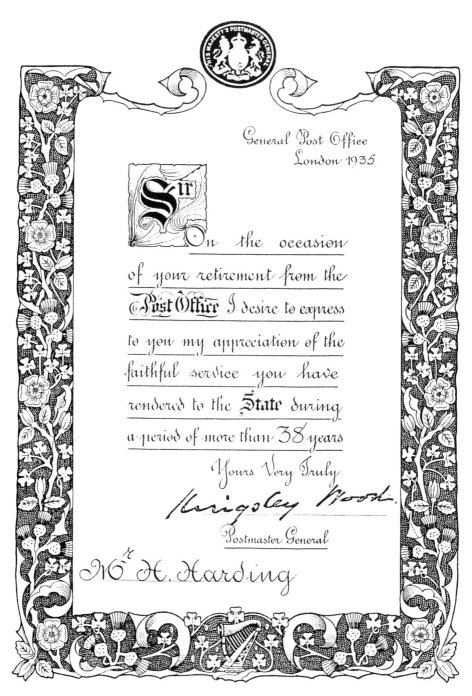

A letter written in 1935 from the G.P.O., expressing their appreciation of Herbert Harding's 38 years of faithful service.

which triggered the siren that would be heard all over the town.

'We didn't expect to be paid. It was something we did for the community. Even if the brigade was called out, the pay was very small. Though the service was already paid for by the rates, as people had fire insurances, after a fire the insurance companies would pay the brigade.

'We would practice at Stockwood Vale as it was quiet. We did our ladder drill at the Workhouse, using the tallest building there. We had a ladder that extended twice, but it was known as 'an escape' not a ladder. In competitions in the South West between brigades, I was the rescue man. As a builder, I was running up and down ladders all day, and could fly up a ladder. However, the rungs between a building ladder were 9 inches apart, but on a fire ladder they were 11 inches, which meant I kept hitting the rungs.

'In a real local fire, any member of the team could do the rescuing, the same as any one could drive. When the siren went, every minute counted, so you didn't wait for any special members. As soon as 5 or 6 men arrived, you went right away. But people in the town were very careful about avoiding fires.

'When the war started in 1939, the National Fire Service started an Auxillary FS Brigade in Keynsham, with their own engine [just a member's own car], trailer and firemen, sited at the Lamb and Lark. So there were two separate brigades, each with its own chain of command. However, an ex-military officer, Mr Gibson, new to Keynsham and this work, wormed his way up and was appointed chief fire officer over all of us. We were so furious that ten of us resigned together, and ten other men had to be appointed,' declared Mr Harding.

An eye-witness account of the Brigade's call-out 25 years later

My wife, Margaret Fitter, recorded the following event in the mid 1960s when the Service still had its station in the High Street.

'The bus travelled through the night and arrived at Keynsham about ten o'clock. As I alighted at the Lamb and Lark Hotel in the High Street, the Fire Siren sounded. The Fire Station loomed nearby in the darkness and I decided to watch the departure of the engine before continuing my journey home.

'Already, a group of people had gathered on the pavement opposite the Station. As I joined them the doors swung open, revealing the Fire Engine in a pool of light, its body vibrating, its driver seated and peering into the darkness from side to side. The town was then not large enough to merit a full-time Fire Brigade, and as we waited, the volunteers came rushing from their homes.

'A motor-bike tore up and was flung against a wall as its owner leapt from the machine, grabbed his jacket and helmet from a peg, and disappeared into the engine. Men appeared from the right and left, running, panting, all in the apparel they had on when the Siren called. The Engine Driver, growing impatient, began driving the vehicle out of the station.

'Then Harry appeared. He was peddling his bicycle as if his life depended on it. He was resplendent in his uniform helmet and jacket over his pyjamas and slippers. I recognised him as our window cleaner, as he half fell, half

Keynsham Fire Station, decorated for King George V's Silver Jubilee, Monday May 6, 1935. Notice on the left the round glass alarm switch, which when broken triggered off the alarm summoning the part-time firemen from their full-time occupations. This building was used during the 1939–45 war as the headquarters of the local National Fire Service. Today the site is 'Currys'. Observe how narrow the pavement was 55 years ago.

Keynsham Fire Brigade at Hamleaze, Stockwood Vale, 1935. Left to right: Fred Harper, Fred Palmer, Les Harding seated, Viv Bateman standing, Chief Officer Jack Bailey seated. On running board, Fred Rayson, Jack Woodham, Phil Harding, Jack Parsons, Cliff Harding, and Harold Robbins below.

jumped from his bicycle. He was too late! The Fire Engine, with bell clanging, moved out of the station without him and disappeared down Bath Hill out of sight.

'A lady standing next to me in the crowd said, with pride in her voice, 'Not bad. Three minutes flat. Not bad at all.' She cupped her hands and shouted across the road, 'Hard luck, Harry, well tried,' then aside to me, 'He could have done with that ten bob, too.'

'I remembered that bronchitis had kept Harry from his work during the winter, and wondered how much his chase to the station would cost him in terms of health.

'I watched him as, still panting, he used the rail to pull himself up the stairs at the rear of the station. I saw him move to another pool of light at the upstairs window, where the telephone operator could be seen seated at the table.

'The crowd disappeared into the darkness, and, the excitement over, the street became again silent and empty. I went home.'

To return to Leslie's resignation from the Brigade in 1939, he said,

'The next day the police were round and asked me to join the special constables, which I did. I wore a flat hat, or a black tin hat if there were raids on. One always went about with a regular constable. I was with Walter Millard, who lived at the top of Albert Road on the same side as this. He had a daughter, Freda. Our main duty was to make people 'put that light out.' Normally I was out twice a week, in the evenings [working for Mrs Wiggins during the day], but if there were raids, you were out every night. We worked from the old Police Station on Bath Hill, which had its front sandbagged.'

'The fine solidly built stone Police Station was in a good state of repair. It had its own magistrate's court. Before the war we even built a new wing on it, part of which was living accommodation. After the war, due to the increased size of the force with Keynsham's growing population, the new larger Station was built to the rear, after which the old building was empty and vandalized,' recalled the former 'Special'.

Protecting homes against the Luftwaffe

'I married Olive Beacham in 1936. When the war came in 1939, help was given by the authorities to make one room safe, possibly just for those with old people or children', Leslie thought. 'Roger, our only child, was a baby then, so we were given a flat-topped metal Morrison shelter, which we had in our back room. In addition, a 14 inch thick blast wall [against exploding bombs], 6 ft tall, was built just outside the rear window. There were a lot of Morrison shelters and blast walls in Keynsham.

'The walls were put up by a local builder named Cooper, who also built the whole of the left hand side of Handel Road, leaving the town. His son Frank lives in Park Road. After the war, I used mine to build our garage, with its concrete roof,' mused Leslie.

The town crier

One thing that Leslie put me right on was Keynsham's designation. 'It was never referred to as a village,' he said, 'but a town'. We had our town council, the KUDC, and were the centre for the local villages. We had our 'Town Band'. It was only the newcomers from Bristol who arrived in the 1920s to work at Fry's who called it 'the village', which compared with Bristol was all it was to them. But we locals always called it 'the town'.'

Yet Miss Fairclough wrote, 'Come to think of it, both my familes were "newcomers" in the nineteenth century! But we did all say "village".'

On the subject of the 'town crier' Leslie recalled that 'He was George Ollis for as far back as I can remember, at least to between the wars. Though he was paid for the job, really he worked for the GW Railway. He would go along the High Street, Temple Street, up Albert Road and Rock Road. In fact he went along all the old roads. He used to live in this road.

'Dressed in his uniform, he would come round in the evenings and ring his bell three times, then shout "O Yez" three times, then read his script. He had a good voice and I could hear him clearly. People would listen through open windows, or go to the gate. When he had finished, he would say, "God save the King". Instead of going to newsprint to advertise matters, you'd take the scroll to him and he would bellow it out through the town.

'His fine regalia and his strong voice helped him win town crier competitions. For three years he was 'All England Champion'. If you went to the pictures, when the Pathe-Victoria news came up, he was the town crier featured.

'Into the Royal Artillery'

'In 1940 I was called up and joined the Royal Artillery. I was in there for 5½ years. I was stationed on the South East coast, and along the Thames estuary, facing Germany. Then I had a spell in Edinburgh. I was on the Heavy Artillery, where you would have a semi circle of four anti-aircraft guns, which fired 3.7 or 4.5 in shells, which we were told had a range of seven miles. As part of a team, we were all able to do any job with the guns.

'As they knew of my fire brigade experience, I was made responsible for fire fighting on the gun sites, with the rank of Lance Bombardier. Also I was the PT Instructor for the unit of some 48 men (4 gun teams of 12) so we did half an hour of physical jerks every day, or went for a run of a mile or more.

'I was one of a gun crew of 12. The guns were a separate unit from searchlights. Behind us was a command post plotting the approach of aircraft. We were kept busy all the time, even if it was only gardening, till the bell went and the call sounded "take posts". Everyone took up the cry, and we had to be ready for action within two minutes, as the planes could be only ten minutes away.

'The large 3 foot long shell cases, 16 inches round, would be carried by hand and placed in the fuse setter, to be electronically activated from the command post, to detonate on impact. On firing, the shell case flew off backwards behind us up to about 100 yards away, but being of thinnish brass, they never hurt anyone. It was the breech that took the force of the firing. Each gun pit was surrounded by a wall of concrete.

'You could be very active or not according to how many planes went over. If a blitz was on, you could be firing for 20 minutes, or if a second wave came over. In the gun pit, you only knew what you were doing, though you could see the other crews. In the gun pit you stored as many shells as necessary for one engagement. Other shells were stored not far behind you in concrete bunkers and you fetched them in the brief spell between firing. The barrel and the chamber of the gun got hot, but not the parts that you touched.

'All you did was to pump one up there. You never knew if you hit a plane, for a circle of guns around a city would all be firing. Generally there was a sergeant in charge of each gun.

'We got dive bombed once. This was at Redcar, beyond the town and the pier, near the bowling green and park. I saw bombs being dropped and quickly looked up and thought, 'This one is for us.' The plane flew straight towards us and dropped a bomb. The next day we discovered that it fell half a mile away. One was not frightened. It all happened so quickly. I never found anything frightening in the army. I might have been if I had been in France and seen men coming towards me with fixed bayonets!

'We would fire as planes approached, generally at night. I can't remember firing in the day. You could only give a quick glance up if you were firing. The command post would give you 'the radius, elevation and fuse', and then the order to 'fire', so you carried on firing until told to 'cease firing'. You tried to get up as many shells as possible as the greatest chance of hitting the enemy.

'I would like to meet the personnel again. I've been to a few London reunions, but they died off. Probably most of them are dead too', sighed the so-helpful old soldier.

Among Mr Harding's awards is the National Fire Brigade's Association 'Long Service Medal', presented to him on May 19, 1940, by the Keynsham Fire Brigade. After the end of the War, he received the 1939–45 Defence Medal, with its green and orange ribbon; and the 1939–45 War Medal, with its broad red stripe.

An octogenarian widower, widely appreciated for his kindness, Mr Leslie Harding died alone in his home on June 17, 1991, aged 82. After a service at St John's Parish Church, he was cremated at Haycombe Cemetery, Bath, where his ashes were buried beside those of his wife.

He was a fine man and a natural gentleman. Rest In Peace, Leslie.

Chapter 17

A family of Builders – in Keynsham and in Korea

The experiences of Lance Bombardier Chris Wiggins, R.A.

The Wiggins are a very old Keynsham family, though unlike quite a few other local families, it is not of Dutch origin, nor is it connected with the brass industry. According to Mr Christopher Wiggins, the family originally came from Oxford, and bought Mulberry Farm, sited just above Cannock's garage on the Bristol Road, when it was still a farm. Though the fields have long been sold off, fortunately the lovely old farmhouse remains, with its own curved baking area still discernible from the road. The house is full of character; its second staircase, narrow and winding, led to the massive roof beams, which were of considerable antiquity. In the ensuing years, the farm was at one time a school run by Miss Oxford, and later this century the Roman Catholic Presbytery, prior to its being renovated as a private house.

Chris said that an entry in the 1851 Census for Keynsham recorded that 'Mrs Wiggins, widow', had two daughters, Elizabeth and Lucy, and an unchristened son. 'He was my grandfather, Edward Wiggins' declared Chris, and showed me two lovely photos of his grandparents, with Edward sporting a gold 'Albert' on his waist coat. He was the founder of the family firm, 'Edward Wiggins, Builder and Decorator', which still flourishes under his grandson.

Edward needed a business with a good income, as his wife blessed him with 9 sons and 3 daughters! But large families were what was expected in those Victorian days. 'My grandfther died in 1917, aged 65', said Chris.

Their second son was Edward junior, born in 1883, who when he grew up and married lived in Westbourne Avenue. The firm expanded under him, and he started building houses in Brislington and in Keynsham, though repairs and maintenance were their main business. Chris has an interesting photo of a group of their men, which includes himself as a young man, standing on a scaffold, during his father's building of a large house in the corner of Westbourne Avenue and St. Keyna Road for Mr Martin Gibbons. The extensive grounds of the house stretched down to a 100 metre frontage on Charlton Road, where I can recall that as late as 1962, wild blackberries grew along the length of the overgrown hedge, before it reached the ditch that flanked the pavement.

Chris wrote that, 'In 1917, whilst I was still a baby, we moved to the family's house at 48, The High Street, a two storey house, where Drummond's now is. Two doors down at 44, was Tredegar House, the three storied home of the renowned 'Dr Claude' Harrison, who had been a Major in the RAMC in the First World War, and who saw service on the continent. 'He was a friend of my father's and in the evenings he would provide entertainment when he brought round his gramophone records, of music and radio plays. He played cricket for Keynsham, and organised matches for all the local children at the Memorial Ground in Wellsway'.

Edward married Winifred Ambrose Ball from Dyrham Park, where her father was the head gardener till he retired around 1928. The marriage was blessed with four children, Christopher, born in 1917, then Sybil, Delia, and, in 1925, Philip. Sadly Chris was only 15 when his father died in 1932, aged 49, after two heart attacks in quick succession.

Edward Wiggins Junior, 1883–1932, son of the founder of the firm, 'Edward Wiggins, Builder and Decorator,' in 1898 as a 15 year old bugler boy in the Somerset Light Infantry Volunteers.

'Quite a dozen Bristol Grammar school boys'

The elder son joined the number of local children who were educated at Mrs Jollyman's, at 37, Charlton Road, until, being a boy, he left at 8. His father did not think much of the other local schools, so Chris was sent to Wick Road School, Brislington, accompanied by other local boys, who all went by train to St Anne's Park Station, then walked. At this time, Mr Gough, the headmaster of Bristol Grammar School's junior section, lived in the large house flanking the old Bristol Road, beside the farm at Hick's Gate, while Mr R J MacGregor, a master at the senior school, who wrote 'boys' books', lived at 'The School House', Burnett. 'I think my father came to know them by doing work for them', commented Chris.

So not unexpectedly, when he was ten, young Wiggins entered the junior section of the Grammar School, and later the main school. 'Other Keynsham boys who made it there, around that time, were the Button boys, Jim and Arthur Taylor, Alfred Pagett, the farmer's son from Burnett, Eric Grey, whose mother ran the Post Office opposite the church, and Reggie Exon, whose parents ran the dairy next to the P.O. A large contingent of us Keynsham boys went there. It was quite a dozen. In the morning we used to catch the 8.11 train to Bristol', Chris recalled. Following his father's death, he left the Grammar School for the Merchant Venturer's Technical College, alas now swept away. He added that Mrs Gough bred Chow dogs at her Hick's Gate home until quite recently. At that time there was no Keynsham Grammar School, nor Broadlands Secondary Modern School; 'Bath Hill' was the only local school for older boys and girls.

At home his mother kept the business going with the help of the foreman/manager, while she did the book work. 'Though we were really Anglicans, we children attended the Victoria Methodist Sunday School. I'm not sure whether it was because our parents thought that we received better teaching there, or just that they gave better parties,' laughed Chris, and added, 'My teacher was Ken Gibbons, the accountant'.

'After leaving the Merchant Venturers I got a post as junior surveyor for Chivers of Devizes, building the hutted army camp on Roundmoor Hill, and when that finished, I moved to Melksham on the RAF hutted camp for John Lang, and whilst there, in March 1941, the calling-up papers came for the Survey Training Regiment, Royal Artillery, at Brighton.'

Lance Bombardier Christopher Wiggins

Apprehensive like everyone else, he went to London by train to join the Royal Artillery. 'On the train I met my future brother-in-law, Alec Pillinger, who joined the REME at Woolwich. Also by chance in the same carriage was Mitchell Bond, who was a traveller for Metal Agencies Company, but we both knew him through his work as Chairman of Keynsham RFC.

'I was then sent to Preston Barracks at Brighton for three months' basic training. Then 'Dunkirk' occurred, and the barracks were taken over. We were moved into tents at nearby Danny Park, with its Elizabethan house, where the Peace Treaty at the end of the first war was drawn up. We were put on

'Beach Defence' duty, which consisted mainly of building up sand-bag defence positions, then taking them down and rebuilding them again in a different manner. A German plane passed overhead at Brighton, dropped a bomb, and we ushered the frightened people into the Aquarium's underground passages,' recalled Gunner Wiggins.

'Then I was posted to the 122 Field Regiment, the 278 Battery, who were mostly Yorkshire 'Terriers', at South Cave, Kingston on Hull. From there we were posted to Aldborough, then to Wolsingham, Co. Durham, then up to Glasgow for overseas service. I was given Embarkation Leave and was back in Keynsham to witness the first raid on Bristol. We went up by car to Queen Charlton, where from the top road you can clearly see the Suspension Bridge. We could hear the German planes quite clearly and see the explosions caused by the bombs dropping.'

'Made up' to Lance Bombardier earlier at Wolsingham, from Glasgow he left with his Battalion on the 'Empress of Japan' for Capetown, Bombay, Ceylon and finally to ill-fated Singapore. 'We were at Pavang, the large open space between the law courts area and the sea, when the surrender came and the Japanese took over. We were marched to Changi barracks, which they used as a prison camp. I was in Singapore for six months, where we were very apprehensive,' the Bombardier recalled.

A Korean Chemical Factory

Then came action. 'We were the first group to be moved from Singapore on the 'Fukkai Maru', Chris wrote.

Corporal JD Wilkinson, of the Australian army, in 'Sketches of a POW in Korea' (Wilkie & Co, Melbourne, 1945) filled in the details of what happened. He wrote, 'After many days of waiting, the 'Japan Party' finally left the Changi Camp, Singapore, on the 16th August, 1942. Travelling over 30 to each truck, we left early in the morning, and were driven to Keppel Harbour. After waiting on the wharf for some time, we were taken aboard a fumigation ship. We bathed in a formalin bath, collected our fumigated belongings, and returned to the wharf. Moving along the wharf, the party went aboard the small Japanese transport the 'Fukkai Maru', 3,000 odd tons. We were then put into one of the four holds of the ship. About 400 senior officers returned to the wharf, leaving about 1,000 British and Australian troops in very cramped and unpleasant conditions.

'The POWs were permitted certain hours on deck for washing and recreation. Due to crowded conditions, it was necessary for half of the men to have their very meagre rice and soup meals on deck, while the remainder ate in the stuffy hold.

'Leaving Singapore on 19 August, we sailed in convoy up the Malay coast and across to St. Jacques, ocean port of Saigon, French Indo-China. We zig-zagged from St. Jacques across to the port of Takao, in south-west Formosa. We spent 16 days unloading our bauxite cargo and reloading with bags of rice.

'On board ship, almost 100 Australian and over 100 members of the Royal North Lancashire Regiment were packed sardine-like into one of the holds.

Lance Bombardier Christopher Wiggins, Surveying Section of Royal Artillery, 1941.

When the hatch covers were on, the air quickly became thick and foul. There were rats, mice, cockroaches and other insects to worry us. The prison ship was a small Japanese tramp steamer, very old and dirty, and of a rather common design.

'On September 22, we finally arrived at Fusan, a port on the south Korean coast. Although rather drab-looking, we were very pleased to see it, as it meant the end of our unpleasant and dangerous voyage. The party was disembarked on the morning of the 24th. After having our belongings searched, we were forced to march about five miles around Fusan. After a short wait at the station, we were entrained in third class carriages, which, after the prison ship, were very comfortable.

'Travelling all night, we arrived at Keijo at about mid-day. We were split into two parties – one of which went to Jinsen, a port about 20 miles from Keijo; ('where we worked for a year digging out the nearby marshes, to extend the port area' recalled Bombardier Wiggins.) The remainder marched from the station about one mile to a newly-prepared prison camp. The camp was in the midst of slum-like Korean houses – very small, very crowded and very squalid. Mostly built of mud, some had thatched roofs, others iron.'

Wilkinson wrote of Roll Call, 'The ceremony of 'rolling the call' took place morning and evening. The squad leader, or 'hancho' made his report in Japanese. The men numbered in Japanese. The Jap Orderly Officer was accompanied by an Orderly Sergeant and interpreter and a British Aide-Officer and Aide-NCO.'

The POWs dormitory was the 'Squad Room', a long, low, flat-ceilinged room, with two rows of mats or 'tatami' [woven straw] just raised off the floor and virtually touching each other, on which they slept. 'In between the two rows were free standing rather inadequate stoves, which we used in the extremely cold winter weather . . . We generally huddled around the stove in order to keep warm. Room temperatures were frequently just a few degrees above freezing point. There were wash-houses, which in winter were completely frozen over.'

Wilkinson explained, 'We had our own men in the cookhouse, which suited both ourselves and the Japs. On Mess Parade, rice and stew was collected from the cookhouse by mess-orderlies. After being 'dished out', each man collected a bowl of rice and a bowl of stew.

'Works Parade. After the Works Bugle was blown in the morning, we went out on the parade ground, and fell in by working parties. We were numbered and searched, then marched off to the factory for whom we worked, about half a mile away. In the bitter winter weather it was very unpleasant standing ten minutes or so with the snow on the ground and the icy blast whistling around us.'

Daily work parties laboured at the freight platform at Keijo Station, entailing a good deal of heavy work. A certain amount of the goods were shifted from one part to another by railway hardcarts, or 'Kurumas'. They unloaded different types of freight, such as iron, flour, rice and timber. Other groups, all usually 30 strong, worked at the lime kilns, with blacksmiths, or tended the furnaces. 'One of the hardest, hottest, most dangerous and most unpleasant jobs was stoking the carbide furnaces, which burnt at a temperature of approximately 3,000 deg.C.'

Bombardier Wiggins was in the same camp as Wilkinson, whom he described as tall, quiet and bookish, and who taught himself Japanese and was then able to read their newspapers, supplied by the Koreans. Describing his work there, Chris wrote, 'Here our main work was to run the furnaces making carbide, which was used to provide acetylene gas in special containers which were used to drive the cars and lorries in place of petrol. Also there was a 'cracking tower' which was used to obtain the high octane fuel for the fighter aircraft, by converting the acetylene. So we were helping the Japanese war effort.'

He recalled that in one group was a young officer, Lieutenant Moore, a Territorial from Halifax. Known as 'Bunny', he escaped from the prison and travelled many miles before recapture. Then he was put into the normal communal prison, where he died.

The bombardier continued, 'We were three years altogether in Korea. We were extremely fortunate in that there was little ill-treatment of the prisoners, compared with some of our regiment working in Thailand and in Japan in their coal mines. But at times when food was short for the Koreans, we were hungry also, and became thin. Occasionally we were knocked about.

'When the war ended in 1945, we were in the northern section, north of the 38 parallel of latitude, about half way up Korea, in the Russian section, when they finally came into the war. The American planes dropped a number of canisters, made by welding two fifty gallon oil drums, on parachutes, right onto the camp. One landed on the hospital, where one of our chaps was in bed, and the drum was suspended just over him by its shrouds. So the Russians devised a different way of receiving food and clothing. When the next USA plane arrived, a Russian plane took off from the nearby airdrome, and requested it to land to unload. The Allied plane refused, so the Russians hit one of its engines, so it had to land there, which increased the number of POWs to be fed. The Americans got in touch with their base, who soon had them out, but we British stayed there for two months after the Peace Agreement.

'The Russians were going to send us home via the Trans-Siberian railway but we went by train to the tip of Korea, then by ship to Manilla, and then sailed to San Francisco, where I remained for three weeks on Angel Island. Then it took us five days to cross America to the Queen Mary. We were in New York for just two hours, which was rather a shame, as we went straight across the city to board the ship. We arrived back in Southampton on November 15, 1945. When we docked, there were thousands on the quayside with the bands assembled. Someone asked, 'What are they there for?' But when the bands struck up, we realised that it was for us, for the ship was full mainly of ex POWs being repatriated. It was quite interesting.'

When I asked him about medals for bravery, he explained that from a fighting point of view, 'I was never in action. I only ever fired three rounds of .303 and that was at the range. I never had a rifle. We were the Surveying Section of the Artillery'.

The following pictures are from J D Wilkinson's 'Sketches of a POW in Korea'. In his foreword he wrote, 'This collection of drawings and sketches, prepared under difficult conditions and with poor materials, represents some of our experiences as POWs. It covers the period from the time the 'Japan Party' left Changi Camp, Singapore, in 1942, up to the finish of the war in 1945. This book is dedicated to those men who died in Korea, and, in particular, to Corporal Reg. Hayter, of Sydney.' The slim book is dated 'October, 1945'.

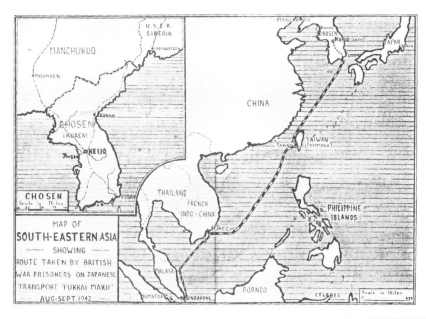

After many days of waiting, the "Japan Party" finally left the Changi Camp, Singapore, on the 16th August, 1942. Travelling over 30 to each truck, we left early in the morning, and were driven into Keppel Harbour.

After waiting on the wharf for some time, we were taken aboard a
fumigation ship. We bathed in a formalin bath, collected our fumigated belongings, and returned to the wharf.

Moving along the wharf, the party went aboard the small Japanese
transport the "Fukkai Maru," three thousand odd tons.

We were then put into one of the four holds of the ship. About 400 senior officers returned to the wharf, leaving about 1000 British and Australian troops in very cramped and unpleasant conditions.

Keijo Station.—Working on the freight platform at Keijo Station, although entailing a good deal of heavy work, had its advantages. A proportion of the freight was foodstuffs, and, of course, the Ps.O.W. took their share of that. The sketch shows sugar being loaded into a truck. Note the P.O.W. getting his sugar behind the stack.

Some of the crates we carried were very heavy and had to be carried
long distances.   We upset the Japs' calculations at times by changing
destination labels.

Roll Call.—The "ceremony" of "rolling the call" took place morning
and evening.   The squad leader, or "hancho," made his report in
Japanese.   The men numbered in Japanese.   The Jap Orderly Officer
was accompanied by an Orderly Sergeant and interpreter and a British
Aide-Officer and Aide-N.C.O.

Wash-house.—There were two Wash-houses, which in winter-time were completely frozen over.

The Stove.—The winter weather was bitterly cold, and we generally huddled around the stove in order to keep warm. Room temperatures were frequently just a few degrees above freezing point.

"A Family at War"

Like the Ashton family in the TV play by the above name, all four of the Wiggins' children played an active part in the war effort.

'My sister Sybil was in the ATS and drove ambulances in France. Later she drove padres as well, though that was mainly in Belgium.

'Delia worked for the Fire Service, which was almost opposite our house in the High Street. I don't think she did any actual fire fighting, but was part of the back-up team. She helped produce the pantomimes which were very popular.'

The jacket of the record, 'Songs that won the war', says that 'In the dark days between 1939–45 only two things united the people of these islands. The first was their indomitable will to win the war, the second was the songs they sang and enjoyed together. Songs that united the housewife in the queue with the PBI sweltering in the sands of the Western Desert or the monsoon mud of Burma, the war worker with the lonely lookout at Atlantic or Malta convoy, the evacuee child with a parent in some underground shelter, and the ATS girl on some lonely gunsite with the man in the air guarding our nation's skies.'

Indeed, I can recall that we sang 'We'll meet again' and 'Roll out the Barrel' with gusto. 'We're gonna hang out the washing on the Siegfried Line' and 'Bless 'em all' were early favourites, together with 'I've got sixpence' and 'Kiss me good night, Sgt-Major'. 'This is the Army, Mr Brown' was humorous, while 'Run rabbit, run rabbit, run, run, run' had overtones of the country side, and was light-hearted and cheerful. But the song that for me epitomized all our patriotism and resolve was, 'There'll always be an England'. They do not seem to write songs of that calibre today. These would have been among the songs that they sang in Delia's fire service entertainments.

Just a young Naval Cadet

Philip, the youngest of the four Wiggins children, was at Bristol Cathedral School when war was declared. He always had a love for the sea, so after Chris was called up, he left school and volunteered.

He joined the Merchant Navy, an unusual thing to do for a Keynsham lad, for in both World Wars, most of the men were in the army. However, he was readily accepted, and within a few weeks was off on his first trip afloat on a convoy to Russia. Unfortunately he did not make it, and his ship was torpedoed off Finland. Luckily Philip survived, and was marched, with the rest of the crew, through Finland and down to a POW camp in Germany, for the rest of the war. What an experience for a sixteen year old boy!

Back in Keynsham at 48, The High Street, a telegram was delivered to Mrs Wiggins, saying that he was lost at sea, believed drowned. If that was not tragic enough, a further telegram was received soon afterwards concerning Chris, stating that he was missing, believed dead. It was not until six months later that she heard that Philip was alive and well, and a year later still before she heard that Chris had also survived. You can imagine the rejoicing!

Incidently, Philip's near drowning in 'The Cruel Sea' did not quench his love for the nautical life. After the war he went on to obtain his master's ticket,

The elder of the sisters, Sybil Wiggins (Mrs C N Benoy), in her ATS uniform, circa 1942/43.

The younger sister, Delia Wiggins (Mrs A G Pillinger), in her National Fire Service uniform, c. 1942/43.

His younger brother, Philip Wiggins, in his Merchant Navy uniform, circa 1941.

captained several ships around Australia, became a ships' pilot at Sydney, and finally captained, then became a pilot, for the new breed of oil-carrying supertankers. Then he retired to live south of Sydney, with a home on a mountain side having a wonderful view.

Chris said that William Brownsey, one of the two sons of the local butcher, was one of the few non-medical officers in the Royal Army Medical Corps. Leslie Davis of Rock Road was also commissioned, while Michael Sparey of Priory Road was an officer in the RAF.

In Korea, when Chris heard of the dropping of the atom bomb, he said, 'We were all highly delighted, though we were unaware of quite its magnitude. The Japanese had orders to kill all prisoners if there was an invasion, while they themselves would fight to the death, as they did on several Pacific islands. So the bomb saved both us and them. With hindsight, it could possibly have been dropped on a slightly less highly populated island.'

Today, with the end of the war now fifty years ago, the fit ex-soldier still continues in business as 'Edwards Wiggins', though at a slower tempo and with one painter on his staff.

Chapter 18

Join the Army and see the World
The experiences of Sergeant Ron Headington

On a cold February day in 1940, a slim-built, bright young man reported at Dorchester to join the Dorset Regiment. Private Ronald William J Headington, 'Number 5729966, Sir', was far from home. That would have been Keynsham, though centuries earlier his family came from Headington outside Oxford.

'Headington is an English locational name . . . the name derives from the personal name 'Head' coming from the Old English pre 7th Century 'heafod' and given to a chief or perhaps to one with a peculiarly shaped head. The suffix 'ing' in this case means 'eldest son' or 'family of'; 'ton' comes from the Old English 'tun' meaning a 'farm' or 'settlement'. The name translates as 'Heads's family farm' and was originally given to one residing in this place . . . In 1379, one Johannes De Hedyngton appeared in the Poll Tax Records of Yorkshire,' according to 'Name Origin Research.'

By the 17th century the 'Head's family' had moved to North Somerset, where one of Ronald's ancestors, a Headington from Corston, was hanged in the Monmouth Rebellion in 1685. Other Headingtons worked in the Keynsham brass works and inter-married with the Ollis family.

Ronald can trace his connection with Keynsham straight back 250 years to Harry and Ann Headington. Harry's son, John, was born and later died in 1771 and is buried in St. John's cemetery where many later Headingtons lie. One was Marie Fray (formerly Voray) born in 1804 and whose daughter, Sarah, married John Headington (1843–1917), Ronald's grandfather.

To return to matters military, the Army has a way of transferring its personnel from one regiment to another. Private Headington had hardly completed his basic training in the 'Dorsets', when they were found to be overmanned,and he was transferred to the 'Queen's Royal Regiment', and was posted to Kent just in time for the Battle of Britain.

Ronald recalled that, 'I had many exciting times there, transporting captured German airmen, watching the coast for wrecks and burying the dead. When I was at Dymchurch, occasionally a German spotter plane would come over and shoot us up at the Martello Tower. I did a stint at Dover, where after the fall of France, the town was shelled from Calais. That was where I first saw Field Marshall B L Montgomery, who inspected us, and under whom I was to serve later.'

The 'History of the 2nd/5th Battalion, The Queen's Royal Regiment, 1939–1945, by Captain P N Tregoning, MC, officially describes how 'the younger members of the Regiment, much to their disgust [instead of accompanying the Battalion to France] . . . were engaged on coast defence and the guarding of airfields until they rejoined the Battalion after its return from France . . . At Dymchurch we were responsible for the coastline from St. Mary's Bay to the Grand Redoubt and were billeted at beach bungalows and holiday camps . . . On 15th August, 200 men and many of the drivers then turned their hands to harvesting for a fortnight . . . This was the time of the Battle of Britain and every night bombers passed over on their way to London . . . The 13th of September was regarded as the probable invasion date, and for a fortnight men slept fully dressed, with vehicles loaded, at thirty minutes' notice to move.

'Journey Overseas'

'On the 3rd May, 1942, we moved to Raleigh . . . and men were sent on embarkation leave. Mobilization was completed at the beginning of August. There was a final review by the King, and on 23rd and 24th August the Battalion moved out of Sudbury Station in three trains for Glasgow Docks. The trains pulled in at the dockside on the afternoon of 24th August. The companies drew mess-tickets and climbed up the gangway of the Johann van Oldenbarnvelt. She was a fairly new ship of 18,000 tons . . . After the usual inspection the men explored the ship and tried not to get lost . . . The convoy formed up and finally sailed in the early evening of Friday, 28th August. Our last view of land showed us the sun setting behind the Scottish hills. One wonders, sailing out of the Clyde, when one will sail into it again.

'On 7th September we had our first sight of Africa. The misty line on the horizon turned to green and took the shapes of hills and trees . . . After a fortnight at sea, everyone is glad to see Freetown; after a couple of days in Freetown everyone is delighted to see the sea . . . Owing to the risk of malaria, no troops were allowed ashore . . . On the morning of 25th September, many of us rose early to see the sun rise over Table Mountain. South Africa from a ship four weeks at sea seems a strange and beautiful world.'

Ronald said the Battalion then sailed on to Bombay where they disembarked and went inland to Deolali for twelve days. 'Parades started early and at mid-morning the heat seemed unbearable . . . During the afternoons it was too hot to move; in the evening the men would walk down to the native bazaars and bargain for silks . . . The march down to the station [of the Battalion, for Bombay] was accompanied by the pipes and drums of an Indian regiment.'

Though 'The Queens' had originally set out to fight the Japanese in the Far East, at Bombay the plans were changed when it was thought that the Germans would come through the Caucasus Mountains and seize the Kuwait oilfields. Accordingly, 'We moved up the Persian Gulf, through a sea of glass, to Basra. After a four-day wait in the anchorage we docked and disembarked. This was 13th November. It was hot and dusty. Winter clothing arrived next day . . . In summer it is heat, dust and flies; in winter it is cold, mud and rain. After disembarking we moved by road to a tented camp at Shaiba. Our final destination was Kirkuk'.

Ronald was by this time a full corporal. He and several of the men were left in Bombay in hospital with mumps, and the corporal was appointed to see that they joined the Battalion when they were all fit. So later the soldiers

Bombay, September, 1942, Corporal Ronald Headington en route for the Persian Gulf and Kirkuk. His Indian photographer insisted that the table, complete with flowers, hat and a book, should be included to enhance the scene. That was nearly fifty years ago, and the corporal, as smart as ever, is still a very active man.

sailed to Basra in a native boat, with its unusual sail. 'The natives fed us with foul tasting food that they cooked in an iron stove in the bows of their boat, which smelt horrible,' Ronald recalled.

Both the Division and the corporal's party, finally reached Kirkuk and stayed there until the following March 21st, when they were relieved by a Polish division. 'We did not know where we were going, but anywhere seemed better than Iraq', continued the 'History'.

The Battalion crossed the desert of Transjordan from Baghdad to Tulquarn in Palestine, and travelled down into Egypt and the Suez Canal. 'The Battalion then learnt its future. It was to organize quickly for battle and leave for the Eighth Army in four days. We exchanged our 2-pounder guns for 6-pounders and were made up to establishment in transport . . . We had changed into khaki drill so the weather was cold and wet'.

From Cairo they went through the Western Desert, through Alamein to Tobruk and Benghazi into Tripoli. 'On 19th April we started the last part of the journey round the Gulf of Gabes to the sound of guns in the Tunis hills. The complete journey from Kirkuk totalled over 3,000 miles, accomplished in under five weeks with seven non-travelling days. It ended after dark on 22nd April and by next morning the Battallion was in action. This must be the longest approach march to battle in modern history.'

Ronald said, 'We drove the Germans out of Tunisia. Their Africa Corps were a tough lot, unlike the Italians, who were nice people but not very good soldiers. There was the amusing occasion when one British soldier alone rounded up 1,000s of them as prisoners of war!

'The Queens', being a London regiment, wore the insignia of a Dick Whittington's black cat on the epaulettes of their shirts and vehicles, so the Germans nicknamed them 'Hell's Kittens'. The Germans feared the Gurkha soldiers as, with their curved daggers, they took no prisoners. When the Germans finally had to give in, they deliberately surrendered to our regiment'.

The Italian campaign

Ronald continued, 'By this time the Americans had joined us. Owing to the fact that they were short on troops that had actually done landings, they put our Division with the American 5th Army under General Mark Clark. This was in September, 1943. Our sea journey from Tripoli to Salerno took us two days.

'For every Battalion, you have an Intelligence Officer to collate all the information coming in. When we landed at Salerno, I had to take over from him as he was put on other duties, so I had to do his job, without any extra pay of course, so that's why they made me up to sergeant to make it look a little bit better, and for which service and responsibility I received a medal.

'Unfortunately, when we landed at Salerno, the Germans there had just finished target practice, and on our arrival they simply unpacked their guns, and caused us heavy casualties.

'I was told that D Company had been dispatched to secure and hold an important bridge. When I arrived at Company HQ, they were nearly all dead. A wounded man said the CO had gone forward to help hold the bridge, where

I found the remaining staff, and the Company Commander, a Major, injured. There being no officer above me in rank, I had to take command and hold the bridge against German attacks for 12 hours. We started with some 15–20 men, and ended with only 6, when the Guards relieved us.

'There we had one large anti-tank gun to defend ourselves against an approaching German armoured car, with troops behind it. As our men were dropping hit, it was important to knock out the car, but I did not know how to fire it. The gunnery corporal showed me how, though saying it had to be set up correctly to get the right range. I said, "Just point the blessed thing at the car," as it drew still nearer. The first shot went over it, but the second scored a direct hit, and the infantry fled.

'Later more heavy firing began, and the corporal was hit. As I went up to him, he murmured, 'Can't go on, Ron, can't go on' and turned his head away. I saw his arm had been blasted by shrapnel and I could see his ribs, and knew that he had had it. I cradled his head for a while until he died. All around him were his dead crew. After that I was so mad and upset that I started loading the shells and blazing away with the gun single-handedly, at nothing in particular, just in the direction of the Germans. Some of the shells would have hit them.

'After this incident, the CO offered me a commission there on the battle-field as a 2nd Lieutenant. I asked, Would I have to leave the Regiment, and go for training? He said 'Yes'. Rather than do this, I refused it, though I knew it was an honour to be offered a commission in these circumstances. The Colonel was greatly disappointed, and kept referring to me as 'wasted material'.

'Some time later I was on the Via Appia in a jeep with the same Command-ing Officer, Lt Colonel JY Whitfield, DSO, OBE, in the front seat, while his batman sat beside me in the rear. The driver was a real character, who had previously been a New York taxi driver and had volunteered to drive the Bri-tish as he had an English mother. Suddenly there was a noise like an express train coming, and that was an armour piercing shell fired by a retreating Ger-man tank. It entered the jeep's fan belt and went right down the middle of the jeep, through the gear box, between the driver and the Colonel and went out through the back of the car, without hitting the petrol tank. The steering gone, the jeep turned out of control and threw us into the ditch.

'The Colonel calmly said, "Don't go out into the road anymore. Stay where you are and you'll be completely safe. We've still got to continue", and sent his batman back to Battalion HQ for another vehicle. He was completely calm, and while we sat there recovering, he asked me if I had any injuries. I said 'No', and then spoke to him in a way not usually done, for they were tin-pot gods. "How ever can you be so calm and confident?" "Well you say your prayers in the morning, don't you?" asked the Colonel. "No, at night". "Then say them in the morning as well.

"In the morning I tell God all that I am going to do and seek His help and protection. Then I go out and leave it in His hands. If He had ordained that I was to die, that's it, so I don't worry about it." Some time later the CO tackled his sergeant about it, emphasizing that he must pray every morning, and keep it up. Later the Colonel was promoted to General.

Ronald participated in the Anzio landing in Feb, 1944, near Rome, adding,

'Later we crossed the Apennines in winter, when the weather was dreadful and the snow deep. The mountains were so steep that we even had mules to carry our ammunition and supplies. Sometimes we sheltered at night in caves occupied by Italians whose homes had been destroyed, who shared their food with us.' Kindly old Keynsham seemed a whole world away!

Earlier, on Jan 1, 1944, at Marrakesh in Morocco the Prime Minister, Winston Churchill, visited his C in C, General Montgomery, and wrote in the General's autograph book, 'The immortal march of the Eighth Army from the gates of Cairo along the African shore through Tunisia through Sicily has carried its ever victorious soldiers and their world honoured Commander far into Italy towards the gates of Rome. The scene changes and vastly expands. A great task accomplished gives place to a greater in which the same unfailing spirit will win for all true men a full and glorious reward.'

The Gothic Line; 29 August 1944 to 10 October 1944

'The decisive defeat suffered by the Germans in May had resulted in the swift conquest of Central Italy, and the advance had continued with diminishing speed through the summer. The resistance stiffened . . . while the Germans prepared in the Northern Appenines their winter line for 1944–45. The Gothic Line guarded the Lombardy Plain.

'On 1st Sept the 2nd/6th Queen's attacked Monte Capello and occupied it, at first taking the Germans completely by surprise. It was now our turn. The 1st September was hot. The Battalion spent it marching up to a concentration area 3,000 yards south-east of the mountain. . . . The intention was to push the enemy off these features before they had time to reorganise,' recorded the History.

Years earlier, in the late 1920s at Bath Hill School, Ronald was a slightly built boy, who somehow attracted the attention of the school bullies. 'The toilets were the worst places. I used to wait for the last minute of playtime to use them, and then got into trouble for being late in the line. One of my close friends was Reg Cook of Park Road, who at 13 was 6 feet tall. Our mothers, who were friends, said, 'Let Reg look after Ron in school, and Ron can help Reg with his homework,' so that is what happened. As friends we joined up together at Dorchester, and were both transferred to the 'Queens' and were in the same company until I was made a corporal.

'As lads, we were on holiday together at Weymouth, where we visited a fortune teller. She said there would be a war and that Reg would not get on very well. She told me as I was leaving that I would always know when I was going to get injured or killed. We both laughed at her words until we were in the army. The absence of the premonition of death or injury gave me a quiet confidence, which the CO said was why he had chosen me for his staff.

'Knowing of our friendship, during the bitter fighting for the Gothic Line, news was brought to me at HQ that Reg had been killed. I asked for permission to bury him, which was granted. After that I had the invidious task of breaking the news to his mother by letter, though she refused to accept the fact until back home I told her of it personally. That was the hardest part of the war for me.

'By now we were in North Italy, level with Florence. It was here, a week after Reg's death, that I suddenly lost my confidence. [Was it delayed shock and grief?] I went forward to an observation post, where I found our man killed from mortar bomb shrapnel. There were two telephone lines there, one

Place: The Army camp of wooden huts outside Cairo.
Year: Summer 1944, on Sergeant Headington's last visit there, a few weeks before being injured in battle.
Occasion: The 'Black Cats' Division were there to regroup and take on new personnel after so many of the 'Queen's Regiment' had been killed or injured at Gemmano. This was in preparation for the final push against the strong German Gothic Line in North Italy.
Front row, left to right.
1. Private Bert Hewitt, 'the strong man', who was also a sniper.
2. Sergeant Headington, wearing the ribbon of his 'MM' and the '8th Army Africa Star'.
3. Lieutenant, later Captain, JM McCarthy.
4. Corporal Moss. He and the Sergeant were the only 2 of the 'Queen's' to survive from the original section of 12 men who came out from England.
Rear row, left to right
1. The USA driver from Texas, seconded at his own request to the 'Queen's.'
2. Private Nicholas Carter, of Anglo-Egyptian parentage.
3. Private Gerald Merson, an Oxford undergraduate.
4. A Yugoslavian private, seconded to the regiment as a linguist and translator, for use as the oncoming offensive gained ground.

for spotting for the artillery, and the other to Battalion HQ, so I stayed and used both. Then one of our runners arrived, with the order that I was to come back as my position had been noticed by the enemy.

'We walked back along the road in the dark until we came to the crossroad, where unknown to us the retreating Germans had an 88 tank gun on a fixed line on the crossing, and every so often sent a salvo over, sure that sometimes it must hit something. Suddenly I saw a flash of light, and a shell exploded near me. I never heard it. You never hear the one that's coming for you. It shattered my left leg, and the runner, a fine man who had given up an Oxford education to fight, helped me to a dressing station 100 yards down the road, with my foot hanging off.

'Later I was taken further back on a stretcher, to a grass landing strip, to fly to Naples. There the plane was too full to accommodate me. I felt so awful that I pleaded for a place, even if I had to leave the stretcher. 'Sorry old chap. It's full up', was the reply. However, my luck held. The plane was so heavy that in taxi-ing to take off, it failed to clear the trees, and came down nose first. They had great difficulty in getting the patients free, some of whom had slid out of their harness.

'The next thing I remembered was waking up in hospital in Naples, with a Queen Alexandra Nursing sister looking at me, in her unusual headgear. The sisters were wonderful. The ward was really macabre. It was called 'the lost limbs ward'. One side of me was a man who had had both legs torn off from the thighs, and had only one arm. The nurses supplied him with a gramophone, with one modern record, which he could wind with his one good arm, and he played it over and over again. We got heartily sick of it, but couldn't bear to ask him to stop it. I never knew if he lived.

'On the other side was a man with gangrene of the leg, which grew worse and worse. One day he was muttering something to the nurse, who came over to me with a request. "Right, you're a sergeant!" "Oh yes, tell me what I've got to do'. "Well, the man dying beside you thinks you're one of his family, and wants to hold your hand." Of course I agreed and they pushed our beds together, and I held his hand till he died.

'Later I was put on Mussolini's pleasure yacht, which sailed to Liverpool. Hundreds were there to greet us. Innumerable dockers pushed lighted cigarettes into my mouth, which as a non-smoker I tried to spit out, which was all the more difficult as my arms were strapped against the stretcher under the red blankets, so they wouldn't get knocked. At Manchester Infirmary I had 12 operations, and finally ended up at St Martin's Hospital, Bath.

'There we walking wounded were given the freedom of Bath. Every morning a bus would come to take those of us who wished to go, into Bath, where in our blue uniforms, white shirts and red ties, we could go into any cinema and almost any restaurant, and nearly anywhere, free of charge. Old ladies would come up and offer us money, though when I looked at them I thought that their need was greater than mine, and declined.'

Ronald was awarded the Military Medal for his great services at the Salerno landing. Unfortunately a letter from His Majesty regretted that he was not well enough to stand for a long period presenting medals. So there was a small parade at the hospital where a line of soldiers and nurses received their

BUCKINGHAM PALACE.

I greatly regret that I am
unable to give you personally the
award which you have so well earned.
I now send it to you with
my congratulations and my best
wishes for your future happiness.

George R.I.

5729966 L.Sjt. R.W.J. Headington, M.M.,

The Queen's Royal Regiment (West Surrey).

The Sergeant receives a personal letter from his Majesty King George VI.

The Queen's Regiment 'Lamb and Flag' hat badge, with their 'Hell's Kitten' insignia of Dick Whittington's cat, worn on their epaulettes.

awards. One of the proudest people there was a lady from Keynsham, the widowed Mrs Headington, who lovingly pinned the Military Medal on her son's blue uniform.

A postage stamp showing first the Military Cross, then the Military Medal, both awarded for 'valour on the field of battle', and always bearing the officer's or the soldier's name on the rim, as does Sergeant Headington's.

Chapter 19

Sergeant Thomas George Williams, SLI, 1895–1974 and his son, Roy Williams, SAS

Tom was born on June 12, 1895, the only child of George Williams, whose wife Susan tragically died just after her son's birth. A broken-hearted George left for London, hardly to be be seen again, and left young Tom to be brought up by his grandmother, Mrs Mary Ann Williams, at the Almshouses in Bristol Road.

Around 1909 at the age of fourteen, he put his age up and enlisted in the Somerset Light Infantry as a bugler boy. He served in India, Gallipoli and Mesopotamia, rising to the rank of sergeant. In 1920 he left the army and in 1922 married a local Keynsham girl, Ethel Neal. Their marriage was blessed with four children, Roy, Audrey, Raymond and Rex.

When Tom was discharged from the army, Ethel was working at the corselet factory, later Strudwick's, and now the Halifax. For a while Tom was employed by Mr Parsons, who lived in one of the big houses at the top of Bristol Road just below the Wingrove. Then he became the chauffeur-gardener to Mr William Thomas, owner of the Albert Mill at Dapps Hill. He stayed in the employment of the Thomas family for the rest of his working life and became the chauffeur-gardener to William Thomas's son, Mr Alfred C Thomas, of St Augustines, Station Road.

During this time, a bright young girl entered the service of Alfred Thomas. This was Violet Pearce, who had been brought up at a small orphanage at Downend. She had no knowledge of her family, but described those who had cared for her as 'a lovely family'. She said of Mr F Thomas, ' He was lovely. We always called him sir. When I left and was engaged in war work, I had to visit him weekly to tell him how I was getting on. He was a true gentleman.'

Young Roy William, born in 1924, described his father as being '5 ft 8 in tall, slim, with thick dark wavy hair, of which he was very proud. He was not a stern man, but his word was law. He was a good story teller about the First World War and old Keynsham. He would talk about his part in the SLI in putting down the Afghan rising in India, and of the inhospitable terrain of the Khyber Pass area around Peshawar.'

Roy went to Temple Street School, then to 'Bath Hill' and, in 1935, aged eleven, he went to Broadlands School, which had just opened that year. Not extra keen on school, when he left he worked for the Hawkins Brothers, builders, who were his uncles. Then he went to Jack Hickling as a plumber's mate. Roy always was a handy man to have about. Then when World War II commenced, Roy joined the local Home Guard. Dad was proud indeed to see his son in uniform.

SERGEANT THOMAS GEORGE WILLIAMS
India, circa 1915, possibly Peshawar, the 20 year old Sergeant in the North Somerset
Yeomanry. As an old soldier commented, 'A typical photo by an Indian – all legs.'.
Mr R William's photo.

Meanwhile, Old Tom was still working for Mr A Thomas and it was quite natural that earlier Roy should have met there the lively Miss Violet Pearce. Romance flourished and marriage followed on Jan 27, 1944. Earlier though, in 1943, came the dreaded 'calling up' papers. Roy found himself in the Duke of Cornwall's Light Infantry and was posted to Egypt. There, later, he applied to join the SAS, the distinguished Special Air Service. Rigorous training followed, but he made the grade and was accepted. 5 ft 8 in tall, he weighed 10 ½ stone, was 20 years of age, and was slim built and fleet of foot. During leave, the matrimonal knot was truly tied.

'It was very tough in the SAS but very satisfying. I enjoyed it. We were fighting the Germans on the east coast of Italy. By this time three-quarters of Italy had been liberated. A lot of my mates from the DCLI had been killed on the west coast, though none of them came from Keynsham.

'We didn't fight in trenches as such, but as 'Specials' behind enemy lines. We wore a simple army uniform, with fawn berets, but devoid of any insignia at all. We wore no stripes, no badges of rank nor regimental flashes. We took no identification papers with us at all. We had no training against interrogation, nor did we carry poison capsules to swallow; we knew that if we were caught we would simply have been shot as saboteurs. I carried a .38 colt revolver and a Tommy gun, though I had received little training in their use.

'We would enter enemy occupied territory, do what we had to and get out quickly. Most of our work was near the coast, blowing up ammunition dumps and airfields. We operated in a team of 24 men, arriving in two-men boats known as kayaks, so we used 12 of them. Our last 'Operation' was at Comacchio, where we lost two men. One was our Commanding Officer, Lt Colonel Andy Lassen. He dropped a grenade into the top of a German pill box but did not get away in time. The second was our cook called 'Ginger' because of his hair. We always brought our dead back with us.

'There were a lot of lakes round there and supplies had to be dropped by air. We arrived one morning at Lake Comacchio, where I had a rather frightening experience. Three of us had to go across the lake in a small rubber dinghy to pick up our supplies. We were about 50 yards from the shore when a German sniper hit the craft. We were sitting targets. The dinghy sank with us in it and all the food disappeared into the water. Fortunately the water was not deep and we managed to wade ashore, looking over our shoulders, fearful of further sniper shots.

'When evening came, we quietly made our way round the lake and knocked out the German post. We waited for their relief party to come, and when they arrived in a single boat, we dropped grenades into it and killed them all. That was the end of the war in Italy, for soon afterwards Germany capitulated to the Allies. The year was 1945.'

When asked if he had personally killed anyone, he raised his hands. 'You never knew. You worked as a member of a team. It was like being in a firing squad – you just didn't know. But in any case, it was kill or be killed.'

August found Roy on a flight back to Keynsham and to his wife, on embarkation leave, before his posting to the Far East. However, during the flight they received the news that Japan also had capitulated. He would not be going east, but his wife still remembers him arriving home in the middle of the night.

After his leave, he was posted to Haifa, in Palestine, for a further year's service. 'We were trying to keep the peace there. The Jews were fighting for home rule. I felt we could not trust the Jews. They fought us with rifles, mortars and grenades. I was hit in the shoulder by shrapnel, but a short time later I was back again on duty.

'A few days after that my B class release came through as I had been in a reserved occupation. I returned to England to be demobilised and reached home again in August, this time on 20th, 1946.'

Violet and Roy were blessed with two sons and two daughters, and are now grandparents. Roy's sister, Audrey, married a Yorkshireman, Ken Spicer, and they have a daughter and two sons. Roy's brothers both have families, and sadly, Raymond died in 1985 and Rex in 1981.

Tom survived both the World Wars, still working with Mr AC Thomas in the local Royal Observer Corps. After the war, when his children and grandchildren wanted him to go on holiday with them to places like Spain, he would retort, 'I had enough of camels, sand and the great heat in the First War. I'd rather stay in Keynsham with relatives.'

He died in 1974, aged 79, a much loved member of the older generation.

He, and the many members of his family, all owe their existence to Susan, their progenitor, who so tragically died after childbirth in 1895.

Chapter 20

Two Soldiers Recall D-Day Drama
Howard Jeffery and Bill Cotter reminisce

Howard Jeffery was born in 1, Temple Street on 24 November, 1922. The son of Winifred Hine, he and his sister, Iris, were brought up by their grandparents, Annie and Henry Hine. Grandfather was known as 'Sooty Hine, the chimney sweep'. Howard attended school at Temple Street, Bath Hill, and then Broadlands.

He now takes up the story. 'In August, 1939, seven of us lads decided to join up together and volunteered for the Territorial Army. We reported to the Gloucester Regiment TA centre in Ashton Gate, Bristol, behind The Rising Sun. The other lads were Stan Phelps, Stan Lyons, Joe Smart, Bill Hembrow, and Fred Clapp. The other lad was from Whitchurch. Smart was rejected as too young, though he was two days older than me. We all put our ages up. Later we separated, and then right through the war I never met another Keynsham person. We joined the Glorious Gloucesters as theirs was the nearest TA unit.

'After training at Churchill Gate, Bristol, I was posted to Banwell, where the Castle and the Abbey had been taken over as a temporary HQ. Then I was sent to London for a survey course as part of a party to go to Greece, but by the time we were ready to go, they had capitulated. During the war I was moved from regiment to regiment as the need arose, though always remaining a member of the Glorious Gloucesters.

'As a Lance Corporal in the Royal Army Service Corps, I had the chance to be in charge of food for the regiment at their base in Wellsway, Keynsham. It was quite a large centre, with probably over a hundred men there. They repaired army lorries and tanks, and built extensive brick ramps to run the tanks up. I refused the job. I wanted to do something more exciting, though I was in the UK until D-Day.

The dawn of D-Day

'I went over on a large boat, the SS Lancaster, with the 15th Scottish and the 51st Highland Division. It was wet when we left Tilbury Docks to sail through the night. It was a rough journey, with a storm in mid-channel. Most of us were seasick and when we arrived off the Normandy beach, I was still dizzy with the world going round. It was just getting light as we were ordered to climb over the side and down the rope nets and into the landing craft. There were already about 40–50 chaps in the vessel. We were all scared stiff, but just tried to concentrate on the job we had been trained for.'

The coastline was divided into 5 sections. To the west were the Utah and the Omaha beaches, attacked by the US 4th, 29th and 1st Divisions of the First American Army under Lt General Omar Bradley. Next were the Gold, Juno and Sword beaches, attacked by the Second British Army under Lt General Sir Miles Dempsey. The 2nd Army included the Canadian 3rd Division, which hit Juno. By 5.30 am the invasion force was preparing the run-in, the craft wallowing in heavy seas.

'Our destination was Gold beach. I was part of a detachment of 13 men of the War Graves commission, and only three of us survived. We had no weapons, as they were in the 15 cwt truck on board and I wasn't going to carry that ashore. Our three officers had revolvers. When the landing craft beached, I stepped into just 6 inches of water. I remember seeing the German sea defences, the steel hedgehogs, though we had different names for them. Many were already blown up. There were a lot of vehicles coming ashore. You couldn't take it all in. As soon as the craft landed, you got straight off and went where you were sent. You didn't notice what was happening around you.

'When we landed, there was the Beachmaster directing the incomers. He was a Major, in a helmet, with a bright sash across his chest. I thought he was a bit of an idiot walking up and down, though he was extremely brave. One beachmaster is said to have had his dog with him. Ours just told us to get out of the way. So we ended up in a field a little way inland and spent the night there. Next morning, D-Day + 1, we sorted ourselves out, that is, our little group of 13.

'Our job was to make a proper cemetery and then a photographer would

Young Howard Jeffery in the early 1930s, with his grandmother, Winifred Hine, ('Mum') outside their home, 1, Temple Street, where Kwik Save now is.

send photos home for propaganda purposes. But it didn't work out like that. We weren't allowed to stay to collect bodies. In any case, most had been removed, but the beach was too full for us to stop. Any bodies there just had to be left. Tanks were coming off the landing craft and drove straight over them. It just couldn't be helped. Our paratroops and commandos, from gliders, had already arrived.'

Airborne divisions were the first to set foot in occupied France. Their objective was to secure both flanks of the invasion area, protecting the assault forces during the early stages of the landings. By 9.00 pm on June 5, Allied airborne troops began boarding their transports. The first to actually land at 12.20 am were the pathfinder parachute troops, followed by airborne units landing in gliders.

During the night the RAF had dropped 5,000 tons of explosives on the formidable coastal batteries. Under the cover of the heavy bombing, the Royal Navy ships HMS Belfast and HMS Warspite were able to lead a ferocious barrage in which thousands of tons of explosives were targeted at beach defences and batteries.

'At Caen we were unable to cross the river because the Germans held the opposite bank, so our planes were called in to do their stuff. But they hit our side of the bank by mistake, so they were called off. They returned later and straffed the opposite bank, by which time we had crossed the river. So we were attacked twice by our own planes. Once our troops had taken Caen, there was no stopping them. There was no resistance for mile after mile.

'Some time later I was hit in the eye by shrapnel from a bursting shell. I had been reconnoitring for a new cemetery site for The Graves Registration Unit to which I belonged. After registering one, an architect would mark it out. Then The Graves Commission unit would bury the fallen according to the architect's plan. I was caught measuring in an open field by a creeping barrage of shells. These are fired from a fixed position. First they land beyond you, then they gradually work backwards. Our troops soon overran their position, but that was the end of my fighting war. When I came to, I was in a field dressing station for the night. Next day I was flown to the 108th General British Hospital in Brussels. After four months I was flown back to England and stayed in different hospitals. I ended up at Woolwich Barracks, and was finally sent to Carlisle, where I was demobbed in 1945 or 46. The biggest mistake I ever made was to come out of the army.'

For a 'demobbed' Howard, all was not lost. Later, working at Smith's Crisps factory in Brislington he met his future wife, Patricia Burke from Bristol. He laughed as he said, 'I was a Salvationist. Pat was a Roman Catholic, so we married in the Church of England. We have a daughter, Jean.

'I remember Len Brewer of St George's Road. He was killed at Dunkirk, and listed as 'Missing, believed dead. No known grave.' Ron Utting, also of St George's Road, became a pilot, a Flight Lieutenant I think, and was shot down and killed on his first solo flight. He was only in his twenties. I remember Reg Exon, who was also in the RAF and was killed. But I don't regret my time in the services.'

Howard lent me a card containing information taken from 'D-Day Operation Overlord,' from Salamander Books Ltd., 1993. It said that 'The Allied

Howard, in the Gloucesters in 1940, wearing an RA tunic. He said of it, 'A bloke who was broke said, 'Want to buy it?' I said, 'How much?' I gave him 10/- (50p) for it, for a laugh.'

Expeditionary Force involved 1,700,000 British Troops, 1,500,000 American Troops, 175,000 Dominion Troops (mainly Canadian), 44,000 Troops of other Allied countries, 1,300 Warships, 1,600 Merchant Ships, 4,126 Landing Ships and Craft, 13,000 Aircraft (including 5,000 fighters and 4,000 bombers) and 3,500 Gliders.'

D-Day afternoon, and the arrival of more supplies

Bill Cotter drove on to Sword Beach, beyond which stood the Pegasus Bridge, captured much earlier that day by the 6th Airborne Parachute Regiment. 'There we formed a bridgehead and were meant to take Caen next day, but it took us 6 weeks. I was with the 3rd British Infantry Division as a transport driver in the RASC. My job was ammunition supplies. We, the British and Canadians, finally entered Caen on July 9, at the cost of 5,000 soldiers wounded or killed.

'I landed after the infantry had made the beach secure. I was driving a four wheel drive Austin lorry, towing a trailer filled with big shells. There were just two of us in the vehicle. We arrived in a tank landing craft which had two decks. I was on the top. Below us were the amphibious tanks which were able to land in deep water with their twin rudders. We had to wait until we were closer and the water shallower, and then it was on to huge steel rafts, powered by engines which towed about 20 vehicles at a time nearer the beach. Despite having our engines specially water-sealed by the ATS, with a vertical exhaust, we could only go up to a depth of three feet of water.

'The German fire was intense at times, but the gunfire from our ships was even more intense and probably helped to keep them down. There was so much going on that we didn't have time to look round. It was the infantry in front of us who were nearer the Germans and were machine-gunned. We were fired at mostly by shells. Every one was scared unless he was an idiot; it was a case of self survival. But we were trained and had a job to do; we didn't know exactly what we were going in to.

'The first person we met on the beach was a military policeman directing us. There were a lot of burnt-out vehicles around us. I can always remember looking up and seeing two houses on the shore, with their windows in, which survived all the shelling. I saw a few bodies but most had already been cleared by the stretcher bearers. If my truck was hit by a shell, it would be 'good night, nurse' for us. We were strafed by the Luftwaffe a few times but they only had a few planes left. I remember them coming over, firing a bit further away from me.

'I had been sent to Middlesex and attached to a machine gun and mortar group. My job was to supply the forward groups in the invasion, so I was very close to the fighting. Sometimes I went up in daytime, other times at night. I never thought that we might be driven off the beaches. It never crossed my mind. It had been bad enough to get ashore, let alone get off.

'I was a lance corporal but gave it up to be a driver. I didn't see any Yanks, thank goodness. It was common knowledge that we didn't appreciate the GI a lot. They made a lot of noise. We did the hardest fighting. A lot felt the same way.

'We crossed over in tank landing craft. We were kept on board for 5 days before we sailed to keep everything secret. We sailed from Gosport, near Portsmouth. We set off in the dark and woke up on June 6 to find we were already underway. We slept in our lorries – anywhere. We certainly didn't have any beds.

'Though it was difficult to feel sorry for Gerry, he must have had a hell of a time from the battering from the ships. I wouldn't like to face those war ships. The noise of the guns was deafening.

'Our planes were brilliant, however you look at it. As the attack on Caen was deadlocked, Sir Arthur 'Bomber' Harris broke the impasse by saturation bombing. They attacked in wave after wave. I saw 1,000 planes go over when they attacked the city. They were mostly British planes. Generally the American planes flew in the daytime, with ours at night, though as Caen was in our zone, they would be our planes.

'We did lose some of our mates due to shelling and bombing (Gerry only came over at night), so we had to have replacements.

'Our uniforms were made of good strong material, so we had no trouble there at all. British khaki was excellent material. It was not as attractive as the Yanks but was very serviceable. But in any case, uniform does not make a man of you.'

* * *

Actually Bill came from Old Market Street in Bristol, where he was called up. After VE day, he went on to see service in Palestine. He has now lived in Keynsham for 40 years so he is nearly accepted as a local man.

* * *

Perhaps a final word, from Winston Churchill himself, would best finish the invasion epic. In Volume VI of 'The Second World War' he described the circumstances of the official end of the war (p 470).

'The instrument of total, unconditional surrender was signed by Lieut-General Bedell Smith and General Jodl, with French and Russian officers as witnesses, at 2.41 am on May 7. Thereby all hostilities ceased at midnight on May 8. The formal ratification by the German High Command took place in Berlin, under Russian arrangements, in the early hours of May 9. Air Chief Marshall Tedder signed on behalf of Eisenhower, Marshall Zhukov for the Russians, and Field-Marshall Keitel for Germany.'

Chapter 21

From the Jockey's seat to the Burma Jungle
Dinah Ruttledge's biography of her brother,
Lieut Desmond Crease, of the Wiltshire Regiment

My father, Charles Crease, was in the Royal Scots Greys in the First World War', recalled his daughter, Dinah. 'He was a Somerset man but my mother, Cordelia, came from Devon. She was a SR nurse, and had been in private nursing. They were married in Bristol and came to Keynsham about 1920, with us two children. My brother Desmond was born in 1915, while I was born three years after him.

Father had a local milk round, getting his milk from Osborne's in Saltford. His pony, Dolly, just 11 hands, pulled his milk cart from which he ladled out skimmed milk from one churn and fresh milk from the other. My parents bought two old semi-detached cottages, Numbers 16 and 18, Bath Road, which stood at right angles to the road. They backed on to what is now the Chandag garage shop, but was in those days the lovely old Ivy Lodge Guest house, run by Mrs Thompson. Gradually my parents knocked the two cottages into one building, with an attractive verandah at the front and side. At the rear of the house was the dairy.

In 1930 when we were struggling, the front room of the house facing the road was made into a shop, from which mother sold cakes and jam, and also did outside catering. Then she combined the shop with a sub post-office section. Naturally she then had to employ someone to help, who lived in. Desmond and I did our bit to help in the shop.

Father dreamed of owning a riding school, and started giving riding lessons on Dolly which proved so popular that he bought another horse, and as more people still wanted riding lessons, he bought more horses until he had fourteen. So around 1936 he bought a plot of land from the Thompsons (now the tyre garage) and had eight loose boxes built, four in one row, and four more in a row at right angles to the first boxes. Opposite, a chaff room and a saddle room were constructed, built by Mr Bailey, who worked for Mr Willcox of Bath Hill. Father sold his milk-round to Mr Exon, who was able to extend his dairy business. With the riding school doing so well, we closed the shop with its PO wing. Dad was so proud. He had arrived. He really had his own horses and stables.

Meanwhile, Desmond, who was mad about horses, had started riding any horse he could find. Then as a family we started going to the Bath races, where we became friendly with the jockeys. Desmond, being short and slim, was just the size for a jockey, so in 1930 at the tender age of fifteen, he left home and was apprenticed to the well known trainer, Fred Pratt, at his stables at Lambourn, Berks. Desmond raced for three years, when he suddenly started

Mrs Ruttledge's photo shows her father, Mr Charles Crease, on the verandah of their lovely old house, 16/18, Bath Road, taken around 1965. Some years after the sale of the house, the Civic Society tried to have it preserved but big business prevailed.

Part of the Keynsham Riding Stables, at the rear of the house, facing the road, around 1938. On the far left is Electric, then Ruby, Sturdy Boy and lastly, Jack. As the house was not on the mains, water had to be pumped by hand from a large well below the kitchen floor, to a cistern in the roof, where it flowed down to the water tank, visible near Electric. The horses learned how to slide the bolts that secured the doors of their boxes, hence the wire frames which were put across to stop their games. They would become excited when their food was coming, and would lean out, and sometimes bite each other. Mrs Ruttledge's photo.

growing and became too tall for a jockey, so he came back home to help with the family riding stables.

When I left school, naturally I was able to help with stables full time, and used to teach and take people out on horses in a string, for a ride to Chewton Keynsham, Compton Dando or to Queen Charlton, along the quiet lanes, down bridle paths and even across fields if the farmers permitted it. On the verges we could break into a canter. The lessons were for one and a half hours duration, priced at four shillings for tuition and the ride, and going up to seven shillings and six pence during the war. Surprisingly, hostilities did not affect our business at all. A number of young men trained prior to joining the Somerset Yeomanry Reserve which was still mounted.

In 1940, Desmond volunteered for the army and was sent to Blandford for training in the Wiltshire Regiment. After six weeks, he was made a lance corporal. Meanwhile, inspired by the courage and death of a pilot in the Battle of Britain, I joined the WAAFs. I was sent to Bridgnorth, Shropshire, where I was introduced to 'square bashing' for two weeks, after which I was posted to Birmingham to train as a wireless operator, learning morse. I enjoyed the experience and found I had quite an aptitude for the work.

I did my training at the Aston Cross Post Office building, and was billeted in the Gravelly Hill Convent, where we were looked after by the nuns, who said they would light a candle and pray for us when we took our exams six months later. I was then posted to the Air Ministry in King Charles Street, Whitehall, not far from Downing Street. Our wireless cabin was way underground, and I was there for 18 months and thoroughly enjoyed being in London. The work was not too demanding, and I was made a Leading Aircraft Woman, a LACW, with two stripes.

In 1942 I was home on a week-end's leave, and, being in uniform, I was persuaded to ride our 17 hands Sturdy Boy at the front of a procession through Keynsham, which set off from one of Farmer Payne's fields near his home by Ashmead roundabout, to St John's Church. The Red Cross and other organisations were in the march, supported by a brass band. It was in aid of the RAF Benevolent Fund.

Later that year, while stationed in London, Desmond was given embarkation leave, and Mother came up and stayed in the city to see him, and we would wait for him in Trafalgar Square. Because of the utmost secrecy, he could not tell us when he was leaving. We realised that one day he would just not make the rendezvous.

He sailed for India in June, 1942, and was sent to the Officer' Training School, Group 75, Senior Division, Bangalore, southern India, due west of Madras. He was there from August 17 to November 14, where his great friend was the jovial Desmond 'Paddy' Ruttlege from Dublin. On December 17 I heard from him about the Passing Out Parade. He wished that I had been there and said that it was a proud moment for all the young officers. He wrote, "It was a moment I shall never forget. We were all marched on to the Parade Ground by a pipe band of Gurkhas, and were inspected by the Assistant Commandant, who took the salute at the march past and then gave us a final address in the main lecture hall. I was one of three in our platoon with an A grade. Because I had not taken Urdu, I will probably be posted to a

British Regiment." Paddy took Urdu and was posted to a different regiment.

Some time after December 17 Desmond left Bangalore for Burma, probably for Rangoon, a distance of over 1,100 miles. If he sailed, it would have taken him several weeks. However, by April, 1943, he was engaged in fighting the Japanese in the Burmese jungle, where the enemy was hidden in the trees. Paddy said that in that far away steaming jungle, sadly, Desmond was killed. He was just 28. He had no known grave.

A letter dated 7 May, 1943, addressed to Mrs C Crease, Keynsham Riding School, Keynsham, commenced,

"Madam

In confirmation of War Office telegram of the 4th May, 1943, I am directed to inform you, with regret, that a notification has been received from an Indian theatre of war that 2nd Lieutenant D C Crease, The Wiltshire Regiment serving with The Royal Enniskillin Fusiliers, was reported missing on 11 April, 1943.

No further information is available at present, but all possible enquiries are

This photo of L.A.C.W. Dinah Ruttledge (nee Crease) was taken probably in 1942 at, she thinks, the Ollis's field (now Gaston Avenue), Keynsham. In uniform and riding Sturdy Boy, she was flanked by a similarly mounted RAF serviceman, as they led a procession through the town in a march for the RAF Benevolent Fund. She recalled that, 'Somewhere behind us there was a band. It was all a bit hectic but very exciting. We only had week-end passes. You just had to jump on the horse and go.' The march led on to a gymkhana, involving among other horses, three from the family's stables, two being held by their former pupils. The boy holds Mischief while Elise Redwood and Dinah hold Dolly (II hands).

being made and any further information received by this Department will be sent to you immediately. Should you receive any communication from 2nd. Lieutenant Crease, or should news of him reach you from any other source, will you kindly notify this Office, and at the same time forward any card or letter you may receive from him, which will be returned to you after inspection.

In the meantime I am to ask you to be good enough to notify this Office of any change of your address.

I am, Madam,
Your obedient Servant,
(Signed) A. Williams."

Broken hearted or not, the war effort had to go on, and I was posted to Leighton Buzzard. The station was a massive purpose-built affair on the outside of the town, covered with wire netting, with imitation trees and foliage growing out of it. There were thousands of us concentrated there where we relayed signals all over the world, compared with Whitehall, where the communications were only within this country. All 'out' messages were in code, as they were in London, so we never knew what information we were sending or receiving. The work was most demanding. We were billeted in Nissen huts with no kind nuns to wait on us.

I finished my WAAF days in 1945 at Leighton Buzzard. Desmond's friend, Captain Paddy Ruttledge of the Royal Ulster Rifles, returned from the war and we were married. We lived in Dublin and Derby before returning to Keynsham in 1950.

My parents gave up the riding school in 1950 as my father was taken seriously ill. It was a sad day for all of us."

WORDS PENNED BY MRS C CREASE ON THE LOSS OF HER SON.

". . . some corner of a foreign field
That is for ever England."

"Smile, my mother, and dry the tear
For I'll be home within a year."
Those dear words to me you spoke
Whilst my heart in anguish broke.
Then for months, I walked beside you,
Dreading the ills that could betide you,
Thoughts to you for ever straying,
Fearing, hoping, praying, praying.

Through a haze of stupefaction
Came the dread words 'Killed in Action'.
You in the jungle lying,
You in the jungle dying.
I heard the guns of the stealthy Jap
Sleeping and waking like Hell dogs yap.
Beloved warm personality
Felled by war's cold brutality.

276

Officer's Training School. Bangalore, India. Group 75, Senior Division, August 17th. – November 14th, 1942

38 British Army officer-cadets training to participate in the Far Eastern War against the Japanese. In the centre of the front row is Lieut. A.A.T. James, the instructor. On his right is Cadet D. St. John Ruttledge. To the instructor's left is Cadet D.C. Crease, with wavy hair.

Days of dull and aching sorrow
But preceded each tomorrow.
Soft and sudden came the calm
On my spirit like a balm
For it seemed you walked beside me,
Your promise you had not denied me.
"Smile, my mother, and dry the tear
For I am Home within a year."

The Army's Roll of Honour

Gunner Reg A G Bailey, of the Royal Artillery, lived in Rock Road, and his father, Reginald Bailey, owned the Railway Inn, with stabling at the rear of it, roughly between the wars. Sadly the gunner was killed in the Italian Campaign toward the end of the war, when his motor cycle crashed into an army lorry.

Lance Corporal David J C Barker, of the Gloucester Regiment (who was recalled as being short of stature) lived in Manor Road.

Gunner Gilbert L Brewer, RA, lived at 34, St George's Road. Before the war he was in the Territorials, and so was one of the first to be called to the colours. He fought in France and was killed at Dunkirk in 1940. A telegram referred to him as, 'Missing, presumed killed.' No confirmation of his death was ever received. There being many G L Brewers, the precise whereabouts of his grave is uncertain. He left a wife, a daughter and two sons.

Sapper Gordon G Camm, of the Royal Engineers, lived at 17, Wellsway, and was the son of Corporal G Camm of the Home Guard, who himself saw service in WWI. Described as a 'tall fine man,' the sapper was killed by the Germans soon after Dunkirk. It is said that he was taken prisoner, and, in trying to escape, became entangled on the perimeter barbed wire, where he was shot.

Private Reginald H Cook, of the Queen's Royal Regiment, lived in Temple Street. His father, Jake, played in the Keynsham band. The private had earlier worked for Mr Chris Wiggins.

Lieut. H E Cottle, of the Gloucester Regiment, though not Keynsham born, was a youngish man who lived in Park Road and had a jeweller's shop beside Mr Nix, the florist.

Corporal S E O Emery, RASC, lived in an old house in what is now Chandag Road and worked for Farmer Payne. He was captured by the Japanese at Singapore.

Gunner Stan G Fisher, RA, had a butcher's shop at 'Cheapside', the row of shops at the top of Bath Hill West, near to where the town hall is now.

Lance Corporal J T Greenland, of the RE, lived on Bristol Hill opposite the Old Wingrove Hotel.

Gunner P W J Howes, of the RA (Airborne), is described as having been seen coming down Rock Road, a big fine fellow, in uniform. He was one of the slightly older men called up, and was killed in France.

Lance Corporal Stan J Phelps, of the South Staffs Regiment, lived in Temple Street, at the end of Cranmore House. He was involved in 'an airborne exercise' as a paratrooper and participated in the 1944 attack on Sicily, 'when the USA airforce dropped them short in the sea.' A telegram stated that 'he was last seen trying to swim ashore', obviously wearing his full uniform, his parachute and heavy boots. He was just twenty one.

Private P W Searle, of the Highland Light Infantry, lived in the Woodbine Cottages.

Private Jack Woodberry, of the RASC, was a Fry's man and lived in Chandos Road. He died just a young man.

Captain R.J.C. 'Bob' Smith was a very popular man who played cricket for Keynsham. His father, Fred Smith of Rock Road, worked for the G.W.R. Bob was educated at Cotham Grammar School, and worked for the Inland Revenue as a tax inspector.

The Royal Marines

Marine Alfred William Hembrow, 'from an old Keynsham family,' was one of the sons of Mr Hembrow who had a haulage business in Wellsway. His sons have been described as 'big boys'. Alfred was killed in 1944 in a landing craft packed with Marines, in an attempted landing on the coast of Holland.

Other Keynsham soldiers who died

Despite diligent and continuous searches, details of other local men who made the supreme sacrifice have failed to produce any information. However, they are not forgotten and at the end of the book, there is a complete list of the men from all three services, from Keynsham and Saltford, who died in the First and Second World Wars. May they rest in peace.

Chapter 22

Warfare on the High Seas
An autobiography by Lieutenant Monty Veale, RNVR

In the past chapters, we have looked at Keynsham men who served in the army in World War Two. In this naval section, Mr Monty Veale has written about his rather sombre experiences in the senior service, The Royal Navy.

* * *

One of my great friends was Henry Phelps, who lived just below us in Temple Street. Henry earned some pocket money from Jack Smith, who kept the London Inn. Greyhounds which raced at Knowle Stadium were kept at the London Inn, and Henry and I used to take them out for exercise. Little did the owners know that we would take the dogs to Queen Charlton where we would often set up a hare and would let the dogs go in hot pursuit. The chase would continue through hedges, ditches and streams until we were all completely exhausted and the dogs were returned limping to their kennels. Although many hares were chased, on no occasion did we catch one!

Those were carefree happy days which were marred as we entered our late teens by the threat of war. Most teenage youths were conscious that they were likely to be called up and when Mr Chamberlain returned from Munich waving a piece of paper, signed by Hitler and saying 'Peace in our time', we were convinced that there was going to be war. It was then a question of what service one would prefer, for it was thought that it may have been a deterrent to the Germans if our forces were considerably increased. The Air Force was in its infancy, I did not enjoy the prospect of marching, so with George Farley of Albert Road, we joined the Royal Naval Volunteer Reserve at HMS Flying Fox berthed at Hotwells.

That was probably in the spring of 1939. We carried out a few drills, made a complete shambles of rowing a boat around the harbour and on 25th August, 1939 we were called up and fitted out with bell bottomed trousers and uniforms at Hotwells and whisked off to RN Barracks, at Devonport. We had very little training as such; we were taught the rudiments of gunnery, how to fire a rifle, and after a short while we were lined up one day and George Farley and a group were drafted to HMS Ardent, a destroyer. I was sent to join an ex Cunard White Star coal-burning liner lying in Devonport Dockyard, HMS Laurentic. We were fitted with Boer War six inch guns and by November, 1939, we were patrolling the Denmark Straits between Greenland and Iceland, and other areas between Iceland and the Faroes. Our job was to intercept all shipping returning to Norway, Denmark and the Baltic and of course, Germany. We would put a boarding party on any suspicious vessel and escort them to Scotland and later on to the Faroes for interrogation.

Our relief from one of these patrols was HMS Rawalpindi and it was with the utmost sadness that we heard that she had been intercepted by German cruisers, had been set on fire and sunk. There was a large number of armed merchant cruisers at that time but they were no match for the U boats or German surface craft, which were usually heavily armed Pocket Battleships. One by one they were sunk and early in 1940 we were returning from what was known as the Southern Patrol in the South Atlantic somewhere about five hundred miles south west of Ireland and we fell victim to the torpedoes of a U boat under the command of Kapitan Otto Kretchmer. He became a famous ace among U boat commanders, but was later sunk and taken a prisoner of war.

On the Laurentic we were hit by three torpedoes. The first made us list, the second straightened us up and the third blew the stern off. Most of the fatalities were stokers working in the engine rooms. At 'Abandon ship' I got away in a Carley float, a primitive inflatable, with the Captain, who when he saw that there were still men aboard, though there shouldn't have been, returned to the doomed ship. There the Captain found a damaged life boat, which with instant repairs, sufficed to take the rest of the men off, even though we had to bail furiously. Two destroyers escorting the nearby convoy were sent to our rescue, HMS Ardent and HMS Acasta. Suddenly they hailed us, 'Back soon. Must attend to a U boat.' I had mixed feelings stranded in a small leaking craft in the middle of a vast ocean. I thought of praying, though I was confident I would be rescued. In due course the destroyer came back for us, by which time our boat, despite frantic bailing, was only just afloat.

We had been in company with another armed merchant cruiser, HMS Protocoulus, which against Admiralty instructions had come to our assistance instead of getting out of the area at full speed, and was also torpedoed as one of our boats drew alongside her, and she sank in minutes. The million to once chance of being picked up by my friend George Farley was not to be. I found myself being shepherded below decks in HMS Acasta and in a line of survivors receiving a tot of rum from their coxswain. I started to tell him that I was under age and 'not entitled' but was cut short with his bark, "Drink this, you silly young so an so", which I did in one gulp, and slept for the next twenty four hours or so.

Some weeks later it was with the utmost sadness that I heard of the loss of HMS Ardent in Norwegian waters and of my friend George Farley, together with another Keynsham former boy scout, Bob Hoddinott, who lived near St Ladoc Road and who served, I believe, in the aircraft carrier HMS Glorious. The Ardent was last seen acting in the true tradition of the service trying to close the range against superior forces in an endeavour to ram, but she sank, on fire but with all her guns still firing.

Very often when I came home on leave, I would meet George Farley's father, who would ask me if I had any further news of George. He never gave up the hope that he was still alive and may have been taken prisoner. It gave me a sense of guilt that I was still alive and I came to find our meetings more and more embarrassing in that nothing I could say was adequate to dispel his grief and despair.

Able Seaman George Farley of 12, Albert Road, a friend of Sub Lieut Monty Veale and of A S Herbert Phelps, RNVR. George served on HMS Ardent which was sunk in Norwegian waters trying to ram a superior German warship. She went down with all her guns still firing, in the true tradition of the Royal Navy. H E Phelp's photo.

My friend Henry Phelps joined the navy as a full time career but unfortunately contracted a chest ailment and was invalided out.

On occasional leaves one caught up with the news of other friends and one soon heard on the grape vine who else was at home. It was a great shock to hear of the death of Stanley Phelps, Henry's brother, at Sicily where he took part in the air landing, and of the injury to his other brother, Fred, who lost a leg.

On one of my leaves I met Reggie Exon, who served in the RAF. Our rendezvous was usually to start at the Talbot and do the rounds of the locals. On this occasion we spent an unusually hectic evening – there was an intensity about it which is hard to explain. We were living for the day! Shortly afterwards Reggie was killed in a bombing mission over Germany.

On another occasion Bert Robe and Bob Smith, who held army commissions, were both home and we all had to return to our units the same evening. Bob's father kindly drove us to Temple Meads and tragically Bob Smith lost his life in Burma.

Many of my friends had been in the Cubs, Scouts or Rover Scouts and they will share my gratitude to Vivian and Reg Turner, who devoted much of their time to moulding the character of many youngsters at that time. Their house in the High Street had an ever open door. Molly, their housekeeper, must have been a saint. She coped with Vivian, who was partially paralysed and confined to a wheelchair, and somehow kept order in a house with an ever open door to all the lads in the village.

When I was called up most people thought that the war would be over by Christmas. How naive we were! Just for the first few months we experienced the lack of reality in the period of the 'phoney war' but we were soon to be awakened to tragic realism.

At the time of Dunkirk we were under repair in dry dock at Belfast, having been damaged running aground on the Isle of Islay on our return from the Northern Patrol. Addressing the ship's company our Captain advised us that in the event of the invasion and occupation of Britain, we would sail to Canada and continue the war from there. That was at the time of Dunkirk and some of our disastrous losses such as the Lancastria returning from St Nazaire, bombed and sunk with the loss of two thousand six hundred lives.

Once we realized that we were going to be in the service for years rather than months the question of advancement arose. This occurred, as far as I was concerned, whilst serving in the destroyer HMS Blankney, which I joined shortly after undergoing another gunnery course after the sinking of HMS Laurentic. A considerable proportion of the ship's company were full-time active service ratings. A number of them decided they would request to undergo examination for advancement to Leading Seaman. A number of us RNVR's decided we were not to be outdone and we also applied and started our studies. Much to my surprise I passed. I then took the bull by the horns and applied to sit for Petty Officer. Once again, much to my surprise, I passed. All this happened over a period of three years. It is unusual for a rating to be sent to train for a commission from a ship but this happened in my case. Perhaps the award of two DSOs, a DSC and Polish Cross of Valour, to my commanding officer during that period had some bearing on my promotion.

Sub-Lieutenant Monty Veale, RNVR, in 1944, when he was on leave from HMS Pickle. The single ring on his sleeve showing his rank, is wavy, which indicated that he was a member of the Volunteer Reserve, as opposed to a regular sailor. Today the distinction has been removed. The photograph belongs to the Lieutenant.

During my service in HMS Blankney we escorted Atlantic convoys during the Battle of the Atlantic. We acted as rescue ship on several occasions, picking up survivors from ships and aircraft. In the days when radar was in its infancy and unreliable, I was often called upon to act as mast-head look out standing on the yard arm at dawn and scanning the horizon for U boats. I enjoyed the experience; I could see everything that was going on, on the bridge.

We escorted channel convoys, battle squadrons and in June 1942 we escorted six merchant ships through the Straits of Gibraltar en route for Malta. We succeeded in getting two ships through, though sadly the other four were sunk. A much larger convoy which set out from Alexandria was forced to return, having sustained high loses.

We visited Gibraltar under strict security in the middle of the night and we were warned that spies from the Spanish border were rife and were likely to be interested in our movements. We were under strict orders not to communicate with anyone ashore. A RAF rescue launch came alongside and one of the Brown brothers [Sir Kenneth, of 69, Charlton Road, and Tom, who owned a sand and gravel company in Bristol] breezily asked if there were any Bristol boys aboard who wanted any mail posted. Their kind gesture and any

This action photograph is taken from a Gaumont cinema news reel, showing HMS Blankney laying a thick smoke screen in the Mediterranean in 1942, to help the Allied convoy from Gibraltar to Malta to escape the shelling from the Italian surface craft. The Blankney kept dodging in and out of the screen to get close enough to attack the Italian cruisers, who had the longer fire range. Sadly only two of the six cargo ships got through. The photo belongs to Lieut. Veale, who was on the ship.

conversation was greeted with icy disinterest. Little did they know how close they could have come to breaching the security of the whole operation.

On the subject of spies and security, apparently my uncle, Horace Veale, did a bit of shooting in the fields off Manor Road and was in the habit of using his binoculars to spot rabbits. On one occasion he was spotted behind a dry wall near the Army camp on the Wellsway, when he was apprehended as a suspected spy and taken to the Police Station. He told them who he was and that he had lived in Keynsham all his life. Several people were asked to identify him but most of them were newcomers and did not know him. Ultimately some one turned up from Temple Street and he was released, but it was a long time before he ever got over the embarrassment.

On one occasion en route to Malta, as dawn broke we sighted the tops of ships' masts just above the horizon. Someone suggested that it was the United States' Navy coming to support us. We soon found out otherwise. It was two 'eight inch' Italian cruisers and escorts which completely outgunned us. Heavy shells sounded like an express train hurtling through the sky. That is exactly how it felt when we were straddled and for the first time during the war, I felt regret that my name may appear on some future war memorial and cause grief to my family.

We carried no torpedo tubes, but the destroyers which did immediately attacked and caused damage to the cruisers and destroyers. In the action HMS Bedouin received damage to her engines and we were forced to sink her. The survivors from the lost ships must look back and feel that their part in this convoy were scarcely recognised in the publicity which the siege of Malta received. It was the 'forgotten convoy' but vital to the continued life of the island at that time. We virtually dropped with exhaustion when we were stood down 'under the protection of the Malta barrage'.

We dropped anchor to seaward of the Grand Harbour, with our surviving two merchant ships. The approach channel had been mined and we had to await daylight for mine sweepers to lead us in. No sooner had we secured our anchorage than we had to weigh anchor and go to the rescue of a Polish manned destroyer. She sank very rapidly, having inadvertently strayed into our own minefield.

At dawn we entered Grand Harbour and were amazed to find the ramparts lined with people cheering us in, singing 'There'll always be an England.' As we lined the upper deck at stations for entering harbour, there was many a moist eye amongst hardened matelots and that welcome made them feel that their part was worthwhile, the loss of lives, injuries and burns and broken limbs forgotten for a short time.

One of the survivors that we picked up from the Polish destroyer had shed his trousers when he had to 'swim for it' and was allocated to my mess. I lent him a pair of trousers and flippantly said, "If we meet again, I'll have them back." It may have been a year later, as we were entering Scapa Flow, when a very important looking launch sped out to us. We all groaned. "Sailing Orders" as a package was sent to the bridge. Next moment the tannoy announced, "Leading Seaman Veale report to the bridge," where the Captain handed me my trousers. I did not know the Polish sailor's name, but he kept faith and I look back with the utmost respect.

From Malta we returned to Gibraltar, then to Glasgow and immediately to Iceland, refuelled and off again to Russia in an endeavour to catch up and support PQ 17, the code name for the convoy to Russia which had been decimated and lost thirty-two ships. The convoy had scattered when its main defence ships had been withdrawn to engage the famous German battleship, the Tirpitz. We spent several weeks patrolling between Murmansk and Archangel before returning to the United Kingdom and then to warmer climes with the invasion of Sicily and later Salerno.

To a degree I had my revenge for the sinking of the HMS Laurentic by Otto Kretchmer. It must have been in 1943 when we joined a large convoy off the Canaries and, as we sailed towards the danger zone, further escorts arrived and several destroyers were detached and placed under the orders of Commander Walker in HMS Stork. Reports of U boats were received from the Admiralty and we left the convoy to intercept and attack. An aircraft from HMS Audacity, a converted carrier, spotted U 151 on the surface and attacked with cannon fire. The U boat fired back and shot the aircraft down with the loss of the pilot. We could see this happening on the horizon and we were sent to intercept. When we arrived at the scene, we immediately received an asdic contact and dropped a pattern of depth charges, gaining contact almost immediately. Our second pattern brought the submarine to the surface like a fish rising to a fly. Apparently our last pattern had exploded one of her torpedoes set for firing and she was virtually jet propelled.

When we had completed picking up survivors and fishing for debris such as signals or any paper which would have been helpful to Naval Intelligence, we rejoined the group and on carrying out a sweep we had another asdic contact. On this occasion Commander Walker directed the attack from HMS Stork, while several ships maintained asdic contact and the remainder were directed to a cross bearing, while we attacked with depth charges. On this occasion we had little immediate success and lost contact. Later the U boat was forced to surface because of the damage sustained during the attack and we all fired at her, and she sank, leaving her survivors swimming in the water to be picked up and returned to Gibraltar. Commander Walker was later to be Captain Walker VC and his directed attacks proved so successful that it turned the tide in the U boat war.

It was with very much regret that I left my shipmates aboard HMS Blankney and returned to the United Kingdom for officer training. This consisted of some six weeks at Lancing College, near Brighton, then some further training on HMS King Alfred. On being commissioned a Sub Lieutenant, I was appointed to HMS Pickle (it bearing a famous name), a Fleet minesweeper. We were involved in sweeping channels for the invading forces for France, Belgium and Holland. After a few months, I was appointed to a minesweeping auxiliary (trawler) as navigator. Our job was to drop down buoys to mark the extremities of the sweep so that the flotilla would remain in safe water on subsequent laps.

At the end of hostilities with Germany, we were engaged in opening up sea routes to Germany and Denmark. For a time we were based at Cuxhaven and swept the approaches to Hamburg, co-operating with German sweepers.

On one misty morning we were on our way to start clearing another mine-

287

field when we heard the high-pitched fog horns of a number of ships followed by a deep resonant note of a much larger craft. Through the gloom appeared a slow-moving escort of destroyers flying the white ensign and following them the awesome towering structure of a German Pocket Battleship, The Prince Eugene. We thanked God that her massive eleven inch guns and secondary armament were trained fore and aft and that peace prevailed, and that we had been spared meeting her a few months earlier.

From Germany we were sent to a small dockyard at Port Dinorwic in North Wales for a refit. As the Navigating Officer I was somewhat surprised to receive a large package of charts which included the Mediterranean, the Indian Ocean, the Malaccan Straits and Japan. We were suddenly told that we would be sailing to Japan to sweep ahead of our invasion forces. We envisaged that there would be high losses and we were not looking forward to the prospect. Fortunately for us, the atom bomb was dropped and our convoy to the Far East was cut short.

A flotilla of minesweepers clearing a channel through the Greek Islands ran into a very dense field and we lost a number of ships, and we were sent out as replacements. En route we revisited Malta and it gave me much pleasure to navigate the ship into Grand Harbour where on the last occasion I was a leading seaman. We cleared the minefield, which had claimed many victims, and on one lap about ten mines came to the surface simultaneously. We were endeavouring to sink them and there was great excitement as I gently gave helm orders to avoid the ones in our path and at the same time keep in the safety of the swept area behind the sweepers ahead of us.

Several months were spent clearing the Islands and I was about a year overdue for demob when my relief arrived. I was asked if I would like to fly home or take passage in a troopship. I decided that possibly I had had 'nine lives' during my seven years service and came home overland with the Army through Italy, Switzerland and France, arriving in London on a Sunday. On reporting to the Admiralty with only Greek money in my pocket, I asked for an advance but was told that this was impossible until next day, but if I went to the Salvation Army Officer's Club, they would no doubt help me. Thankfully they lent me a fiver and gave me a bed for the night and earned my lasting gratitude.

* * *

In due course the Lieutenant was awarded the standard campaign medals, which included The Atlantic Star, The Africa Star, The Italy Star, and The France and Germany Star.

Later Monty married Miss Jennifer Hitching from Saltford, who during the war, in The Girl's Auxillary, helped as a teenager on the land with such work as potato picking. Their marriage was blessed with two daughters and a son. Some five years ago Mrs Veale was awarded the OBE for her public and political services.

Ian Newman, 1931–1985

Ian, the elder son of Mrs Gwen Newman, was born in Steel Mills. Educated at St Mary Redcliffe, he served his apprenticeship in the printing trade. His aunt, Mrs P Robinson, described him as "a bright lovely boy who was always young looking. He was keen on fishing." He was in the scouts and connected with the Methodist church, though in the pub he was one of the lads and enjoyed darts. His brother, Ray, described him as being always well dressed, "a nice, smart, good bloke".

His national service in the Royal Marines, 1949–51, took him from Scandinavia in the north to Australia in the south. He was based on the Indefatigable and spent much time in Gibraltar. Ray said it was a hard life in the Marines, but in uniform "he looked the cat's whiskers. I can remember his coming home in uniform with his rifle. With a great sense of pride, he was always polishing his boot and his buttons."

By 1952 he was back in printing at ES & A Robinson in Bristol. Later he married Gwen Attwood and they had two daughters, Susan and Julie, and lived on the Chandag estate. Sadly, in 1983 he developed cancer of the throat and suffered terribly until he died in 1985, aged just 54.

Royal Marine Ian Newman, far right, on board the Indefatigable, 1950.

Chapter 23

'D' Day drama, the experiences of Able Seaman Herbert Phelps, Croix de Guerre

1918 marked the end of World War I. But July 29 1918 also marked the birth of Herbert Ernest Nelson Phelps at Ivy Cottage, attached to Cranmore House, at 96, Temple Street, Keynsham. Perhaps the name Nelson was a portent of the future. He was one of seven children. Herbert followed the custom of the majority of the town's children born at that time, and went to Temple Street Infants' School, followed by Bath Hill School, and left at fourteen.

At first he worked for Hickling, the well known ironmongers, for a year, and then went to Keynsham Paper Mills. But at 19, just before Chamberlain's famous speech in October 1938 about 'Peace in our time,' and with his parents' consent, Herbert joined The Royal Navy Volunteer Reserve. As he said later, 'I wanted to see the world and I certainly saw three parts of it'.

Herbert was one of the four Phelp's boys who served the country in WWII and is the only one alive today. Fred was in the SLI and made the mistake of stepping on a mine in France, which blew off his leg. He recovered, though, and wore an artificial limb. Henry was 'in submarines' and was invalided out with TB, yet he lived until 1991. They both died of heart trouble. Like his brothers, Stanley Joseph was also born at Ivy Cottage and joined the South Staffs. Parachute Division. He died in the prime of life when, at 21, the Parachute Division participated in the invasion of Sicily in 1943. Tragically they 'were dropped short by the USA Airforce, so that they landed in the sea'. As Herbert added, he was last seen trying to swim ashore – in full uniform and with heavy boots on.

Having been a cadet in the RNVR since he was nineteen, he was actually called up for full-time service two months before the declaration of war. By that time he was in training at Weymouth and was on board HMS Caradoc, part of the reserve fleet. Able Seaman Phelps said, 'I was on the Caradoc for two and half years on the North Atlantic. At first our task was not escort duty, but patrolling the area looking for stray German vessels that were trying to get through. We 'captured' one, the Emma Frederick, but they scuttled their ship before we boarded it. Their crew became prisoners of war. There were about ten of them, which our patrol boat picked up out of the sea. They knew how fair minded the British were, so even when they climbed up the ropes to come aboard, they did not look scared, not even their fourteen-year-old boy.

'When I was home on leave in April 1942, I became engaged to Miss Eileen Allen of Bristol. Then it was back to the Devonport Barracks, Plymouth, until I was on leave again in August, when we were married. Returning from my eventful leave, I was sent to the Stoke Damerell barracks, formerly a Girls' High School, where, while awaiting a ship, we practised our drill.

Lance Corporal Stanley Joseph Phelps, of Ivy Cottage, 96, Temple Street. He served in the South Staffs. Parachute Division, and was one of four brothers in military service. He died in action aged 21, when at the invasion of Sicily, his parachute company were dropped into the sea.

'I had already been trained as a gunner, hence my partial deafness. The Caradoc was a light cruiser with four six-inch guns, four torpedo tubes and two Oerlikon (Swedish) anti-aircraft guns, mounted one each side of the bridge. The gunner's responsibility was to clean the guns and keep them in good order, to practise loading, firing and unloading, and to carry the heavy shells from the 'cordite' magazine. The shells were about two feet long by a foot thick. After loading them into the barrels, lengths of cordite, which were very inflammable and longer than the shells but not as thick, were pushed in behind the shells, the breeches slammed shut, and the gun was ready for firing. In battle, my action station was in the magazine, issuing the shells and the cordite.

'Later, the Caradoc, with its complement of some one hundred men, sailed, under Captain L Cook, for New York. There we collected some hush hush constructions built in America called 'Landing Ship Tanks'. The LSTs were large metal, tank-carrying vessels. They had an upper and a lower deck, with a lift, and could carry some twenty tanks, or a combination of tanks and Bren-gun carriers, arranged one behind the other. Obviously they were pretty big and had their own engines, and were flat bottomed with landing ramp bows.

'Captain S Bethel then took command of the Caradoc but in October 1942 we sailed without her for England, on board a valuable LST, fully laden with tanks. Instead of names, the LSTs all had numbers and I was on number 419. This time we sailed in convoy, with the protection of destroyers. There was a crew of about thirty of us on 419. It was equipped with two Oerlikon guns and a small gun on the quarter deck and on the stern. It was a slow moving convoy. All the LSTs, possibly thirty in number, had a blue light on their stern and our responsibility was to follow the light in front of us. The weather was foggy and my duty was to stand on the bows and to shout to the Captain if we were getting too close to the LST in front of us. We had to keep a safe distance behind each other. We docked at Falmouth, but other LSTs moored at various other ports along the south coast. It was all very 'hush hush'. We did not want to draw the attention of the Germans to our build-up for the invasion.

'In 1943 we set off for Africa in 419, loaded with Bren-gun carriers. We sailed from Malta with our valuable cargo aboard and discharged it in the landing at Sicily, which was quite easy going. Then it was back to Malta, reload and off to Salerno. Later, at the Anzio beach, we had a lot of trouble from the Italian gunners and one shell hit our LST. A soldier on the upper deck lost a hand, while fortunately, I was at the other side of the deck. Shrapnel splintered one of our life boats.

'After that it was back to England, to wait in Dover for D Day. When the day arrived in June 1944, the sea was rough and the weather poor, but even worse weather was expected. It was now, or not for several weeks. We sailed, the LST crammed full of tanks and Bren-gun carriers and their crews. But this time we were also towing a twenty ton pontoon consisting of fifteen tanks welded together to float, to carry a further twenty Bren-gun carriers.

'In daylight, in the middle of the English Channel, with a very choppy sea running, the two-inch wire towing-rope to the pontoon broke and the craft quickly drifted away. Without a moment's thought, I dived overboard to swim to the craft. I was still fully dressed so I swam breast stroke. The water was very cold and the pontoon was about seventeen feet away. Behind me the deck

Able Seaman Herbert Phelps, awarded the Croix de Guerre in 1945.

By the KING'S Order the name of
Able Seaman Herbert Ernest Nelson Phelps,

was published in the London Gazette on
14 November, 1944,
as mentioned in a Despatch for distinguished service.
I am charged to record
His Majesty's high appreciation.

First Lord of the Admiralty

was lined with cheering crewmen and soldiers leaning on the guard rails. I was intent on getting there and I used to be a good swimmer, having learnt at the Jubilee Baths on Sunday mornings. I was not frightened as I was sure I could do it, but it was hard work and took me longer than I thought. Around me high waves lifted me up for a moment at a time. Gradually I got closer and, with an almighty effort, I reached the vessel and clambered aboard.

'A thin rope was thrown to me, which I caught. Attached to it was a thicker rope, and finally a wire rope. I stood and pulled on board the wire rope, which was heavy because of the length of it from the ship and the pontoon going up and down all the time. However, I made it secure to a bollard as the LST finally came alongside. The Captain sent for me on the bridge, where he congratulated me and gave me a glass of something very strong to warm me up.

'Finally we reached the Normandy beach, to find ours was nearly the only LST to make it. We stood off the beach until a drifter came and towed the pontoon in to unload. Then we went in, the ramp went down and our fifteen Bren-gun carriers drove down it into battle, with our infantry men too. As we were beached, one of our planes, hit by fire, ditched in the sea just near us. There was a lot of gunfire and dead men lying on the beach, including a German pilot wearing high boots. There were rows of the infantry landing craft stretched along the beach, as the Germans fired from the houses. Then it was straight back to Dover to load 419 again and return to Normandy. We made quite a number of these trips.

'Some time later I received a letter from the Admiralty. It said,

"By the KING's order the name of Able Seaman Herbert Ernest Nelson Phelps was published in the London Gazette on 14 November, 1944, as mentioned in a Despatch for distinguished service. I am charged to record His Majesty's high appreciation. [signed] A V Alexander, First Lord of the Admiralty." I had lived up to the name of Nelson!

'To return to the war. When that part of the invasion was over, I was later involved in landing LSTs at Ostend to help in the freeing of Holland. In preparing to unload, we landed in water too deep for the first ramp. So five of us pulled on the chains to bring down the second ramp. Unfortunately, it released itself and ran down out of control. The other four men escaped but I being the last man, it crushed my ankle. I was taken to Tilbury Hospital for setting and plaster, and sent to Southwold, near Lowestoft, for convalescence.

'When I was quite fit, it was back to 419 again, until the cessation of hostilities. Then I returned to England to the Fleet Air Arm base at Winchester to await my release. I was finally demobilised at Portsmouth in September 1945, and happily returned to Keynsham, my wife Eileen and our daughter Jean.

'As I had served in several spheres of the war, I was awarded the Atlantic Star, the Africa Star, the Italy Star, and the French and German Clasp War Medal. Obviously I was given the 1939–45 Star, and, of course, also the Long Service and Good Conduct Medal. I had been on active service for six years.

'When I arrived home, a letter in French was awaiting me, which translated says,

RÉPUBLIQUE FRANÇAISE

Guerre 1939-1945

C I T A T I O N

MINISTERE DE LA MARINE

ETAT-MAJOR GENERAL

N° 634   E.M.G.O/REC.

PARIS, le 11 août 1945

Le Vice-Amiral LEMONNIER
Chef d'Etat-Major Général de la Marine
Commandant les Forces Maritimes et Aéronavales

C I T E

=-=-=-=-=-=

A l'ORDRE DE LA DIVISION :

ASSAUT FORCE " S "

(L.S.T. 419 3rd Flotilla) A.B. Erbert Ernest Nelson PHELPS D/BD/X 1602

     " Le 6 juin 1944 s'est porté volontaire pour poser des amarres à bord d'un bâtiment en dérive malgré une mer grosse et un vent très fort. Il permit ainsi de ramener sur les plages de Normandie un matériel de valeur ".

     Cette citation comporte l'attribution de la Croix de Guerre 1939-1945 avec Etoile d'Argent.

Signé : LEMONNIER.

The Citation of the Croix de Guerre awarded to Able Seaman Herbert E N Phelps, 1945. The translation is to be found in the chapter.

"French Republic, 1939–1945 War CITATION. Paris, 11th, August 1945. [from] Naval Ministry, Chief of Staff, No. 634. E.M.G.O./REC.

Vice Admiral LEMMONIER, Chief of Naval Staff, Commander of Naval Forces and Fleet Air Arm.

Mentioned in Despatches, Operation 'S'. (L.S.T. 419 3rd. Flotilla)

A. S. Herbert Ernest Nelson PHELPS, D/ BO / X 1602.

On 6th June 1944, he volunteered to make fast a drifting vessel despite heavy seas and gale force winds, thereby making it possible to bring on to the Normandy beaches valuable equipment.

This recommendation merits the award of the CROIX DE GUERRE of the Second World War with the Silver Star.

[Signed]   Lemmonnier"

'I felt very humble at this honour bestowed upon me. Then I thought of my poor brother, Stanley, who perished in the Mediterranean, and gave thanks for simply being spared.'

Chapter 24

Brothers in War

The biography of Ordinary Signaller Derek Renshaw, RN, written by Brian, his younger brother

It was a Sunday morning, September 12 1943. I was in the garden of my home in Rock Road occupied with my usual weekend jobs. This time it was chopping firewood in preparation for the winter. I heard a knock at the front door followed by a silence. Then my Mother appeared looking very pale and shaken, a yellow telegram clasped in her hand. 'Derek is dead,' she blurted out and hugged me to her. My Father was there; I heard him groan in sheer grief. I could feel nothing. Derek was my big brother, four and a half years my senior, a hero to me. It was his birthday. Now I would never see him again.

During the early stages of the war, Derek, who was a member of the 1st Keynsham Scouts Troop, acted as a messenger for the Civil Defence Organisation, doing evening duties at the end of a day working as a clerk for Keynsham Urban District Council in their offices on Wellsway. This meant that during the evenings, both he and my Father, who was a member of the Local Defence Volunteers, were quite often out on duty, leaving my Mother, Grandmother, younger sister and myself at home. I was the man of the house then.

During the war I attended Bath Hill School where Mr Mycock was the head teacher, and who had had a gate inserted into the playground's stone wall, providing access to what is now Keynsham Park. Even then it was known as the park although it was only a field belonging to Mr Clothier, where a few cattle grazed. When the sirens sounded we pupils would be marshalled through this gate and were then to run to allocated spots on the banks of the River Chew where there was room to scramble down the banks to shelter, before reaching the actual waterline.

Then it was decided that if you lived within half a mile of the school, you could run home, and, if your parents agreed, take home with you a child who lived further away. So when the sirens sounded, I and some of my friends would run to my home and take shelter in a cupboard under the stairs.

Fifty years later, I was called to my old home to convert one bedroom into two. My attention was drawn to the under-stair cupboard which had become a downstairs toilet.

Still clearly to be seen was the pencilled record I had made of the many air raids that had been spent in that small space. In some instances I had filled in if and where bombs had landed. The present owner was reluctant for this little piece of history to be lost, so it has been varnished over and thus preserved for possibly the lifetime of the house.

Our sister, Diane, was born about a month before war broke out. She would

Ordinary Signaller Derek Renshaw on sick leave from HMS Anson. This photo was taken in August 1943 in the back garden of the home of Mr Vivian Turner, the greatly respected Scout District Commissioner, who lived in Charlton Road almost opposite the cinema. A very popular sailor, Derek received many 'get well' letters from his friends on the Anson. At the end of August he returned from leave to HMS Helicon at Aultbea, Scotland, where he died on September 12, 1943, on his 19th birthday, from a stomach complaint. (B Renshaw.)

remember Derek perhaps for the last two years of his life, sadly mostly during the comings and goings on 'leave'. She still cherishes the one china doll he brought home for her and can still recall the rough feel of his uniform as he carried her upstairs to bed.

During the later stages of the war our family was issued with a Morrison shelter – this curtailed the recording of air raids – probably because it was constructed of heavy rusting girders and anti-shrapnel iron grilling. The raids were very frequent at this time due to the importance of the Bristol docks, aircraft manufacture at Filton, etc . . . We got into the habit of sleeping downstairs to save as much disturbance as possible. My bed was actually made up in the shelter and, for the most part, was quite comfortable and tinged with a certain excitement, but one night I had a terrible dream about a German pilot in his airplane telling me he was coming to kill me. I 'watched' as he climbed out of his cockpit and floated down on a parachute, but by this time there was only the lower half of him with black jackboots. He came into the house, entered the shelter and sat across my chest, his hands went round my throat and I woke up! There, right in front of my face, was a pair of black Wellington boots.

Derek was educated at Wick Road Junior School at St Anne's, then for a short while at Broadlands, Keynsham, and later at Cannings College, Bristol. I remember he was very popular with all his associates and I always envied him his talents as an artist. The sketch of the Sailor is one he did for me during his later days in the Navy, while the Brassmills was done at an earlier age, during the time when he and I used to play in the disused buildings.

My brother also gave me a gift that I treasured and regret not still possessing – we were looking in a toy shop window and admiring Hornby '0' gauge Model Railway items and I was very thrilled and excited when my brother told me to take my pick – up to a certain price, of course.

The sketch of Hitler is pierced with holes, evidence of the fact that it was pinned to the door of the out-house and made a most suitable dartboard target. 'Tommy' was another of his sketches of about the same time.

It was during his time working as a clerk that Derek expressed his desire to go to sea. This naturally was to the great dismay of our parents but they would not stand in his way and he volunteered for the Navy at the age of sixteen. He joined HMS St George near Douglas on the Isle of Man and completed his initial training and qualified as a boy signaller. He was eventually posted to HMS Anson. This battleship was engaged in escort duties to the Russian convoys. The photograph gives some idea of the appalling conditions faced by these convoys and many sailors suffered severe frost burns from handling the thickly iced metalwork.

The terrible conditions experienced on these trips took their toll of his health and I remember how ill he looked on one of his leaves. Because of his health he was posted to Defence Boom Station at Aultbea on the west coast of Ross & Cromarty on the shores of the bleak Lock Ewe, Scotland, where he was occupied on lighter duties.

On his last leave, he brought home a puppy for me – it was an Old English Sheepdog and although great fun to have whilst young, we did not have space enough for such an animal when fully grown. So it was a sad outing for my

299

Dad and me to take it to a new home in the country shortly after Derek's death.

The war continued. We like many others had our very personal war.

A feature that is still very apparent around Keynsham as a result of the War Effort, is the lack of ornamental railings on front garden walls. Still to be seen,

Derek was quite an artist. 'The sketch of Hitler . . . made a most suitable dartboard target', recorded Brian.

THE BATTLESHIP HMS ANSON. Ordinary Signaller Derek Renshaw, aged 17, joined the ship in 1941 and served on her for about 18 months. Though life was hard on her, he never complained, and as his brother said, 'He was proud to be on her and was happy enough'. (B Renshaw.)

The back of the photo that Derek sent home states, 'Ice formed on the Anson during Russian Convoy duty, 1942'. As it crossed the Arctic Circle, protecting food convoys en route for Russia's northern ports, spray iced over the ship's decking many inches thick. It must have been hell for the crew. (B Renshaw.)

however, is where they were once embedded in the stone. The railings, along with saucepans and any other old iron and steel objects, were commandeered for re-use in the manufacture of tanks, airplanes and munitions.

Above, around and within us, the war rolled on to its eventual end. Keynsham and its people played their part.

'Blackouts' a school Composition by Derek A Renshaw September 29, 1939

Crash! Down comes the window-covering. The drawing pins have failed to hold the weight of the thick brown paper and someone else is having trouble with the Blackout. It is a source of exasperation as well as fun, as many folk have already discovered.

After sun-set people spend their evenings apologising to lamp posts, injuring themselves with hammer blows while blacking out, finding their way in a fog, as it were, and generally enjoying themselves or otherwise.

The inhabitants of the country are the lucky ones, for they are used to the dark and there are few lamp posts to collide with! Although the County Councils are splashing gallons of white paint on protruding obstacles and drawing thick white lines on the highways, travel is still difficult. Hitler has succeeded in making cyclists buy rear lights. This is proving a great difficulty, for there are only a limited number manufactured.

Car enamel is being covered by thick layers of white, covered torches are being used and there is a boom in the light shade trade. Millions of sheets of brown paper are being pasted over windows and people are growing tired of struggling in the pitch blackness.

The one good of the blackout is to make people use their brains and have recourse to rough and ready measures.

* * *

A Letter to an Imaginary Pen-friend –

School Composition by Derek A Renshaw November 15, 1939

61, Rock Road, KEYNSHAM.

Dear Michael,

As in England at the present time we are having rather a dull time, I can only wish I was with you on your Father's sheep farm. I will give you a brief outline of an English Saturday now the war is being fought.

Eight o'clock. Having arrived downstairs we proceed to breakfast off bread and Government butter. The morning is spent alternately chopping wood and listening to complaining neighbours and news broadcasts.

One o'clock. Dinner consists of moderately good potatoes (having come from our own garden) Government butter, meat (very fatty) and cabbage, also from our own garden.

Three former Keynsham scouts on leave in August 1943. The soldier was John Williams of 77, Charlton Road, the sailor Derek Renshaw of 61, Rock Road and the airman Trevor Tyler of Stockwood Vale, whose grandfather (?) had been the local brushmaker. The photo was probably taken in Stockwood Vale. Sadly Derek lost his life in the war from stomach troubles which were believed to have been brought on by the pressure and strain of serving on the Arctic convoy duty the year before. He died aged 19. The finely carved oak lectern at Victoria Methodist Church was given in his memory, where a plaque records that it was presented by 'his family, his messmates and his friends'. (B Renshaw.)

Derek, aged 18, drew this fine sketch of a soldier while in Keynsham on sick leave in July 1943. Two months later he was dead.

The afternoon is spent in various ways and is the brightest part of the day (if it is not raining). Then comes tea of bread, Government butter and jam, cake and tea (with no sugar). Next, the blackout. Up go the black curtains and out goes Dad to see if any chinks of light are showing.

We often go out on Saturday nights and I remember one night, having lent my torch to Dad, stepping into a deep puddle and so extinguishing my few good spirits. If we do not go out, the evening is spent arguing and listening to propaganda reports from station DJA. All I can say is 'Oh, for Australia!'

Yours,

Derek

* * *

The Royal Navy's Roll of Honour

'It is upon the Navy under the Providence of God that the safety, honour, and welfare of this realm, do chiefly attend.'

Charles II, 'Articles of War,' Preamble.

Able Seaman CHARLIE T CLAPP was born and lived at 101, Temple Street, the cousin of Herbert Phelps, but was not related to the farming family

'The Brass Mills was done . . . during the time when he and I used to play in the disused buildings', wrote Brian about Derek's sketch.

305

of the same name. He served on the destroyer HMS Valentine and went down with the ship in the North Sea when it was bombed.

Able Seaman GEORGE V FARLEY. He was born at 12, Albert Road, and served on HMS Ardent. He died on active service in the North Sea, when the Ardent was sunk by a German warship. It went down with all guns blazing.

Able Seaman 'Bob' H HODDINOTT was not connected with the family of the same name who ran a public house in Temple Street. Able Seaman 'Bob' Hoddinott, a son of the family who lived in Wellsway opposite Rock Hill House, joined the Royal Navy in 1936, when 17 years old. He was serving on the aircraft carrier H.M.S. Glorious and died when she was torpedoed North of Norway when escorting King Haakon and his Cabinet in April 1940 after the Nazi invasion. He was just 21.

Signalman DEREK A RENSHAW was born at 61, Rock Road, in September 1924. At HMS St George, at Douglas, Isle of Man, he trained in morse and semaphore.

He was then posted to the battleship HMS Anson, then captained by Sir Bruce Frazer, later Admiral Frazer. Still a teenager, he was with the Anson on its protection role on the Arctic Convoy route to Russia, where there was sometimes as much as eight inches of ice on the guns. The crossing of the Arctic Circle was duly ceremonially celebrated. After a while he was granted sick leave in Scotland, where sadly he died, aged just nineteen. With his parents' agreement, he was buried at sea with appropriate military honours. At Victoria Methodist Church, an oak lectern stands in his memory.

Gunner G D COOKSLEY, Wireless Electrician, A J PALMER, and Air Mechanic R G WAYMOUTH also served in the Royal Navy and bravely died for their country.

Chief Engineer E HARDY was in the Merchant Navy, and his memory is also honoured as yet another Keynsham naval man who gave his life for his country.

Chapter 25

Flying in the Royal Air Force

'Never in the field of human conflict was so much owed by so many to so few,' declared Sir Winston Churchill in Parliament on August 20, 1940. He was, of course, referring to the bravery of the young fighter pilots in the face of the massive strength of the Luftwaffe. The Sunday Times of 9 September 1990 recalled that on 26 August 1940 during the Battle of Britain (c. 10 July to 31 October 1940) 1,000 German planes were launched in a mass daylight assault, and were attacked by 21 squadrons of RAF fighters, so that 41 Luftwaffe planes failed to return.

It is difficult to say exactly how many Keynsham men were in the RAF at that time. The late Councillor Len Ellis was in the RAF and was not very impressed with the experience. The late Gordon Reed also saw wartime service in the RAF. One Keynsham airman bailed out once, only to crash later, and is still alive and living in Keynsham. Some airmen understandably do not wish to talk about their service; fortunately others are more forthcoming, for without their co-operation this chapter could not be written. Their help is indeed appreciated.

Sergeant Geoffrey Sherwell reminisces

David G Sherwell, his father, was born in Brislington, and in WWI was a mule driver, though David's brother, Arthur, was a Surgeon Lieutenant who went down with the battleship HMS Barham and perished with 900 other crewmen. David married May Edwina, and Geoffrey, their only child, was born in Bitton in 1914. In 1915 the family moved to 47, Bristol Road, and in 1920 to No 51, 'Welford House' nearby. In the large house with sundry out-buildings, almost opposite Cannock's garage, and happily still there, David started a pickle factory around 1924. The business flourished and built up a wonderful reputation. At first the firm sold to retailers as far away as Yeovil, Weymouth, Plymouth and Gloucester; to licenced premises and fish and chip shops. Gradually they switched to supplying wholesalers instead.

After WWII again they were able to obtain the ingredients of vegetables and onions from Holland, Egypt and Italy, and the business expanded. Sadly David had developed cancer by the time that Geoffrey was demobilised, so he then took over the firm, with May, his strong-minded mother, always in the wings. The firm prospered and became so big that business had to be turned away. As they expanded, they were about to become a limited company when in 1973 the Government's credit squeeze devastated them. They were forced to sell their business, and Elgood and Dye bought it and transferred the firm out of Keynsham.

To turn to Geoffrey's school days, he was in the OTC at Bristol Grammar School, and as war was declared on the Sunday, so he volunteered on the Monday for the RAF. Within a week he was at Uxbridge for testing and was then sent home for six months on 'deferred service'. Finally he was called up and sent to Babbacombe, Torquay, for two weeks, then to Preston. Next he was sent to the old Bristol Flying School at Yatesbury, near Calne, for two weeks, before going to Weston-super-Mare for three weeks. Eventually he arrived at Blackpool, where he learnt the morse code with 500 other airmen in a massive former tram shed.

In 1940 he married Betty Chiswell from Knowle, and their marriage was blessed with baby David in August 1941.

Meanwhile Empire Flying Schools abroad were being formed, while he was getting older and without flying experience, so he applied to go to Northolt Aerodrome, where the famous Polish 'fighter wing' was stationed. Under Squadron Ldr. Raymond who was in charge of Fighter Control there, Geoffrey was trained as a fighter controller, using radar. He now takes up the story.

'By the end of 1943, I had finished my training at Uxbridge, and during one of my breaks, which we all needed because of the pressure of the work, I was assigned to the 'hangar room', a box-like room at the top of a high ladder, situated on the roof of a hangar, like a crow's next. There I was responsible for counting all the aircraft that flew out and the number that returned. This was a double check on the WAAF's plotting, and also I would inform them if any planes were damaged. Watching radar was like sitting in front of a television, and when I was trained I was sent to the radar centre. There, 80 ft below ground at Uxbridge, as 'Acting Sergeant Sherwell', I became part of the team in the Night Fighter Plotting Control Department, at HQ Group Control of No 11 Group, but in no way were we controlling night fighters. We were to build up for D Day by switching over to day control, and were known as Area Control.

'Around the large table containing the outline of Britain, WAAFs were on duty, and plotted the positions of all aircraft. They worked four shifts with 40 girls on each, with 40 girls to relieve them and a further 40 girls in reserve. Though officially they did a six-hour day, sometimes they worked day and night. They were wonderful girls, all of them. They were of above average intelligence, and performed a dedicated task. Mainly in their twenties, their job was very stressful, and they were damned dedicated. When Biggin Hill Aerodrome was on fire and their lives in danger from the collapsing building, they had to be forcibly carried out from the table. They knew that as long as they were doing their job, they could keep the fighters flying.

'The girls used long magnetic rods and pushed triangular plane markers about, with ear phones over their heads to receive the latest reports from the Observer Corps, and a telephone mouthpiece hanging from their necks. From a gallery above them, the Area Control Officer, who was responsible for the scrambling of fighters, looked on and gave orders on the strength of what he saw. Our markers had white numbers on red bases, while the Germans had black numbers on yellow bases. The enemy markers, initialled H for Hun, indicated the different number allocated to each raid, the number of planes involved, their height and an arrow showing their direction. On the wall was a

This photo of Sergeant G Sherwell was taken in 1940 when, as a young RAF cadet in the Initial Training Wing, he was sent to Preston, where the Air Force had taken over a large hotel. The white 'flash' in their caps indicated they were trainees. He is in the third row from the front, and fourth in from the right. (G Sherwell's.)

board listing the strength of the different squadrons, so that the famous leader, 'Stuffy' Dowding, knew at any one time just how many aircraft they had in reserve – if any.

German reconnaissance

'In the preparation for the 'D Day' invasion at Normandy in 1944, the Americans, in overall command, moved to Clifton College, Bristol, to formulate their plans, while Clifton College was evacuated to Bude, Cornwall. Meanwhile the German PRU photograpic reconnaissance planes, Focke-Wulf 190s, which were very fast and carried no weapons, came over very high at 35–40,000 ft to ascertain our movements. We moved our 124 Fighter Squadron back to the North Weald to give them more time to intercept the PRUs. Unfortunately our Spitfire Mark 6 had difficulties due to lack of oxygen at that height. Even if they bailed out, they had a small bottle of oxygen to keep them alive. Lack of air pressure could make the pilot's responses slow, and even cause him to burst out of his skin. A later version, the Spitfire Mark 7, had a pressurised cabin, still having Merlin engines, and so the difficulty was overcome.

'Two officers and another airman and I were instructed to set up an Area Control Anti-PRU unit, with authority to work out a suitable system for tracking, intercepting and destroying these craft. Flight Lieutenant A V Homes was a dedicated man and I was his deputy, as 'deputy area fighter controller'. My responsibility was to obtain and collate information for the controller. I worked like mad, with two telephones on my desk. It was a very stressful time.

'Fortunately the Germans were very consistent, and flew in from Cherbourg over Beachy Head and Dungeness, or up the Thames estuary. Dover-Calais being the shortest distance, the Germans expected us to invade across there, a belief we encouraged. Our fighters were painted duck egg blue to blend in with the sky. Below 30–40,000 ft horizontal visibility was eight miles. Above that height, the PRUs looked like mere spots and difficult to see. In any case, our fighter pilots were really flying blind as they had no maps and no time to read them, as they were going so fast. They just depended on information via the VHF RT phones. So with limited visibility, the warning was 'Look out for the Hun, coming out of the sun'.

'Normally we tried to get our fighters above the Germans, with the sun behind them. Our fighters began to trail 'vapour' at 18–20,000 ft so we flew planes in pairs, one behind the other, and if the rear one shouted 'Smoking' they dropped down, so they were then below the Germans, who in any case, if they saw our trailing, would usually go home. Using radar, we tried to keep the Luftwaffe incoming planes, and our fighters approaching in the opposite direction, about eight miles apart, with our boys below to avoid trailing. At a given signal our chaps would turn to port or starboard onto the same course as the Hun, and if he was above them, they would climb through his 'trail' until level with him and the Hun would never even know that they were there.

'The Germans were very quick to lock on to any conversations, and so work out the position of our planes, so silence was golden. The trouble with the

Poles was that they would chatter so, but they were never used in this Anti-PRU role.

'In the end, we established a 'standing patrol' of two aircraft always in the sky, ready to intercept PRUs up to D Day invasion. Actually there was a very effective spy network known as the 'Y Service', the Maquis, in France. Each morning it supplied us with information regarding what German spy planes were going to take off next day, and just when and where from. Mostly the Luftwaffe used Focke-Wulfs, with cameras replacing their guns. Warned in advance at our Anti-PRU base, by 8.30 am the first plot of them appeared on the radar. In passing, it is interesting to know that the Luftwaffe used St John's Church, Keynsham, as a navigational reference point, though not the PRUs.

'Our unit was wanted only until 'D Day' after which we were disbanded and I was sent to Blackpool, where I was billeted out. It was a happy time there, out in town every night, and usually, being in uniform, one did not have to pay for the entertainments.

'We were inoculated against yellow fever and on December 23 1945, we left on board HMS Andes from Liverpool, going north round the top of Ireland as German submarines were still operating. I was in charge of a lot of chaps as I had joined the service early. On Christmas Day we were off the coast of Morocco when a Sunderland flew in with our Christmas dinner of turkey, cake and pudding – from Australia! From a passing Russian ship, they called out, 'Joe for king'. There was dead silence among the 1,500 men on board the Andes as we listened over the tannoy to the King's Speech, which was very touching with its connections with home, and at least brought a lump to the throat. This was followed by a tot of rum.

'At Gambia we took on supplies and in four or five days arrived at Freetown, where we disembarked, put on our packs, and marched to the barracks at New England, Freetown. It was very humid, and 90 degrees in the shade. One's webbing would rot in six weeks. I was 'Deputy Controller, Combined Operations'. There were still German submarines in the district, so I organised a 'square search' for them if necessary, and also I handled the coded messages.

'I was severely reprimanded when on receiving a 'May Day' distress call from a Wellington bomber which had ditched nearby in the sea, I ordered the Vice-Admiral's pinnace to go out and rescue the survivors. Initially I had directed the Air Sea Rescue launch to go, but the conditions at sea made it unsuitable. Later the Vice-Admiral sent for me, with the Wing Commander present, and demanded just who I thought I was to commandeer his personal boat which would take months to replace. I replied simply that 'men's lives were at stake, sir'.

'Twelve months later, I sailed for England on the 'Eastern Princess', a stinking army boat, with Colonel Scott in charge. The conditions were bad, and the food included black potatoes. But at least I got back home to Keynsham, and to Betty and to young David, whom I had hardly seen for six years. Gratefully, I had survived the war.'

Keynsham's First XI fifty years ago

Mr Les Whittock said that for many years the Keynsham Football team's First and Second Eleven played their home matches on the open land opposite the large Edwardian houses in Charlton Road. The First XI's pitch was beside the fine row of poplar trees that grew to a great height, and the Second XI's pitch was in the next field further up the road.

Les added that among the committee who ran the teams were Jack Exon, chairman, Jack Woodham and Arthur Brown. In 1941, the land on which the games were played came up for sale. Due to the doubt by some of the committee members of their ability to raise the whole sum required, they lost the land. Future matches had to be played on the Crown Field, which is their home today.

The photo below shows the First XI in 1941, in the early years of World War II. Tom Carpenter is shown in his RAF uniform on his first home leave.

Keynsham's First XI, 1941

Front Row, left to right.
Leslie Whittock, a Brislington man, another Brislington lad, Maurice Ryan and Peter Ollis.
Second Row.
George Parsons, a Wellsway man, and Percy Robbins.
Rear Row.
Wally Blue, George Box, the late Ron Herniman, Ron Vile, the goalie, Leonard Lloyd and Tom Carpenter.

He was the son of the wealthy Tom Carpenter senior, of Carpenter's Lane fame, who had a large haulage business in Temple Street, first of horses and carts, and later of lorries.

Chapter 26

Per Ardua Ad Astra

The experiences of Flight Lieutenant M Sparey and Corporal Les Harvey

To few boys is it given to be born with a father who really was a railway station master, with access to those wonderful GWR steam engines. Yet that was the lot of Michael Sparey, who was one of the family of four sons and six daughters of Keynsham's station master and his teacher-wife. They lived in Hawthorn Villa, in the row of stone houses at the beginning of Chandag Road (named after an Indian village), when the terrace practically constituted the only houses in that muddy lane. Not far away at 26, Manor Road lived the Stone family, later to become well known through a marriage to one Leslie Crowther. Some of the children of the respective families used to play together before WWII.

Station Master Sparey was responsible for both Keynsham and Saltford stations, though he did not live at the station master's house at Keynsham station, nor had his predecessors since an earlier station master's wife had hanged herself there.

Sadly, one of the Sparey brothers, Ronald, died when he was but sixteen. A second brother, Peter, born in 1922, joined the merchant navy when he was a young man and truly saw the world. During WWII many times he sailed across the Atlantic as part of convoys. On one occasion a German torpedo hit the rudder of his ship but fortunately, being a dud, it did not blow up the ship but made a hole and the ship slowly sank. Fortunately, another vessel took the crew off, and Peter lived to sail the seas for many more years.

A third brother, Robert, from Cotham Grammar School, trained in the RAF and became a Navigator Sergeant in WWII. On June 15 1942 he was one of the North African squadrons deputed to give a merchant navy convoy aerial protection. Tragically, that day, he was one of six planes from his squadron who were shot down by trigger-happy MN gunners. Sadly, Robert was killed. Some very straight talking ensued between the Air Ministry and the Admiralty about the conditions for future protection of merchant navy vessels.

Despite this tragedy in the family, Michael, the fourth brother, wanted to follow in Robert's footsteps. From Temple Street Infants to Bath Hill Juniors, he won a scholarship to the City of Bath Grammar School, at Beechen Cliff.

Michael remembered that before the war, Farmer Payne would deliver the milk in a small Austin Seven blue van, from which he ladled out milk from a churn. You could tell when the farmer was at the local cinema, by the sound of his loud hearty laughter. From his fruit shop, Mr Aslin would come in his open cart selling his wares. Another trader, Mr Skuse, in his old truck, would pass by selling paraffin.

In connection with WWII, Michael said there were many occasions in which RAF fighters shot down our own planes. One particular member of an aircrew was due to be court-martialled for such an event, but the Germans got him first! When planes were flying in close formation, one could easily just bump his neighbour, with fatal consequences, particularly when night flying. When the RAF attacked Cologne with a thousand planes, all concentrated over a small area for a short time, great care was essential to avoid collisions with those beside or above you, and to make sure bombs did not land on planes below you.

In 1942 Michael joined the RAF, but there was a long queue of would-be pilots, so he had to wait until he was called up in 1943, when he was whisked to London for his uniform and injections. Rather unusually, he and his fellow aircraftmen grade two, AC2, (= 'privates') had their meals at London Zoo, of which he has memories of queueing up for breakfast at six o'clock outside the monkey house, china mug in hand, while the animals ran round their cages.

The Initial Training Wing

He was then posted to the ITW at Stratford-on-Avon, and was billeted at the Elizabethan 'Falcon Hotel' though still just an AC2 on three shillings a day, less deductions. The twelve weeks' course, apart from marching, consisted of endless lectures on navigation, meteorology, aircraft recognition [How necessary!], engines and weapons.

They learned to take a Browning .303 machine gun to pieces and reassemble it, metaphorically, with their hands tied behind their backs. On the ranges, they also shot twelve bore tracer ammunition, so that they could see how far away they were from the targets. And just in case they were mentally tired at the end of a gruelling day, they ended up with a three mile run, to keep them fit.

For those trainee pilots who had successfully passed their exams in the above subjects, it was on to the Grading School, the GS, for three to four weeks. There they would do twelve hours flying in a Tiger Moth with an instructor, to see if they were suitable for pilot training. They were expected to fly solo after six to eight hours. Michael really enjoyed flying 'Tigers', which to him were more interesting than later sophisticated machines. 'In a Tiger, at 45 mph, in a strong contrary wind, you could almost hover.'

In his book, 'A Thousand Shall Fall,' M Peden [1979, Canada Wings Inc. Spitsville, page 30] described the Tiger as 'With a wing span of 29 ft, she was a graceful, rather delicate looking biplane, with a perspex coupe top to cover the two tandem seats. She weighed only 1,115lbs empty, and had a 145 hp gravity-fed inverted Gipsy Moth engine, which was extremely reliable. Being a Training Command Aircraft, she was painted the standard (and beautiful) shade of yellow'.

Back in England, the GS at Clyffe Pypard, south of Swindon, was such an isolated place that it did not even have a pub. The teachers were experienced air crew who had done their thirty sorties (bombing raids over the continent), and having survived, were removed from 'operations' for six months. If trainees at GS were not found to be suitable, or failed their exams, they were 'out' as pilots, and were posted elsewhere in the RAF, with visible or invisible tears of disappointment.

An unexpected meeting

During the war, pilot training schools were set up at least in Canada, Rhodesia and the USA, where the better weather than ours facilitated many more days of flying practice. Michael was posted to Canada, and arrived at Moncton, New Brunswick, where newly-arrived AC2s were assigned into groups for lectures and training, prior to selection for the Elementary Flying Training Schools, the EFTS.

Pedan recalled that during his training there was painted on the wall at his EFTS in Canada, near his newly assigned locker, in heavy black script, the simple message that 'There are old pilots, and bold pilots; there are no old, bold pilots'.

In 1943, another Keynsham man was also posted to Moncton, Corporal 'Les' Harvey, the son of Henry and Jemima (nee Ollis) Harvey of 10, Fairfield Terrace. He was called up in May 1940 just before his twentieth birthday. At Moncton he was appointed to No 31 Personnel Disposal Unit where he received lists of the names and home addresses of the new intake of pilot trainees. One evening he was not a little surprised to read the entry, 'AC2 Michael Sparey, Keynsham, Somerset'. The two men were glad to see each other, so far away from home but united in a common aim to destroy the Nazi War Machine. Michael was only there for two or three weeks before being posted to EFTS but Les remained there until 1945.

Michael found himself at Saskatchewan, on the Canadian Prairies, with no cities for many miles around. At the EFTS, there were endless written exams, and flying tests. The chief instructor sat behind Michael, carefully watching how he took off and landed, not to mention how the would-be pilot dealt with instructor-created difficulties such as cutting out the engines, or forced landings. His temperament under stress was recorded and the speed of his reflexes, and any proneness to air sickness. Not a few instructors and trainee pilots died in training accidents.

Having satisfied the Royal Canadian Air Force authorities of his initial ability, it was on to the Service Flying Training School, the SFTS, at Souris in Saskatchewan, with more lectures and exams, and many more hours of flying, learning advanced flying skills. Then he graduated to flying 'twins', twin-engine planes. If one passed all the written exams and the flying proficiency tests, one could win the coveted 'wings', and according to the level of their marks, some men were then made flight sergeants or sergeants, and others, Pilot Officers. Murray Pedan described how, at the Wings' Parade, the band led the parade into the large hangar.

'Inside the hangar, the graduating class would be called up, one at a time before a visiting VIP, usually a visiting Air Commodore, who would acknowledge the cadet's salute, pin the coveted wings on his chest, then shake his hand and give him a verbal pat on the back before the cadet marched off. I never tired of the drama implicit in the cadet's marching up in his plain unadorned blue tunic, then turning about smartly and marching back toward

A Spitfire Mark IX, the fighter aircraft that many pilots in training had hoped to fly. Together with the Hurricane, they caused havoc among the Luftwaffe during the war.

Leslie Harvey of St George's Road in his uniform as a corporal in the Royal Air Force. This photo of his was taken in Saltford in 1943 before he was posted to Canada for the next two and a half years.

the crowd of spectators with the clearly visible and impressive set of white centred wings fairly gleaming over his left tunic pocket. Parents and relatives of the graduates were welcome at these parades and their obvious pride and enjoyment added to the exultant atmosphere radiating from the graduating platoon.' [page 13.]

Later, the slim Pilot Officer Sparey looked very smart in his new uniform, proudly bearing the one narrow ring on his sleeve, and on his chest his wings. All USA pilots were officers but not so in the UK. The next rank above Pilot Officer was Flying Officer (= 1st Lieutenant). By now it was early 1945 and the war was just finishing. He had signed on for the DPE, 'Duration of the Present Emergency' and so was in the RAF until his demobilisation number came up.

He returned to England on the ship 'The New Amsterdam' and took a Physical Training course at Cosforth, Wolverhampton, where he became a parachute instructor. 'It was quite interesting work, though it became a monotonous regularity. Yet there was always excitement when you were standing waiting to jump and in the first few seconds in the air. One fell in different positions, and at a rate of 2–300 feet per second, you fell a long way in the first few minutes.' He participated in jumping exhibitions at the prestigious Farnborough Air Show.

Michael recalled that the excitement of parachute jumping got into the blood of the instructors who would go mad with it, and were unable to resist it and became 'jump happy', and jumped whenever they possibly could. Some planes had side doors from which to jump, while others had panels on the floor. As a pilot, while the parachute was strapped on your back, part of it trailed below you, and was sat on in the cockpit, which made ejection difficult, even when sitting in a training plane in a hangar. How very much more difficult it would be if your plane was on fire and hurtling groundward at an increasing speed! In action, most fighter pilots only survived a dozen or so flights, though there were the famous exceptions.

The Pilot Officer then extended his length of service by eighteen months and was posted to Rawalpindi, India, which he described as 'cold and wet, as well as hot'. There he taught the Indian Army how to parachute. As the air was hotter there, one descended more slowly and if one sprained an ankle on landing, it was usually through carelessness. Today's parachute has changed from that of fifty years ago.

In 1947 Michael, now a two ring Flight Lieutenant, and still a single man, returned to Lytham St Annes to be demobilised. There he was given a horrid blue suit and that was it. There was no party, no speeches, and no word of thanks. 'It was all a bit of an anti-climax,' he said.

But at least he was still alive. 'I can't think of anyone in Keynsham with flying service who survived. The casualty rate was high even in training, as one was so high up and things happened so quickly, and there was no second chance. The proportion of pilots who survived was far fewer than other airmen as it was so hard to get out with heavy parachutes and there were no ejector seats in those days.'

* * *

The expression 'tour' in the following poem (written in 1975) refers to the war-time number of compulsory bombing operations undertaken by aircrew. Warrant Officer Brand commented that 'Tragically, a large number of men never survived their basic quota of 30 or more 'ops' over enemy territory'.

The end of the tour

Time on target,
Collect your kit,
The aircraft's ready,
The flarepath lit,
Men in brown leather, woollens and boots,
With maps and protractors to plan out their routes,
Huddle together, their secret no shame:
To get to the target and safe home again.

The Flight Engineer sits watching his gauges,
And flowing of fuel through its various stages,
With details of distance, diversion and track;
Of his precious cargo he'll see there's no lack.

The trio of Air Gunners, each in his place,
Will warn of the fighters that dare to give chase;
Belching out tracer, yellow and bright,
These daggers of flame are lost in the night.

The Wireless Op sits with transceiver aligned,
Its Morse and the like which are filling his mind,
With little time free to leave his post,
Dependent are the crew on their electronic host.

The Pilot is moving his eyes to and fro,
Selecting the area far down below,
In which lies the target they have to destroy;
With flak and the searchlights it's no bloody joy.

The bombs have been dropped and the photoflash taken,
But the crew don't relax, for they could be mistaken,
As enemy fighters out stalking alone
Might just sight the bomber as it sets course for home.

Over the Dutch coast, the North Sea below,
With thermos flasks empty, an hour to go,
The Nav makes a landfall: it's England's shore;
This op's nearly over, a crew not quite sure.

A call to the tower, the circuit left hand,
With Port outer feathered they come in to land;
The wheels touch the runway, twin bursts of black dust,
As rubber meets concrete, reduction in thrust.

Along it they speed, slight touch on the brake,
The dawn that's just breaking, a crew more awake;
They halt for a moment – eyes survey the land,
The hangars and tower, the figure-waving hand.

And now at dispersal, they quietly wait,
Discussing with Ground Crew the night and its fate,
Of friends that are missing, bailed out or got chopped,
And the ones who returned to carry on with more ops.

Some take the transport, others they walk,
Talking with WAAFs of things other than work,
Consoling the women of men not returned,
Those who are wounded, blinded and burned.

Now very tired they arrive at the Mess;
The debriefing over, it's bacon and eggs;
And on such occasions as they've done times before,
The WAAFS in their midst, bread-jam and what's more,
Large white mugs of hot steaming tea,
They talk of the flak, wizard prang, what a spree!
But this one was different, such horror no more,
Last night's operation,
The end of the tour.

WO Rick Brand – Wing Radio Officer
Herts & Bucks Wing ATC.

'Their names live on'

The Memorial in St John's Church lists Keynsham's fallen as 16 men in the Army, 9 men in the Navy (including the R Marines and the MN) and 17 men in the RAF, a total of 42. Their names are also on the War Memorial by the Park Gates, where the Roll records 49 servicemen.

The Royal Air Force's Roll of Honour

We have read that Sergeant Robert Sparey was killed in his Bristol Beaufighter, last seen flying west of Crete. The tall thin Flight Sergeant Reginald Exon, whose father ran the local dairying business, died in a tactical sweep over France around 1942. He was in his twenties.

AC2 Eric Thompson was killed by a taxi-ing plane running into him in Saskatchewan and is buried there in Canada. His brother Graham was a Quarter Master Sergeant in the Royal Artillery and was captured by the Japanese at Sumatra, Malaya. They imprisoned him for four years nine months, and he was one of only 8 out of 124 who survived the captivity. His family describe him as 'happy-go-lucky, and able to eat anything', which surely enabled him to endure the suffering. Today he lives in Australia.

Sergeant Observer Edgar Downton of Avon Road was killed on active service.

Flying Officer Hugh Coverley of Wellsway flew a Spitfire and was shot down in the Battle of Britain, on the famous day in the autumn of 1940 when the greatest number of German planes were shot down. His father was killed in WWI.

Sergeant L A Oldfield lived in Chandos Road and worked at Fry's. He was only 22 when he died.

Flight Sergeant J E Parsons was a wireless operator and died aged 22. He was the son of Mr Parsons, the cobbler who lived in Station Road.

Pilot Officer Ronald Utting lived in a cottage attached to Lays farm. He was described as a 'bright, quiet and reserved boy'.

Sergeant Flight Engineer Jack Wilson was an adopted son, who worked at Fry's. He is remembered as a lively lad with a fresh complexion. In Bomber Command he was involved in the nightly raids over Hamburg and other German cities.

Only those involved in such missions could know the tremendous pressure on the aircrews. They knew how well the cities were defended by a ring of guns, and the almost fanatical ferocity of the German night fighters they were setting out to face. If they did not kill you outright, your plane could be so badly damaged that it would crash. Or it could catch fire, or your engines cease to function correctly. Damaged planes could limp home, only to crash on trying to land. The dangers were legion. Terrifying fears were endured. Any trip might be your last. Anyone who was awarded a DFM or a DFC very much merited it indeed.

Because of the great loss of life in bomber crews, leave was granted every six weeks, if you survived that long. When Sergeant Wilson came home on one such occasion, it was noticed that 'his hair had gone white and he looked an old man'. He died circa 1942, still a young man.

Flying Officer 'Vic' C Williams, of Charlton Road, was, according to the St John's memorial, the only airman in Keynsham to be honoured with the award of the Distinguished Flying Cross.

Sergeant Les Harvey said that five lads in his class at school alone died in the war. To the tragedy of armed conflict was the further sadness that so many killed were only in their twenties.

The names of the other Keynsham men in the RAF who made the supreme sacrifice are listed at the end of the book.

For the men of all three services who bravely laid down their lives for kith and kin, we remember the well known words of Laurence Binyon, from 'Poems for the Fallen',

'They shall grow not old, as we that are left grow old:
Age shall not weary them, nor the years condemn.
At the going down of the sun and in the morning,
We will remember them.'

Chapter 27

Fifty years later

'We all fell in love with the place. We walked from the railway to the hospital, where we stayed for two weeks while we waited for billets. It was from the workhouse to school and back each day. We slept on mattresses on the floor, which was quiet and peaceful after eight months of bombing. We were treated wonderfully, so much so that none of the family wanted to go back to London. There was immediate integration. We thought we had come to paradise,' recalled Mr Percy Kilburn speaking of his arrival in Keynsham as an evacuee.

'My elder brothers and sisters were separated from mum and were billeted locally in Temple Street and Charlton Road, the two boys in one home and the two girls in the other. I went to Frome to where my old London school, 'The Cooper's Company School' had been evacuated, and only came home at the weekends, when I stayed with mother in The Avenue. There I joined in the games and played other Keynsham teams at football, firstly at the Charlton Road pitch, then in 1945 at the Crown Fields.

'Coming home through Bath by bus, I saw the bombing there and the grotesque damage. But I was not frightened or concerned, as I had come from Bow, which was heavily bombed and where I had seen so much. Later I went to work for the BAC, which became Bristol Aerospace.'

I met Percy and others at a reunion held at Cadbury's on Saturday 26 September 1992, of 'old Keynsham' people who lived in the town in the 1940s, organised by Mr H Dominey and I was kindly allowed to attend. Mr John Clarke was also there, and contributed the following memories.

A thousand planes over Keynsham

'My grandfather, Arthur Gullis, used to drive a horse and cart to Queen Charlton and Compton Dando for George Chappel. He killed pigs in Rock Road and cut them up. He started early in the morning and worked into the evening.

'My grandmother, Minnie, came from Wales and went into service at Rockhill House, where she met Arthur who used to deliver there. They married and bought 2, Albert Road. My mother, Rita, was born there in 1912 and went to Bath Hill School and left in 1928. At Number Two there was a cess-pit which had not been used for many years, which during World War II, grandfather, aided by his three sons, cleaned out. They reinforced the roof with concrete. Metal being impossible to obtain, they used old bedsteads and similar objects around which to concrete. Bunks were put in for the whole family, children on the bottom and Mum and the aunts above. I can remember aunts' legs hanging over the side.

'When the siren sounded, we would walk the long distance from our house in St George's Road down Handel Road to Albert Road. Dad used to carry Bill, the youngest. I used to watch the searchlights and see the flash of shells. It was a frightening walk for Dad but not for us children. If there was not time to walk, he would unhinge a door and put it over the wringer and the table. It was a tight squeeze. By the time of the Bath raids, we had a Morrison shelter, so Dad reinforced the joists under the shelter.

'Later Dad went to Southampton and helped build the Mulberry Harbours. I was the eldest of the four children and took Father's place. One night there were a lot of incendiaries. But the most exciting event was about tea-time one summer afternoon when I was in St George's Road and looked up and saw hundreds and hundreds of planes passing over to bomb Germany. Being in the Air Cadets I recognised them as formations of Halifaxes and of Stirlings, wave after wave. I was dumbfounded.

[Mr Doug Dyson, who had some connection with the squadrons of planes, said that it was the occasion of the ill-fated Arnhem Operation. 'The Stirling and Halifaxes were pulling gliders full of red bereted Commandos. The planes came from the Gloucester and Wiltshire aerodromes, and they met up to fly off in formation. They had no fighter protection over this county. There were literally thousands and thousands of them. I also saw them go. The first glider to come down lost its tail, crashed in Paulton, and killed all the twenty-four men on board, a tragedy the village still commemorates once a year.']

'During the Bristol raids, Father and my two uncles, Norman and Les Gullis, and Percy Phelps, were in the Auxiliary Fire Service at the Lamb and Lark. When I left school in 1944, the army pronounced me grade four and would not take me.'

An unwelcome 'bread basket'

Another man that I met at the reunion was Mr Gerwyn Thomas, who had come over from Radstock. He commented, 'I came to Keynsham in 1934 from South Wales. I went to the Infants' School, then from Bath Hill to the City of Bath Boys' School and later on to college. I played rugger and cricket for Keynsham.

'We lived at 4, Stockwood Vale, a large house named "Clovelly". Mr Ford was the nearby market gardener, and he used to ring a hand bell at lunch time and at the end of the day when it was time for the men to finish.

'One night during the war, a container, known as a breadbasket, containing a cluster of many incendiary bombs, had fallen into the soft wet ground without going off. Though they were meant to explode if you touched them, we boys were just going to pick one up to investigate, when the Army arrived to collect them. If they hadn't arrived just then, possibly I would not be here tonight.'

The Keynsham Air Training Corps

'Locally, the ATC started in Brislington in 1937, and in Keynsham in 1940. We were 2043 Squadron under our CO, Pilot Officer Ken Grimes, RAFVR, assisted by Pilot Officer Dicky Bird, the local police officer. I joined in 1942,' said Mr David Wilson.

'There were about fifty cadets and just the two officers. We used to visit the various RAF camps such as Colerne, Weston-super-Mare and Locking. With three other cadets I had the opportunity to fly in an Avro Anson with its seats ripped out, flown by a civilian pilot. He was a member of the Air Transport Auxiliary, fine men who as civilians delivered aircraft all over the globe, frequently flying from Britain to Canada. We were up all day.

'There were spinoffs being in the ATC and as a boy of fourteen I had a ride in a Flying Fortress that had been repaired. Later I flew in a Tiger Moth, a Mosquito, a Beaufighter and a De Haviland Dominie.

'At the back of Avon Road (now Dragon's Hill Court) were tennis courts, on which we used to drill, and we used the club house as our base. This was around 1942. Later the ATC transferred its premises to a wing of the Drill Hall in Bath Hill.'

A display of wartime photographs at the reunion showed some 25 ATC cadets marching past Victoria Church, with more cadets in front and behind those actually shown, I was told.

A Girls' Training Corps

'I came to Keynsham when I was five, during the depression,' recalled Mrs Rosemary Hurlow. 'Dad, Archibald Bathe-Taylor, was a master craftsman from Cheshire and made tennis racquets in our front room at 37, St Ladoc Road. He ran the Keynsham hockey team.

'There was a lot of glass at the 'New School', as Broadlands was called at first, and we were told that if the siren went, we were to run up the road and lie in the ditches. But as the school survived the raids on the BAC and the aerial 'dog fights', it was decided that during future raids we should stay in the school.

'The raids were exciting but not frightening. When the Wellington bomber crashed in Wellsway, the boot of one of the airmen fell in our garden, and the police came and collected it. I was a volunteer casualty at the Temple Street dressing station.

'I was in the Girls' Training Corps, the pre-Service training organisation and was taught how to shoot beside the drill hall. We started the Corps by approaching Miss Gough (who lived at Hick's Gate), saying we wanted to do something in the war. We wore white blouses, navy blue skirts and bomber jackets, with forage caps. There were about forty of us, aged between 14 and 15, who had just left school and we used to giggle on 'the parade ground' when an army sergeant drilled us at the new school after the pupils had gone home.

'My brother, Ramon, was one of the ARP messenger boys, who were issued with a black helmet and an armband. Mr B T Turner, the local scout master, turned his home into the centre for the operation. The boys were about 15–16 though some were only 12–13. They worked on a rota basis, using their bicycles to carry their messages.'

After talking to Mrs Hurlow, I looked at the display of photos, and saw one of the Keynsham Army Cadet Force. However, the photo showed some 50 lads, aged from about 8–14, many in khaki uniforms, sitting higgledy piggledy on a grass bank. Their HQ was the Drill Hall. A fascinating collection indeed.

The memories of Percy from London and Gerwyn from Wales, together with those of John, David and Rosemary, are a reminder of the momentous events that happened here over fifty years ago. Suffering and sacrifice, fears and fortitude, camaraderie and courage, were then the experience of many ordinary local people, both on The Home Front and at The Battles' Front. 'Lest we forget' is the aim of 'The War over Keynsham'.

Chapter 28

V E Day Celebration Parties

'I remember the party celebrating the end of the war, held in Albert Road, below the school-end and just past the turning to the hospital. There were long trestle tables down the middle of the road, about four in number. They had white tablecloths on them, with sandwiches, cakes and jelly (but no ice cream as you could not get it), all supplied by the mothers,' recalled John Baker.

Though born at 44, Albert Road himself at the home of his grandmother, Mrs Adelaide Godfrey, during the war he lived at 9, Queens Road. He said, 'After the meal, the trestles were cleared away and there were games. Later, in the evening, there was a large impromptu bonfire, consisting of such things as old bits of furniture and chair legs, in the middle of the road, which scorched the road surface.

'I was nearly 13 at the time of the celebrations and felt that I was too old to sit down with the younger children. Instead I wandered off with some of the lads to see what else was going on in the town. There was another bonfire in Temple Street, where 'fireworks' were let off. Actually these were tubular smoke cannisters that produced bright lights of red and other colours. Also there were military type flares. Proper fireworks and rockets were not obtainable.

'I can't remember any streamers but there were possibly some flags hung out. Generally there were a lot of people milling around. I didn't notice any music, just people joyous and chatting generally.'

Another lady who can recall that day is Miss Gwendolene Bennett. She and her younger brother, Douglas, lived with their parents, Lena and Henry Bennett at 46, Park Road. A young teenager then, she recollected, 'There was a party for the children in the garden of one of the old cottages in Park Road, Number 90, the home of Mrs Adams, beyond the turning into Albert Road. Part of the garden has now been built on. There were a number of children present, but I don't know where they all came from as there were few children in Park Road. We all sat down for tea at a long table. I can't remember what we ate – the food was probably a bit sparse, as it was in those days, compared with today. But I know that mother provided a chocolate cake.

Gwen wrote of the war, 'We had two longish spells without electricity. One was for about a week. The cable from Bristol was cut by bombing. Fry's had their own cable, so they were alright, and the cinema still functioned as they had their own generator. I can remember my mother cooking on the coal fire, as we had an electric cooker.

'It was in the winter and as there was no electricity, there was a great shortage of candles, and as we only had one candle, I was unable to do my home-

326

work. Despite this, at school next day (I was at Colston's Girls' School at the time) I was soundly told off. War or no war, school work was still top priority. And of course, not being at a local school, I didn't know the local children very well, apart from other Keynsham girls who went to Colston's. These included the Stone girls, Jean (Mrs L Crowther) and her sisters Pat, Valerie and Lesley; Joyce and Cynthia Light and Barbara Tucker. We all travelled by train as buses were so chockablock full that you couldn't get on them.'

Someone else who remembered the celebrations was the London evacuee, Stan Kilburn. He said, 'I was evacuated to Mrs Williams of 40, Temple Street. She was the caretaker of the Methodist Church and well known as "Deaf Mrs Williams" (to distinguish her from the number of other local Mrs Williams). I was fifteen at the time and working for Mr E T Harding, the butcher, whose shop was at the beginning of Temple Street.

'I can remember accordion players outside The Ship Inn, in Temple Street, with a lot of people singing and dancing in the road, arm in arm, doing The Hokey-cokey and similar types of dances. It was not organised, just spontaneous. There were fireworks, but I can't remember a bonfire or a children's tea party. People were just making jolly.'

Some people that I have spoken to simply have no recollections of the celebrations. Of those who do have memories, not unnaturally there are conflicting stories, but then even the Synoptic Gospels differ in places.

'There were wonderful parties going on all over Keynsham,' said Roger Bees. 'We lived at 67, The High Street (now Currys), which was a lovely old cottage with stables at the back with a large loft over them. This was reached by a passage between us and the old Fire Station. Our front door was at the side of the house. Dad was a painter and decorator, a proper one, who used to make his own paints. I remember his large tin of red lead.

'I can remember the jelly and blancmange at the street party. There were lots of games going on such as "Pass the parcel". There were also running races, sack races and three legged races, with prizes. I won a fortune in florins (10p) and half-a-crowns (12½p), so that dad had to take it all home. I was only seven and quite a dap on my feet in those days. Generally it was like a mad house, with everybody going crazy.

'There was a lot of ale drunk that night I can tell you. There were four pubs in Temple Street alone. The races, largely spontaneous, were on the recreation ground at the back of Temple Street. I kept going from one area of Keynsham to another. The celebrations were mainly grouped in areas, such as Pittsville, Brick Town, Park Road and the Temple Street areas. There was a lot of bunting about. The doors of a lot of the houses were open, though in any case we never locked them in those days. It was a freerer time altogether. It was pitch black when I went home.'

* * *

Following Lily Harrison's excellent chapter on schooling in Volume I, perhaps it is only fitting that her words should bring Volume II, with its war time memories, to an end.

The Memoirs of Mrs Lily Harrison

V E Day, 8th May 1945, was declared a public holiday. At that time, I was employed working in the office of Willoughby Brothers, one of the large grocery shops in Keynsham. By law, all women up to 35 years of age (the age was raised later) without any children or other special responsibilities, had to work for the war effort. It is worth noting at this point, that the majority of married women did not work outside the home in those days, as it was regarded as demeaning that the husband could not afford to support his wife.

When hostilities in Europe finally ceased we were not totally unprepared. Radio and other communications kept us reasonably informed of how the war was going. Listening to the 9 pm news became a 'must' for almost every family. So, as the end of the war began to draw near, people talked about what they would do and how they would celebrate when the time came.

My brother Frank (Supervisor for the distribution of coal), a very well known and popular person, decided on his own type of 'Town Crier' announcement. Accompanied by my sisters, Evelyn and Clara, he set off touring the streets, ringing a large handbell, and calling out that the war was over. This created much fun, and soon many other people joined with them. Clara gave me confirmation of this.

In record time shops and houses were decorated with red, white and blue. Flags were brought out from attics and cupboards, and everywhere began to take on a look of festivity. I was living then in Queens Road, which was a cul-de-sac with an unmade road, and only one street lighting standard. Under these conditions, it was not possible to hold a children's party, but they were invited to other parties where relatives lived.

Albert Road party was held on the forecourt of Mrs Vi Jarrett's grocery shop (where Hall's now have their hairdressing salon). It was a grand success, as it included a fancy dress parade for the children. My niece, Jean, who was 12 years of age, decided at the eleventh hour that she wanted a costume! I made her one bearing the title, 'No more strikes'. Similar costumes had been made, and worn, by other members of my family for the Keynsham Carnival prior to the war.

Some doubt remains as to whether there was a bonfire on this occasion. They were more in evidence for the Queen's Coronation in 1953. Incidentally Queens Road had been made up by then, and one of the best parties in Keynsham was held there – my photograph album is a record of that day.

Another street party was held in Temple Street organised by Mrs Hilda Green. After nearly six years of rationing it was amazing what was provided. Because of the years of austerity, films for cameras were difficult to come by; therefore few snap-shots were taken of the events.

There was a sense of jubilation everywhere throughout the day. In the evening, crowds gathered in Temple Street, being a central point of the village, for singing and dancing which was mostly for the adult population. Service personnel in uniform all joined together in hilarious fun. Quite a few Service people had been billeted with civilian families so there was quite a family atmosphere.

Everyone joined in the Lambeth Walk, Hokey-cokey, and Knees up

Mrs Brown, interspersed with favourite war-time songs, such as 'Kiss me goodnight, Sergeant Major'. At times service caps were thrown into the air that night, and many must have been lost or mislaid, but no one seemed to care. The thing uppermost in people's minds was that the war was over. Some Service personnel who were fortunate enough to be stationed fairly near their homes, were granted leave to celebrate with their families.

It is difficult to adequately put into words the spirit of friendship, comradeship and sociability that existed, not just that night, but throughout the war years. It was like being a member of one big family, sharing everything together, all having been affected in one way or another because of the war.

We did not forget during our celebrations those who would never again come home, our friends and relatives, and the brave way families were carrying on living without them. It is worth reflecting how sad it is that the freedom these men and women died for, in two World Wars, is gradually being lost to our nation.

* * *

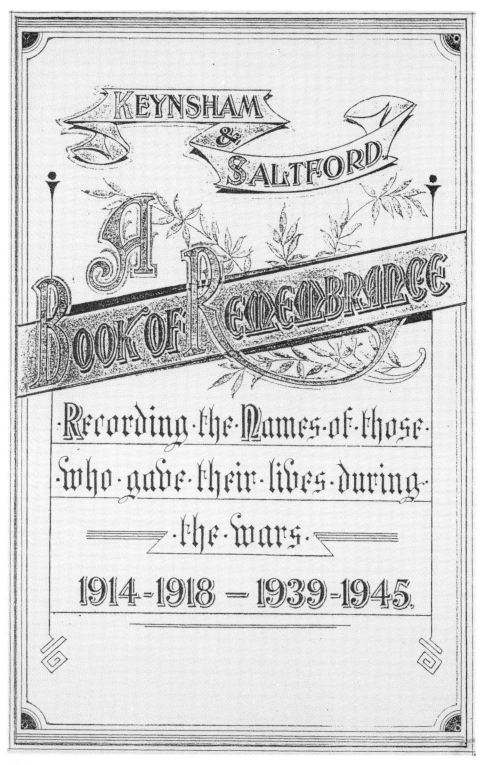

This photostated copy of the 'Roll of Honour' is kept in a glass-topped cabinet in the reception area of the Town Hall, Keynsham.

·1914 = 1918 · War. ·
·Keynsham. ·

Andrews, W. T.
Atkins, D. N.
Baker, E. S.
Baker, C. H.
Beck, T.
Blunden, E. J.
Bowring, R.
Bray, F. W.
Brookman, A. T.
Brown, W.
Burchell, A.
Bush, R. E.
Cantle, R.
Carpenter, D. C.
Chappell, A. L.
Clarke, W. B.
Coombs, E. H.
Ethell, W.

Forster, H. K.

Frankham, W.

Gale, H.

Gough, H. B.

Gunton, J.

Harding, R.

Harris, E.

Harvey, H. A.

Harvey, W.

Head, W.

Headington, A.

Joyner, G.

Knight, H.

Lear, W.

Macfarlane, R. G.

Newell, F. J.

Newman, T.

Newport, T.

Ollis, J.

Ollis, J. A. W.

Parsons, W. H. L.

Payne, J.

Phillips, E.

Price, D. V.

Rayson, F. R.

Rayson, A. E.

Richardson, G.

Roberts, W. O.

Rogers, R. J.

Shortman, T.

Stokes, D. M.

Stokes, H. N.

Tipney, P.

Thomas, A. W.

Thomas, W.

Travers, H. E. K.

Tucker, D. C.

Waters, E.

Westwood, R. B.

White, A. E.

Willcox, J.
Williams, C.
Williams, E.
Wood, C. H.
Woodward, W. H.

Saltford.

Andrews, H.
Barnett, E. G.
Dukes, O. G.
Gale, H. J.
Gilmore, J. K.
Goddard, M. A.
Goddard, S.
Goddard, W.
Haycroft, F. A.
Hobbs, A. H.
King, L.
Lock, H. J. H.
Lowman, R. J.
Mitchell, H.

Skinner, A.

Tarr, H. C. H.

Weymouth, F. G.

1939-1945 War.

Keynsham.

Bailey, R. A. G.

Barker, D. J. C.

Brewer, G. L.

Camm, G. G.

Clapp, C. T.

Cook, R. H.

Cooksley, G. D.

Cottle, H. E.

Coverley, W. H.

Crease, D. C.

Cross, S.

Downton, G. E.

Emery, S. E. O.

Exon, R. H.

Farley, G. V.

Fisher, S. G.
Fricker, A. W.
Greenland, J. T.
Habgood, F. H.
Hardy, E.
Harvey, R.
Hembrow, A. W.
Hoddinott, R. H.
Howes, P. W. J.
Jones, W. H.
Lusher, V.
Oldfield, L. A.
Oxford, E. T.
Palmer, A. J.
Parsons, J. E.
Phelps, S. J.
Renshaw, D. A.
Searle, P. W.
Sparey, A. R.
Smith, G. W.

Smith, R. J. C.
Steer, R. M.
Thompson, E. F.
Utting, R. M.
Waymouth, R. G.
Williams, V. G.
Wilson, J. W. G.
Woodberry, J.

Saltford.

Hamilton, G. R.
Hethey, J. H.
Kelly, J. V. K.
Lewis, J. C.
Rogers, A. M.
Steer, V. C. J.

INDEX

'It is, perhaps, the end of the beginning'	May 31	Company Ceremonial Parade at Hunstrete before Battalion Commander.
Japanese fleet suffered severe defeat at Midway	June 9	Compulsory enrolements into H.G.
From El Alamein Montgomery drove Rommel back	June October 23	Sgt. W.M. Bond (later Lieut.) in King's Birthday Honours List.
	Nov	Col. Parke of U.S. Army addressed H.G. at Drill Hall.

1943

	March	'Wing's for Victory week.' Broadlands School raised £506.10.6.
British forces occupy Tripoli	April 8	Spitfire crashed Newton St Loe
German retreat from Russia	May	General Sir H. Elles visit to H.G. re their part in Civil Defence in air raids.
	July 3	H.G. Training Camps at Hunstrete for series of week-ends re battlecraft, battle drill
Invasion of Italy	Sept	bayonet fighting, reconnaisance, defended locality, combined attack & camouflage.
Mussolini driven from power Churchill/Roosevelt at Casablanca		
They meet Stalin at Teheran	Nov	
General Wingate's offensive in Burma		

1944

	March 5	H.G. exercise 'Raider'.
	March 24	Widespread attacks over this area generally 60 H.G. transferred to A.A. Battery.
	April 15	Salute soldier week. Ceremonial parade and inspection at cricket ground by Duke of Beaufort.
Allies enter Rome	June 4	
D-Day	*June 6*	
V1 rocket attacks launched Assassination attempt on Hitler		New bombing range for live grenades, at Burnett
	July	Issue to H.G. of chevrons (one for each year
Paris liberated	August 25	of service) and wound stripes.
	August 26	Wellington Bomber crashed Uplands. Crew 6 killed